Guibert

C&C
CAMPAIGNS & COMMANDERS
GREGORY J. W. URWIN, SERIES EDITOR

CAMPAIGNS AND COMMANDERS

GENERAL EDITOR
Gregory J. W. Urwin, *Temple University, Philadelphia, Pennsylvania*

ADVISORY BOARD
Lawrence E. Babits, *Greenville, North Carolina*
James C. Bradford, *Texas A&M University, College Station*
Robert M. Epstein, *U.S. Army School of Advanced Military Studies, Fort Leavenworth, Kansas (retired)*
David M. Glantz, *Carlisle, Pennsylvania*
Jerome A. Greene, *Denver, Colorado*
Victor Davis Hanson, *Hoover Institution of Stanford University, Stanford*
Herman Hattaway, *Leawood, Kansas*
J. A. Houlding, *Rückersdorf, Germany*
Eugenia C. Kiesling, *U.S. Military Academy, West Point, New York*
Timothy K. Nenninger, *National Archives, Washington, D.C.*
Bruce Vandervort, *Virginia Military Institute, Lexington*

GUIBERT
Father of Napoleon's Grande Armée

JONATHAN ABEL

UNIVERSITY OF OKLAHOMA PRESS | NORMAN

Publication of this book is made possible through the generosity of Edith Kinney Gaylord.

Library of Congress Cataloging-in-Publication Data

Names: Abel, Jonathan, 1985– author.
Title: Guibert : father of Napoleon's Grande Armée / Jonathan Abel.
Other titles: Father of Napoleon's Grande Armée
Description: Norman, OK : University of Oklahoma Press, [2016] | Series: Campaigns and commanders | Includes bibliographical references and index.
Identifiers: LCCN 2016009810 | ISBN 978-0-8061-5443-5 (hardcover : alk. paper)
Subjects: LCSH: Guibert, Jacques-Antoine-Hippolyte, comte de, 1743–1790. | Military scientists—France—Biography. | Military art and science—France—History—18th century. | France. Armée. Grande Armée. | Generals—France—Biography.
Classification: LCC DC135.G85 A25 2016 | DDC 355.0092[B]—dc23
LC record available at http://lccn.loc.gov/2016009810

Guibert: Father of Napoleon's Grande Armée is Volume 57 in the Campaigns and Commanders series.

The paper in this book meets the guidelines for permanence and durability of the Committee on Production Guidelines for Book Longevity of the Council on Library Resources, Inc. ∞

Copyright © 2016 by the University of Oklahoma Press, Norman, Publishing Division of the University. Manufactured in the U.S.A.

All rights reserved. No part of this publication may be reproduced, stored in a retrieval system, or transmitted, in any form or by any means, electronic, mechanical, photocopying, recording, or otherwise—except as permitted under Section 107 or 108 of the United States Copyright Act—without the prior written permission of the University of Oklahoma Press. To request permission to reproduce selections from this book, write to Permissions, University of Oklahoma Press, 2800 Venture Drive, Norman, OK 73069, or email rights.oupress@ou.edu.

1 2 3 4 5 6 7 8 9 10

Interior layout and composition: Alcorn Publication Design

To the memory of Jack P. Abel Sr.

Contents

List of Illustrations	ix
Acknowledgments	xi
Introduction	3
1. The Evolving French Army	13
2. Guibert's Early Life in the Twilight of the Old Regime	34
3. The *Essai général de tactique*	55
4. La Gloire par tous les chemins	77
5. The Council of War under Saint-Germain	98
6. War, Home, and Abroad	118
7. Commencement d'une vie nouvelle	140
8. Guibert's Revolution	156
9. The Father of the Grande Armée	175
10. Legacy	194
Notes	205
Bibliography	247
Index	269

Illustrations

Figures

Basic deployment on the square	23
Deployment on the square by quarter-wheel versus deployment on the oblique	43
Deployment using Guibert columns	44
Camp of Vaussieux, maneuvers of 9 September 1778	127
Camp of Vaussieux, maneuvers of 21 September 1778	129
Camp of Vaussieux, maneuvers of 28 September 1778	131

Maps

The Battle of Rossbach, 5 November 1757	29
The Battle of Minden, 1 August 1759	30
The Battle of Vellinghausen, 15–16 July 1761	32
Napoleon's *bataillon carré*, early October 1806	185

Acknowledgments

My father, Jack Abel, ignited in me a passion for learning, for which I will be eternally grateful. My mother, Rosemary Abel, has been a diligent copyeditor and sounding board for all of my projects, large and small. Together, they gave me the learning and love to achieve this publication.

David Brinkley inspired a lifelong interest in history and developed the critical-thinking skills necessary in the field during his history classes at Notre Dame. James King shepherded my budding historical career at Midwestern State University and provided much encouragement for me to pursue a graduate education.

Michael Leggiere has been a superior patron. This work, and my scholastic career, are as much a product of his paternal guidance and excellent direction as any of my own meager skills.

Marilyn Morris, Robert Citino, Walter Roberts, and Marijn Kaplan have provided excellent feedback and mentorship throughout my graduate-school career and this project. Geoffrey Wawro and the Military History Center at the University of North Texas gave generously for myself and my fellow graduate students to develop our scholarship, particularly in attending international conferences and achieving publications. Richard McCaslin's direction of the Department of History provided me with the funding and position to undertake this study of Guibert.

Chloe Northrop and I began graduate school on the same day, both similarly lost and confused. Her banter, support, and more-than-occasional ribbing have been the best companionship for which a graduate student could ask. My colleagues Jordan Hayworth, Chad Tomaselli, Nate Jarritt, Paul Strietelmeier, Eric Smith, and Casey Baker—the Frenchies—have been my traveling companions and intellectual sounding boards for years. Much of their thought has helped shape the arguments of this work. The Interlibrary Loan staff at Willis Library has tirelessly and skillfully responded to my requests for obscure documents, including a good-faith effort to secure a print copy of the entire eighteenth-century edition of the *Encyclopedia*. Charles Rankin, Adam Kane, and the rest of the staff at the University of Oklahoma Press deserve much credit for shepherding me through this process and publishing the resulting manuscript.

Alexander Mikaberidze's passion for history and learning is unequalled. No matter the time of day nor the medium, he has responded promptly and intelligently to any question posed regardless of the level of research or effort required. His support and friendship are deeply appreciated. Marshall Lilly, Will Yancey, Paul Golightly, Javier Lopez, and Chaz Gober have kept me sane throughout my research, comps, and dissertation through many drinks and trivia victories. Mark Gerges, Michael Bonura, and the other senior members and associates of the Masséna Society deserve recognition for their warm and generous nurturing of budding Napoleonic scholarship. Rafe Blaufarb generously gave his time and energy in advising me on the direction of my research when it was in its early stages, drawing on his own expertise regarding the French army before 1789. James Hathcock at Tarrant County College has been another excellent friend and mentor, particularly to my teaching. Any errors or omissions herein are of course my own.

And naturally, my appreciation extends to Emperor Napoleon I, "the man who pays all the bills"!

GUIBERT

Introduction

The eighteenth century marked a time of intense upheaval in France. The opening of the War of Spanish Succession in 1701 saw Louis XIV's state at near-hegemonic heights, having defeated the League of Augsburg and seeking to place a Bourbon prince on the throne of Spain. France's army became the most feared in Europe, sallying forth to fulfill the Sun King's ambitions.[1] Only fifty years later during the Seven Years War, 1756–63, France experienced one of its most ignominious defeats on 5 November 1757 at Rossbach.[2] This swift reversal brought low the kingdom that had dominated Continental politics for generations and set it on a path toward reform and revolution.

Fourteen years before that battle, one of the most important military theorists of the period was born in the south of France. Jacques-Antoine-Hippolyte, comte de Guibert, was born in 1743 in the provincial city of Montauban. In his youth he received the typical education of the lower nobility, first at a regional *école*, then in Paris. During the Seven Years War, he entered the army, serving as an aide-de-camp to his father, Charles-Benoît Guibert. Guibert witnessed the French defeat at Rossbach, after which his father was taken to Prussia as a prisoner of war. During the later years of the conflict, Guibert participated in the Battles of Minden on 17 August 1759 and Vellinghausen on 15–16 July 1761, winning a decoration for valor in the latter.[3]

The Seven Years War, which saw the beginning of Guibert's military career, ended as abjectly for France as it began, with the humiliating 1763 Treaty of Paris affirming the military superiority of Great Britain and Prussia over the once-great kingdom. This disaster revealed deeper, systemic problems in the French army and state. Louis XV, whose reign began with the near-universal acclaim of the French people, evinced an increasing disinterest in administering the government by war's end.[4] The burgeoning Enlightenment increasingly questioned the existing order. Its call for rational government included an end to absolutist rule and an enumerated constitution. Various groups within the nobility and the common classes warred with each other for power, prestige, and profit. The decades that followed would be a time of great upheaval and change, both for Guibert and for France.[5]

After the war Guibert's father joined the ministry of Etienne-François, duc de Choiseul, as an advisor. Guibert himself advanced through the ranks of promotion to colonel by 1768. That year he participated in the French pacification of Corsica as an aide-de-camp to General Noël Jourda, comte de Vaux. Guibert commanded operations during the island campaign, which culminated with the sanguinary Battle of Ponte Nuovo on 8–9 May 1769.[6] The colonel remained on Corsica until mid-1770, composing a work on military theory and readying it for publication; he returned to duty in the metropole the same year. His childhood friend Charles-François du Périer Dumouriez introduced him to a salon on the mainland, marking Guibert's first entry into the Republic of Letters.

The *Essai général de tactique* was published anonymously in late 1771 or early 1772, launching Guibert's literary career. It proved popular in the salon culture of Paris by offering a stinging critique of the existing order and promising wholesale political, social, and military reform. In it Guibert provides the first systemic infantry doctrine in French history, proposing wholesale changes to create an army that could face the Prussian juggernaut and return France to its rightful place as the superior army in Europe.[7] As a result, he became the toast of literary Paris. Between 1775 and 1777 and again from 1787 to 1789, Guibert served in the Ministry of War as a member of the Conseil de la Guerre, or Council of War, which oversaw the implementation of his doctrine as codified in the 1791 *Réglement*, or Regulations.[8]

The traditionalist picture of France portrays the period between 1763 and 1789, Guibert's active years, as the decline and failure of the ancien régime, when social, political, and military pressures on an increasingly anachronistic government caused its inevitable collapse. This distinction often remains in accounts of the French military of this era and those that followed.[9] Yet beneath the surface of decay and apathy lay the theoretical foundation for reform. The Enlightenment encouraged philosophes not only to question the existing system but also to improve upon it. Montesquieu and his fellow philosophes did not simply attack absolute monarchy, they presented a comprehensive series of reforms designed to regenerate the state. After 1763 these efforts emerged from within the government, society, and salons as France worked to recover its prestige. Political thinkers proposed wholesale change to the absolute monarchy. Social philosophes like Jean-Jacques Rousseau questioned centuries-old practices like childrearing. New forms of art, literature, and music fed France's cultural and linguistic dominance of the Continent. The intellectual, cultural, and political elite of the world gathered at Paris's famed salons to share in the Republic of Letters. Taken together, these trends portray the Old Regime not sinking into the abyss of its inevitable demise, but rather struggling and innovating solutions to avoid it.[10]

No other institution of the French government epitomized this effort like the army. Theoretical debate proliferated, leading to frequent changes in doctrine. The period was one of the most remarkable in the history of the French army, mirroring innovation in philosophy, government, and society. Military theorists participated in the Republic of Letters and the larger Enlightenment, bringing the rationalist and reformist elements of both to their own profession. Great change occurred not despite the often-contentious theoretical wrangling, but because of it. The oscillation between schools of theory allowed the army to test elements of each proposed system, accepting those that proved effective and rejecting those that did not.

This debate sought an institutional army and professional doctrine, as distinguished from the decentralized and personal doctrine of the feudal army that still existed in France through the eighteenth century. On the surface of the debate, each faction contained proponents who refused to compromise and often used their positions to subvert opposing arguments, a tactic common throughout the French government. Nevertheless, this opened the door for true change.

Throughout his life, Guibert sought to completely regenerate the state, returning France to its rightful position atop the European state system. Being a military man, he naturally focused on army reform. Most historiographical scholarship on his life focuses on this point. Yet Guibert cannot be described as a mere technical reformer, like so many of his contemporaries. Others of his day had recognized similar problems in the army as early as the 1720s and had proposed a variety of solutions. While Guibert's reforms stood on a more solid footing than theirs and eventually became the *Réglement* of 1791, his tactics and operations merely marked the most prominent examples of the deep and systemic nature of the transformation.[11]

Although referred to as a "military constitution," or in modern terms, a new doctrine for the French army, little about Guibert's proposals was revolutionary. Indeed, Guibert openly decried the anarchy of popular participation in government and looked askance at the early days of the French Revolution. Rather, his doctrine marked the culmination of an evolutionary process that commenced decades before his time and reached fruition in the *Réglement* of 1791, which remained in force until the 1830s.

Guibert founded his doctrine on sound military precepts: discipline, simplification, rationalization, and maneuver. Most of his fellow military reformers had done so as well in their own reforms to some degree. But his doctrine differed in its foundation. Not content with changes only in the military, Guibert demanded a political and social constitution to match. His system required these changes, needing a disciplined, service-oriented society and a functional, rational government to assist his reformed military. He delved deeply, like no other contemporary writer, into the linkages between society, politics, and the military throughout his career and his writings. "The military success of nations," he wrote, "depends, more than we think, on their politics, on their [social] morals above all, and it is this linkage that is never shown adequately by military or philosophical historians, let alone both at once."[12]

Guibert exerted an overwhelming influence on military thought across Europe for the next fifty years. His theories provided the foundation for reform during the twilight of the Old Regime. Revolutionary France, which adopted most of Guibert's doctrine in 1791, continued his work. A new army and way of war based on his reforms emerged to defeat the nation's major enemies. Napoleon added his own operational and organizational genius to Guibert's system, leading the army to conquer much of Europe by 1807.

This work adopts a biographical approach to examine Guibert's life and influence on the creation of the military system that led to Napoleon's conquest of Europe. As no biography exists in Anglophone literature, such a work will fill a crucial gap in understanding French military success to 1807. It examines the period of military reform from 1760 to the creation and use of Napoleon's Grande Armée from 1803 to 1807, illustrating the importance of

Guibert's systemic doctrine in the period. Moreover, it argues that Guibert belongs in the ranks of authors whose writings exerted a primary influence on the French Enlightenment and Revolution by examining his work in the Republic of Letters between 1770 and his death in 1790.[13]

Guibertian historiography began shortly after his death. His friend and fellow historian François-Emmanuel Toulongeon authored a 1790 biography that appeared as an introduction to an edition of Guibert's work. It provided basic biographical information, including details of his life and military service, that established the foundation for future studies.[14]

The nineteenth century contained periods of intense interest in Guibert's life and works. The literary markets of the First Empire and the Restoration demanded edited volumes of his letters and writings, which his widow, Alexandrine, provided. The earliest extant collection of his letters to Julie de Lespinasse first appeared in 1809, edited by the former Terrorist Bertrand Barère.[15] The remainder of the century saw brief biographies published in a variety of works, including the efforts of Etienne-Alexandre Bardin and Emerand Forestié.[16] These tended to be produced only for the army and those interested in technical military studies, a relatively small community in France and Europe at large in the first half of the nineteenth century.

Guibert's influence, particularly through his emphasis on doctrine and pragmatism, penetrated nineteenth-century military studies chiefly through the work of Antoine-Henri, baron de Jomini. Like his intellectual predecessor, Jomini championed systematic doctrine based on endemic principles. In contrast, the contemporary work of Carl von Clausewitz sought the novelty of each war, eschewing systematic principles and doctrine in favor of a matrix of political, social, and moral forces that drove military theory and practice. While Guibert had written much on the linkages between society, politics, and the military, Clausewitz found much less of value in his work than did Jomini.[17]

A second field of Guibertian historiography joined the military studies in the latter half of the nineteenth century. The occasional publication of the correspondence between Guibert and Julie de Lespinasse captured the Romantic sensibilities of the era.[18] The most significant of these is Pierre-Marie-Maurice Henri, marquis de Ségur's *Julie de Lespinasse*. Ségur's sympathetic portrayal of

Lespinasse depicts Guibert as a distracted and craven figure, playing on her attraction to him to advance his own career. Many works on Lespinasse adopt this argument, largely under Ségur's influence.[19] The development of this line of study divides Guibertian historiography into two separate and distinct fields, one loosely focused on his military work and the other on his social interactions. This divide remains to the present.

The intense focus on the study of militaries and military history after 1880, prompted in no small part by the work of Hans Delbrück, produced another wave of Guibertian study before the outbreak of the First World War.[20] Officers in the French army, particularly those serving in staff positions, wrote numerous works on all aspects of military history and theory, among them Jean Colin and Albert Latreille. Colin's *L'infanterie au XVIIIe siècle* (1907) draws on the works listed above to examine Guibert's primary role in shaping military thought after 1760. Colin's earlier *L'éducation militaire de Napoléon* (1901) projects this influence forward from Guibert's later career and death through to the great curators of Napoleonic military theory, Clausewitz and Jomini. Albert Latreille's *L'œuvre militaire de la révolution* (1914) relies heavily on the extensive Archives de la Guerre to produce a history of each secretary of state for war between Etienne-François, duc de Choiseul, and the Revolution, encompassing the years 1760 to 1791. His work, which includes lengthy reflections on Guibert's terms in the Ministry of War, provides much of the available archival material for accessible study.[21]

As with the biographical studies, these works were written in French and remain without translation. Shortly after the appearance of Colin's books, British scholar Spenser Wilkinson adapted many of their ideas for his Anglophone trilogy on French military history. *The French Army before Napoleon* (1915) is essentially a condensation and translation of Colin's *L'infanterie au XVIIIe siècle* and represents the first English-language examination of Guibert's influence on French doctrine.[22]

The world wars largely curtailed Guibertian studies, particularly the first, which devastated the ranks of soldier-historians serving on the French staff, notably including the death of Colin. They resumed only slowly, chiefly after 1945, due to Peter Paret's seminal collections *Makers of Modern Strategy* (1952 and 1986). Among the included essays, R. R. Palmer's "Frederick the Great, Guibert,

Bülow: From Dynastic to National War" particularly reinvigorated the field, presenting Guibert to a new generation of scholars in the English-speaking world.[23] Many modern scholars, particularly military historians, first encountered the French thinker in this work.

The modern age of Guibertian historiography began in the 1950s in both English and French. Robert Quimby's *The Background of Napoleonic Warfare* (1957) synthesized the work of Colin, Latreille, and Wilkinson into a study of French military theory of the eighteenth century. Quimby examines the importance of the polemical debate between the various "schools," especially the great dispute between proponents of *l'ordre mince* and *l'ordre profond*.[24] This debate forms the crux of Quimby's analysis, in which he finds that Guibert charted a middle path between the two to create a hybrid system. Quimby followed Colin's lead closely in examining the work of the Department of War and the *Réglements* of 1787, 1788, and 1791 as well as the training that took place at the Camp of Vaussieux held in 1778.[25]

Modern biographical studies began with Matti Lauerma's *Jacques-Antoine-Hippolyte de Guibert* (1989), which focuses on Guibert as a military figure and contains extensive analysis of his military writings.[26] Lauerma's work is the first true biography of Guibert, greatly expanding on earlier biographical treatments. David D. Bien began his studies of the French army shortly after the publication of Quimby's work. In various publications Bien has examined the important links between the French army, government, and society of Guibert's time. He has argued that the French army of the period was not reactionary, as many have contended, particularly with the passage of the Ségur Decree, mirroring the shift in larger Enlightenment historiography away from a coherent "Aristocratic Reaction."[27] Rather, Bien noted that the army and its theorists, like Guibert, sought to professionalize the French military by eliminating incompetent officers, which largely meant nonnobles at the time. Including financial, social, and political examinations of military history, Bien's work represented the first entrée of "new military history" into Guibertian studies. Bien also provides an excellent framework for the understanding of *mentalités*, particularly the thought processes and biases of Guibert and his contemporaries.[28]

French authors resumed Guibertian studies in the 1970s, producing many important works by the following decade. Lucien

Poirier's *Les voix de la stratégie* presents a philosophical examination of Guibert's work in the context of the eighteenth century and the work of his intellectual successor Jomini. Poirier finds Guibert to be an important focusing agent of theory during the period, epitomizing the theoretical examinations of the eighteenth century and producing a model that would inspire both Napoleon and Jomini.[29]

Jean-Paul Charnay conducted a variety of studies in Guibertian historiography, the most significant being *Guibert, ou le soldat philosophe*. This work collects the studies presented at a conference on Guibert held by the University of Clermont-Ferrand. Its various essays illuminate the importance of Guibert not only to military history but also to social, political, and literary studies.[30]

The latter half of the twentieth century produced an explosion of works focusing on the eighteenth century, particularly in the field of "Enlightenment studies." Throughout the eighteenth century, a rising tide of publication and public discourse produced the "public sphere," an arena for discussion and particularly for criticism of existing systems, most notably the government.[31] Contemporaries argued for a more "rational" government, founded on a written constitution and allowing for promotion by merit alongside social equality and political access to the disenfranchised lower classes. Guibert's call for a more ordered army and supporting doctrinal system echoed these sentiments and embodied the Enlightenment zeitgeist, particularly its calls for reform.

Many works that examine the period elaborate the larger arena of Guibert's working environment, society, and influence. Dena Goodman's study of French salons provides an excellent introduction to their importance in contemporary social and political life. She notes the primacy of Lespinasse on the Parisian social scene, providing Guibert an important avenue to fame and success. Daniel Roche and Peter Gay separately explored the larger considerations of the Enlightenment to which Guibert belonged. Roger Chartier's *Cultural Origins of the French Revolution* (1991), along with Roche's work, examines the process whereby the Enlightenment gradually eroded the legitimacy of the monarchy, leading to its dissolution in 1792.[32]

These works gird the separation in Guibertian studies, building on the previous examinations of Lespinasse to create the social historiography of Guibert's life and career. From this field has come the most recent biography of the reformer, Ethel Groffier's *Le stratège des lumières* (2005), which concentrates on rehabilitating Guibert's image as a writer.[33] Groffier focuses on his literary and social activities but does not shun his importance to military history. She argues that Guibert's literary achievements are underappreciated and that he was a premier writer of the period. This analysis pairs invaluably with the more traditional approach of Lauerma's biography.

Military scholarship began its own revival around the same time as Enlightenment studies, particularly with the rise of the "New Military History" and the classification of the operational level of war by Western historians.[34] These studies in military history closely examined Guibert's career and influence, much as their social-history counterparts did his social activities. Primary among these are the works of Rafe Blaufarb and Julia Osman, both following the lead of Bien in examining the social and political aspects of Guibert's writings. Blaufarb narrowed Bien's focus to the institution of the army. Following Quimby, Blaufarb argues that the reform process inaugurated by Choiseul and adopted by Guibert largely produced the army of the French Revolution, particularly with regard to the destruction of social barriers within the officer corps. Osman's work echoes Blaufarb's examinations, particularly by illuminating the mindset of the members of an institution in transition.[35]

Beatrice Heuser and Claus Telp contributed important works to Guibertian studies, both interacting with Palmer's essay. Heuser's recent work situates Guibert's influence among discussions of total war, following the tradition established by Palmer in examining the nature of such warfare and its implications, particularly during the Revolution. Telp examines Guibert's importance to the development of operational-level warfare, arguing that he played a primary role in the development of operational warfare by adopting Frederick II's battlefield exigencies into a coherent doctrine that emphasized mobility, organizational articulation, and firepower. This contrasts sharply with Palmer, who argues that Guibert fundamentally misunderstood operational warfare.[36]

Other works of military history illuminate the wider scope of theory and practice between 1760 and 1807, the height of Napoleon's military prowess and the end of the great campaigns of the original Grande Armée. These include Rory Muir's *Tactics and the Experience of Battle in the Age of Napoleon* (1998), Gunther Rothenberg's *Art of Warfare in the Age of Napoleon* (1978), Paddy Griffith's *The Art of War of Revolutionary France* (1998), and Steven

T. Ross's *From Flintlock to Rifle* (1996). Jean-Paul Bertaud's *The Army of the French Revolution* (1988), Samuel Scott's *The Response of the Royal Army to the French Revolution* (1978), John Lynn's *Bayonets of the Republic* (1984), and John Elting's *Swords Around a Throne* (1988) examine the French armies in depth.[37]

Primary sources provide a nearly complete picture of Guibert's thought and its influence. His own works naturally serve this goal best.[38] Guibert's spirited romance and correspondence with Lespinasse provide the only surviving collection of his letters in print, while his official papers are contained in five cartons at the Archives de la Guerre, Château de Vincennes.[39] Numerous other primary sources illuminate Guibert's life and career, including works by Charles Dumouriez and Germaine de Staël-Holstein, two of his closest friends.[40]

The materials discussed above offer only an incomplete portrait of Guibertian historiography. The comte de Guibert left a complex legacy that scholars often divide into three categories: military, literary, and social.[41] While these approaches are valid, the man's true nature and tremendous influence can only be understood when his work is examined as a whole. Although a military theorist, Guibert did not confine himself to that realm. He proved a master of the polite sociability of the salon, commanding the attention and respect of most who heard him. In addition, he remained largely unique among his fellow philosophes in that he represented himself as a military man in addition to being a leading social and literary figure.

This sophisticated nature elevated Guibert from the morass of lower nobility and the myriad of officers who sought elevation or struggled to promulgate their own military theory. His social and literary activities granted him access to the upper levels of government, access that would have been largely closed after the fall of his father's patron, Choiseul, in 1770. Literary markets remained opened to his writings, as evidenced by the numerous printings during his lifetime of the *Essai général de tactique*, a work that epitomized the military wisdom of the great eighteenth-century reforms. Guibert himself served as a lens, focusing these reform efforts into a coherent and systematic doctrine. His writing and constant advocacy for the implementation of his doctrine vis-à-vis the Council of War led directly to the *Réglement* of 1791, which in turn established the organization and doctrine of the armies that would virtually conquer Europe between 1792 and 1807.

CHAPTER I

The Evolving French Army

Guibert's career occurred near the end of a centuries-long period of debate and reform. As early as the medieval period, France began a lengthy shift from armored cavalry to missile infantry as its basic weapons system. This produced massive changes in military theory and practice, particularly as formations of missile infantry required a much more organized and standardized doctrine to operate.

By 1700 the transition was complete, as all French infantry were armed with muskets affixed with socket bayonets. The soldiers also were supported by artillery and cavalry, the latter's weaponry and organization much more standardized from past practice. These changes now allowed for the beginnings of institutional doctrine. A few theorists began to work on this, proposing to remove doctrine from the purview of individual officers and commanders and instead propagate a single system for the entire army.

The process of doctrinal development was greatly accelerated by the rise of Prussia. Frederick II's disciplined battalions proved indomitable during the War of Austrian Succession, 1740–48. While France and Prussia were allied in that conflict, many on the French side came away with a favorable view of their partners. Practitioners and theorists alike came to view Prussia, not France, as the leading military power after the war, touching off a wave of polemical debate and reform.

The rise of Prussia produced a two-fold response in France. Institutional doctrine developed at a much more rapid pace, with the first elements appearing by 1755 at the tactical level. This produced in turn an emphasis on rigid discipline and organization, much to the dismay of many within the Ministry of War. As a result, a doctrinal debate erupted, with various groups advocating their unique views and accusing the others of unpatriotic sentiments. More importantly, the rise of Prussia produced a new adversary for France. Confronting Prussia for the first time during the Seven Years War, France was humiliated. The combination of these two developments produced a time of great angst and reform in the French military, in which Guibert would be an active participant.

The origins of France's eighteenth-century army can be found in a long process touched off by the development of gunpowder weapons during the early fifteenth century. Beginning in the later phases of the Hundred Years War, 1337–1475, infantry gradually replaced shock cavalry, famously personified by the medieval knight. Affecting more than events on the battlefield, the development of firearms also considerably influenced both government and society. Taken together, this trend is known as the Military Revolution.[1]

Relying on the system of vassal service, medieval armies required little organizational training. Knights trained extensively as warriors, but armies rarely, if ever, practiced tactics or operations. Battles largely consisted of individual combats fought with sword and spear, with knights confronted by their opposite numbers in the enemy army. Medieval soldiers provided most or all of their own equipment as a portion of the feudal obligations they owed their lord. This defrayed the cost of war from the state to the nobility, enabling relatively poor monarchs and lords to conduct campaigns that otherwise would have been cost prohibitive.[2]

Missile weapons gradually brought an end to this system of warfare. As technology developed in the high medieval period, bows and crossbows followed by gunpowder weapons became relatively cheap compared to the armor systems of heavy cavalry. These weapons also required much less individual skill and training to use than the weapons system employed by medieval knights. Due to their ease of use, missile weapons could be wielded by peasants, a trend begun on a small scale by the English longbowmen of the Hundred Years War. As technology developed, firearms came to be the dominant missile weapon, particularly given the training required for use of the longbow. Many Europeans recognized the potential for a resulting power shift. This process originated in the mid-fifteenth century, particularly during the Hundred Years War and the subsequent French campaigns for hegemony on the Rhine.[3] For the first time since the fall of Rome, large numbers of nonelites could be equipped and used in battle. According to John Lynn, this marked the transition from a medieval system to an "aggregate contract," whereby monarchs assembled quasi-feudal venal regiments or hired mercenaries to man their armies.[4]

Arming commoners with firearms had a double effect on military establishments across Europe. In society it marked the beginning of a gradual change whereby commoners ultimately rejected feudal social and political systems. For militaries, the shift to firearm-wielding infantry necessitated the development of higher-order organization and tactics. Soldiers could no longer rely on personal martial prowess or superior equipment to best their foes. The extreme vulnerability of firearms-bearing soldiers to cavalry required large numbers of troops to work together in disciplined formations to remain safe and effective. This fact, along with the increasingly complex machinery used in firearms, required technical knowledge and training to operate under battle conditions as the period progressed. When combined, these factors necessitated an army composed of soldiers who could maneuver and fight as a unit rather than individuals. Consequently, early modern armies required organization to practice tactics.[5]

But such developments rarely occurred immediately or even concurrently. The period between the adoption of gunpowder weapons and the appearance of infantry tactics and organization began in the late medieval period but took up to three centuries to take hold throughout most of Europe. Various states adopted intermediate steps between medieval and early modern tactics, most notably Spain. In the fifteenth and early sixteenth century, the Spanish mixed pikemen and gunmen in a dense, rectangular formation known as a *tercio*. Although these combined-arms formations enabled the Spanish to conquer much of their empire during this period, the tercio proved tactically inflexible. For protection from cavalry, the pikemen needed to remain near the gunmen, thus preventing rapid maneuver.[6]

As a result of this evolutionary process, France produced an army based on infantry armed with gunpowder weapons and pikes by 1700. Other branches included mounted infantry (dragoons), shock cavalry (cuirassiers), and artillery. Cannon had developed alongside infantry firearms, particularly in the great age of sieges that occurred roughly between 1500 and 1740. Louis de Bourbon, prince de Condé, used artillery in battle as early as 1643, but the type of mobile guns that dominated the battlefields of the nineteenth century had yet to be developed. As a result, artillery remained largely stationary on the battlefield, grouped into batteries of various sizes and used largely for suppressive and counterbattery fire.[7]

Fighting in this transitional system required both discipline and careful organization, particularly as fire weapons increased in power, range, and accuracy. French generals of the period arranged their armies by infantry regiment and cavalry squadron. The regiment remained the highest permanent organizational body within the army from the development of firearms until the mid-eighteenth century. Infantry was organized into companies, which in turn were formed into battalions within the regiment. Ad-hoc formations like platoons and "divisions" proliferated as regimental commanders sought to better organize their men, but none persisted in the French army's official regulations.[8]

Likewise, battles retained a ritualistic aspect in large part because of the lack of unit organization above the regimental level. To both provide order and to pay homage to the noble tradition still in place, French armies deployed not according to battlefield conditions, but rather by precedence. The commander who led the most prestigious unit always deployed on the right of the formation, with other units following to his left according to declining order of merit. To maintain this precedent, battle order had to be drawn up before the fighting commenced, meaning that often orders were drafted before the battlefield was chosen. French units marched in battle order, requiring an arcane system of maneuvers and evolutions to move across country and into action.[9]

As a result of this method of warfare, or perhaps driving it, noble tradition remained the most important aspect of the army before 1700. Wealthy nobles purchased regiments for their sons, fulfilling the ancient obligation of military service to the crown. General officers also paid for their commissions. This mirrored the increasing purchase of both noble patents and state offices within French culture at large.[10]

Due to the feudal nature of the army, the development of systematic doctrine proved nearly impossible. Although the crown periodically issued *réglements*, or regulations, they remained largely general instructions rather than the specific and detailed manuals that provide the basis of modern tactics. Regardless, the nobility jealously guarded its prerogatives within the army, particularly the right to command units as individual nobles saw fit. Virtues inherent in the medieval service like chivalry, personal valor, and martial prowess formed the "national character" in their minds and would remain sufficient to lead France to victory over its enemies, as they had for centuries. In addition, nobles were the best-educated subjects of the crown during the period, supplementing the argument of innate virtue with education, particularly the mathematical and physical skills needed to lead and maneuver military forces.[11]

Thus at the end of the seventeenth century, the French army remained a pastiche of medieval tradition and early modern organization and tactics. The latter developed often in spite of commanders and the government, relying instead on individuals to formulate their own doctrines and tactics. Therefore, the army relied on the personal ideas of commanders rather than the institutional doctrine of the state. By 1701 the French generally fought in formations of four ranks, which was often reduced to three in action. Battle order consisted of battalions formed by regiment into two lines, a forward line and a reserve line. This also dictated march order, with two columns corresponding to the two battle lines marching abreast onto the field, wheeling right through a complex series of evolutions, and marching into place, wheeling left, and preparing to fight.[12]

This system greatly hampered organized combat. While colonels were liable for training their men in basic march and weapon use, they often abrogated the responsibility.[13] Soldiers frequently appeared for the campaign with little to no training and had to be instructed on the march. Early modern armies also lacked the basic organization required to execute all but the most basic maneuvers and evolutions. The French army had no cadenced step, resulting in regiments and even battalions marching at a rate dictated by individual officers rather than regulated doctrine.[14]

The lack of a cadenced step serves as a microcosm of the absence of institutional doctrine, which in turn severely limited French forces, particularly in battle. Unwieldy block formations and lack of training necessitated simplistic maneuvers in action, conducted at the processional speed and deployment of the parade ground. As noted, units deployed by precedence according to a prearranged plan rather than to the circumstances of terrain or the battlefield.[15]

Battles proved elusive during the period from 1600 to 1700, generally occurring when both parties sought combat, which proved a rare occurrence. For example, Henri de la Tour d'Auvergne, vicomte de Turenne, commanding French forces in the early years of the Dutch War of 1672–78, only fought two major battles during that conflict. Combat, particularly during the wars of Louis XIV, often involved sieges rather than pitched battles. Even in engagements, infantry attacks rarely took place. Often, the decisive blow was delivered by shock cavalry, always the preferred arm of a noble class that highly prized martial honor.[16]

As a result of this evolution, the French army possessed limited organization, tactics, and doctrine on the eve of the War of Spanish Succession, 1701–13. With the transition to gunpowder weapons largely completed by 1700, military authorities sought a more sophisticated doctrine. Lynn argues that this represented a shift from the aggregate contract army to a "state commission" system, whereby monarchs relied on the growing state bureaucracy to recruit armies from within their kingdoms, largely eschewing foreign mercenaries.[17] But significant challenges remained in the creation of an institutional army. Organization and discipline lagged behind technical developments, particularly given the decentralized nature of the military. Reformers labored over the next several decades to reform the system and lay the foundation for the development of the truly regular army required by the state commission system.

The first step in this process was the appearance of the fusil in the seventeenth century, which made significant improvements on the design of the musket by rendering it more stable and effective.[18] The adoption of Vauban's socket bayonet in 1698 transformed the basic infantry shoulder arm into a system capable of delivering both shock and fire. As a result, pikes all but disappeared from the French army over the next two decades. This greatly simplified tactics and theory, as neither would have to account for foot units of different type. Instead, infantry would be standardized, capable of utilizing both fire and shock as well as a variety of formations, depending on circumstance. Consequently, the socket bayonet laid the foundation for the development of modern doctrine by simplifying the variables of infantry warfare to a single type of soldier.[19]

France participated in four major wars between 1701 and 1755, winning or drawing all of them. Due to this success, doctrinal development and reform proceeded slowly. Yet a movement toward reform represented a nascent call not only for regeneration of the military but also of the state and the society it reflected. The implications of these changes reached into the latter two areas, sowing the seeds of wrenching debate within the army. The first author in this field was Jean-Charles, Chevalier Folard. Folard's various works, most notably his *Traité de Polybe*, reached only a small audience before 1740, largely because most within the French military establishment remained suspicious of theory. Yet his writings inaugurated an important school in the great debates that would follow. Folard argued for a primitive system of dense columns mixing shot and pike. Although these resembled the fabled Spanish tercio in form, Folard's columns were to be fast moving and of sufficient strength to break the opponent's lines. He intermixed cavalry and infantry, ideally forming a combined-arms unit that could resist enemy action.[20]

Folard's treatise established the *ordre profond* school of thought, which would prove vital in the reform debates of the century.[21] Like many of his contemporaries, he hearkened to Greece and Rome for support, which explains in part the almost complete absence of artillery from his calculations. Folard's system was visibly deficient even to its supporters and later proponents. Without cadenced step and regular battle drill, soldiers formed in column were largely incapable of advancing under fire. "The advocates of the *ordre profond*," Robert Quimby concludes, argued "that tactics [were] primarily a matter of geometry and should be governed by it rather than by the properties of the weapons employed."[22]

Yet Folard's genius and lasting legacy were to capture the *kulturgeist* of the nobility and transfer it to a tactical system. His l'ordre profond was an explicitly French system, drawing on élan and the initiative of the individual soldier to press forward in column. More so than any technical consideration, this aspect vaulted Folard's system to the apex of the French military mind for the remainder of the century.[23] It also ignited a polemical debate that would dominate military theory between shock, embodied by l'ordre profond, and fire, or *l'ordre mince*.

At the same time, however, a new military power rose outside of France, marking a development that would have significant consequences for doctrine and practice throughout Europe. Organization and discipline developed significantly in the eighteenth century as a direct result of the influence of the Kingdom of Prussia and its army on military thought. Beginning with the elevation of the elector of Brandenburg to king in Prussia in 1701, the Hohenzollern rulers constructed an army that could contend with the larger Continental powers. As Prussia lacked the manpower of its larger neighbors, its monarchs emphasized military quality over quantity. This produced a small but highly skilled army, disciplined through many hours of training and drill. Unlike the French tradition, with its decentralized organization, the Prussian system emphasized discipline and provided an organizational structure from the crown down to the lowest organizational levels.[24]

The first king of Prussia, Frederick I, as well as his son and successor, Frederick William I, largely refused to engage in combat during the wars of the early part of the eighteenth century, which saw France extend its control over Continental politics. Throughout his reign, Frederick William I slowly built a small yet highly disciplined army as well as a large war chest for future conflicts. His death in 1740 brought his son, Frederick II, to the throne. Determined to make use of his military, the new king immediately launched an invasion of Austrian-held Silesia. This sparked the War of Austrian Succession, which developed into a general European war that lasted for eight years. Frederick's disciplined battalions proved superior to more-numerous enemy forces, holding off the British-Austrian coalition; France generally supported the Prussian cause.[25]

The War of Austrian Succession ended in a minor French-Prussian victory. More importantly for the military, Frederick's success in the contest ignited a wave of debate in Paris. French military ideology remained the pinnacle of Continental theory throughout Louis XIV's reign. Austria, France's "hereditary enemy," had little tradition of military debate, and British thought did not gain much traction in the considerations of French theorists. The rise of Prussian methods threatened the hegemony of French military ideology after 1740. Nearly all commentators noted the Prussian army's efficiency and discipline. Some advocated a shift to a more formalized and disciplined system in France, aping that of Prussia; they became the proponents of l'ordre mince. Others, chiefly Folard, demurred, insisting that the "national character" of the French soldier prevented such a system's use; they preferred l'ordre profond. But all of these thinkers concluded that Prussia's unique factors served as force multipliers to provide Frederick military power far out of proportion to the size of his state, perhaps eclipsing France as the premier power on the Continent.[26]

These admissions launched French military thinkers into a decades-long polemical struggle, uniting all of the disputes that had risen within the army establishment. Reformers strove to remake the army into a modern institutional force rather than the "aggregated contract" of prior practice. Theorists and practitioners alike became occupied with the search for a unified, systemic doctrine, leading to fierce debates between l'ordre mince and l'ordre profond.

In addition, groups within the nobility strove to retain their traditional position of honor within the military, resisting centralizing efforts that threatened their privilege. This divided theoretical circles into two groups, one focused on each state—institutionalization or decentralization—and its methodology. The essentially noble origins of the French army raised concerns over its inherent "nature" and its doctrine. Writers like Folard preached the benefits of the "national character," most notably élan and individualism. Folard's works appeared before the Austrian Succession, but they came to prominence in the new intellectual climate after 1748 as a result of the increasing ideological division between French and Prussian "schools" of theory.[27]

The work of Jacques-François de Chastenet, marquis de Puységur, built on Folard's example in the "French" school of theory. His *Art of War by Principles and by Rules* epitomizes French tactics and discipline in the era before the adoption of the cadenced step. Its system contains numerous complicated evolutions and movements, most of which functioned beauteously on a parade ground but rarely so well under fire. These processional movements were necessary for an army lacking a cadenced step, which provided the basis for all discipline, particularly the stringent order required by a Prussian-style system.[28]

Folard and Puységur remained the chief theorists of the French army until the mid-1750s. Their works presented academic and polemical studies, but few within the Ministry of War or the government at large contemplated implementing elements of them as doctrine before 1740. Only after the Austrian Succession and the rise of Prussia did calls for reform increase and the theoretical works gain a wide readership as military philosophy.

The period of the early 1750s saw limited efforts at reform within the Ministry of War, particularly as theoretical writing proliferated. The various secretaries of state for war began to push for a more institutionalized and regular doctrine. One, Marc-Pierre de Voyer de Paulmy, comte d'Argenson, transitioned the debate from theoretical circles to French army doctrine with the *Réglements* of 1753 and 1754. Both sets of rules promulgated the system championed by Puységur and Folard by institutionalizing l'ordre profond. This produced widespread consternation, for many within the army noted the inutility of its preferred column formation, known as the *plésion*, in combat.[29]

More fundamentally, these regulations, as well as those that followed in 1755, substantially altered French doctrine. These changes began at the level of petty tactics. The 1754 document established a standard cadenced step, a first for France, fixing march and battle step for the entire army rather than leaving to commanders the responsibility of determining the rate used by their troops. In addition, deployment on the firing line was established at three ranks, which would remain the French standard for the remainder of the century.[30]

These changes in petty tactics produced commensurate alterations to grand tactics. Columns of maneuver had previously operated as open formations, leaving a significant gap between each unit to allow it room for executing movements. This gave individual commanders the authority to dictate the pace of march in their column to keep each unit in loose contact with its neighbors. This system remained necessary in an army without a cadenced step. The implementation of a doctrine specifying a cadenced step allowed for a shift from open to closed columns of maneuver, closing the intervals between units.[31] These alterations marked a shift away from an autonomous, decentralized "French" system to a more disciplined and uniform "Prussian" one.

The regularization of doctrine at the tactical level led officers and theorists to realize the difficulties of commanding an army with no institutionalized subdivisions. They thus combined a traditional emphasis on the precedence of elite units with this new formalism, linking march order to battle order for the first time in recent memory. As a result, increasingly complex systems of organization and maneuver became the norm to compensate for the loss of lower-level autonomy. March and battle order now had to be planned in advance lest the entire army collapse into chaos. Layers of processional maneuver were added to layers of geometric deployment, producing a nigh-impenetrable system that functioned best on a perfectly flat parade ground.

The resulting grand tactics proved difficult in the extreme for officers to manage. Battalions organized into march columns to reach a battlefield. Upon arrival, the march column used a single axis of deployment. In typical circumstances this required the entire column to proceed to either the rightmost or leftmost corner of the front, approaching at a perpendicular angle to the enemy. Each battalion would perform a quarter-wheel and march along the front until it reached its predetermined position in line, where it would

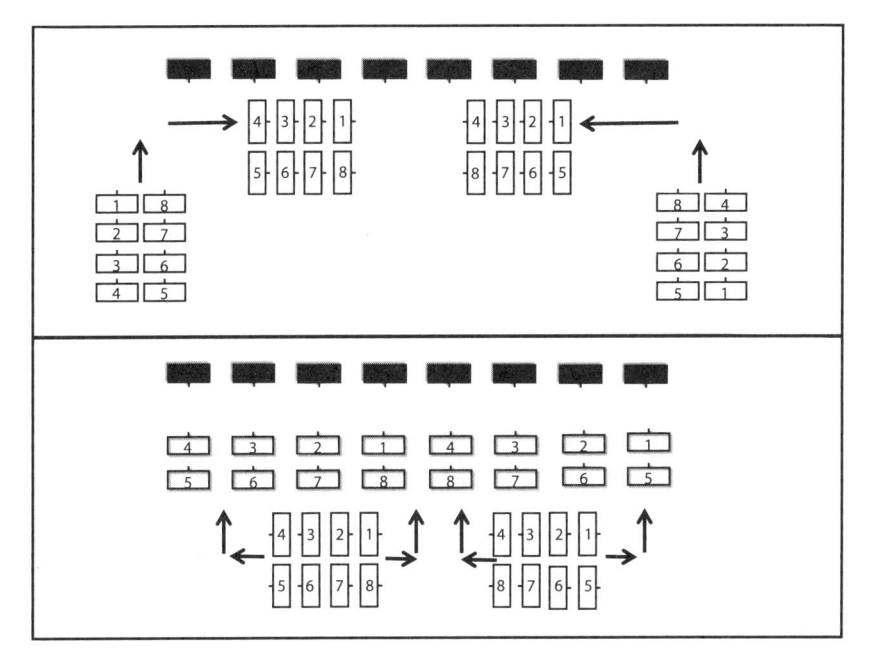

Basic deployment of twin march columns on the square. The upper figure illustrates deployment of columns from the flanks, while the lower shows the subsequent deployment from the center.

perform the opposite quarter-wheel into position, thus forming a parallel line.[32]

This produced a deployment whereby the entire army marched across the enemy's front in a large and complex maneuver. Alternatively, an army could be broken into twin march columns, each approaching from the flank of the battlefield and reaching deployment point at the edge of the enemy formation. Each would then perform quarter-wheels by battalion as above, with the twin columns marching toward each other until they met in the center. The entire formation then executed its quarter-wheels to face the enemy. This maneuver was considered to be the most difficult to perform and therefore the most elegant.[33]

These reforms provided the impetus, both positive and negative, for all theory that followed. On the negative side of the ledger, the complicated nature of the new uniformity produced much polemical squabbling, as different theorists joined rival schools and quarreled with each other over the minutiae of their increasingly complicated and arcane systems. On the positive side, the reforms provided the foundation for the institutional army by generating the germ of a codified doctrine. The cadenced step standardized march and maneuver, allowing for the implementation of systemic doctrine. Battle drill became possible, as the entire army marched and maneuvered at the same pace. This also would allow much greater flexibility and mobility at the tactical level.

The considerable steps of the reforms of the 1750s marked a significant advance toward the institutional army, but further theoretical development proved necessary to expand on this foundation, particularly at the operational level. The most significant theorist to emerge from the immediate post–Austrian Succession period had been a key participant in the conflict itself. Maurice de Saxe committed his experience as a high-level commander and marshal general of France to his memoirs, *Mes rêveries*, which appeared posthumously in 1757. Historian Thomas Carlyle has described Saxe's book as "a strange military farrago, dictated, I should think, under opium." Unlike most of his contemporaries, Saxe produced no coherent system, in large part because of the disorder of his memoirs. Rather, he collected his thoughts about his wartime experiences and how he envisioned the French army of the future. Consequently, Saxe's chief contributions came in the areas of discipline and organization. He advocated the adoption of the cadenced step, which would allow for tighter maneuvering and more organized evolutions. He drew from his experience fighting the Austrians and observing the Prussians advocate the use of skirmishers—light troops who fanned out in loose order ahead of an advancing army to harry and disrupt enemy formations—and pursuit.[34]

Saxe also addressed the growing debate between shock and firepower. He denigrated the role of fire, noting that only a Prussian-style discipline could produce an effective volume. While he preferred shock, Saxe eschewed Folard's pike-laden columns, though noting their importance as an object lesson in effective maneuver. He concluded that shock better utilized the capabilities of the French soldier by embodying his "national character."[35]

Saxe's writings, which provided the spark for much debate, included a brief section on army organization in which he proposed to organize the army into "legions" composed of autonomous combined-arms units that could function independently of the larger formation for brief periods of time. Although he intended the legions to be no more than a battlefield exigency, the idea would prove to be the seed of the division system that would emerge over the next century.[36]

The theoretical works of Puységur, Folard, and Saxe proffered the opening salvoes in the great debate of theory in the eighteenth-century French army. They created the basic arguments that occupied theorists for the remainder of the era. "All the military of France was divided between the two systems," recorded Alexandre-Marie-Eléonor, prince de Montbarey et du Saint-Empire.[37] The army, and those who shared an interest in the military, continued to develop along the two schools of thought.

Moreover, deeper flaws underlay the state and society. Eighteenth-century France stood amid a great evolutionary transition. The age of the Sun King had long since faded, and fissures threatened to shatter French society and government. These originated with the inability of either to adapt to the rapidly modernizing world, particularly in the areas of finance and social structures. Enlightened reformers sought sweeping changes to many areas of the government and society, while much of France clung to its traditional past, including many within the military. Above all, interest groups sought their own advancement and power, often at the expense of the state. These groups supported change or reacted against it as benefited their own interests, providing corollary arguments to the established schools of thought.[38] This inaugurated a great age of internal social and political conflict that spanned decades and rendered any attempt at the systemic reform of France rancorous at best.[39]

The major effect of this turmoil was the blow it dealt to the kingdom's finances. After the declaration of bankruptcy between 1648 and 1666, generations of finance ministers struggled to balance the budget in the wake of the various dynastic wars fought by Louis XIV and Louis XV. By the end of the War of Polish Succession in 1738, state finances were in hand, perhaps even operating on a surplus.[40] As the century waxed, however, deficits reopened, thanks in large part to spending on the War of Austrian Succession. For the remainder of the century, the crown's major concern was to contain the mounting financial crisis. Near-constant warfare, the burdens of a colonial empire, and the need to maintain prestige on the Continent only exacerbated the situation.[41]

This extended to the armed forces, one of the major sources of expenditure for the royal government. The midcentury wars upset the fragile fiscal balance struck by the budgets of earlier ministers. In 1765 the Trésoriers généraux de l'extraordinaire des guerres (Extraordinary Treasurers-General for War) owed almost 59 million livres, with the artillery and *génie*, or engineers, owing an additional 22 million to various state and individual creditors. In addition, the debt of the Marine rose sharply during the same period as France strove to compete with Great Britain's growing monopoly on maritime trade and naval power. This all represented a significant portion of the state's budget, perhaps as much as one-quarter to one-third of the total. It also did not include further military expenditures, which continued to contribute to the debt. Borrowing and taxation could not cover the deficits, which became increasingly onerous.[42]

Concurrent with the financial crisis and the military-reform debate, another feud arose within the army in the area of traditional privilege. Beginning in the seventeenth century, nobles of ancient lineage deeply resented those of more recent promotion, particularly any who had purchased a noble patent and the *paulette* to retain the title within their families. This produced a much-divided Second Estate in French society. The traditional aristocracy decried the purchase of patents as denigrating to the very principle of nobility, which was ideally demonstrated through fealty and military service to the crown. Within the army, this debate centered on the propriety of the wealthy *anoblis* purchasing commands for their sons, thus producing an officer corps that contained thousands of supernumerary officers, particularly within the *Maison du roi*. The older nobility resented the diminution of privilege and status that came with the newer and often bourgeois-moneyed aristocrats who supplanted them within this venal system.

Nearly every group within the army assailed these corrupted and entrenched interests. Certain nobles wanted to regain the military positions, and therefore the prestige, for themselves. Others welcomed a new source of revenue and sought to attach themselves to the rising power associated with wealth rather than birth. Yet others decried the waste of time, resources, and operational ability present in an army imbued with officers who had little to no military training, regardless of their extraction. But all groups used rhetoric drawn from French tradition and the Enlightenment to portray their enemies as craven, un-French, and disruptive to the kingdom and its army. These debates became part of the discussions on military reform and doctrine, adding a layer of complexity and rancor to the increasingly polemical disputes raging in print and within the Ministry of War.[43]

The opening of these rifts destabilized the state at a critical point in international politics. Prussia's victory over Austria in 1748 provided an opportunity for France to profit diplomatically and perhaps even materially by gaining territory in Germany; dividing the region more or less evenly between Prussia and Austria benefited France. Should it remain allied to the enigmatic Prussia, formally or informally, against its "hereditary enemy" Austria, France could ideally make gains along the Rhine in pursuit of the nation's natural frontiers. After 1748, the kingdom's Continental position appeared to be as secure as it had been for decades. Its major attention, both politically and militarily, remained focused on Austria and Britain, particularly in relation to the ongoing conflict with the latter informally known as the Second Hundred Years War.[44]

Frederick determined to press Prussia's advantage and secure its seizure of Silesia, which Austria had not formally renounced. At the same time, Britain sought an alliance partner on the Continent to protect Hanover from French predation, leading in part to the "Diplomatic Revolution."[45] This included an Anglo-Prussian entente and a subsequent Franco-Austrian alliance, pitting the "hereditary enemies" against the northern powers. Russia joined the latter coalition, which then virtually surrounded Prussia. The Seven Years War erupted in 1756 as a result.

France marshaled its forces throughout 1756 and into the campaign season of 1757. In September 1757 Frederick advanced into Saxony at the head of an army of 25,000 Prussians. Charles de Rohan, prince de Soubise, led the 18,000 men of his own army and 12,000 men detached from the army of Armand de Vignerot du Plessis, duc de Richelieu, to the north. The French arranged a rendezvous with an imperial army of 12,000 soldiers commanded by Joseph Maria Frederick Wilhelm of Saxe-Hildburghausen, duke of Saxony, near the Saale River. By October the Franco-imperial army had done little but shadow the Prussians, always remaining to their west. Frederick now resolved to attack. On the night of 4 November the Prussian king encamped within striking distance of the coalition army, which camped near the village of Rossbach. Unbeknown to Frederick, Soubise and Hildburghausen quarreled over the proper course of action: the former counseled caution, while the latter demanded immediate action.[46] Although technically subordinate to

Hildburghausen, Soubise's dominant and quarrelsome personality led to a breakdown in command.

The following morning, 5 November, Hildburghausen reluctantly allowed Soubise to execute a march east against the Prussian left. Slow deployment and movement on the part of the French afforded Frederick time to shift his men to the south to meet the assault. As the coalition army neared the Prussian line, Major General Friedrich Wilhelm von Seydlitz's cavalry succeeded in halting the column's advance. Frederick positioned his artillery on a nearby ridge and brought up his infantry while the allies wasted time debating whether to attack in line or column. Deciding on the latter, the French soldiers formed into a tightly packed mass, not unlike Folard's attack columns, to assault the Prussian lines. Frederick responded with an artillery bombardment that savaged the enemy formation. Despite a heroic advance under withering fire, the French attack faltered before disciplined Prussian infantry and began a disorderly retreat. Seydlitz's cavalry pounced, shredding and routing the disorganized survivors.[47]

The most lopsided major battle of the eighteenth century, the fighting at Rossbach inflicted allied losses as high as 20,000 men to only around 1,000 Prussian casualties.[48] Rossbach devastated French morale and would prove a turning point with ramifications stretching into the years after the war. But the battle's immediate effect was to extend fighting along the Franco-German front for the remainder of the conflict. French armies probed for openings in the Prussian defenses as Frederick maneuvered his forces to counter their moves.

In the summer of 1759, the 54,000-strong army of Marshal Louis Georges Erasme, marquis de Contades, pushed into Hanover and captured the town of Minden. Commanding the Prussian army of 43,000 men in the region, Prince Ferdinand of Brunswick maneuvered to contain Contades and force a battle. Throughout the last week of July, Brunswick demonstrated across the French front, inviting an attack. On 1 August Contades obliged. The marshal deployed his army in an arc to the south of Minden, with its left flank anchored on a swamp and its right along the Weser River. Early in the morning, Contades ordered his right, under Victor-François, duc de Broglie, to turn the Prussian left and roll up that flank as Contades himself menaced the Prussian center. Brunswick deftly maneuvered his forces to contain the French attack, repulsing Broglie's assault with artillery and pushing several units against the

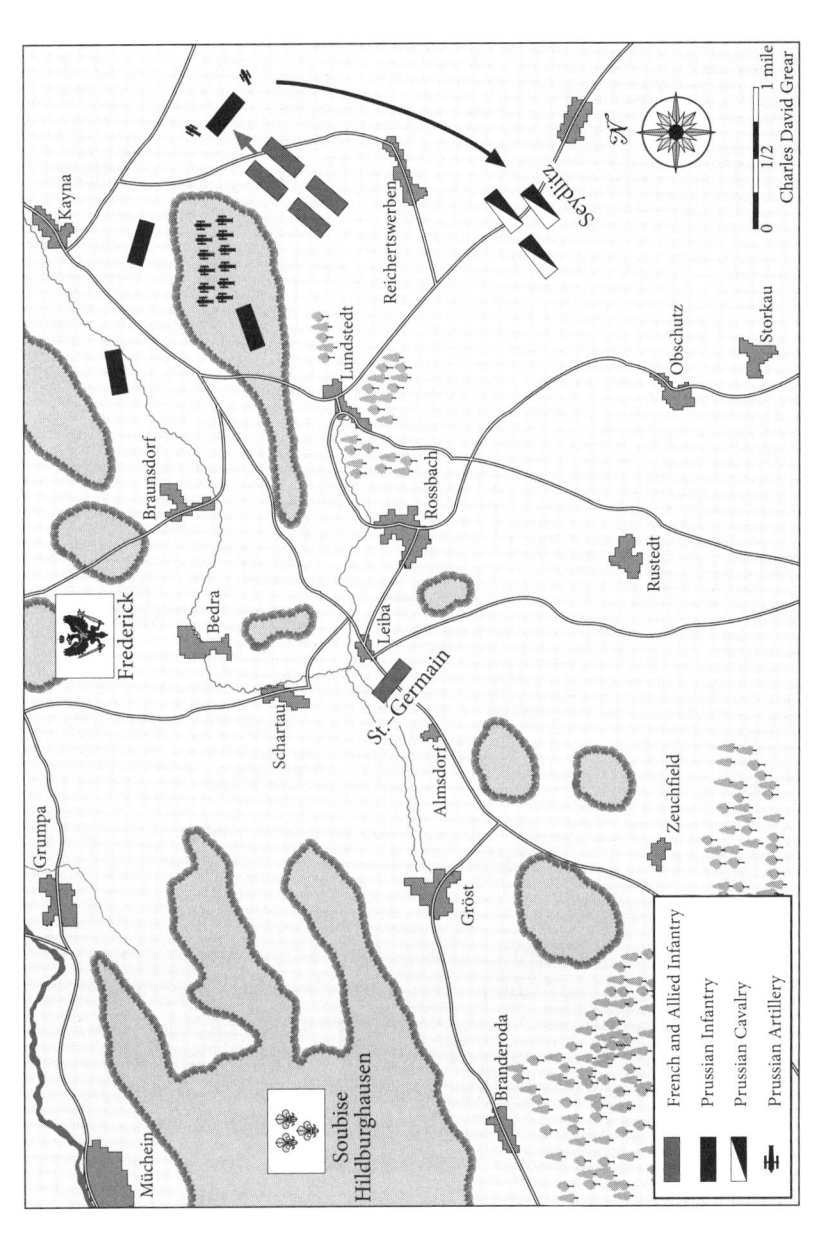

The Battle of Rossbach, 5 November 1757. The disastrous French attack goes forward into Frederick's prepared position, while Seydlitz's cavalry waits to pounce on the survivors. Map by Charles David Grear. Copyright © 2016 University of Oklahoma Press.

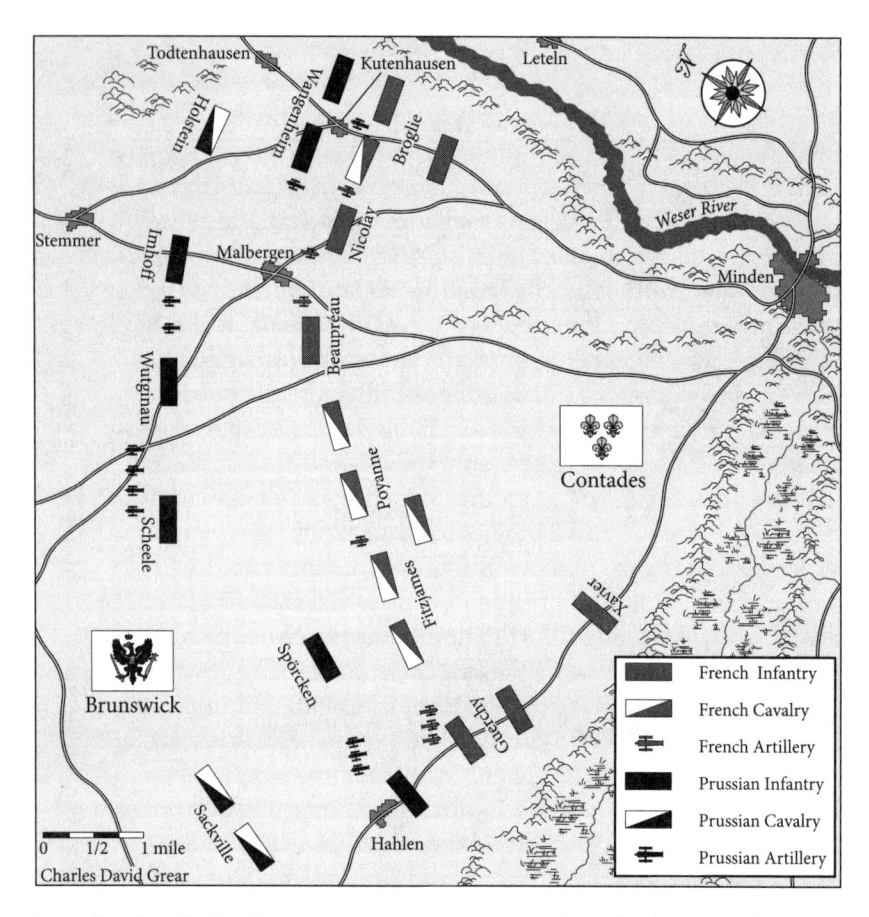

The Battle of Minden, 1 August 1759. Map by Charles David Grear. Copyright © 2016 University of Oklahoma Press.

French center, blunting Contades's advance. Broglie proved unable to act with equal energy. At one point during the battle, he traveled to the marshal's headquarters to explain personally a minor command decision. The battle concluded with a French cavalry attack that broke up against the Prussian center. The Battle of Minden ended with 2,800 Prussian casualties to 7,000 French.[49]

The summer of 1761 opened in much the same manner as the previous summers of the war. Two French armies under Soubise and Broglie pushed toward the Rhine, where Brunswick prepared to meet their attacks. By early July, the duke had interposed his army of 65,000 men between Soubise's 58,000 and Broglie's 32,000 in the vicinity of Hamm. Failing to prevent a union of the two French armies on 8 July, Brunswick fell back on the town in an attempt to sever the enemy line of retreat. He positioned his forces in a defensive arc, with his left anchored along the Lippe River to the north and his right on a hill south of the Ahse River.[50]

Broglie and Soubise approached from the east and squabbled over the proper course of action, eventually deciding on a general attack led by Broglie. Late on the afternoon of 15 July, Broglie began his action against Brunswick's center and left between the Lippe and the Ahse. His advance made headway, capturing the village of Vellinghausen by midnight, but was halted after the Prussian commander shuttled forces across the Ahse to shore up his center. Broglie renewed the attack early the next morning, expecting Soubise to pressure the Prussian right and draw forces away from the heavily engaged center. Unfortunately for the French, Soubise failed to act with vigor, launching an ineffectual attack before ultimately withdrawing. Bereft of support, Broglie also retreated. The French lost a combined 5,000 men, only 300 of whom were under Soubise's command; the Prussians suffered 1,400 casualties.[51]

The Seven Years War ended in 1763, with France admitting defeat and ceding its North American possessions to Britain in the Treaty of Paris. The French military establishment would live in the shadow of the conflict, particularly of Rossbach, for the remainder of the century. The tactical dispute that preceded the attack on the Prussian lines at Rossbach provided a blatant example of the flaws of personal doctrine over institutional regulation. That disagreement illustrated the consequences of the lack of an overarching doctrine that otherwise would have prevented such a quarrel on the eve of battle. Continuing that argument on the battlefield blunted the force of the attack before it began; the unwieldy formations ceremoniously shifted, giving the Prussians time to prepare a proper defense. After the discussion was resolved and the attack proceeded, Frederick's artillery and disciplined infantry demonstrated the ineffectiveness of the attack column against a well-defended position. The subsequent slaughter and breakdown in discipline enabled Seydlitz's cavalry to rout the survivors.[52]

The French army's performance during the remainder of the war did not recover the glory lost at Rossbach. At both Minden and Vellinghausen, French attacks were stymied by a lack of coordination,

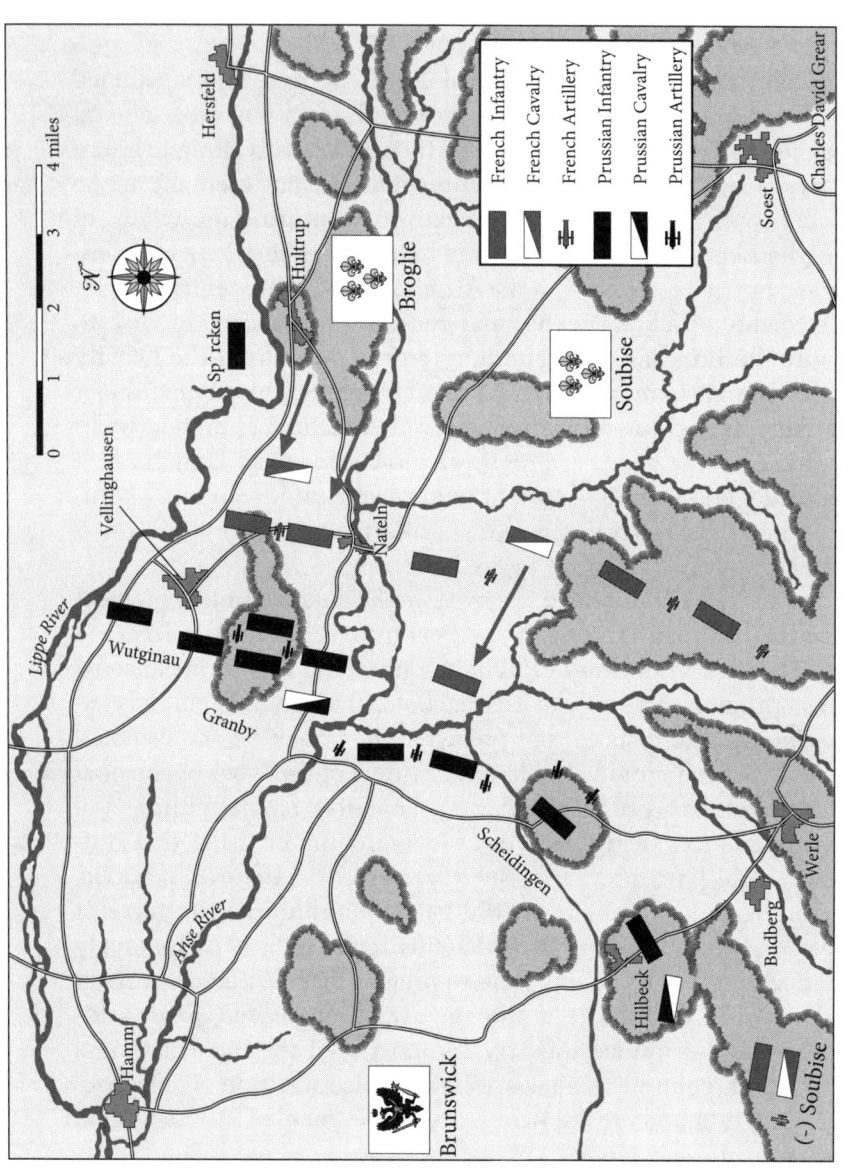

The Battle of Vellinghausen, 15–16 July 1761. Soubise fails to support Broglie's robust attack, resulting in the battle's loss for the French. Map by Charles David Grear. Copyright © 2016 University of Oklahoma Press.

central direction, and military effectiveness. These defeats for a military that largely had been undefeated for centuries indicated the deflation of France's honor and international position. The sudden and sharp shock of losing the war punctured the army's pride and sense of propriety. Both the performance in battle and the considerable casualty list that resulted indicated the sorry state of the army by the early 1760s.[53]

The humiliation of Rossbach elevated the ongoing theoretical dispute to a wrenching debate about the nature and future of the French army. The competing French and Prussian schools offered their tenets as the solution, providing an immediate and existential impetus to the polemical debate. This drew elements of the financial crisis and the question of nobility into the discussion, broadening it to include various groups and beliefs on either side of those issues. Thus, France's quest for an institutional army grew by fits and starts during the eighteenth century in both victory and defeat.

CHAPTER 2

Guibert's Early Life in the Twilight of the Old Regime

The humiliation of France in 1763 provided the impetus to increase the fervor for reform. In the decade after the war, this issue merged within the army establishment with the crises facing the state. Each secretary of state for war following the Battle of Rossbach attempted to rectify the financial crisis within the Ministry of War, the growing isolation of the nobility, and the polemical debate on the nature of the French military constitution.

Guibert's upbringing and early experiences shaped his thought and career. The education he received at his father's hands proved to be vital in the construction of his military thought. Between 1760 and 1770, Guibert aided his father in producing the third and final piece of the theoretical foundation for the institutional army. In the *1769 Instructions for Light Troops*, the two men, led by the younger, created a formation that had radical implications for doctrine going forward. This period prepared Guibert for his major theoretical and practical reforms to follow. His battle experiences during the Seven Years War and on Corsica demonstrated the principles that his father had taught him and further developed his own personality and superior military mind. They prepared him for the construction of his own military constitution, which would shake the army establishment to its foundations and provide a blueprint for French military success in the coming decades.

Aside from the defeat at the hands of the Prussians, mid-eighteenth century France also produced the most important military theorist of the period: Jacques-Antoine-Hippolyte, comte de Guibert. Historians have uncovered little of the family's background or origins. Information on the Guiberts first appears in the southern French city of Montauban in the mid-seventeenth century. The earliest notable member was Jean Guibert, living from 1666 to

34

1733, who purchased the offices of conseiller du roi (king's councilor) and garde des sceaux (guardian of the seals) of Montauban in 1707 from the government of Louis XIV.[1] Like most government positions, these offices required substantial capital investment and a noble patent, although no documentation of the latter exists. Jean may have been ennobled in the early decades of the eighteenth century through venality, but more probable is the speculation of one scholar that he cemented his status through his offices and via marriage to a local noble.[2] Jean's marriage gained him the estate of Fonneuve, which remained the Guibert family home until the nineteenth century.

Jean had three daughters and four sons. His youngest son, Charles-Benoît, was born in Montauban in 1715. Charles entered the military at an early age, as was customary for the sons of provincial nobles. He began his studies at Strasbourg's *Ecole militaire* in 1729 and was promoted lieutenant in the Regiment d'Auvergne in 1732. Charles participated in the War of Polish Succession, most notably in 1734 at the Battle of San Pietro, where he demonstrated personal bravery and was wounded. He rose through the ranks following the war, being promoted to aide-major in 1738 and captain in September 1739.[3]

After the outbreak of the War of Austrian Succession in 1740, Charles again saw combat. Serving in the Flemish and Bohemian theaters throughout the conflict, he distinguished himself during the French defeat at Dettingen in 1743 and the French victory at Rocoux in 1746. War again led to promotion, with Charles attaining the rank of major in January 1744 and lieutenant colonel in 1747. During the war, Charles also found time to start a family. In March 1742 he married Suzanne Thérèse de Rivail, daughter of local noble François de Rivail. The union fetched a 40,000-livres dowry, a substantial sum indicating both the Rivails' wealth and the rising social status of the Guiberts. Suzanne bore Charles five daughters and one son, Jacques-Antoine-Hippolyte.[4]

Jacques-Antoine-Hippolyte was born 11 November 1743 on the rue d'Elie near the center of Montauban. Three separate birth certificates exist, listing the boy's name variously as "Jacques-Antoine-Hippolyte" or "François-Appollini/Apolline." No satisfactory explanation for the discrepancy exists. Guibert took the former name, although he often demonstrated a fondness for the name "Apolline." On 2 May 1748 Guibert was named a cadet in the Regiment d'Auvergne at the rank of lieutenant, thus formally beginning his military career before his fifth birthday.[5]

After the Austrian Succession, Charles sold the Montauban estate in 1750 and moved the family to Fonneuve. Placing great importance on raising his only son, he retired from the army in 1752 to direct the boy's education. Charles imparted to him a love for military science, from the minutiae of petty tactics to the political intricacies of grand strategy. Guibert already had received an elementary education at Montauban, learning his letters, basic mathematics, and language. After Guibert reached the age of eight, Charles arranged for the boy's education to continue at a school in Paris. There, his studies provided him the skills necessary to succeed in the army and in society: rhetoric, logic, and higher mathematics. Graduation led to an assignment in an active line unit. The young Guibert was promoted to first lieutenant on 7 May 1753.[6]

The Seven Years War had significant effects for both France and the Guibert family. Following the declaration of war in May 1757, the War Ministry recalled Charles to active duty and appointed him aide–major general to Soubise. Charles Guibert's duties were akin to those of a modern staff officer: operational and organizational planning, topographical study, and overseeing the execution of operational plans. At thirteen years old, the younger Guibert had reached the age of service and accompanied his father as an aide. Soubise's army was tasked with the defense of the upper Rhine and penetration of Prussian territory if practicable.[7] The experience of serving on Soubise's staff provided Guibert an intimate view of the French army and its doctrine.

After the Battle of Rossbach in November 1757, Charles found himself among the thousands of prisoners taken by the Prussians during and after the fighting; his son appears to have avoided capture through unknown means. Charles's captors sent him to Prussia, where he spent the next eighteen months. Despite the lack of freedom, he found tremendous opportunity in this situation. By all accounts, the prisoners were treated well and allowed a large measure of personal freedom. Charles utilized his inactivity to closely observe the internal workings of the Prussian army, which was fast becoming Europe's premier military institution. He spent his days studying the army and its methods by attending military exercises. In his spare time he dissected the Prussian art and science of war to determine exactly how it had overcome the French army with such ease.[8]

The Prussians released Charles in May 1759. During his father's absence, the younger Guibert had been promoted to captain on 1 October 1758. On 20 February 1761 Charles was promoted to brigadier and named chef d'état-major of the Army of the Lower Rhine under Marshal Contades. Guibert again followed as his father's aide. From 1759 until the end of the war in 1763, Brigadier Guibert served in a planning role on the army's staff. Meanwhile, Captain Guibert distinguished himself through personal bravery and battlefield competence.[9] The Battles of Minden and Vellinghausen cemented the lessons of Rossbach in Guibert's thought and provided invaluable combat experience.

Minden provided one of the more memorable and important moments in the military experience of the young Guibert. In the course of that battle, he was tasked with delivering an order to place a battery on the line. As he arrived, the captain noted that the situation had changed and decided that the execution of the order would be detrimental to the French position. Consequently, he altered the instructions to fit the new situation. "The courageous solution of the young captain later proved to be the correct one," noted one contemporary account.[10]

Guibert's experience in the Seven Years War played a significant role in shaping his military career and theory. Its many negative examples laid bare the inherent contradictions and inefficiencies of the French service. More importantly, they provided the seeds of the reforms that would germinate into Guibert's doctrinal system in the years following the conflict. For both Guibert and the French army at large, the Battle of Rossbach proved to be a watershed. The allies' assault had gone awry from the start, doomed by a lack of leadership and an obsolete military constitution. Army commanders had quarreled incessantly; as a member of Soubise's staff, Charles Guibert undoubtedly had been privy to these discussions in addition to Hildburghausen's inability to control his subordinates. The younger Guibert probably observed the breakdown of command at headquarters; his position as an aide to his father also would have allowed him to witness the ineffectiveness of French tactics and operations. These lessons were reinforced through the teachings of his father, which continued throughout the war. For Guibert, Rossbach demonstrated several fundamental shortcomings in the French art of war that he later sought to rectify through his military writings, most notably the intense need for institutional doctrine to resolve the "state of utter confusion" in French military methods.[11]

As noted, Minden and Vellinghausen also influenced Guibert's military thought. In both battles he again witnessed French commanders displaying the worst of their "national character," as he would later term it, bickering incessantly over questions of command and operations. While this same "national character" drove soldiers to acts of bravery and heroism, it remained a relic of a feudal age, one of individual doctrine by which commanders acted with impunity and rarely in cooperation with each other. With the rise of Prussia and more modern methods of warfare, particularly requiring operational coordination and cooperation, the French system appeared outmoded. Prussian soldiers were more disciplined and their commanders rarely suffered the same ambiguities of command as their French counterparts.[12]

The French cavalry, long the most glorious branch of the service and favored by the upper nobility, proved consistently ineffective throughout the Seven Years War and revealed the inability of commanders to grasp battlefield realities. Contades opined, "I never thought to see a single line of [Prussian] infantry break through three lines of [French] cavalry ranked in order of battle, and tumble them to ruin." To the eye of the young Guibert, the fact that France had lost at both Minden and Vellinghausen was no accident. While quarrelsome commanders could assume some of the blame, they could not account for the entirety of France's devastating defeat in the war. He concluded that the military constitution itself had proven fundamentally inferior to its Prussian counterpart, most notably in the areas of discipline and flexibility.[13]

In addition, Guibert's experience imparted in him a special dislike for the bloodshed he witnessed. He would later "remember especially the horrors of the campaign of 1757; brigandage was at its height; hospitals were charnel houses."[14] The carnage of war made a deep impression on Guibert and shaped his military and political discourse. He realized the links between society, military, and the state through this particular means. This resulted from his recognition that armies did not operate in isolation on the battlefield and that reducing the destructiveness of war required a combined effort from all three areas, not just the military. Unlike contemporary theorists, who tended to view war in a vacuum, Guibert understood that it could not be extricated either from the society that fought it or the politics that drove it.

The Seven Years War also provided positive experience for the young officer. For example, the decision not to relay his superiors' orders to position the battery at Vellinghausen, and altering them when they proved incorrect for the situation, took a large measure of courage. Had the outcome gone awry or been noticed by a commander seeking a scapegoat, his career might have been cut short. As it was, Guibert was fast winning recognition as a competent and brave officer.[15]

Ending with the 1763 Treaty of Paris, the Seven Years War marked Guibert's maturation into his adult life. While he began the war as little more than an aide to his father, by its end Guibert had endured combat, received recognition for his bravery, demonstrated martial skill, and most importantly witnessed the structural and operational failings of the French army. These last experiences would remain with him and form an integral part of his drive to provide his kingdom a sound military constitution.

Following the Treaty of Paris, both Guiberts shifted to inactive duty and returned to the family estate at Fonneuve. Charles spent this period instructing his son in the practices of the Prussian service as observed during his captivity. This would have provided the young man with an inside glimpse of the military system that had bested the French in the war. In the spring of 1765, Louis XV appointed Charles to the office of lieutenant du roi and garde des sceaux at Perpignan, a moderately sized city on the Spanish border near the Mediterranean coast. The fortress there was of minor importance to the kingdom's security, being sited on the Franco-Spanish border. Guibert remained assigned to the Auvergne Regiment but went to Perpignan to continue serving as his father's aide. More importantly, father and son persisted in their discussions of military theory and the failures of the French military constitution. Charles remained at Perpignan for only a short period before his political connections drew him back to Paris. Having reached brigadier in January 1766, Charles was made maréchal de camp on 16 April 1767.[16] Later that same year, Secretary of State for War Etienne François, duc de Choiseul, transferred Charles to a position in the Ministry of War.[17]

Guibert followed his father to Paris, continuing his role as aide as well as his military education. While his father busied himself with administrative duties, Captain Guibert sought his own promotion. In 1766 he applied to Pierre-Joseph Bourcet's "Officiers employés à la reconnaissance du pays," a topographical unit assigned to map and study France's military frontiers. After serving in a variety of staff positions during the War of Austrian Succession and the Seven Years War, Bourcet emerged with the reputation as one of the premier military strategists of his day. Guibert's request to join his mountain-warfare bureau was denied for unknown reasons.[18]

Following this refusal, Guibert fell back on his family connections, both in the government and the military. His father proved a man of no social ambitions, preferring the minutiae of the army and political office, which limited the family's opportunities to rapidly rise to wealth and influence in a culture heavily dependent on political patronage.[19] Yet it was not without its resources, especially within military circles. One family in particular would aid the Guiberts, elevating them to significant roles within the Ministry of War.

The most important French military figure to emerge during the Seven Years War was Victor-François, duc de Broglie. A senior general in the army, Broglie came from a family that had remained well connected politically throughout the eighteenth century. He commanded a portion of the French army at Rossbach, sharing in the taint of its humiliation. For the remainder of that war, he commanded armies on the Rhine frontier, largely fighting against the armies of Frederick II's subordinates.[20]

The static nature of combat on this front had granted Broglie the opportunity to test a variety of innovations, particularly in the area of command. He often divided his army into as many as six march columns, dispersing them on different roads if necessary. This challenged the tradition of unitary marching order in favor of more-rapid convergence and deployment, which the general repeatedly emphasized. To achieve an effective dispersed march and deployment, Broglie required a regular organization within his command largely absent from the French system. To accomplish this goal, he created temporary organizational units composed of infantry and artillery with cavalry support. These units marched individually and deployed by small column into line.[21]

As a result of his experiments during the Seven Years War, Broglie's army was one of the most mobile and flexible in recent French history. Yet it could not overcome the Prussian forces arrayed against it, despite often having numerical superiority. More fundamentally, Broglie's system remained a personal doctrine rather than one applied to all forces after the campaign's end. The structural problems inherent in the French military system ran too deep for any single commander to rectify, particularly on the battlefield.

Decades of reform efforts, from the top down, would be required to make headway against the problems of divided command, anachronistic traditions, and noble reactionaries.

Guibert had more than a passing acquaintance with Broglie, having served near or under him during the 1759 and 1761 campaigns. Broglie's ideas, particularly on organization, would influence Guibert enormously. The notion of the autonomous division and the small column of maneuver provided the prototype for an organizational system that divided the unitary army, allowing it to maneuver more fluidly. Closer at hand, the influence of the Broglie family's patronage would provide support for both Guibert and his father.[22]

In the waning years of the conflict, Louis XV had added the position of secretary of state for war to the portfolio of the duc de Choiseul, who already served as secretary of state for the navy and foreign affairs and de-facto first minister.[23] Choiseul selected Charles to preside over army regulations; the elder Guibert applied his customary energy and competence to this task.[24]

Choiseul's ministry, which extended from his position as first minister, largely concerned itself with repairing France's image and military after the disaster of the Seven Years War. France had lost its colonies in North America, including both the prestige inherent in their possession and the revenues from mercantilist enterprises. The war also had exacerbated the financial crisis, destroying an ostensibly balanced budget and incurring massive deficits that would have disastrous consequences for the French state and monarchy in the following decades. More immediately for Choiseul and those serving under him, the conflict destroyed the kingdom's prestige throughout Europe as the premier military power, one that had nearly achieved hegemony in the wars of Louis XIV. Choiseul's tasks were to reform the army to match the newly established Prussian standard. This marked the transition to a truly systemic doctrine, so clearly lacking in the French service during the Seven Years War. He was also to cut the army's costs, particularly as it represented one of the largest expenses of the crown's ballooning deficit.[25]

To this end, Choiseul's ministry introduced a number of structural changes to the French military via the *Règlement* of 1764 and 1766. These combined the platoon and the company into a single unit, uniting the administrative and tactical organizations for the first time for efficiency. While deployment was definitively decreed on three ranks, a formation of six ranks now was permitted. This was a paean to the proponents of l'ordre profond, who desired strength in depth, believing that only solidity would lead to victory. For the first time, Choiseul dictated the use of double march columns to replace the unitary column of past practice and the theories of Jean-Charles, chevalier Folard, and Jacques-François de Chastenet, marquis de Puységur. The 1766 *Réglement* devoted much ink to the deployment of troops. Deployment on the square remained the norm, but much debate and experimentation occurred in the latter half of the 1760s, particularly with regard to deployment on the oblique and open deployment. Both methods lacked the technique for deployment in battle, particularly within the fog of war, when unitary or double columns would prove unwieldy.[26]

As noted earlier, the grand tactical process of deployment in closed column was laborious, especially with the increasing emphasis on army-wide uniformity of petty tactics. Deployment on the square required a Byzantine series of maneuvers and commands, which necessitated absolute precision in march and maneuver. March order and battle order were identical, particularly given the traditionalist emphasis on deploying the most prestigious units in the positions of most honor, regardless of battlefield reality. As such, battles were planned in advance, and units were largely locked into a required deployment. This rarely functioned well in the fog of war, rendering preparations within the extant system largely ineffectual. As a result, battlefield maneuver during the Seven Years War often devolved into individual doctrine, as officers and commanders discarded regulations in order to meet contingencies on the battlefield.

The Guiberts, working under Choiseul, determined to rectify the problem on the level of grand tactics. Their solution appeared in *L'instruction de 1769 pour les troupes légères*. Although Guibert collaborated with his father on the work, it bears a resemblance to many of his later writings. More than a simple instruction for light troops, the document is a prototypical military constitution of the type that would occupy the remainder of Guibert's career. In it he dispenses with complex and processional deployments on the square. Instead, platoons within the column would maintain a space of three paces between them, with two between each rank. Deployment would occur in small columns of platoons rather than the unitary or dual columns of past practice.[27]

These small formations became known as "Guibert columns." They deployed not on a fixed pivot, the standard of parade-ground

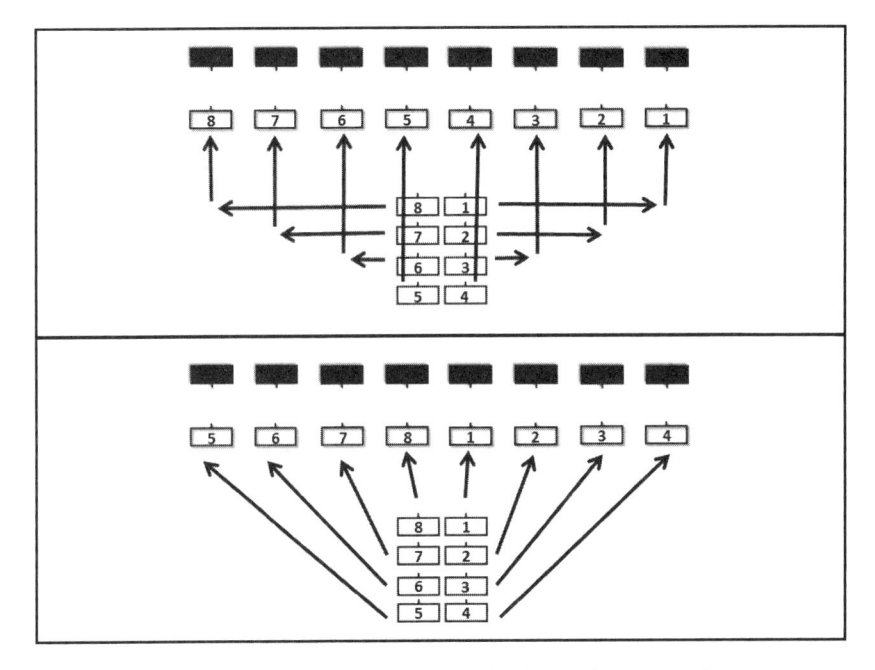

Deployment on the square by quarter-wheel, in the upper figure, versus deployment on the oblique, in the lower figure.

maneuvering and the basic method of deployment on the square, but rather adopted the moving pivot from the Prussian practice, allowing for a more flexible distribution. They also were not required to move in perfectly maintained lines or by precedence, as was the traditional practice. Instead, columns deployed as needed on the battlefield, including in nonlinear formations as dictated by terrain. Guibert columns also moved on the oblique, which greatly accelerated deployment and also allowed for tactical planning during the approach to the battlefield. These formations allowed for commanders to maneuver their armies into a position of tactical superiority before and during deployment, an immeasurable advantage, especially when the battlefield did not resemble the perfectly flat parade ground.[28]

The *Instruction* also introduced minor reforms that refined the use of Guibert columns. Complex instructions for columns of march, retreat, and advance were eliminated, essentially reducing deployment and maneuver to a single multiuse column. The new regulations increased march and battle step to a potential of 240 per minute, further reducing processional movements in favor of those more appropriate to real-world applications.[29]

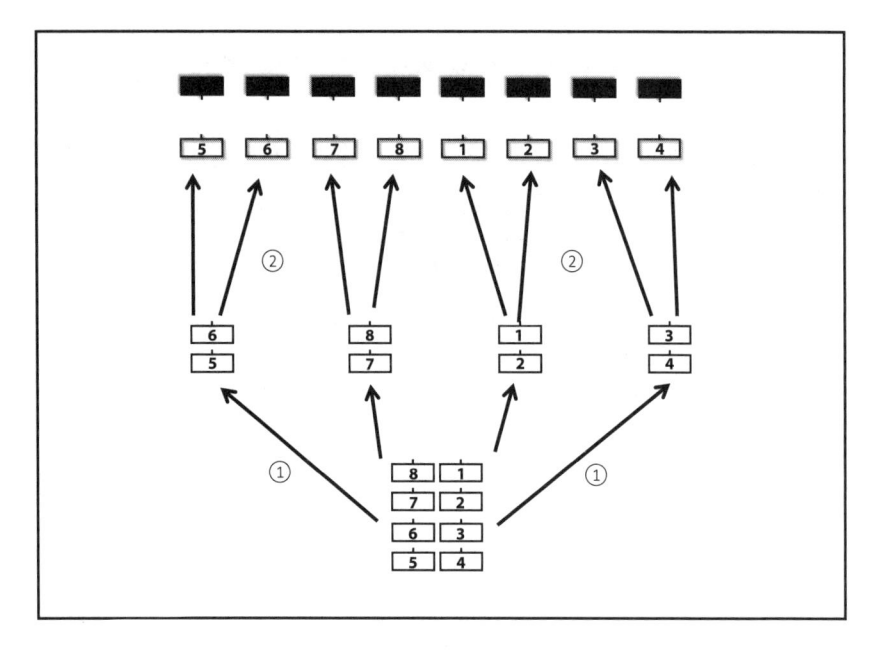

Deployment using Guibert columns. The march column is first (1) broken into separate smaller columns, which then (2) deploy as necessary on the battlefield.

The introduction of Guibert columns added the final foundational element to the first half of France's eighteenth-century military reforms. Along with the system outlined for their use, they liberated tactics and maneuver from the stilted processional movements of prior decades. Thus constituted, French forces gained the ability to meet battlefield exigency rather than rely on processional movements, allowing them to deploy and maneuver quickly in a variety of formations rather than the simplistic, block arrangements of previous wars.

An intriguing point of discussion arose during this period regarding the precise authorship of *L'instruction pour les troupes légères*, originating with Louis-Pierre de Chastenet, comte de Puységur, son of the famous theoretician. As an official document issued by the Ministry of War, the *Instruction* bears no enumerated authorship. In a little-read treatise on Chinese military theory published in 1773, Puységur argued that Guibert played no role in the formulation of the 1769 regulations; rather, they were authored solely by his father, "qui ont donné occasion à la lettre de M. le Marquis de Puységur" (who had given occasion to the letter of the Marquis de Puységur). This letter, along with others Puységur purported to have in his possession, contained a draft of the *Instruction* in Charles's hand.[30]

Puységur's speculation illustrates the veiled nature of the work of Choiseul's ministry, particularly in the absence of primary accounts from either Guibert on the subject. This attack, coming after the publication of the seminal *Essai général de tactique*, accused Guibert of having plagiarized the entire work from his father. Military historian Jean Colin has decisively refuted Puységur's charge by noting that the *Instruction* bears evidence of Guibert's hand, particularly the writing style and certain metaphors used in his later works, including those composed after his father's death.[31] Given Puységur's role in the later polemical debates of the period, his argument, hidden in an obscure work of little note, likely represents an ad hominem attack of no veracity on the young Guibert.

Regardless, Choiseul and his advisors made significant progress in army reform. Via the *Instruction*, they established the precedent that laid the foundation for the formation of the institutional army. But Choiseul's ministry was not without its enemies. In 1768 Louis XV took Jeanne Bécu, comtesse du Barry, as his *maîtresse-en-titre*, replacing the deceased Madame Pompadour. An ambitious social climber of common ancestry, Barry wielded considerable power at court. She joined with Emmanuel-Armand de Vignerot du Plessis de Richelieu, duc d'Aiguillon, to oppose Choiseul. Together, the two argued that Choiseul mismanaged his ministry, particularly in light of the mounting debt crisis and France's waning military prestige.[32]

An international incident finally provided the ammunition for Barry and Aiguillon to convince the king to oust Choiseul in 1770. Five years prior, British explorers had landed on the Malvinas Islands, which France and Spain both claimed. France ceded its claims to Spain by 1767, and Spain pressed Britain to remove its growing settlement from the islands. Britain refused, precipitating an international crisis in June 1770. Acting on his national-security objective of containing the British, Choiseul mobilized elements of the French army and navy for war alongside the Spanish. Prompted in large part by Barry and Aiguillon, Louis XV refused to support this hard line. To defuse the crisis, he ordered the military to stand down and dismissed Choiseul.[33]

The experience of the Choiseul ministry proved to the reformers how difficult implementing true, lasting change would be. From his position at his father's side, Guibert witnessed the contentious political debate, an experience that likely impressed on him the importance of court politics in military reform. In this atmosphere he garnered his first taste of Parisian intrigue, which was equal parts diplomacy, rhetorical skill, and networking. It also laid the pattern for Guibert's own political service. From the Choiseul ministry until the Revolution, reformers and reactionaries alternatively held sway at court and in the War Ministry. Guibert would emerge as a leading reformer, thrusting him to the forefront of court politics through his advocacy of change.[34]

In addition to his political connections with the Broglie family, Guibert also profited from his regimental associations and the combat experience he had earned early in his career. Through the Auvergne Regiment, he was introduced to a variety of officers who would prove influential in the coming decades. These included the Chevalier François-Jean de Beauvoir, marquis de Chastellux, a famous writer of history and philosophical works who won election to Seat Two of the Académie française. Chastellux also dabbled in military service, most notably as a general in the French Expeditionary Force during the American War of Independence.[35] Guibert perhaps absorbed Chastellux's affinity for the career of the philosophe, a path generally eschewed by most military reformers of the period who preferred to confine themselves to military writings.

Guibert also cultivated a friendship in his childhood and young-adult years with Charles-François du Périer Dumouriez. "His father . . . and the father of Dumouriez lived in great intimacy together. The career of the two sons was similar," Dumouriez recorded. "They always lived on good terms and their friendship was never crossed by jealousy." He and Guibert served together at times during the Seven Years War and in the Auvergne Regiment. After the war they formed a friendship built on their childhood association.[36] Like Broglie, Dumouriez provided Guibert access to advancement, particularly in the social sphere.

Guibert and Dumouriez served together during France's military expedition to the island of Corsica. Situated in the north-central Mediterranean Sea, Corsica sat astride the major trade routes from western Europe to North Africa, Egypt, the Levant, Persia, and the Far East. Genoa's struggle to maintain control over the historically recalcitrant Corsican people in order to influence a large portion of Mediterranean trade ultimately failed. After having lost its major

North American colonies as a result of the Seven Years War, France looked to strengthen commercial ties with the East. Although many trade routes ran through Corsica, the island's instability threatened French trade, as did its management by the Genoese. Freed of the obligations of the prior war, France resolved to ameliorate the situation.[37]

Mid-eighteenth-century Corsica was a hotbed of internal unrest and violence. That the Genoese held the island for decades despite massive military and economic setbacks attests to its strategic importance. Never strong, though, Genoese control evaporated completely around 1755. A revolt led by Pasquale di Paoli and Carlo Buonaparte soundly defeated the Genoese and inaugurated a republic based on Jean-Jacques Rousseau's theories.[38]

In May 1768 Genoa sold Corsica to France, which moved quickly to replace the existing government. To enforce French rule, Choiseul assembled the "Royal Legion" from the Grenadiers of Languedoc and other units. The initial engagements went poorly for the legion, as Paoli's ragtag Corsican army hounded the French invaders throughout the autumn, pushing them back to their coastal strongholds. On 7 October Paoli cornered the largest French force at Borgo. A series of hard-fought engagements over the next two days ended in ignominious defeat for Louis's troops.[39]

The following spring Choiseul appointed General Noël-Jourda, comte de Vaux, to assume command of the Royal Legion. Vaux was another acquaintance of the Guibert family and appointed the young captain to be his aide–major general. The two reached Corsica in spring 1769 and immediately set about reversing French fortunes. A careful campaign of maneuver succeeded in confining the Corsican army, securing much of the island under French control.[40]

Vaux finally cornered Paoli in late April. From 26 to 30 April, both armies took positions, with the Corsicans defending the town and the French preparing a concentric assault. On 4 May Vaux pushed one column into the village of Rapale, where it was halted by devastating fire from entrenched sharpshooters. Nevertheless, French pressure forced Paoli to withdraw the majority of his troops to the right bank of the Golo River. Token forces were left to guard the bridges as Paoli attempted to consolidate his forces. During the night, French troops overran the bridges, disordering the Corsicans as undisciplined militiamen ran to the aid of their compatriots but were swept aside. By the morning of 5 May, the French had established a secure foothold on the right bank of the Golo. Paoli threw increasingly desperate assaults at this position but could not dislodge Vaux's men. A dispirited retreat followed, after which Paoli fled for England on 12 June. Known as the Battle of Ponte Nuovo, the confrontation cost the Corsicans 500–600 casualties to some 50–90 French.[41]

Corsica proved to be a turning point in Guibert's career. "The war in Corsica furnished him the occasion to practice that about which he had thought," records Toulongeon. Finally emerging from the shadow of his father, Guibert had served directly under the expedition's commander, allowing him to witness Vaux's competence in operational planning and tactical execution. Freed from the onerous task of running dispatches, he observed a campaign from its highest levels. The efficiency with which Vaux maneuvered the Corsicans into an unwinnable situation stood in stark contrast to prior French efforts and undoubtedly left an impression on the young captain.[42]

Nevertheless, the pluck of the Corsican freedom fighters deeply affected many who fought against them. Heavily outnumbered, the rebels managed to defeat the French during the opening engagements of the war, utilizing superior operational skill, rough terrain, and what the French Revolutionaries would later refer to as love of *la patrie*. This last point was noted most famously by Voltaire: "[The Corsicans made] a rampart of their dead. . . . [V]alor is found everywhere, but such actions as this are never seen except among a free people." The Corsican citizen-soldiers, fighting of their own free will in defense of their nation, made a good accounting of themselves despite crushing numerical inferiority. Guibert was duly impressed with their tenacity and fighting spirit, taking from Corsica a strong belief in the efficacy of an army composed of citizen-soldiers.[43]

The climactic battle of the campaign also brought military honor to Guibert. For his actions at Ponte Nuovo on 4–5 May, he received a citation for personal bravery and a promotion directly to colonel on the eleventh. The following August, Guibert was named colonel-commandant of the newly christened Corsican Legion.[44] For an officer of only twenty-six years of age and not of a high noble pedigree, this command marked a significant rise in status and fortune. Vaux initiated a review of Guibert's conduct on Corsica, which resulted in his being awarded France's highest military order, the Cross of St. Louis, in September 1770. Around the same time, the Corsican Legion was transferred to metropolitan France, headquartered at Tarascon.[45]

During his service on Corsica, Guibert also devoted himself to a study of military theory, including the works of Maurice de Saxe, Broglie, Folard, and marquis de Puységur. In addition, a series of reformers who wrote and worked post-1750 deeply influenced Guibert's thought. Chief among these were Bourcet; François-Jean de Graindorge d'Orgeville, baron de Mesnil-Durand; and Jean-Baptiste Vaquette de Gribeauval. Mesnil-Durand elaborated on the ordre profond of Puységur and Folard, ostensibly updating it for future use.[46] Bourcet arguably contributed much to the development of operational-level warfare in France, with profound effects on military theory, including Guibert's. Gribeauval was the premier technician of the French army in the late eighteenth century, creating a system of artillery that promised to greatly enhance the speed and maneuverability of the arm.

Mesnil-Durand was born on the family's ancient noble estate in Lower Normandy. Like Guibert, he entered the army at an early age, rising through the ranks to become colonel en second of the Regiment of Navarre during the 1770s and 1780s. He did not tally any notable service during the Seven Years War, appearing instead to devote himself to writing.[47]

A disciple of Folard, Mesnil-Durand adopted much of the former's work for his own theoretical system. His first study appeared in 1755. In it he adapted Folard's *plésions* into a more contemporary system, acknowledging the impropriety of creating an army of pike and shot in the eighteenth century. But he continued to denigrate the importance of fire, particularly that of artillery. As a result, the ballistic arm remained almost entirely absent from Mesnil-Durand's tactics. He also reduced much of the fire role of the infantry, insisting on Folard's principles of speed and shock. Perhaps as a sop to those who argued for a more disciplined army based on the Prussian model, Mesnil-Durand's model contained numerous technical points and maneuvers to properly function, requiring a complex geometrical system bordering on pedantry.[48]

Mesnil-Durand offered hardly more than a rehash of Folard's ideas from three decades prior. Nevertheless, he benefited immensely from the growing polemical climate in military theory. Proponents of the noble position and those who argued for a "French" system rallied to Mesnil-Durand, arguing that his constitution embodied those virtues in contrast to others that proved too "Prussian." Almost singlehandedly, Mesnil-Durand reignited the polarizing debate between his own l'ordre profond and the growing school of l'ordre mince, which had lapsed during the Seven Years War. Thus began a second generation of debates built on the arguments put forth between the 1720s and 1750s.[49]

Of the major eighteenth-century theorists, Bourcet possessed the most military experience after Saxe. Born in 1700 in the village of Usseaux, then a part of France but now in Italy, Bourcet entered military service at a young age, became a staff officer, and gained particular expertise in mountain warfare along the Franco-Italian border. Focusing his career on the military problems posed by the Italian Alps, his many writings on the subject included detailed staff planning for invasions across the treacherous mountain passes. During the Wars of Polish and Austrian Succession, Bourcet served on the headquarters staffs of the French armies stationed in the Italian theater, chiefly creating maps and planning campaigns. From the 1760s to his death in 1780, he devoted himself to writing memoirs and studies of mountain warfare in Italy.[50]

Bourcet's most important work appeared sometime in the mid-eighteenth century. Entitled *Principes de la guerre des montagnes*, he wrote it for internal use by the French officer corps.[51] In the pamphlet he advocates the division of the army into autonomous units that could traverse the mountain passes more rapidly than conventionally organized forces. By dividing an army into sections, Bourcet suggests that it could move more efficiently and quickly. Due to the intrinsic instabilities of mountain warfare, he also advocates a "plan of many branches," with various attacks and maneuvers designed in case one or more mountain passes were blocked.[52]

This study had titanic repercussions on military theory. Bourcet is almost universally credited with expounding the foundations of operational-level warfare with this treatise. The parceling of an army into "divisions" shattered the unitary organization that had remained the basis of tactics and operations in European armies since the Roman period. His "plan of many branches" originated with operations in the Alps on the Franco-Italian border: "Any proposed campaign must have several branches and be so well planned that one or another of the branches cannot fail to complete the operation. Here is how one would form them, for example, in three: one to open the debouche on the right, which necessarily carries with it the siege of a [fortified] place; the other [second, in the center] to make itself master of the Tendi Pass, which opens onto the plain, and for which the diversion is located on the left; and the third to master the passages that relate to the Esture valley."[53] Bourcet's theories were applied to mountain warfare, largely as an effort to grapple with the particular operational challenges of crossing the Alps to reach the plains of northern Italy via the few dangerous passes that an army could use.

The utility of Bourcet's proposals in a wider context became apparent in the decades after this work appeared. His recommendation to divide an army into separate "branches" laid the foundation for autonomous operations along separate routes regardless of the presence or absence of mountains and passes. Bourcet's model army, marching on separate routes and uniting only shortly before contact with the enemy, possessed operational articulation, arguably for the first time in French history. A commander skilled enough to keep such a force in hand and maneuver it effectively could use Bourcet's methods to dictate the pace of a campaign and force favorable battles.[54]

Jean-Baptiste Vaquette de Gribeauval was born at Amiens in 1715 and entered the French service in 1732 as an artillerist. The technical branches would remain his occupation for the remainder of his life and career, including service with sappers and miners during the 1750s. In 1757 he was promoted to lieutenant colonel and assigned to make a study of the Austrian artillery, both as an effort to warm relations with Louis's new ally and to bring the French artillery in line with the Austrian branch, which was considered to be the best in Europe at the time. During his tour, Gribeauval founded the Austrian Sapper Corps.[55]

Following the Seven Years War, Choiseul appointed him inspector of French artillery and tasked him with redesigning the artillery system. Gribeauval began by adopting the Dutch method of drilling cannon bores in a finished piece rather than casting the bores with a mold. This greatly reduced windage and strengthened the barrel of the gun, improving both the accuracy and distance of each firing. It also had the benefit of providing standardized calibers, which reduced the overall weight of the siege train by eliminating many extraneous-sized shot. Following this line, Gribeauval also disposed of all but three calibers of field artillery (twelve-, eight-, and four-pound guns) and four calibers of siege artillery (twenty-four-, sixteen-, twelve-, and eight-pound guns). To this he added a six-inch howitzer and several types of mortar.[56]

Gribeauval constructed his guns and other equipment using interchangeable parts, heretofore a prohibitively expensive proposition. But the burgeoning Industrial Revolution now lowered the price of both labor and industrial production, allowing for parts to be made separately and later assembled into a finished product rather than being created wholly by an artisan. While Gribeauval did not originate the concept, he proposed the first recorded instance of using interchangeable parts in weapons manufacturing, representing an important step in the evolution of the science.[57]

The net result, which became known as the Gribeauval system, greatly reduced the cost and weight of cannon while simultaneously increasing their efficiency. Yet many within the army objected to the loss of both heavier and regimental guns provided in the extant Vallière system, named for fellow artillery theorist Louis-César de la Baume le Blanc, duc de Vaujours et de la Vallière. The latter regimen remained in force throughout Choiseul's administration despite the minister's effort to institute Gribeauval's changes. Gribeauval lost favor at court after the fall of Choiseul, and his reforms remained unimplemented.[58]

Armies that are generally successful tend not to produce reform movements that are as radical as those for armies that have been defeated. France had not experienced significant defeat in decades, arguably centuries.[59] The Seven Years War proved different. The humiliation of the army in that conflict illuminated the deep divisions within its structure, illustrating its doctrinal deficits. More fundamentally, the fissures in the state and society began to widen during the period, in part because of the crushing defeat. In addition, a financial crisis mounted as military spending spun out of control. Noble and bourgeois groups championed a variety of solutions, including the merit of education rather than birth, calling into question the basic assumptions of French society and the state built on it.

By the late eighteenth century, the cracks inherent in the system had widened past the point of easy correction. In particular, the anachronistic web of royal and state revenues proved inadequate to the financing of an early modern government, particularly one under the intense strain of maintaining both a colonial empire and a Continental military. The massive expenditures paid out on the War of the Austrian Succession and Seven Years War pushed the state into virtual bankruptcy and stimulated numerous reform efforts to rectify the situation.[60]

Financial concerns became the impetus of every attempted reform between 1760 and 1789. This produced a second crisis, one with profound social and structural roots and implications, as the nobility's position in French society eroded. A rancorous polemical debate followed, particularly in the wake of the defeat of 1763. Within the officer corps, reactionaries dug in as nonmilitary philosophes and other officers endeavored to lever them from their positions. Another debate emerged after the rise of Prussia as a military power. Writers like Johann Ernst, baron von Pirch, lauded the methods of Frederick II, counseling the adoption of Prussian-style discipline and methods within the French army.[61] Others demanded the return to "French" methods, emphasizing the works of Folard and Saxe that called for troops fighting with loose discipline and élan. This produced the most significant polarizing discussion, culminating in a crisis of military theory, within the military of the late eighteenth century. As is de rigueur in French debates, proponents of both positions crafted polemics defending their position and assailing the opposition.

On the surface these debates appeared to paralyze the French army as much as they did the state and society. Yet the two movements diverged, particularly after 1760. Society and the state remained mired in discussions over power, corporate coherence, and proposed reforms, particularly of the financial system. Their refusal to consider bankruptcy allowed the debates to fester without accomplishing real change. Conversely, the debates of the latter half of the eighteenth century within the army did not illustrate its weakness but rather its strength. Military defeat, especially at Rossbach, bankrupted the military. It forced theorists and practitioners alike to face the harsh reality that French doctrine did not compare favorably to the Prussians, much less the other great powers. Therefore, the ensuing debate drove reform within the army, sharpening it and bringing into focus the lack of institutional doctrine. This allowed reformers to propose competing theoretical systems for discussion. Others, chiefly Guibert, epitomized those reforms, drawing the best from each system into hybrid doctrines. Together, they laid the foundation for the creation of the institutional army.

Three major developments occurred before 1770: the adoption of the socket bayonet around 1698, the use of cadenced step in 1754, and the development of Guibert columns in 1769. Together, these served to greatly advance the discipline, organization, and professionalism of the French army, a necessary step from medieval to modern. This provided the foundation for the development of doctrine that dictated the discipline, organization, and tactics of the entire military that would develop after 1770. Taken together, these represent the continued push to create an institutional army.

CHAPTER 3

THE *ESSAI GÉNÉRAL DE TACTIQUE*

Guibert's magnum opus, the *Essai général de tactique*, originated in the 1760s. It was likely drafted during his time under his father with Choiseul and in lax periods while on Corsica.[1] It drew heavily on the preceding decades of military reform and also benefited from the works of Guibert's fellow military theorists, particularly Saxe and the duc de Broglie, from whom Guibert pulled much of his organizational and operational thought.

Mesnil-Durand, Bourcet, and Gribeauval all gave important background theories and information for Guibert's work. Mesnil-Durand provided the foil to his ideas before and after its publication. Bourcet's operational warfare combined with the young officer's experience under Broglie to shape the organizational and operational changes he advocated. Gribeauval's artillery system, despite its rejection by the army establishment, laid the foundation for Guibert's doctrine in that field. Together, they added to the spectrum of eighteenth-century reform providing the backdrop to the *Essai général de tactique*.[2]

Guibert's youth and training inculcated in him a deep understanding and experience of military theory and its practice in war. It also ignited a desire to modernize French society and government, in accordance with Enlightenment principles, to be better defined and more rational and functional. As his career advanced throughout the 1760s, Guibert composed his treatise on military theory, dubbing it an "encyclopedia . . . of the military science" in keeping with the Enlightenment quest for definition and enumeration.[3] Like his previous work on the 1769 *Instruction for Light Troops*, Guibert intended the *Essai général de tactique* to be a wholesale plan of military reform, not simply a technical document or a polemical entry into the growing tactical disputes of the late eighteenth century. He created a prototype for French doctrine, embracing all levels of war from petty tactics to grand strategy, and its effects on the state and society. Guibert declared with the *Essai* his

55

intention to create a modern institutional army and military doctrine for France.

The *Essai* begins with a discussion of French politics and society. The "Discours préliminaire," an introductory piece to the larger work, elaborates much of Guibert's thought in these two areas. To the young philosophe, reform of the army could not proceed without first recreating its parents: the state and society. The "Discours" establishes the basic principles for constitutional reforms in politics. Drawing from Enlightenment thought, Guibert demands a state and a military founded on rationality, pragmatism, simplicity, and adaptability. The primary virtue of this system was discipline, without which ministers and soldiers alike would squander their power in petty disputes. He calls for strong control of the army, chiefly to maintain discipline.[4]

Guibert demands a unitary state grounded in virtue, reason, and discipline, believing that a state should be well founded on a political constitution, much as an army be founded on a military constitution. Moreover, Guibert finds the two to be codependent. A state without a well-built constitution could not produce an effective military, as he concludes the French had proven in the Seven Years War.[5]

Battlefield success, he argues, came as a result of training, discipline, organization, tactics, and leadership. Yet these proved fleeting when drawn from a commander's personal rather than an institutional doctrine. A great general might lead his army to victory, but his successors, devoid of his genius and abilities, would watch it tumble to ruin. This is precisely what occurred in Sweden after Gustavus Adolphus and in France after Louis XIV, Guibert asserts: their successes proved transitory because they did not rest on a firm institutional foundation. While new methods and doctrine were vital to the military's regeneration process, they were meaningless without social and political reforms.[6]

Guibert found the unity of politics, society, and the army to be sorely lacking in the contemporary world, particularly in France. He unearthed an explanation for this absence in the period of Louis XIV's reign. Effective ministers under his service, like Jean-Baptiste Colbert, placed the kingdom on a firm financial and political footing. Other ministers, jealous of Colbert's skill and power, actively combatted the progress of the state in order to aggrandize themselves. Guibert blames François-Michel le Tellier, marquis de Louvois, for robbing Colbert's Department of the Marine of needed resources, thus undermining the power of the French navy due to a petty political dispute. Louvois's actions granted Louis XIV a large and powerful army, enflaming his territorial ambitions and embroiling Europe in decades of disastrous and costly wars. During these decades, armies expanded and destruction spread, bankrupting states with no discernible return on the investment of money and blood. The reign of Louis XV proved worse as he continued his predecessor's destructive policies with none of his skill or innovative ability. France plunged into the abyss of debt and military decline, Guibert maintains, not only because of its anachronistic doctrine but also because the state and society proved corrupt and in need of change.[7]

That reform, according to Guibert, could only come from strict discipline in both personal and governmental conduct. Like many of his contemporaries, he longed for the discipline of the classical period, particularly Republican Rome, lauding its virtues and civic sensibilities. Young men, motivated by patriotism, volunteered for national service. They dedicated themselves to discipline, producing political and military leaders of dedication and patriotism who refused to feud with each other like Louvois and Colbert. Rather, they developed their political and organizational skills to better serve their countries and their institutions.[8]

Each of Guibert's governmental reforms represents a branch of the same tree, all striving for the betterment of society, the state, and the army to achieve success. This formula had enabled Rome to soar to hegemonic heights under the Republic. Later, during its imperial period, men forgot their virtue and discipline, descending into vice and laxity. Corruption entered politics as each official sought to enrich himself at the expense of others within the same government. Rot spread from the core, and Rome succumbed to the barbarians.[9]

Guibert undoubtedly drew inspiration for his idealistic portrayal of Republican Rome not only from his contemporaries but also from the military theorist Flavius Vegetius Renatus. Vegetius's *De re militaris* contains a critique of late-imperial Rome that has remarkable similarities in tone and style to Guibert's analysis of his own day. The Roman set the example for many Enlightenment writers by castigating late-imperial society for its decadence and lack of dedication to patriotism and duty. His work remained popular among military circles for its thorough examination of theory and discipline, creating a constitutional system of the type Guibert proposed.[10]

Vegetius provided much of the impetus for Guibert's criticisms and proposed reforms. Building on that foundation, he constructed his "constitution." It begins at the lowest level of society, with the citizen. He theorizes that young men must dedicate themselves to either the militia or the army to create a firm foundation for both. The latter institution would be small, only large enough to act as a deterrent to enemy aggression and to allow the government limited foreign intervention. The former would serve to deter enemy invasion by mobilizing the entire young-male population of the threatened region. All citizens would be dedicated to virtue and discipline, striving to use their abilities for the betterment of the nation. This social and military linkage was mirrored in politics. Like Guibert's military, his government would be administered by skilled and knowledgeable men dedicated to the state.[11]

Discipline, professionalism, and skill informed the actions and policies of the administrators in Guibert's ideal state. When combined, they would produce a society that embodied the virtue and discipline he sought:

> Suppose that there was elevated in Europe a vigorous people, of intelligence, of means, and of government; a people who combine austere virtues, a national militia, and a fixed plan of aggrandizement, who would not forget the [larger] view of the system, who know how to make war at little cost, and subsist on their victories, not reduced to laying down their arms by calculations of finance. We should see that people subjugate its neighbors and overthrow their feeble constitutions like the north wind bending the frail reeds.[12]

Many commentators have noted the air of revolutionary thought in this passage—the most famous from the *Essai général de tactique*—particularly the notion of a nation-in-arms rising up to overwhelm its enemies. The last line is often presented as a prophecy of the French Revolutionary army, which supposedly overcame its enemies with élan and superior numbers.[13] But this analysis misrepresents Guibert's intent. If the text preceding it is related as well, the meaning becomes clear:

> What is now the result of our wars? States have neither treasure nor excesses of population. Their spending in peacetime already exceeds their revenue. Therefore, they declare war. They take the

field with armies that can be neither recruited nor paid. Victor or vanquished, they are eventually exhausted. The mass of national debt increases. Credit falls. Money is lost. Fleets have no sailors and armies no soldiers. The ministers from both sides sense it is time to negotiate. Peace is made. Some colonies or provinces change hands. Often the source of disputes is not resolved, and everyone rests on the debris [of their efforts], occupied by paying their debts and sharpening their weapons.[14]

To Guibert, the "vigorous people" was not a call for revolution but rather a pipe dream, or perhaps an unattainable Utopian standard for which to strive. The famous passage, quoted out of context, appears to be a prophecy of the Revolution's mass armies. Yet it makes no sense in Guibert's doctrine without its context.[15]

Guibert did not intend to prophesy a revolution. Throughout the work, he never wavers from his conviction that governments need a strong guiding hand and that popular participation must be avoided. He argues that all men should dedicate themselves to militia service. Yet not only did he fail to predict the mass armies of the Year II, but the very idea ran counter to the fundamental principle of his reforms—discipline. In the passage Guibert calls for small, professional, disciplined armies rather than large, popular, mass legions. Nowhere in his doctrine is found a call for citizen armies to bathe the Continent in blood and flame. He clearly delimits his popular participation to the militia, which he restricts to operating in its resident region. The line army was to remain the province of disciplined professionals.[16]

Rather than an instrument of revolution, Guibert views his militia as a means to an end: the disciplining and betterment of society. But those in power could not help but feel threatened by an armed citizenry. Thus, the citizen militia in Guibert's system would serve only the needs of national defense. He carefully places parameters around its deployment, requiring its members to remain in their birth cantons and forbidding its units from use as a ready reserve during wartime.[17]

This argument, perhaps better than any other, demonstrates Guibert's political naivety. An ideal minister, perhaps in the mold of Nicolas Catinat or Guillaume de l'Hôpital, might seek to leave the militia to its intended purpose.[18] But a savvy and ambitious politician could easily take advantage of the aggregation of state power in the militia. An armed citizens' militia, properly employed, could shake the foundations of the French state and possibly effect a transfer of power. In fact, the Enlightenment emphasis on classical education offered a plethora of examples of Roman emperors crowned and deposed by the Praetorian Guard. To place similar power in the hands of ambitious politicians in contemporary France and rely on their goodwill and "virtue" smacks of political gullibility, perhaps understandable given Guibert's youth. He seems to have disregarded the specter of Caesarism, which had brought an abrupt end to the Roman Republic he idealized.[19]

Guibert's careful consideration of political and social reform underlay his technical reforms of the army. Without the "regeneration of the state," a reformed army would not properly function. Although the bulk of the *Essai général de tactique* contains military reforms, Guibert placed the political and social concerns first to illustrate their primacy. After enumerating them, he moved to his proposed military constitution.[20]

An army "better constituted and more maneuverable..., easy to move and to conduct ... [with] simple, analogous, [and] flexible tactics" was the goal of Guibert's systematic doctrine. He based his constitution on three major principles: simplicity, flexibility, and speed. Each was integral to the system and was present at the tactical, operational, and strategic levels. The concept of pragmatism underlay the entire constitution rather than the "pretention to precision and perfection on many points, meticulous and ridiculous," for which many contemporary armies were noted, particularly the Prussian but also the French. He removed almost all processional maneuvers in favor of a simple and flexible organization. These changes aided Guibert's third principle—speed.[21] Accelerated march step and the liberation of march order from battle order would lead to increased mobility.

Guibert begins with a reform of tactical organization, advocating the efficacy of line infantry and constructing his ideal army around that branch. He ordains the battalion his preferred tactical unit, for "battalions reunite the properties of fire, shock, simplicity, lightness, [and] solidity," providing the all-purpose organization for his system. Guibert rejects the Old Regime tradition of dividing battalions into two or four sections. Instead, he proposes dividing battalions into three divisions of three companies each, thus providing a natural division of left, center, and right within the basic tactical unit.[22]

Guibert argues that "the natural and habitual order is the proper order of fire, that is to say l'ordre mince." According to this idea, a line would offer more firepower than a column: "The primitive, fundamental, and habitual order of infantry will be on three ranks of depth; the momentary and accidental order will be the column." Lines formed on three ranks of depth, per the *Réglement* of 1754, providing a much wider front than the formations of l'ordre profond.[23] This multiplied the volume of fire from an army deployed in such a formation.

Moreover, Guibert rejects the primary virtues of l'ordre profond, arguing that fire proved superior to shock because it could be used from a variety of formations and circumstances. The formal attack columns of l'ordre profond were designed to hit enemy lines with deep physical force, creating a breach. But Guibert argues that the effects of incoming fire would upset the column's close formation, robbing it of its physical momentum and rendering it ineffectual at best. He also takes into account the morale of the soldier on the battlefield, unlike many of his contemporary theorists, noting that a closely deployed unit tends to panic when under fire, losing its formation. Taken together, these deficiencies rendered the entire ordre-profond system inoperable.[24]

For his part, Guibert suggests that battalions deploy into lines of between 140 and 180 men in length, as a line any longer would be beyond the ability of the commander to control. This provides for battalions of approximately 400–500 men, which one scholar notes were "considerably smaller than any advocated by previous writers."[25] Small battalions, and smaller formations in general, appealed to Guibert's sense of order and flexibility.

The *Essai général de tactique*'s detailed fine tuning of the size and shape of a battalion is pure pedantry in the vein of contemporary polemical debate, however, Guibert's small battalion represented a principle rather than a maxim. Armies before the 1760s relied on large, unwieldy formations. Guibert's battalion was intended as a polemical argument to skew theory to the direction of smaller, more maneuverable units, whether they conformed to the exact specifications he gave or not.

Continuing his reforms, Guibert argues for a faster march and double step for his battalions, 80 and 160 steps per minute, respectively. The increase in double-step speed would lead to greater maneuverability, as this was the slowest pace suggested for use in battle. Guibert also calls for a triple step, although he does not provide a specific pace for it. Essentially a run, triple step would allow units to remain in formation while attacking in column, retreating in good order, or deploying to another sector of the battlefield.[26] Guibert's smaller, quicker battalions would be more flexible and maneuverable, thus more easily commanded and much more easily adapted to counter any situation encountered in combat.

Guibert's organizational reforms on the grand tactical level strongly reflect his work under Choiseul, particularly the *Instruction for Light Troops*. His smaller battalions and quicker march speed were to be employed by the "Guibert columns" of that earlier document. Instead of the unitary or double column of march and deployment of standard practice, in the *Essai* Guibert calls for small columns of maneuver, separated by a short distance and screened by light cavalry. The columns would advance at normal step, gradually increasing pace as they neared the enemy's line, officers maintaining order and separation between the columns to prevent bunching. If the attack succeeded, the light cavalry would pursue and harass the enemy to prevent a counterattack. Consequently, his proposal effectively reduced the various types of columns then employed to a single, all-purpose column.[27]

Guibert believed that the Old Regime concept of keeping the infantry line perfectly intact while on the march or while deployed was nonsense. He also rejected the processional movements that had developed in the last few decades that emphasized rigid adherence to march orders and parade-ground precision. Instead, he argues for "movements that are by battalion and never by regiment," essentially devolving march and battle order to the battalion level. While the larger administrative units would provide an outline and even the arrangement of the march, Guibert expected the battalion to maneuver around obstacles on its own authority. The *Essai* allows for a formation disrupted by terrain as long as the army as a whole maintained its cohesion. Battalion commanders could act autonomously, thus improving overall flexibility.[28]

Guibert's evolutions, or the methods of deployment from march to battle order, reflect his push for simplicity and pragmatism.[29] The *Essai* proposes four basic evolutions to function in all situations: "doubling the ranks, making movements of conversion, forming in column, and deploying *en bataille*."[30] These encompassed the possible uses of his battalions on a battlefield. The first served as a defense against cavalry, a median step between the deployed line and the later cavalry square. The second, movements of conversion, included all the individual and unit maneuvers required to orient forces within the larger army; for example, quarter-wheels by individuals or by battalion that preceded a line march into position. Deployment in column included both march and battle columns. Deployment en bataille consisted largely of maneuvers into line from march column and vice versa. Guibert notes that deployment should not be held to a rigid standard. The first company of a battalion could deploy to the left or the right rather than always to the right, which was common practice in contemporary armies.[31] The result stripped away the complicated, scientific maneuvers of the Old Regime in favor of a simple, flexible system.

"The circumstances, the nature of the terrain, the situation of the enemy," Guibert notes, "can require that one go without fire and that one engages in shock action." He argues for the use of attack columns under these circumstances particularly when attacking a fortified position, commonly referred to as a "point." Yet he rejects the organization of l'ordre profond for his attack columns since it required a series of complex maneuvers to maintain the closed formation of the attack column when deploying. Instead of one or two attack columns in close order, Guibert instead promotes the methods he helped craft in the *Instruction for Light Troops*, providing for a series of smaller columns with intervals between them. His system of attack columns was far more flexible and maneuverable than those of l'ordre profond. He also all but eliminated the processional movements of that system by breaking his columns with intervals.[32]

Contrary to extant theory and the growing debate, Guibert here insists on adherence to neither l'ordre mince nor l'ordre profond, not confining himself to a single argument or polemical system. Rather, he creates a dynamic doctrine that would allow either column or line formations to be used, including by the same unit, as circumstances dictated. He names this system *l'ordre mixte*.[33] An important historiographical point must be made with regard to this term. Unlike l'ordre profond or l'ordre mince, l'ordre mixte was not a rigid system, nor was it a tactical formation. It was a combination of organization and tactics that allowed a variety of formations and tactics to be used at the discretion of officers to meet battlefield conditions. While Guibert preferred a linear formation that maximized firepower, he did not dismiss the use of shock through attack columns. This was the crux of his doctrine: removing processional, traditional, and rigid procedures in favor of those that were far more flexible and adaptable.

While the line infantry remains the foundation and primary tool of Guibert's theoretical army and constitution, cavalry serves several important roles. These duties include disrupting enemy lines of communication and supply, scouting, raiding, screening, shock attacks, and pursuit. Just as Guibert's basic tactical infantry unit is a subunit of the regiment, so too his basic tactical cavalry unit is the smaller squadron. His squadron consists of eighty men, a reduction in size from contemporary squadrons, to be more flexible.[34]

Guibert divides his cavalry into two types, light and heavy. Light cavalry consisted of dragoons and hussars who perform all but shock attacks, which he leaves to the heavy cavalry. Of the two, Guibert prefers light cavalry, as it would be more maneuverable and adaptable to rapidly changing battlefield situations. But he acknowledges the usefulness of heavy cavalry while advocating significant changes for it. He makes his cuirassiers more mobile by the removal of the traditional cuirass in favor of a series of draped chains to protect the cavalryman from enemy saber blows. This serves to make the cavalryman lighter and necessarily more maneuverable, amplifying speed without sacrificing defense in Guibert's estimation.[35]

Like many of his points on infantry, Guibert's cavalry instructions contain much pedantry, particularly the notion of dismissing with the cuirass. His draped chains, even in the form of chain mail, provide no conceivable use, particularly over the extant cuirass. Heavy cavalry, chiefly cuirassiers, continued to play a vital role in warfare during and after the publication of the *Essai général de tactique*, particularly as the *masse de décision*. But Guibert's pedantry conceals a deeper meaning. He does not tie the cavalry to the infantry's formation, negating its maneuverability, as many of his contemporaries had, including most of the proponents of l'ordre profond. His doctrine incorporates cavalry in a dynamic interchange with infantry, with each supporting the other depending on circumstances. As Robert Quimby notes, this was virtually unknown in military theory before Guibert.[36]

As with the cavalry, Guibert includes the artillery in his doctrine as a fully functioning branch of the army, albeit one with a less significant role than infantry or cavalry. To do so he adopts the principles of the Gribeauval system, particularly its promise of lighter, more mobile guns to support the other arms. Guibert subordinates artillery to the rest of the army, as it was "a utile and important accessory of the troops that compose armies . . . [because it] cannot fight alone and by [itself]," which the other branches could. As with cavalry, he sought to reduce the amount of artillery as a percentage of the army at large, soundly rejecting the practice of building grand batteries and the use of battalion guns, both of which contributed to a proliferation of artillery throughout the period. He argues that these hindered armies and prevented maneuver as the ponderous guns forced the entire army to move at a slow pace.[37]

Instead, Guibert advocates the use of small, maneuverable batteries of Gribeauval guns within his model army. These proved more maneuverable because they were lighter than normal, allowing them to more ably find the appropriate place on the battlefield where they were needed. Only these small batteries would leave the artillery park, leaving a large group in reserve. Guibert counsels this approach because he believed that dispersing guns across the front reduced maneuverability and bogged an army down. His system, Guibert concludes, would create mobile artillery units better designed to support infantry and cavalry.[38]

Light infantry, which was generally distinguished from line infantry during the Old Regime, composed the fourth arm of Guibert's contemporary army. As such, he designed his doctrine to encompass the use of this newest arm of European militaries. Light forces originated in the early years of the 1700s, likely born of the Austrian *Grenzers* drawn from the Habsburg-Ottoman border region. Their efficacy in the first wars of the century led most states, including France, to adopt their use in increasing numbers.[39]

Guibert notes the loss of many line soldiers to the light infantry, pointing out that up to 20 percent of an army's line could be lost in this way. He disapproves of this, noting that skirmishers serve their specialized role well but could not fight in any other manner. His doctrine centers on the line infantry, and the drain of manpower to the ranks of skirmishers thus diminished that core. He includes greatly limited numbers of light infantry, who would serve an auxiliary role much like that of light cavalry. These skirmishers scouted, screened the army, and harassed enemy forces both beyond and within the battlefield. Most importantly, Guibert advocates for training line infantry in the skills of skirmishing, further reducing the number of specialist light troops in favor of multipurpose soldiers. Together, this system would be far more flexible than those currently employed, allowing battalions to fight in closed or open order as the battle dictated rather than by preordained plans or roles.[40]

The reductions in the three supporting arms in favor of the line infantry indicate the thrust of Guibert's doctrine. He sought to create a unitary army that concentrated its force rather than dispersing it into rigid formations. He accomplished this, paradoxically, by providing the mechanisms by which the line infantry, supported by cavalry, artillery, and light infantry, could break into small and maneuverable units. An army thus constituted could use superior maneuverability and flexibility to concentrate against enemy weak points like no contemporary force could.[41]

The organizational and tactical reforms of the *Essai général de tactique* provide the foundation for the higher levels of war. Much of Guibert's analysis concerns the operational level, particularly his design of a prototypical battle using his system in theoretical practice, further elucidating its principles. Borrowing from Saxe, he notes that "all the secret of exercise, of war, is in the legs." The basis of operational success mirrored tactical success in that both were based on speed and mobility. He argues that "for a large mass to be moved with the most ease, it must be divided . . . into many parts; then each of the parts is susceptible to more movement and action; then one can, by these forces combined and multiplied, act on all the parts at a time; this is therefore an army."[42]

To accomplish this goal, Guibert uses an ad-hoc formation that had appeared during the Seven Years War in Broglie's army: the division. Just as the battalion serves as Guibert's tactical unit, the division serves as the basic operational unit of his army. Divisions are combined-arms units composed of infantry, cavalry, and in some circumstances artillery, thus providing greater march security, discipline, and operational flexibility.[43] But Broglie's use of divisions never became a permanent formation in the larger army because it was a personal doctrine unique to the commander, not to the institution.

Guibert remedies this by implementing the division in his doctrine. Like his battalions, Guibert's divisions are smaller than those of large enemy detachments, and like the battalions, make up for this weakness with superior mobility. On the level of petty tactics, the increase in march step enables his divisions to move much faster than enemy formations. At the grand-tactical level, Guibert columns would allow units to deploy from march to battle order within their divisions as needed. This greatly increases speed and flexibility as it eliminates the complicated maneuvers necessary in an Old Regime army to deploy from march to battle order. It also allows divisions to disperse and use different march routes to arrive at the same destination. "[These] principles ... will be able to render march more rapid and easier, will separate the army in many bodies that reunite on a point, or to within range of a prepared point," Guibert concludes.[44]

Unitary march necessitated a lengthy process delaying movement; dispersed march allowed units to maneuver at a much more rapid pace. As Bourcet had envisioned in the Alpine passes, divisions marched within support distance of each other and only converged into battle formation once the enemy was sighted and the battlefield selected. Past practice preferred a dispersal along a cordon line: units generally occupied a fortified "place" until march orders were received and then formed the march column through a tedious series of processional maneuvers. Guibert's operational system borrows from his tactical organization, creating an articulated operational system. His divisions would maneuver on the enemy flanks, together or separately, to find a weak point in the same manner as his battalions at the tactical level. Above all, use was dictated by practicality rather than predetermined formation or tradition.[45]

This portion of Guibert's constitution most clearly illustrates Bourcet's influence. His dispersed divisions bear a remarkable resemblance to his predecessor's "plan of many branches." Guibert drew much of his operational philosophy from Bourcet's work, creating a dynamic interchange between the two that would play out over the next generation of military theory.[46] This leads to an important historiographical debate. Operational-level warfare, as conceived by modern scholars, originated at some point during the eighteenth century. Various scholars credit different armies and commanders with this development. Many look to Frederick II of Prussia, particularly his campaigns between 1740 and 1759.[47] Other scholars argue that Bourcet and Guibert developed the practice. Claus Telp credits Guibert with being "particularly important for the 'discovery' of the operational level of war." Yet to the contrary, R. R. Palmer argues that while Guibert's theory is "more Napoleonic than Frederician," he did not grasp the core principles of operational-level warfare and wrote most often in terms of a unitary army.[48]

Guibert and his contemporaries certainly did not speak in terms of "operational warfare." Yet the conceptual leap from Guibert's tactical envelopment of an enemy's flanks to a flank attack via operational maneuver is small: "by the disposition of march one can carry a part of the army on the flank of the enemy, while one carries the rest of the front," he concludes.[49] Thus, Guibert did think in terms of a unitary army and not the independent commands of Napoleonic warfare.

Nevertheless, Guibert's true innovation came in the institutionalization of doctrine rather than in any particular discovery of operations. In the *Essai* he provides the army-wide grammar by which later practitioners would build phrases and sentences. His system established the framework that allowed future leaders to develop the operational art. In particular, his tactical and organizational reforms freed commanders from the processional strictures of past practice.[50]

As a result, Guibert's organizational reforms, along with his emphasis on discipline, potentially could grant his army an operational flexibility not seen in many contemporary forces. He uses these changes to describe a model attack, illustrating his system in practice. His new army would deploy from column to line on the battlefield using simplified evolutions and Guibert columns, stressing that units should never deploy under enemy fire, for this could not be executed in the disciplined order required for any linear maneuver. Light infantry, cavalry, and line infantry trained in the art of skirmishing would be placed in advance of the main body to disrupt enemy formations and attacks. After army deployment, the main attack would proceed. Drawing from the example of Frederick II of Prussia, Guibert's system generally prefers the tactical offensive based on maneuver against the enemy's flanks and local numerical superiority.[51]

His army would accomplish the first—maneuver on the flanks—primarily through "oblique order." Following contemporary conventional wisdom, Guibert declares that this formation style was developed by Frederick and used to great effect during his wars. In Guibert's oblique order, one flank of the army is re-fused, inviting enemy attack against a reinforced position. The other flank is then pushed forward against the enemy's subsequently weakened flank.[52]

In addition to his oblique order, Guibert also provides for a more general tactical envelopment of an enemy's flanks. An army deployed in Guibert's l'ordre mince would have a broader front than most enemy forces, particularly those deploying on four or more ranks. Spread in a thin line three ranks deep, his model army could wrap its flanks around the enemy's flanks and thus turn them.[53]

Local numerical superiority provided the key to Guibert's hypothetical operations. His articulated battalions would be able to maneuver more rapidly than standard militaries of the time, allowing his army to have greater numbers of men and greater volumes of fire at critical points on the battlefield. After achieving this local superiority, Guibert advocates "unit[ing] the most fire possible on the point that one attacks or defends." Fire from troops deployed in line, skirmishers, artillery, and cavalry would be focused on the enemy's weak point. Guibert's nimble attack columns also allowed for a tactical assault on a weak position, exploiting what would later be called the *Schwerpunkt*.[54] The flexibility and maneuverability of the system allowed his proposed attacks to go forward at great speed with expected success.

Continuing the model battle, line infantry would bear the brunt of the attack, with light infantry, cavalry, and artillery in supporting roles. But the shock charge by heavy cavalry still remained one of the best methods of breaking an enemy formation, according to Guibert. His cavalry assault would be performed in much the same manner as the infantry charge in column: gradually increasing in pace as the horse approached the enemy line, reaching the fastest pace just before contact. Yet this charge would be made in line rather than in column, as Guibert insists that cavalry could not properly act in closed column. Like his infantry battalions, Guibert's smaller squadrons were more maneuverable than their larger counterparts. This allows for the concentration of force on the enemy's weak points, of which a skilled commander could take full advantage with the more maneuverable Guibertian army.[55]

Formed in small rather than grand batteries, the model army's artillery would be employed against the enemy line, concentrating fire on its weakest point. The psychological effect of bombardment against infantry, he contends, would create local disruptions for attacking infantry and cavalry to exploit. Additional guns would remain in the artillery park to be brought up if necessary to support the infantry. Guibert notes that the best firing position for artillery was the oblique and on a slight rise, as these two factors allowed for the maximum damage from solid shot or canister.[56]

Guibert expected an army using this flexible and maneuverable system to sweep an enemy from the field. His organizational reforms would allow an army to move more swiftly and easily across terrain and into battle formation. His tactical and operational reforms provided the foundation upon which individual commanders could exercise their skills at their discretion. Only by using this system, he concluded, could French armies win and sustain victory.[57]

The role of the commander was a vital aspect of his system. Like the operational level of war, the strategic remained nebulous in contemporary theory. Guibert's "science of generals" combined the art and science of strategy, particularly as executed by commanders. As such, Guibert did not have the nuanced view of strategy that modern theorists possess. Nevertheless, in the *Essai* he establishes many of the foundational elements of the strategic level of war. The most fundamental of these principles is his belief in the strategic offensive. Guibert rejects the defensive as a matter of course when speaking of states' actions toward other states: "one does not reflect enough that there is not a good defensive, that the [good strategy] is the offensive." To this end, he abandoned Old Regime positional warfare in favor of a strategy of annihilation. In practice, this meant the abandonment of fortresses, defensive strongholds, and cordons, collectively referred to as *points d'appui* in contemporary parlance. He replaces these previously vital posts with a mobile, unitary army whose goal would be the destruction of the enemy army.[58] This concentration of force is made possible by the division system and the increased mobility of Guibert's army.

Logistics play a central role in Guibert's strategy. He argues that an important aspect of strategic mobility was the rejection of the Old Regime magazine-and-depot system. Guibert notes that such supply points slowed an army considerably, greatly reducing its mobility. Quoting Cato, he asserts that "it must be that war nourishes war."[59] This would liberate the army from lines of supply, granting it a greatly increased strategic mobility. The *Essai* does not advocate wholesale pillage of the countryside; such a system would run directly counter to his principles of discipline. Rather, Guibert calls for an orderly system of requisitions, overseen by officers and perhaps alongside civilian or government officials. In this way an army would abandon its magazines and depots for more-rapid movement while retaining its ability to nourish itself.[60]

These two arguments coalesce in Guibert's rejection of one of the principles of Old Regime warfare: the siege. He notes that the investment of a fortress required an army to maintain a static position for a lengthy period of time, greatly reducing its operational and strategic mobility. Leaving a fortress to the rear of a strategic advance would be possible only if the army could operate independent of lines of supply and communication, which Guibert's army could do in theory via the division and requisitions systems. These principles play an integral role in Guibert's strategic offensive.[61]

Guibert's system relies on the education of its practitioners, grounding them in discipline and the principles of the system. Throughout the *Essai*, he removes the systematic approach of the Old Regime in favor of a simpler, more flexible approach. This necessarily places greater responsibility on the individual, which in turn requires greater discipline. Guibert advocates constant drill to hone both a soldier's instincts and a general's battlefield command, drawing from the lessons of the reforms of the 1750s.[62]

Fire tactics much concerned the reformers of the period, including Guibert. These writers spilled much ink about the proper method of fire, whether by ranks or files, individual or alternating units, and volley or at will. In keeping with his general principles, Guibert stresses training to increase the battalion's fire discipline and thus its firepower. He also offers a number of maxims, bordering on pedantry, as to the exact nature of fire in combat.[63]

Despite his occasional stodginess, Guibert's fire principles remain a vital aspect of his doctrine. By rejecting the Prussian model, Guibert preempts critics who accused him of enslavement to that state's rigid discipline. His call for individualism in voluntary fire falls under the category of "French national character," which emphasizes individuality. To improve discipline, he argues for continual training with live ammunition to improve the soldier's aim, a rarity in the budget-challenged armies of the period. He also lobbies for bayonet training, as the psychological effects of cold steel could shatter enemy formations with minimal effort or casualties. Guibert's drill is simple, reinforcing the concepts of discipline and maneuver as a unit rather than processional movements or Prussian-style discipline.[64]

Guibert wholly rejects the Prussian practice of disciplined volleys, including on the march. In reality, as contemporaries knew and modern studies have elucidated, soldiers in battle rarely conform to fire practice and often resort to voluntary fire regardless of training.[65] Instead, he favors voluntary fire, or the *feu à volonté:* "This fire is the liveliest and deadliest of all; it stirs the mind of the soldier; it inures them to danger; it agrees perfectly with the vivacity and the skill of the French; its essence is only to accustom the soldier to stop on signal and to maintain silence."[66]

The same concepts of tactical training translated to operational and strategic education in Guibert's system. This would be accomplished via the training camp. Guibert devotes much of the second volume of the *Essai* to a discussion of these camps. Modeled on Frederick's annual Prussian exercises, Guibert's camps would be the "continual exercise of the work of war . . . where one can undertake a complete education" of both officers and men. He rejects the Old Regime tradition of using training camps as a quasi-Roman triumph designed to show the splendor of the French military. In the wake of the Seven Years War, such displays would ring hollow, if not laughable. Rather, he adopts the efficient model of the French service since the 1750s, which emphasized the education through maneuver of both individual units and the entire army.[67]

Guibert's camps, lasting for three months, were to be held annually in an isolated region. He specifies in great detail the composition of the opposing armies, both of which would use his tactical and organizational systems. These camps would educate all soldiers and officers in the practice of enumerated doctrine and include maneuvers by battalion, regiment, and division, both alone and against opposition. After putting them through the paces of basic maneuvering, Guibert would have both armies engage in a number of operational actions, demonstrating and testing his doctrinal principles. These exercises would train the junior officers in the minutiae of tactics and the senior officers in the principles of operational warfare. All officers would receive the pragmatic education that came from commanding their soldiers in combat-like situations.[68]

Guibert's model commanding officer was *un homme de génie* who could unite the art and science of warfare, a strong guiding hand for his army. This "man of genius" was an educated individual capable of inspiring his troops in battle, "rarely rest[ing] in action." He would possess superior *génie* and *moyen*, which correspond to the science and art of war. Training camps would serve as a valuable educational resource for instilling Guibert's system but hardly the beginning of an officer's education. This began with his génie, or the innate skill of command unique to officers and generally believed to be imparted through noble blood. According to Guibert, this was acquired through years of education, both civilian and military, which mirrored his own training in mathematics and the other skills necessary for an officer. To supplement this natural génie, an enlightened education in the technical aspects of warfare was necessary to impart moyen, or the technical knowledge required to understand the mathematical and physical principles of contemporary warfare. This flexibility in training and education would lead to more-skilled officers and qualitative continuity in their replacements. These officers would command army units as well as serve as staff.[69]

While an army constructed on Guibert's system could function adequately without such a leader, an homme de génie remained necessary to fully institute the doctrine. This commander would lead the army to victory, and his subordinates would direct their own units within the larger battle plan. Crucial to this leadership was *coup d'oeil*, which would allow the gifted commander to "perceive many objects, embrace many combinations; and therefore by consequence, where the mediocre general does not see the position to defend or the possibility of acting, [coup d'oeil] presents to the imagination of [the homme de génie] an advantageous movement" in both time and space. He would maneuver his forces in such a way as to take full advantage of this moment, leading to the defeat of the enemy. All officers would be educated in schools and training camps in the principles and precepts of Guibert's system.[70] This would produce the trained and skilled men who would lead the new army to victory.

Throughout the *Essai général de tactique*, Guibert often laments the destruction that accompanies war. He decries the human and financial costs and notes its terrible consequences on civilians, societies, and political systems. He remarks often on the need to ameliorate this destruction.[71] The carnage of war made a deep impression on Guibert and shaped his military and political discourse. Both his reform plan and its resulting doctrinal system were based in large part on this desire to minimize the damage. By creating a small, professional army, he hoped to remove warfare from society and isolate it to the battlefield. While he counsels forage for supply on campaign, he notes the need for a regular system of purchase rather than a reliance on looting and brigandage in order to maintain discipline and to reduce the effects on civilians. He also recognizes the disruptive nature of conscription on society. Although noting that wars are inevitable and occasionally desirable, Guibert sought to reduce their toll through discipline, professionalism, thrift, and a superior army that would overthrow the enemy quickly and with minimal human or financial costs.[72]

This minimization informs much of Guibert's tactics, operations, and strategy. An army better trained and organized could execute the variety of maneuvers detailed in the *Essai*, illustrating his flexible and maneuverable tactical system. In turn, this would allow the army to triumph over its enemies on the battlefield in short order, reducing casualties and the costs of campaigning. Similarly, his culling of the complex march formations greatly simplified operational maneuver, as did his insistence that "war should nourish war," meaning self-supply through an orderly system of purchase and requisition. In addition, Guibert's strategic thought reflects the need to reduce destructiveness. He firmly rejects the endless hegemonic wars of Louis XIV, preferring instead limited attacks according to a "fixed plan of aggrandizement." He writes that his army would function first for defense, defeating any enemy incursion; if required to conduct offensive action, it would sally forth to defeat the enemy in his own territory. Crucially, however, Guibert places diplomacy and international relations ahead of military action. In the *Essai* he argues that after demonstrating itself to be the superior force on the Continent, his new army would deter aggression from other states and encourage them to submit to France. This would render fighting moot, as the clearly superior French army would deter smaller states and lesser forces from even attempting resistance. Those who did fight would feel the full might of France.[73]

Guibert's true intent in the famous "north wind bending the reeds" passage becomes clear in the wider image of his entire reform project. His army's success depended on "a fixed plan of aggrandizement" and a "system" rather than the chaos of mass armies. He joined social, political, and military reforms in a doctrine that would subsist within the French army and state. It would outlast rulers, ministers, and even uniquely gifted generals, charting a blueprint of success for generations.[74] Guibert's ultimate goal was to provide France an enlightened, rational military doctrine based on social, political, and military reform.

Taken as a whole, the *Essai général de tactique* is a work unlike any other of its time. Guibert was little different from Bourcet, Mesnil-Durand, or Broglie in that he wrote military theory as both a philosophe and a practitioner of war. Yet his study stands apart because of its completeness. No other treatise of the period, and for many years following, would embrace every aspect and level of war in the manner of Guibert's. Although containing the pedantry typical of works of theory, Guibert's writing generally eschewed the complicated systems and precision of other systems, particularly those that relied on l'ordre profond. His analysis of politics and society, so clearly drawn from the Enlightenment tradition, also marked out Guibert among his contemporaries. In particular, he noted the dynamic linkages between state, society, and the army.[75] Guibert's simple and penetrating analysis created a true doctrine for the first time in French history, the single most important step in the creation of the institutional army.

The *Essai général de tactique*'s path to publication is obscure and probably will remain so. Much speculation abounds as to the precise reason for its anonymous publication, but a plausible explanation suggests itself: the work contains a scathing attack on the French military and political establishment. Despite the need for reform demonstrated by the appointment of the Choiseul ministry, the army remained an inherently conservative body. A public attack, however warranted, exposed its internal flaws to neutral and hostile observers.[76] Any military institution naturally would want to conceal its faults, if only to preempt a first strike by enemies cognizant of its weakness. On a more personal level, Guibert was intensely aware of the possibility of the publication's failure. Always hyperconscious of his reputation, he undoubtedly published the *Essai* anonymously in order to ensure plausible deniability if it failed as a literary work.[77]

Despite its author's apprehensions, the *Essai général de tactique* proved a rousing success from the moment of its publication in several editions around 1772. The following year it achieved publication at Geneva and Liège; in 1774 it was translated into German and published at Dresden. Its enormous success was a watershed for Guibert. At the relatively young age of twenty-nine, his theories were the talk of every military establishment from the wilderness of North America to the court of Persia.[78] Frederick II of Prussia wrote a lengthy response praising the work in the *Journal littéraire de Berlin*. He demurred to Guibert's adoration of his art of war, noting to d'Alembert that he had "withdraw[n himself] in some measure from the noble profession on which Guibert gives such eloquent instructions."[79]

The king also discussed the young philosophe and his work at length with his most famous correspondent, adopting some of Voltaire's gently mocking style: "Guibert sees me with young eyes that have rejuvenated me. My hair is white, my force dissipated, my fire wanes. It is given only to rejuvenate them. The protégés of Apollo are more favored than those of Mars. . . . I believe that once Guibert has left his murderous art in your hands, he will become a capuchin or philosophe, and he will find in you a powerful protector."[80] While Guibert's later writings would refine his military constitution, the *Essai* was the most widely read and influential of his military works. Its effects would prove to be profound for both its author and the French army.

CHAPTER 4

La Gloire par tous les chemins

With the end of his assignment in Corsica, Guibert returned to the Continent in the hope of gaining fame and recognition as well as a position that would allow him to influence doctrine. To achieve military and political success required him to build a network of social, political, and military associates to advance his own interests, both personal and professional. In the particularist military of the late Old Regime, influence with the crown played a significant role in promotion and appointment to more prestigious commands. Court influence also dictated the disbursement of government pensions, which provided the major source of income for many in Guibert's station and profession, including the young officer himself.[1]

A simple path to achieve fame might have been through family connections, as was typical for the period, especially among noble families. Although Charles-Benoît Guibert was a prominent officer in the army and had many political connections, he appeared to eschew social interaction.[2] This left his son largely to his own devices for gaining entry into Parisian society and the Republic of Letters.

Over the next four years, Guibert would largely achieve the recognition he sought. He would rely on personal and military connections to gain admittance to the Republic of Letters and salon culture, where he found himself the object of admiration and curiosity. He took up romances with a number of women, including the famous *salonnière* Julie de Lespinasse. He continued his literary career during this time, publishing and debuting a theatrical work. Most importantly to him, many famous people like Voltaire and Frederick II of Prussia spoke of him in public and in private. This rise to fame would open many opportunities for Guibert, including the ability to travel across Europe in 1773 to observe the Prussian maneuvers that year and to join the French Ministry of War in late 1775. These years would serve as a crucial transition as he built his social network, gained recognition, and began to parlay both into power and influence, gaining "la gloire par tous les chemins" (glory by all paths).

During his formative years, Guibert had made several important relationships, both personal and professional. His father's network in the government, which included the powerful Broglie family, provided access to many of his earliest friends and connections.[3] One of these family relationships came in the person of Guibert's friend Dumouriez.[4] On their return to the Continent, Dumouriez introduced Guibert to his first literary *cercle*. Its membership included Claude Prosper Jolyot de Crébillon; Charles Collé; François-Augustin de Paradis de Moncrif; the duc de Richelieu (probably Louis-Antoine-Sophie de Vignerot du Plessis, duc de Fronsac); Jean-Louis Favier; and Emmanuel-Félicité de Durfort, duc de Duras. Like most salons, its members involved themselves in politics as well as literature. At the beginning of the crisis of the *parlements* in 1771, Guibert and the others published a memorandum requesting a meeting of the Estates-General. The members of this circle eased Guibert's entrée into the larger world of Parisian society. His *Essai* carried his name and reputation, opening every door for advancement.[5] Salongoers recognized his talents and welcomed him.

In addition to his precocious and burgeoning military and literary success, Guibert profited from a number of personal attributes that would aid his rise in the Republic of Letters. "A high head, a sharp tone, revolted by mediocrity . . . , Guibert was violent of character and impetuous of spirit," recorded one famous admirer, Germaine de Staël (née Necker). "[H]is conversation was the most varied, the most animated, the most fecund that I ever knew." Rarely described as handsome, he nevertheless managed to draw the attention of many ladies of the Parisian elite. "He pleases me greatly," remarked Lespinasse; "his soul is painted with all that he says, he has force and high ideals [*élévation*]; he does not resemble anyone else. . . . [His writing] is full of vigor, high ideals, and *liberté*."[6] Fellow salonnière Suzanne Necker echoed these sentiments:

> Guibert received at birth . . . all the advantages of memory and faculties of intelligence, vivacity, activity, imagination, in a word the indications of superior talents; more fortunately gifted than the most fortunate in this way. One admired his marvelous faculties and his absolute individuality, which no man before him had yet possessed. Who has ever begun a glorious career with such éclat, force, and maturity? [He] became the object of admiration of both sexes, and at twenty-four years, he brought new glory to his nation.

... Guibert received supernatural gifts more than natural gifts. ... [H]e seemed to be of a separate species, of which he was the only individual.[7]

Above all, Guibert's oratorical ability and charisma elevated him above his peers. "[He] spoke with extreme ease. This talent, which can only give, in a public meeting, an influence to be envied, added to his desire to appear [in public]," recorded Staël.[8]

Guibert also possessed two qualities that made him attractive in society. The first was an eidetic memory, as he demonstrated the ability to recall obscure facts, statistics, and quotes at will: "Endowed with a vast memory, he rarely presented new works; the first word made him recognize every page, and he would pass the work to the next [person]." These qualities made him appealing to most salongoers, particularly women, who often expressed admiration for and attraction to the dynamic young man. "A young duchess of eighteen," recorded the *Correspondance littéraire*, "not knowing how to sufficiently express the admiration with which she was impressed [after Guibert's public reading of the *Connêtable de Bourbon*], said, with much naïveté: 'Oh! Heaven! How happy a lot it is to be the mother of such a man!'" In the female-led salon culture of the time, these attributes proved vital to success.[9]

Another key to Guibert's personal success came in the form of his insatiable drive to accomplish his goals. These varied depending on his position, but they generally included his own advancement and the accomplishment of his reform program. As Lespinasse wrote, "One could say about him what he said about the *Connêtable de Bourbon*: 'his talents agitate and weigh on his soul,'" and in letters to Lespinasse, he often expounded on his frustrations with the traditions of playing politics and remaining in his place at Versailles. "These features all combined to grant Guibert a special place of recognition in the salons as well as the path of his future career. His passion for reform and his ambition would carry him far beyond the traditional slow advancement through the military, but it would also hinder him in places, particularly as it offended more-established figures.[10]

The salon as the center of social life had developed first in Paris, then spread throughout France and Europe in the late seventeenth century. By the latter half of the eighteenth century, they had evolved into simple, furnished rooms provided by their owners as a place for intellectuals to gather and discuss art, literature, politics, drama, music, theater, philosophy, and nearly every other subject in a relaxed environment. Thus they provided a generally friendly atmosphere for discussion, readings, and debuts of literary works. A typical salon opened its doors once or twice per week, usually after sundown. Salongoers maintained a rotating attendance throughout the week, visiting those that were open on the appropriate day.[11]

Salons were unique in that they were largely administered by women. These salonnières, typically members of the nobility and the upper bourgeoisie, attracted men and women from across Paris and Europe to their homes. They opened their salons usually on a specific day of the week and oversaw who attended, the material presented, and the direction of discussion. This last task proved the most important. A salonnière was more than an administrator and thus expected to stimulate and facilitate conversation. She performed all the functions of a social hostess to a widely varied cast of personalities and tastes in addition to her intellectual obligations to her clients. As the dean of salon studies, Dena Goodman, explains: "[A]s governors, rather than judges, salonnières provided the ground for the *philosophes'* serious work by shaping and controlling the discourse to which men of letters were dedicated and which constituted their project of Enlightenment. In so doing, they transformed the salon from a leisure institution of the nobility into an institution of the Enlightenment."[12]

Playing a vital role in the Enlightenment, the salon served as the breeding ground for its ideas and philosophies. By the late eighteenth century, they could be found in every major city in Europe. The salons in Paris, however, remained preeminent on the Continent. Philosophes, artists, writers, statesmen, and military figures from across Europe came to the Parisian salons, including Rousseau; Charles-Louis de Secondat, baron de la Brède et de Montesquieu; Voltaire; David Hume; d'Alembert; and Diderot.[13]

Guibert's work, character, and connections enabled him to enter this environment around 1771. He frequented the three leading salons of the period: those of Marie Thérèse Rodet Geoffrin, Suzanne Necker, and Julie de Lespinasse. Their names "were recorded and praised again and again in the letters and works of the *philosophes*," notes Goodman, "[their salons] formed the social base of the Enlightenment." Geoffrin's salon, the oldest of the three, served as the training ground for salonnières. Her and Necker's establishments served to assist philosophes in the development and proliferation of their works. Lespinasse's was "more literary than that of the Marquise du Deffand, more aristocratic than that of the bourgeois Mme. Geoffrin."[14]

Guibert quickly became recognized as a philosophe by the social and military elite of Europe and was "a lion of the salons," according to Palmer. Necker's daughter, Germaine de Staël, numbered among the officer's friends and admirers, who also included "Voltaire, Buffon, Rousseau, Diderot, d'Alembert, [and] Thomas"; Voltaire penned a poem gently mocking the young man entitled "La Tactique."[15] Although Guibert was now over the age of thirty, many established philosophes referred to him as "young," indicating both his newness on the social scene and the precocity of his career.

Guibert maintained a busy schedule, making the rounds of the salons. Lespinasse noted this in a letter to him:

> Sunday, you will work all morning without going out, you will dine with Mme. de M . . . ; you will return at 5:00 to work, and at 8:00 you will come to my house.
> Monday, dinner at M. de Vaines' and supper with Mme. De M. . . .
> Tuesday, dinner at the Contrôle Général and supper with Mme. de M. . . .
> Wednesday, dinner at Mme. Geoffrin's, and supper with Mme. de M. . . .
> Thursday, dinner at the comte de Crillon's, and supper with Mme. de M. . . .
> Friday, dinner at Mme. de Chatillon's, and supper with Mme. de M. . . .
> Saturday, dinner with Mme. de M . . . , and go to Versailles after dinner, and return on Sunday evening to spend the evening with me.[16]

Through this busy schedule, Guibert contacted many of the leading figures of the Enlightenment, many of whom became his close associates and friends.

In particular, his relationship with Lespinasse and his regular attendance at her salon greatly aided his networking. D'Alembert proved to be her closest associate; many referred to him as "Julie's secretary." He led the group of Encyclopedists who frequented the salon, including Denis Diderot and the marquis de Condorcet. The latter took rooms with Lespinasse and won an informal position as her "vice-secretary." Added to this group were Jacques Turgot and Jacques Necker, future French ministers of finance.[17] These men formed close associations with each other and with Guibert. Drawn from the bourgeoisie or lower nobility, they embodied the latter two decades of the Old Regime, contributing to philosophy and literature, chiefly through the *Encyclopedia*. But their interests moved away from the metaphysics of Voltaire and Rousseau to a more self-consciously political orientation.[18]

Guibert joined this august group and gained recognition as their intellectual and social equal. D'Alembert found him to be "a young soldier, full of enthusiasm, wit, and knowledge."[19] He wrote of the officer to Frederick II of Prussia in 1773, lauding the young man's personality and work: "I assure you that Guibert is worthy in every way of the honors which are accorded him, by the extent and variety of his knowledge, by the honesty of his character, the simplicity of his morals, and the nobility of his soul. Whatever he does, by right, the study of his profession and dearest occupation, he has given to literature and philosophy, and with the greatest success, every moment that this study has accorded him."[20] Frederick apparently remained unconvinced, leading d'Alembert to write, "I share very strongly the recognition of Guibert . . . that your majesty has witnessed; he needs no recognition other than himself."[21]

The other members of the circle shared d'Alembert's admiration of Guibert. "His verse is not written in an easy manner," Turgot noted, "but the ideas are quite beautiful, and they are composed on the spot; [their] being written more carefully would certainly cause them to be better."[22] The sense that Guibert's spirit exceeded his literary skill seems to have pervaded both their group and the Republic of Letters at large.

Guibert's lack of literary ability to match the great writers, combined with his rapid rise in status, led to the impression of him by some as a fervent, ambitious self-promoter. "Witness this Caesar," noted Jacques-André Naigeon in a letter to Diderot. "I would swear to you that this is the first time he has worn this clothing. Witness this ship. It has been launched into the water; her golden bow resembles that of Guibert's house. He does not know that the draperies are heavy and crude, thrown on the canvas, freshly drawn from the boiler; they make a poor first impression, which becomes a little worse over time." Diderot, protecting his associate, cautioned his collaborator, "I wish, my dear Naigeon, that you would reserve your bile and your furor for the gods, for the priests, for the tyrants, for all the imposters of the world."[23] Despite the negative cast of Naigeon's comments, Guibert's embodiment as a metaphor indicates his ubiquity within the Republic of Letters.

As he increased in fame and prominence, Guibert became something of an affectation for salonnières and other women, the young army colonel of charming voice and sweeping intellect. The attention he drew from many ladies who patronized the salons came not from his physical attractions, which were rather limited, but rather from "the all-powerful charm of [his] personality."[24] Guibert was intensely passionate and relayed that passion through his discourse to eager listeners. He conversed with philosophes on a broad range of subjects, particularly politics, the military, literature, art, architecture, and gardening. Perhaps more importantly, Guibert was young, dynamic, well known, and appeared to have a bright future. "He exercised over women a special fascination," claims his most recent biographer.[25]

His attractiveness granted Guibert the opportunity to engage in romance, perhaps for the first time in his life. He sought the attention of women who fascinated him, not only as a young man but also for the remainder of his life. The first of these was Jeanne Thiroux de Montsauge, wife of financier Philibert Thiroux de Montsauge. She and Guibert met in 1771, probably at a salon.[26] Montsauge was the prototype of the woman he would prefer throughout his life: "a remarkable beauty," older, highly intelligent, and demure. But Montsauge was of no great importance in the Parisian social scene and did little to advance his career. Nevertheless, she captured his attention for a significant period of his life. Despite other romances, Guibert never remained long from Montsauge and seemed to have carried on a regular correspondence with her until his marriage.[27]

Guibert's most significant romance, and a foundational element in his legacy, came with Julie de Lespinasse. The two met at a garden party hosted by Claude Henri Watelet at Moulin-Joly in 1772. "She was far from beautiful," recalled Guibert, "and her features were still further marred by the small-pox; but her plainness had nothing repulsive at the first glance; at the second the eye grew accustomed to it, and as soon as she spoke it was forgotten. She was tall and well-made." Her "plainness" seemed not to deter the colonel, who developed an attraction to the salonnière. "Guibert resembled a cat and Lespinasse the mouse," noted Louis-Henriette-Charlotte Philippine de Durfort, duchesse de Duras.[28]

Lespinasse was the illegitimate daughter of Julie d'Albon, herself a salonnière of note. Given her birth, Lespinasse at first felt herself consigned to the unhappy life of an illegitimate noble and resolved to enter the convent. She was rescued from the cloister by Marie Anne de Vichy-Chamrond, marquise du Deffand, a cantankerous character of the mid-eighteenth century who maintained a popular salon. During one of her many journeys to the countryside to improve her health, Deffand encountered Lespinasse at Chamrond around 1747. Taken by the young woman, the marquise brought her to Paris, where Lespinasse became her protégée. From Deffand she learned the art of the salonnière. Perhaps more importantly, by standing in Deffand's shadow, Lespinasse learned the fine arts of tact and grace in social situations: "Look at the education I received: madame du Deffand . . . , the Président Hénault, the abbé Bon, the archbishops of Toulouse and Aix, M. Turgot, M. d'Alembert . . . , such are the people who taught me to speak and think."[29]

Eventually, the relationship between mentor and protégée soured, and Lespinasse broke away to establish her own salon in 1764. She took lodging on rue Saint Dominique at the corner of rue de Belle-Chasse, the front room of which became her salon. Lespinasse furnished it simply and tastefully on a budget granted by her late mother and several wealthy acquaintances, including Geoffrin, and it soon became a leading institution in Paris.[30] Her personality remained key to the atmosphere of her salon. Lespinasse was almost universally adored, save perhaps by those who remained loyal to Deffand. She was demure, self-effacing, highly intelligent, and well spoken. In Guibert's words,

> She was always free from personality and always natural. She knew that the great secret of pleasing was in forgetting self to give one's interest to others, and she forgot herself perpetually. She was the soul of a conversation, but she never made herself its object. Her great art lay in showing the minds of others to advantage; she enjoyed that more than to show her own. . . . [T]he charm of her circle was so in *her* that the persons who composed it were not the same as they were elsewhere. It was only in her presence that they had their full value.[31]

Lespinasse's salon, buoyed by her personality, attracted the leading figures in Paris. Its intellectual nature drew a number of Diderot's followers: "If the official assizes of the Encyclopedia were housed in Rue Saint-Honoré, the little apartment in Rue Saint Dominique contained its 'laboratory,'" wrote Philippe-Marie-Maurice Henri, marquis de Ségur.[32]

Lespinasse also gained a reputation as the arbiter of the Académie française; the candidates who won her approval often won appointment. Such was the case with Jean-Baptiste-Antoine Suard, who owed his seat to her and remained a close confidant until her death. D'Alembert also owed a portion of his renown to Lespinasse, in addition to harboring an attraction for her.[33] She perhaps viewed him as a kind of eunuch, valuable for his discretion and gentle manner without the danger of sexual attraction. Throughout their interaction, he would serve as her doorkeeper and closest friend.

The meeting between Guibert and Lespinasse inaugurated a relationship that would greatly benefit the former. To Guibert, Lespinasse represented the seasoned salonnière who ran one of the most celebrated salons in Paris. She could open many doors for him, including those at the highest levels of government. She also possessed the traits he seemed to have valued in women, including an inquiring mind and vivacious manner.

Lespinasse demurred from a romance with Guibert despite their growing attraction for each other. This was due in large part to a prior unresolved relationship. In 1766 she had met Don José y Gonzaga, marquis de Mora, son of the Spanish ambassador. Much like Guibert, Mora was highly intelligent, charismatic, and passionate. He and Lespinasse began an affair in 1767, with a promise of marriage after he could disentangle himself from an unfortunate engagement. In 1771 Mora's father was recalled to Madrid, and he was forced to leave Paris. The following year Mora fell gravely ill and remained close to death for a lengthy period. At the time Lespinasse met Guibert at Moulin-Joly, she harbored unspoken fears for Mora's life and may have viewed Guibert as a kind of French replacement for him. Yet their relationship would remain nothing more than a deep friendship while Mora languished at Bordeaux.[34]

During this period, Guibert engaged in other pursuits, chief among them the furthering of his military career. An opportunity for the colonel to conduct a "military voyage" through eastern France, Germany, and Austria presented itself in late 1773. Throughout the journey, Guibert acted as an informal ambassador and official military observer. More importantly, it removed him from Paris at a politically dangerous time. Reactionaries had taken control of the Ministry of War after the fall of Choiseul and reasserted their power over the army. Guibert's outspoken nature and the contentiousness of the *Essai* threatened to sabotage his career, and it appeared that a royal reprimand might be forthcoming for "le colonel insolent." On the advice of a family friend, the prince of Soubise, Guibert removed himself from Paris, which helped calm the tension.[35]

Drawing on the long tradition of travel narratives, Guibert kept a detailed journal for publication. In it he details his travels and observations on the military, political, and cultural situations of the various states that he visited. Guibert departed Paris on 20 May 1773 and traveled east, reaching Strasbourg on 26 May. He noted the disrepair of the villages and the plight of the peasants, a repeated observation of every region Guibert visited. The next day he crossed the Rhine into Baden and continued east. Passing through Mannheim, he recorded the poor condition of the troops, which were maintained with Prussian discipline. From 30 May to 1 June, Guibert toured the battlefields of Lützen and Leipzig, where Gustavus Adolphus and Charles XII of Sweden had fought legendary engagements. On 4 June he reached Dresden, where he enjoyed the hospitality of the Saxon court.[36]

There, Guibert began the intensive work of examining the military constitution of the state. He found the Saxon army to be populated with "beautiful soldiers, well maintained, but poorly instructed." He noted the disrepair of the city's fortifications and doubted the locals' claim that the city's walls could be held with 30,000 men. He conducted several meetings with government officials, including the royal family. Guibert concluded that Saxony was ill governed, with "vices without number; financial disorder; poorly paid and maintained troops, . . . the Court [having] cabals, disorders, infamy of every kind."[37]

After a short stay at Dresden, the colonel departed for Berlin on 8 June. Two days later he reached the great city. "Berlin [is] an immense city; its grandeur cannot be seen at first glance," Guibert noted, awed at the prospect of reaching the object of his boyhood military admiration. He traveled the city, taking in its sights and recording his observations. He observed soldiers laboring, seemingly on every street corner: "Berlin has the air of a grand quartermaster-general, of a military metropolis." Guibert watched many military parades, remarking on the lack of uniformity in Prussian dress and manners. When he was not occupying himself with military affairs, the military intellectual toured the city's gardens and artistic displays. Much of what he found he described as "de mauvais goût" (in poor taste), illustrating a very French sense of cultural superiority.[38] After nearly a week at the Prussian capital, Guibert received word that his request to meet the king had been accepted. On 14 June he left the city for Potsdam, which housed the court of Frederick.

On reaching Potsdam, Guibert was interrogated by a series of officials and aides, culminating in an audience with Frederick's close associate and military philosophe, Karl Gottlieb Guichard, better known as Quintus Icilius.[39] The two spent several days discussing the military situation in Europe. Quintus argued forcefully that Frederick's success was due in large part to luck rather than skill, convincing Guibert on the point. Following his audience with Quintus, Guibert passed several days with the crown prince, Frederick William, to whom the Frenchman took a liking. Frederick William and Quintus introduced Guibert to the various ambassadors and diplomats who inhabited Potsdam; the colonel found them "more French than [their] country," a notion that both pleased and surprised him. Finally, on 17 June Guibert received his audience with Frederick. He was transfixed: "A sort of magic vapor seemed to me to envelop his person; it is, I believe, what one calls the halo of a saint, and the glory around a Great Man. I remember his face now as if I had seen it in a dream; these are all the details that I know of his private life, of his character; it is the likeness that I have before me, that I find that I saw with confusion and with trouble." Guibert recovered and spent an hour in deep discussion with the king. Frederick revealed that he had read the *Essai général de tactique*, which "had given him a great desire to know its author." Impressed with the author's military acumen, Frederick invited the young officer to maneuvers in Silesia in the fall, an offer that Guibert eagerly accepted.[40]

After the audience, Guibert dined with the royal family before returning to Berlin. There, he encountered Prince Henry, the king's brother and erstwhile rival for military and social acclaim. He greatly enjoyed Henry's company, finding him to be intelligent, educated, and insightful on military and political matters.[41]

At the end of the month, Guibert departed Berlin for Vienna. He passed through Saxony and into Austria, where he witnessed the poor living conditions of the peasants and castigated the Austrian government for not aiding them. Reaching Vienna by 1 July, he found the Habsburg capital to be a city impressive only in size, with little artistic merit and a corrupt court to match that at Dresden. Commenting on his audience with Empress Maria-Theresa, he noted that she appeared to be "a good member of the bourgeoisie." Guibert finished his tour of Vienna with a visit to the city's arsenal, which he praised for its organization, adoption of Gribeauval guns, and the quality of its saltpeter and powder.[42]

After a lengthy stay at Vienna, Guibert departed for a tour of the military border between the Habsburg and Ottoman Empires on 19 July. The farther he travelled south, the more savage and beautiful he found the countryside, echoing Rousseau and several other philosophes who found beauty in primitive, natural surroundings.[43] On reaching the border, Guibert discovered a highly militarized zone that stretched from the Adriatic Sea to the forests of Romania. He dined with several provincial officers and lauded the militarization of the land's citizens, who were forced to be on constant alert against Ottoman incursions. While the colonel praised their dedication, he judged that the system could not be exported because it required a long border that remained hostile for years or decades.[44]

In mid-August Guibert reluctantly left the countryside and journeyed north for Frederick's Silesian maneuvers. He reached Breslau, the site of the exercises, on 15 August. By this time, Frederick's maneuvers had become something of a legend in military circles. The king conducted them every year from summer to autumn in peacetime and when he could during war. He intended them to expand small-unit drill onto a larger scale, allowing his officers to test operational theory and practice in close-to-accurate conditions. These maneuvers were a critical element in the success of the Prussian military constitution, a fact that did not escape Guibert's notice.[45]

For the next month, Guibert attended a variety of maneuvers, often in the presence of the king and his leading generals. He studied the various exercises with a critical eye. Observing basic drill, he found the Prussian infantry to be "capable of perfect movement, when properly commanded" and noted the cavalry's "perfect alignment." After witnessing several small-unit tactical exercises, Guibert was treated to a series of operational maneuvers presided over by the "prodigious activity of the king." These took place on a variety of terrain and pitted armies commanded by Frederick and "Anhalt" against each other.[46] These exercises included the king, with infantry formed in square, defending against cavalry; Anhalt placed in a superior defensive position while Frederick demonstrated his favored "oblique order" attack; and Anhalt staging an assault on a fortified camp commanded by Frederick.[47]

Despite his praise for Prussian technical precision, Guibert's opinion of Frederick and the Prussian constitution decreased as the exercises went on. He criticized the king for their unbalanced nature, noting that the maneuvers often gave Frederick's army an insurmountable advantage of numbers or position. The maneuvers also lacked the confused conditions that often presented themselves on a battlefield, the fog of war.[48] More damningly, Guibert castigated the entire Prussian system constructed by Frederick, noting that the parade-ground precision for which his military had become a byword disappeared after the maneuver progressed beyond its opening volleys. "Since I have been in Prussia," he concluded, "I have been increasingly confirmed in the opinion that the king has pressed neither the theory nor the practice of the [military] art to its perfection, and there are many objects on which one could think and do better."[49]

At the beginning of September, Guibert took his leave of Frederick. He had intended to visit Poland and perhaps Russia but was stricken with fever and forced to turn back. On 16 September he returned to Vienna, still weak with illness. Over the course of the next month, Guibert slowly made his way west, along the way paying homage to Voltaire at Ferney before crossing the border on 18 October.[50]

Upon his return to France, a curious incident took place. Guibert's old friend Dumouriez had been arrested following a failed attempt to remove Russian influence from Poland. Jean-Louis Favier, a friend of both men, was also arrested.[51] Evidence, now largely lost, implicated the two in the plot. Rumors swirled around Versailles that the two were members of Louis XV's famed "Secret du roi," a shadowy cabal of agents who undertook secret missions for the king. Dumouriez and Favier did belong to the Secret du roi, and some evidence suggests that Guibert might also have been involved with the group.[52]

The "difficulties without number" that Guibert faced at the various customs stations on his voyage lend credence to the argument.[53] Regardless of his suspected complicity in the plot, the colonel fell under suspicion because of his close association with Dumouriez and Favier. He first learned of their arrests while at Vienna and claimed innocence himself: "I had a clear conscience; I held my head high. Nevertheless, I [was] agitated at times." Despite his fears, Guibert was never arrested or officially accused of impropriety. Ethel Groffier attributes this to timely intervention by Charles-François de Broglie, marquis de Ruffec, who was head of the Secret du roi. Broglie intervened personally with the king and likely burnt all incriminating evidence, saving Guibert's career and bright future.[54]

His return to Paris allowed Guibert to resume his social activities. In particular, it led to a shift in his relationship with Lespinasse. Despite their disparity in age and their respective romantic entanglements, the relationship deepened. On the night of 10 February 1774, the two attended the opera, which they watched from a box alone. Ségur conjectures that "in the ensuing silence their lips were drawn together; they drank, as Julie writes, the cup of 'delicious poison.'"[55] No published version of this quote exists, but the two certainly began a romance around this time. "I shall enjoy them [the operas *Iphigenia* and *Orpheus*] with you in that *chamber* where I heard so little of the *Village Sorcerer* and *Vertumnus and Pomona*," wrote Lespinasse.[56]

The relationship between Guibert and Lespinasse typified the great romances of the period. Selections from her letters reveal the intensity of their passion: "Must I not love you, must I not cherish your presence? You have the power to divert me from so sharp and so deep-seated a pain: I wait for, I long for your letters." She continued later, melodramatically: "my dear, I suffer, I love you, I wait for you." Her feeling soon reached hyperbolic heights: "doubtless, I have been kept in bondage by the same charm which drew me to you, by the all-powerful charm of your personality, which intoxicates my mind. . . . [M]y friend, you are more powerful than God."[57]

Their early letters strike not only many notes of romance but also a subtle undercurrent of impending disruption. "You had no need to be loved as I know how to love," noted Lespinasse; "no, that is not your style; you are so perfectly loveable, that you must be or become the prime object of all those charming ladies who place on their heads all that they had within them, and are so loveable that they love themselves in preference to all else. You will be the pleasure, you will satisfy the vanity, of almost every woman." More ominously, she declared, "I love you to desperation, and yet something tells me that that is not how you ought to be loved."[58]

Much of their correspondence follows this pattern. Lespinasse wrote most often of her feelings for or about him, usually addressing his faults. Guibert responded in kind on occasion, but most often spoke of his work and possibilities for his own advancement. She offered him constructive criticism on his projects, particularly the development of his budding interest in the theater.[59]

Despite their visibility on the Parisian social scene, Guibert and Lespinasse's intense relationship was remarkable in that it never became public during their lifetimes. "People must suspect my interest in you," she recorded, "for when I was told of the importance of the secret, my informant added: *A secret for everybody, for M. de Guibert*. I laughed at this condition and said: so he is not included in *everybody*? 'No, no, not for you!'" Lespinasse likely kept the affair quiet in order to preserve her reputation for tact. She pleaded with Guibert to burn her letters after he had read them and promised to do the same.[60] His motives for secrecy remain unknown, although the continuation of other affairs was a likely factor. Even more remarkably, Lespinasse's intimate companion d'Alembert, who often composed her letters to Guibert, never deduced the affair.[61] While d'Alembert was perhaps blinded by his own romantic attraction to her, his lack of discovery speaks to the extreme tact of the couple.

As the romance proceeded, problems appeared. Despite promises to do so, Guibert never dropped his dalliances with Montsauge, prompting angry recriminations from Lespinasse:

> My friend, I ought to hate you. Alas! For how long a time have I no more done what I ought to do, what I wish to do! I hate myself, I condemn myself, and I love you. . . . But how comes it about that [she] does not love you to desperation? As you would like to be loved? As you deserve to be? On what then can she spend her mind and her life? Ah, yes, she has no taste, no sensibility, I am sure of it. She ought to love you, if it were only from vanity. But in what am I going to interfere? You are content, or if you are not, you love the ill she does you. . . . So why should I pity you? But that other wretched creature, she *does* interest me; have you written to her? Is her unhappiness still as profound as ever? . . . Only come to me when you have no more to say to *her*.[62]

This excerpt captures the tone of Lespinasse's letters to Guibert, both her passion and her occasional vituperation.

His continuing liaison with Montsauge reveals a fundamental flaw within the relationship. Guibert and Lespinasse were both intensely passionate people, but as their relationship advanced, she became the more passionate of the two; he returned the sentiment with equal fervor only occasionally. While both were engaged in numerous social activities, Lespinasse considered Guibert to be her first priority personally: "I feel so positively that I am not *I*; I am *you*." He seems not to have shared her depth of sentiment, remaining primarily focused on his work rather than on his relationship with her. Many of his letters reveal Guibert to be distracted by events at Versailles, rarely returning the sentiment with which her missives were filled. "A king, an emperor, armies, camps, make you forget she who loves you, and, what perhaps touches a sensitive mind more nearly, those whom your friendship sustains and consoles," wrote Lespinasse. Only when she railed against his liaisons with Montsauge or mentioned her opium use did Guibert return her passion and eloquence.[63]

Letters of this type reveal an element of Lespinasse's personality that few had seen in public. As a salonnière, she was measured, lively, and gracious. As a lover, she was wild, fiercely possessive, jealous, and irrational. Lespinasse demanded constant attention from Guibert when he was in Paris and regular letters when he was not. When she did not receive the latter, she castigated him for not writing as often as she wrote him. Guibert managed to pacify her on the wilder occasions, reeling in her widely flung emotions. His eloquence saved Lespinasse's regard more than once, particularly in situations dealing with Montsauge.

While the two appeared to be an ideal match, their romance seemed destined to fail. Lespinasse was an older woman, bastard daughter of a dead salonnière, who was highly attractive as a mistress but not as a wife. While Guibert carried on a number of affairs, he likely held Lespinasse above his other mistresses, given the time and effort he devoted to the relationship. She was everything he desired in a wife: humility, passion, intelligence, and the ability to be the model hostess.

Yet Guibert was an ambitious member of the lower nobility, needing a good marriage to cement his social standing and finances, as he noted on 9 September 1774: "The easy circumstances of my family are dependent on the King's beneficence, which may cease at any moment on my father's death, or by cessation of payment. . . . [I]n my perplexity as to the future which I foresee, marriage is perhaps the only means of escaping my debts, of strengthening the fortunes of my family, of gaining the power to be of some help to it."[64] Again, later in the year: "So the comte de Crillon is married irretrievably. A wife, a great fortune: what shackles on one's liberty! He had fifteen thousand francs a year and was free: if only I had as much! And I too shall have to marry! I shall have to, Good Heavens! The comte de Crillon had fifteen thousand francs a year and I have half that; he was at his ease, but I am in debt: everything attached him to Paris while in my present position everything drives me from it."[65]

Unfortunately for Lespinasse, Guibert's marriage prospects remained largely out of his own hands, as his parents determined to make for him a good social and financial match. In early 1774 they contacted Hayes de Courcelles, a member of the Berry nobility, regarding the availability his daughter, Alexandrine-Louis Boutinon des Hayes de Courcelles.[66] The families arranged a meeting between her and Guibert at the family estate. He appeared to take a liking to the young woman, and she accompanied him to Paris for integration among his social network. Lespinasse wrote to Guibert that she "found her charming and well worthy of the interest that she inspires in you; the manners, face, the style of her mother, are equally amiable and interesting." The following May the families contracted a marriage. Guibert and Alexandrine wed on 1 June 1775 at Courcelles.[67]

Guibert's marriage proved fruitful. The Courcelles family held little influence at court, but its provincial wealth remained irresistible to the well-positioned Guibert family. The union reportedly resulted in an increase of 12,000 livres per year in the colonel's income.[68] Alexandrine proved to be the ideal wife for a man of his ambitions. She seemingly harbored none of her own, instead deferring to her husband in all public matters; after their marriage she all but disappears from the public record until after his death. No letters between the two appear in Guibertian historiography. Unlike Lespinasse, Alexandrine seemed to have made no protest to her husband's continuing intimacy with a variety of women, including perhaps Montsauge and Lespinasse herself.

The salonnière did not hide her distaste, becoming inconsolable at Guibert's marriage: "I see you today as you are, I see that you have committed a vile action for the sake of 12,000 francs a year; I see that you were not afraid of reducing me to despair, if you could use me as a stop-gap during a period which you wanted to use for breaking a connection which you could not keep up when you married.

... [Y]ou cared little whether you dragged me in the mud, and made me lose the only thing left to me: my self-esteem." Her recriminations knew few bounds: "You know quite well that my heart does not understand moderation: so, to want to make me take an interest in you is to condemn me to the tortures of the damned. You would like the impossible: that I should love you madly, and yet that reason should govern all my emotions.... You know quite well, you can see it clearly, I have not even the use of my intelligence with the man I love."[69] Her vituperation continued throughout the period; unfortunately for posterity, Guibert's responses have been lost.

In the months following the marriage, Lespinasse's letters alternate between icy condemnation and sorrowful pleading. She attempted suicide on more than one occasion; after each attempt, Guibert soothed her in person or via letter. The two settled into an uneasy friendship, with Guibert seeking her advice on his many projects, and she supporting his cause at nearly every juncture. No evidence exists of a continued sexual liaison, and indications are that such activities ceased with the marriage.[70]

Guibert refused to confine himself to a military career and advancement in the Republic of Letters. To add to his fame, he began to explore the theater in 1774. He penned a number of dramatic works to hone his skills and to serve as projects for future performance and publication. Foremost among these projects was the production of the *Connétable de Bourbon*, which would be his first public foray into the genre.

The *Connétable de Bourbon* was composed on Corsica around 1769. It tells the story of Charles III, duc de Bourbon, Constable of France. Charles was a tragic figure in history; appointed constable in 1515 by Francis I, he led French armies in battle until the king grew uneasy of Charles's power and began to confiscate his estates. Charles fled to the Holy Roman Empire, where he was given command of an army to cow Pope Clement VII in 1527. His forces mutinied and killed Charles outside the walls of Rome, after which the troops sacked the city.[71]

The play, like all composed by Guibert, was poorly written but conveyed much of his political and personal philosophy. While Charles and Bayard are well-rounded personalities, the other characters are elementary archetypes. Charles "is torn between love and patriotism on one hand and ambition on the other," a statement that proved an excellent autobiographical description.[72]

Guibert may have circulated copies of the *Connétable de Bourbon* as early as 1771, although first public mention did not occur until early 1773. In the spring of that year, Guibert staged a performance in a small Parisian theater. It was received with success and the piece became moderately popular in the salons. The *Correspondance littéraire* recorded that "M. de Guibert read the piece . . . at the Palais-Royal, the Palais Bourbon, and in all the great houses of France. Everywhere he was showered with praise."[73]

With his finances secured through marriage, Guibert sought an outlet for his theatrical work, increasing his own fame in the process. The Comédie française contracted to perform the *Connétable de Bourbon*, its production debuting on 23 August 1775 and running for four days to generally positive reviews. Young Queen Marie-Antoinette attended the play during the summer and took a liking to it, arranging royal patronage for the work as well as a court performance. On 27 August she presented the play at the wedding of Charles Emmanuel of Piedmont to Marie Clothilde, King Louis XVI's sister. The production was lavish, costing an estimated 300,000 livres for set designs and hiring the best actors, designers, costumers, and staff in Paris.[74]

The performance was panned by literary critics, particularly Jean-François de la Harpe, who would become Guibert's harshest literary detractor and something of a personal nemesis. Undeterred by the criticism, Marie-Antoinette arranged for a second production at another royal wedding on 20 December. In the interval between performances, Guibert revised the play, significantly altering its final two acts. This time the criticism was unstinting, as literary figures across Paris lambasted the play and its author.[75]

The failure of Guibert's theatrical work indicates that his precocious career was not immune to criticism. Voltaire viewed him as a gifted upstart: "I found even more genius than the [*Essai*] in his tragedy [the *Connétable*]," he wrote to Deffand, "and even more boldness. What delighted me was that, in this doctor in the art of killing people, I found in society a most polite and gentle of men. . . . I cordially detest the art of war, and yet I admire his [*Essai*]." Voltaire celebrated both the *Essai* and the *Connétable*, often comparing their merits and their reflection on their author: "This book [the *Essai*] is full of grand ideas, like his tragedy *The Connétable de Bourbon* is full of beautiful verse."[76]

Voltaire's criticism, however, did not remain entirely laudatory. By 1775 Guibert had involved himself in the running of the

Ministry of War, the production of the *Connétable de Bourbon* by the court, his relationship with Lespinasse, and several writing projects. During this busy year, he apparently let the attention he paid to the great philosophe lapse: "I was a little piqued that Guibert did not honor me with an example of his *Elegy of M. le maréchal de Catinat*," wrote Voltaire. "I was so charmed by this work that I pardoned the author his indifference to me."[77] While Guibert's inattention did not result in any loss of regard the older man had for the younger, it would prove an indication of the officer's ambition overriding his ability to play politics. Other figures would prove to be less kind than Voltaire in their response to such pretentions. "Guibert . . . loves to hear himself talk [and] say a good deal to prove that he knows but little," recorded Gouverneur Morris on one of his many visits to France.[78]

Voltaire's status as the leader of the philosophes was matched in Guibert's mind by Frederick's dominance over the military realm. This recognition did not escape the notice of the colonel's friends. "He merits," d'Alembert wrote to the Prussian king, "to admire in you the general and the writer, the monarch and the philosophe." Voltaire and Frederick both viewed Guibert as a noteworthy member of the Republic of Letters who perhaps took himself too seriously but remained a leading philosophe of his day.[79]

The early half of the 1770s proved a decisive period in the life of the military philosophe. At its beginning, he remained in a Corsican idyll following the conclusion of the island's subjugation. He used this period to finish drafting his magnum opus, the *Essai général de tactique*. He also devoted his time to other literary pursuits, including theatrical works.

Over the next four years, Guibert transitioned from Corsica back to the metropole. There, with the guidance of men like Dumouriez, he entered Parisian society. This gave him access to a wide range of personalities and experiences, including Voltaire, Diderot, d'Alembert, and Condorcet. His personal attractions, including his excellent memory, endeared him to the salon culture that dominated Paris. His penchant for romance also enabled him to advance quickly in that female-centric society. This environment fostered his literary career, providing a source of support, criticism, and an audience for his efforts. Guibert parlayed his skills into a position as a figure of rising importance and notice in the Republic of Letters. From 1770 to 1775, he concentrated on building his social network, seeking "glory by all paths: receiving the applause of armies, the theatre, and women."[80] These efforts combined to make him one of the most prominent figures of the age.

Salon culture provided many additional opportunities for the young philosophe. He encountered many women, including those he would carry on romances with throughout his adult life, among them leading salonnière Julie de Lespinasse. Guibert also encountered many of the leading figures of the day in the salons, including Turgot and Necker. In particular, they provided a third path to fame for him, namely politics. The stinging critique of France's government in the *Essai général de tactique* resonated with many in the salons. They acknowledged the truth of Guibert's analysis and began to envision his role in reform, not only of the military but also of the government.

These experiences elevated Guibert and provided numerous opportunities for further fame and advancement. His theatrical career began in 1775, when the *Connétable de Bourbon* won the attention of the queen, resulting in two royal performances. Despite his social success, Guibert remained primarily a military theorist. The same year that his theatrical career began, he received an opportunity to join the Ministry of War and further expound and implement his military reforms to build the institutional army.

CHAPTER 5

THE COUNCIL OF WAR UNDER SAINT-GERMAIN

Guibert's rise to fame occurred near the end of a decades-long trend in French politics, one that would both bring him to power and exile him from it. The state experienced a number of crises during the eighteenth century, most importantly financial difficulties. The mounting problems of the past few decades threatened to drag the entire state into the abyss by the 1770s. Most immediately, the royal government found it increasingly difficult to secure foreign loans. Shortfalls in tax revenue, long the bane of the monarchy, exacerbated the situation. Bankruptcy loomed, as it had in the mid-seventeenth century.[1] But the state demurred from this dangerous path, opting instead for internal reforms designed to reduce costs and increase revenue. Many of these changes concerned the increasingly bloated state and society, particularly areas of traditional privilege that were increasingly at odds with rational, ordered Enlightenment principles. Cutting costs and increasing efficiency required paring down the decentralized model of past practice, which necessarily produced a crisis for those who benefited from the status quo. Many resisted the intrusions on their traditional rights, leading to contentious political debates and court intrigue.

Within the army, these threads met in the ministry of Claude Louis, comte de Saint-Germain. Nominated secretary of state for war in late 1775, he convened a *conseil de la guerre*, or council of war, to oversee sweeping reforms in three areas: finance, the entrenchment of the conservative nobility, and technical improvements of the kind debated for decades and instituted in the *Instruction for Light Troops*. All were intended to restore the French army's prestige, which had been shattered on the field of Rossbach.

Guibert served on this council alongside a group of reformers and theorists, playing a central role inspiring and driving change. Under Saint-Germain, they worked for almost two years, hoping to remake the army, state, and society in the image of the *Essai général de tactique*. They introduced a number of measures addressing the army's education, system of promotion, regulations, and punishment methods. But they pressed too far and too fast. Opposition coalesced around a number of particularist groups and interests, including a "pro-French" party that accused Saint-Germain and the council of introducing Prussian-style discipline to the detriment of the kingdom. In 1777 Saint-Germain retired, the council dispersed, and Guibert fell from power. His first taste of politics proved fraught but productive.

As Guibert pursued fame in the mid-1770s, the challenges for the Old Regime reached crisis levels. The combined efforts over decades to reduce or eliminate the debt, and the larger push to modernize the French political economy, were in danger of failing spectacularly. In his later years Louis XV had increasingly endeavored to assert royal authority by centralizing power in his own hands or those of his ministers. His efforts in this regard mirrored Louis XIV's attempts to concentrate power in the hands of a small number of officials.[2]

Yet Louis XV's reign, and that of his successor, differed greatly from his great predecessor's in many ways. The most significant of these contrasts was the shifting political landscape that sustained a variety of particularist opposition groups rather than the largely unified politics of the Sun King. Noble groups fought to assert their powers, often relying on traditionalist arguments. In addition, groups within the *parlements* also fought to gain power and influence, particularly relying on Enlightenment arguments to press their case. From 1740 on, the thirteen judicial bodies sought most strenuously a more representative government, chiefly through their acquisition of true legislative power. Using the words of the philosophes, the *parlementaires* argued for a more rational and representative system than the purported absolute monarchy. As they gained a voice in literary publications like the Jansenist *Nouvelles ecclésiastiques*, they increasingly appealed to public opinion to support their stance.[3]

Opposition by the parlements increased throughout the 1760s, reaching its apex in the early years of the following decade. The specific issue that sparked action from the crown came in the continual refusal of the parlements, particularly that of the Parlement of Paris, to register edicts designed to reform and provide greater oversight of the tax farmers. *Les fermiers-généraux* proved both corrupt and inefficient, taking much of the tax revenue for themselves. When questioned on the shortfall, they often claimed that hardship on the part of the populace resulted in lower revenues. *Parlementaire* interests closely coincided with the Farmers, as many were familial relations and a significant number of Farmers served in the parlements and vice versa.[4]

Louis XV's chief minister, René-Nicolas-Charles Augustin de Maupeou, began a crusade against the parlements at the king's direction in late 1770. This culminated with the January 1771 exile of the Parlement of Paris and the suppression of the other twelve regional parlements; they remained so until Louis's death in 1774. Maupeou's actions represented the most significant and visible example of royal efforts to address the mounting state crisis, particularly in the area of finance. Louis's motives for suppressing the parlements for nearly four years remain nebulous. The most salient element of the dispute were the questions of reform and taxation. Many groups resented the crown's lurch into "despotism," envisioning a further weakening of noble privilege in the mode of Louis XIV, particularly with regard to the aristocracy's eroding status and influence within French society and the state.[5]

These three threads united in the ongoing reform efforts of the French government for the next two decades, with the financial crisis remaining the chief danger and motivation. This continuing dislocation of the nobility, particularly within the context of the military, created an interest group that argued for a return to "traditional" privilege to advance their own interests. Finally, the crushing defeat in the Seven Years War illustrated the backward nature of French doctrine, which would need to be modernized via the institutional army to restore international prestige.

Within the Ministry of War, Maupeou's policies meant that reactionaries moved to end the progressive reforms pioneered by Choiseul. These individuals tended to have vested social and economic interests in maintaining the status quo and were opposed to each other until united in their opposition to the chief minister. Many were upwardly mobile members of the bourgeoisie seeking to purchase their way into the aristocracy. They partnered with the nobles who populated the upper echelons of the officer corps, even though they were ideological enemies. These men formed a particularist group arguing against the idea of merit-based advancement in both the army and society, insisting that only nobility of long extraction held the necessary military ability. They attempted to form a closed caste to jealously guard its membership and social privilege against the bourgeoisie.[6]

Yet both groups had a vested interest in preventing any changes they could not bend to their own ends. Choiseul's grip on power and insistence on pressing reforms dislocated both groups, thus forcing them together. Like most political appointments, Old Regime military commands had to be purchased. The grades of colonel and above remained far beyond the reach of all but the oldest and wealthiest noble families. The crown also maintained a large number of household regiments, which served little purpose on the battlefield but functioned as a haven for scores of supernumerary noble officers.[7]

Choiseul's de-jure elimination of venality within the army struck a serious blow to noble privilege, as did his proposed reduction in the number of household regiments and supernumerary officers. As Louis began to assert royal power in 1770, groups within the army joined the rising chorus of opposition to Choiseul. The minister resigned that same year, replaced by Louis François, marquis de Monteynard, who reversed most of Choiseul's reforms.[8]

Louis's death in 1774 ended the reassertion of royal power. His grandson inherited the throne as Louis XVI and promised enlightened reform in place of his predecessor's despotic tendencies. Maupeou duly received his dismissal, and the new king invited the parlements back to their prior service, albeit without granting them the legislative power they desired.[9]

Guibert witnessed these events from Paris. He attended the leading salons, participating in discussions on the Maupeou "revolution" and other questions of reform. The *Essai général de tactique* contained almost as much political as military thought, indicating Guibert's abiding interest in politics and the workings of the state. His rising popularity, aided by the influence of Lespinasse and his father, vaulted Guibert's name to the top of the lists for political office.[10]

During the same period, his father proved adept at balancing personal ambition and court politics. Charles Guibert had closely aligned himself with Choiseul, who had reigned as virtual prime minister throughout the 1760s. In subsequent years the elder Guibert was promoted to maréchal de camp and named governor of the Invalides, a prestigious if not powerful position. He would also remain one of the chief *doyens* of the *logis*, or the army's quartermaster organization, with a special expertise in organization and logistics.[11]

Charles Guibert undoubtedly wielded at least limited influence within the Ministry of War, though not enough to have his son named to a position of power in the young king's government. Louis XVI appointed his childhood companion, Louis Nicolas Victor de Félix d'Ollières, comte de Muy et comte de Grignan, to head the Ministry of War in June 1774. After an unremarkable term, Muy died in 1775. As summer turned to autumn that year, Paris and the court buzzed with talk of who would succeed Muy. Charles Eugène Gabriel de la Croix, marquis de Castries; Noël-Jourda, comte de Vaux; and the comte de Broglie emerged as the leading candidates.[12]

Guibert shuttled almost daily between Paris and the court at Fontainebleau. He became caught up in the excitement over the appointment, perhaps hoping to secure patronage for himself. He noted the strong candidacies of Vaux, with whom he had had a falling out, and Castries, whom he considered the most probable appointment.[13] The anxious days waiting at court proved nearly intolerable for the ambitious officer. He wrote to Lespinasse often, expressing his frustrations at the political machinations of the government. His biting critique in the *Essai* of government ministers resurfaced as he noted the Machiavellian scheming:

> These people are men of intelligence, and that is all. They have no love of fame; they have only a passive love of what is good; they grope their way, they make composition with abuses; in short, I suspect them of having taken a liking for their positions. . . . Great men—and I only call "great," men who have energy—love, and hate; they have no doubt, weaknesses, passions; they sometimes act on the spur of the moment and immoderately; they pile benefits upon their friends; but the mass of humanity whom they make happy forgives them the debts which they pay to nature. Believe me, your passionless, cold, people, your so-called virtuous people, are not cut out to rule.
>
> I, who would travel ten leagues to dine with ministers in disgrace, always regret the distance I have to come to meet those who are in office. Their power weighs heavy on me; it seems to me at once that they hold it at my expense, that they have usurped it from me. The idea comes into my head that they do nothing good, nothing big, with it, while I—.[14]

The young Guibert believed that his own reforming zeal, manifested in the "Discours préliminaire" of the *Essai général de tactique*, would triumph over entrenched political interests and political infighting.[15]

In the intense political climate at Fontainebleau, the comte de Saint-Germain emerged as a dark-horse candidate for the position of secretary of state for war. Like the other contenders, Saint-Germain had an illustrious military record, having served in the armies of Bavaria, the Palatinate, Prussia, Denmark, and France, the last under Maurice de Saxe. After the Seven Years War, in which he served with both Guiberts, he retired to his estate in Alsace, removing himself from the pitfalls of court politics and blame for his participation in the defeat at Rossbach.[16]

After a financial crisis eliminated his pension, the old soldier reluctantly returned to court. Saint-Germain had no stomach for politics and rarely pursued a dispute when confronted by even minimal opposition. He had largely exited the public arena by 1775, and his name did not appear on the short list for the position.[17] But after negotiations at court failed to produce a viable candidate, young Louis looked outside the establishment for his new minister.

Saint-Germain finally bent to the will of the court and submitted his candidacy. Along with his offer of service, he produced an outline for the comprehensive reform of the French army. He later acknowledged Guibert as the virtual coauthor of the document, admitting that the influence of the *Essai général de tactique* provided the foundation for his reforms. Saint-Germain's plan called for a leaner, more cost-effective army stripped of its noble pretentions and bloated officer corps. He also requested the convening of a conseil de la guerre that would oversee the changes and also eventually evolve into a permanent general staff.[18]

To the new king, the nearly colorless veteran seemed the perfect candidate to enact military reform. Louis bypassed the pool of favorites and appointed Saint-Germain on 27 October 1775. This likely came at the instigation of another reform-minded minister, A. R. J. Turgot, who served as controller general of finances from 1774 to 1776. Guibert consulted closely with Turgot on his initial reform plan for the army, much of which formed the basis of Saint-Germain's own proposals as presented to the king.[19]

Louis assigned two official charges to Saint-Germain: reform the army to return France to military dominance while simultaneously reducing its cost by a significant amount. These indicated the daunting task facing the new minister. Budget reductions would hopefully ease the crisis, ideally combining with Turgot's efforts in the Ministry of Finance. Reform of the army via implementation of an institutional doctrine would restore France's prestige. "The necessity," Albert Latreille notes, "of completely modifying the constitution of the army was not in doubt by anyone." But reform threatened to run afoul of some traditionalist nobles who sought to maintain their own rights and privileges. Therefore, a determined Saint-Germain trod a dangerous path. To accomplish this task, he began by assembling a group of prominent reformers to serve on his Council of War. Among them were Louis-François, baron Wimpffen-Bornebourg; Chevalier Louis de Jaucourt; and Gribeauval.[20]

Born in 1732, Wimpffen hailed from a family of high German nobility "mais pauvre et très-nombreuse" (but poor and very numerous). Five of his brothers entered military service in France or the neighboring German states. Like Guibert, Wimpffen had spent his life in the French army. During the Seven Years War, he won the Cross of Saint-Louis, France's highest award for valor. That led to his promotion to maréchal de camp in 1771, which would remain his rank until the outbreak of the Revolution. Wimpffen's reputation as a military philosophe and outspoken reformer during his work in the Ministry of War in the early 1770s made him a natural choice for Saint-Germain's council.[21]

Jaucourt was perhaps the most famous member of the council. Born in 1704, he became in turn a celebrated physician, writer, and sometime philosopher. The last two came in large part because he contributed more articles than any single writer to the *Encyclopedia*. These included essays on war, monarchy, and society, all of which formed the nucleus of an institutional army. Jaucourt's role with the *Encyclopedia* made him one of the premier military theorists of the period. Yet his attention remained divided between his military and literary work, rendering his service on the council negligible beyond lending his prestige to the proceedings.[22]

Gribeauval was born in Amiens in 1715. As noted previously, his career primarily focused on the technical aspects of the army, particularly the artillery. His system of lightweight guns using interchangeable parts superseded the extant Vallière system, making French artillery lighter, more maneuverable, and standardized. These reforms occurred under Choiseul, thus Gribeauval fell from power alongside him in 1770. He remained the chief technician of the French army, though, advocating for the adoption of his system, which Guibert stridently endorsed in the *Essai général de tactique*.[23]

Together, these men were the drivers of the reform movement. Wimpffen contributed his military knowledge and not inconsiderable literary and rhetorical skill to the Council of War. Jaucourt brought his prestige and, at least in theory, his ideas. Gribeauval brought the elements of his system, whose cost savings and efficiency were a microcosm of the task the new ministry had determined to accomplish.

In early autumn 1775 Saint-Germain requested that Guibert join the council as its recording secretary and his own confidential advisor. In his memoirs Saint-Germain describes an unnamed figure who desired to serve on the council as its recording secretary: "a young colonel, also distinguished by his talents, known for his knowledge, his spirit, the warmth of his soul that perhaps sometimes exceeds the goal; but [this] can be justified by his most ardent love for good and the rarest patriotism."[24] This can only be Guibert, whom Saint-Germain had already acknowledged as charting the course of his reform plan.

Guibert was initially skeptical of the position and delayed responding to the invitation. He had married the previous June, and his lingering affair with Lespinasse required a delicate touch and a large measure of his attention. He was also distracted by the debut of the *Connétable de Bourbon* at the Comédie française in August and its impending production before the court. Moreover, he expressed frustration with Saint-Germain and the existing political structure, fearing that his own reforms would be unpalatable. The colonel remained skeptical that Saint-Germain's energy and determination would overcome dissenting viewpoints: "He is weakening, he is giving in to the suggestions people make to him. The cabinet has already spoiled him." Later in the month Guibert expressed his distaste over Saint-Germain's initial proposals, noting that they differed substantially from his own. This prompted him to write "a fiery letter" to the minister and solicit a similar missive from Wimpffen.[25]

Despite his distractions and skepticism, Guibert eventually agreed to join the council.[26] In December he "hand[ed Saint-Germain] a general sketch of the new plan of military organization." His skepticism and frustrations with the minister would remain throughout their association, but they settled in to work. Guibert became the "primus motor" of the council, driving its reforms through his dedication and zeal. Saint-Germain and his confidential advisor embarked on a "campaign of austerity" for the French military.[27]

Facing a daunting task, the council commenced work in the winter of 1775–76. Its first step was to reduce the army's overall cost, which began with the Maison militaire du roi, the king's royal household regiments. During the ongoing transition from a feudal to modern army, it assumed the responsibility of raising, equipping, and maintaining elite regiments. These units, including the Maison du roi, Maison des princes, gendarmerie, and several light-horse regiments, became a major source of friction between reformers and reactionaries. After Louis XIV had reduced the aristocracy's influence on the government, the nobles had agitated for the return of their traditional roles leading the military.[28]

By the 1770s, conservative members of the upper nobility had formed a bastion of aristocratic privilege within the Maison militaire. Commands in these units could be purchased only by the wealthiest nobles and members of the bourgeoisie, thus excluding the majority of poorer, provincial nobles from the most illustrious and lucrative positions. Most of the royal household regiments served no purpose on the battlefield and indeed were excluded from action in the Seven Years War as a result of poor performance during the War of Austrian Succession. In the late eighteenth century, these units became a byword for corruption and leisure. Few actually contained any soldiers or junior officers, most consisting of a few troops and numerous supernumerary officers.[29]

On 15 December 1775 the Council of War issued a series of ordinances reducing the *mousquetaires* and the *grenadiers montés* by three companies each. These directives also reduced the numbers of *gardes du corps*, gendarmerie, and the *chevaux légers*.[30] The measures cut few costs, as the officers who had purchased commissions in these units had to be reimbursed for the expense. But the elimination of numerous supernumerary positions from units was expected to pay dividends both financially, by saving money in the long run, and in the army's performance, by eliminating unnecessary positions whose holders' authority often overlapped that of other officers. Guibert provided the impetus for these reforms, including collecting much of the data concerning the changes.[31]

The council followed its reduction of the Maison militaire by turning its attention to the Invalides, which Louis XIV had founded as a hospice for wounded soldiers. By the 1770s, several units were attached to it, nominally manned by those with injuries that did not incapacitate them. Rarely in Paris, these units instead served as garrisons for the many fortifications on the kingdom's frontiers. Guibert's father had commanded one such fortress at Perpignan in 1767, which may have planted the idea in the colonel's mind that such postings were largely unnecessary. While performing a valuable duty by releasing line troops for combat, their inflated numbers, particularly within the officer ranks, concerned the council. Like the royal household units, Invalides commands had become havens for inept supernumerary officers. On 17 June 1776 the council issued a directive reducing the number of officers and men attached to the Invalides. This measure eliminated many of the various political positions for officers, although it reduced few costs for the same reasons as the Maison militaire reductions.[32]

The Council of War continued its assault on the bloated officer corps by examining military education. France had long relied on the Catholic Church, particularly the Jesuit schools that populated the country, to provide the basic education for most within the kingdom. But the expulsion of the Jesuits in 1764 had ended their grip on education, and the increasingly secularist philosophes looked outside the church for the vital imparting of Enlightenment thought to new generations. This required a revamping of education across the country, including the military.[33]

Education became increasingly important to the French army in the eighteenth century as war became more regulated, defined, and technical. This produced a dichotomy within the reform movement, particularly with regard to the status of nobility. More conservative members of groups within the nobility insisted that the skill of an officer lay in his blood rather than his head. They looked with disdain on the increasingly technical education of the Enlightenment, preferring instead a basic clerical education to supplement their innate abilities.[34]

Like most reformers and philosophes, Guibert firmly believed in combining the technical education (moyen) of an officer, with the innate ability (génie) that noble officers claimed ran in their blood. While they did not necessarily reject noble leadership, reformers believed in ordered, technical systems. Following the newer tradition of Enlightenment thought, they insisted that officers needed to have a minimum of technical education and expertise to conduct a successful military campaign. While the concept of aristocratic leadership seemed positive in theory, it proved ineffective in practice. Guibert himself had witnessed its downfalls, most spectacularly at Rossbach, where a noble, courageous advance was shredded by the technical, disciplined fire of the Prussian army. As Prussian doctrine had demonstrated, eighteenth-century warfare was far more technical than in prior centuries. Guibert realized this and sought to reform the French system from within, an argument largely adopted by the council.[35]

Throughout late 1775 and early 1776, Guibert gathered data and crafted a systematic reform of the military-education system. He worked closely with Etienne-Charles de Loménie de Brienne, archbishop of Toulouse, and Jean-François Joly de Fleury to craft these reforms, which were then remitted to the council. Thus, educational reform concerned much of the body's work in spring 1776. Edicts issued on 2 February and 28 March completely revamped the system. The first decree eliminated the central École militaire, replacing it with ten (later twelve) smaller provincial écoles. These schools were designed to provide the technical, enlightened education Guibert and other reformers believed was necessary to form a good officer. The establishment of provincial écoles intended to supplant religious education, replacing it with a technical, logical education that was affordable to all, particularly impoverished provincial nobles.[36]

Another breach between particularist groups concerned the purchase of offices, both civil and military. From its earliest feudal origins, the army had been an aristocratic institution. Nobles maintained retinues that served the king in times of war, making the command of a unit one of the most prestigious elements of aristocratic privilege. When the Bourbon kings began to sell commissions in the late medieval period, the nobility bitterly resented this loss of privilege. Aristocratic groups argued for their traditional roles, while the purchasing bourgeoisie saw the system as a much quicker path to prestige and power. Venality, like most matters of reform, thus became an issue of contention. As with political office, *anoblis* members of the upper bourgeoisie could purchase military commissions and their accompanying noble patents. Given the close association between honor and military service, men of this group sought commissions to grant legitimacy to their questionable aristocratic status. Noble groups in turn resented this intrusion and loss of social power.[37]

Many nobles clung to France's feudal military system, which the anoblis adopted as they strove to rise to true nobility. Both presented arguments supporting their position by relying on Enlightenment principles, particularly the philosophes' quest for order, efficiency, and centralized control. Traditionalists emphasized their moyen, while more-progressive groups lauded the technical education imparted by the schooling generally disdained by much of the older nobility.[38]

While venal commissions conferred honor and defrayed costs, they proved far from being cost efficient in the long term. Purchased regiments demonstrated their unsuitability on the battlefield with the shift to modern professionalism. In medieval feudal warfare, a purchased regiment could engage the enemy autonomously within a larger battle plan. As professional warfare developed, this method became increasingly obsolete. Infantry fighting in more complex tactical and operational formations required highly skilled and educated officers who possessed the moyen of operational and tactical warfare. Venal officers, particularly the bloated ranks of supernumeraries, proved entirely incapable of leading basic drill, much less directing units in battle. These skills could only be found in a technical education provided by the reformed educational system and were vital to the formation of the institutional army. Choiseul had attempted to eliminate venality a decade earlier, but court opposition supported by both the upper bourgeoisie and the nobility guaranteed his failure.[39]

Saint-Germain and the Council of War determined to rectify the situation. Once again Guibert provided much of the research on the issue and the impetus for reform. On 25 March 1776 the council issued an edict that gradually ended the purchase of commissions. Instead of wealthy nobles and members of the bourgeoisie buying rank, the Ministry of War would select officers from the graduates of the regional schools. With this measure, the noble génie of Guibert's constitution and the moyen of a technical education were united in the process of officer selection and promotion.[40]

The elimination of the École militaire and commission purchases left the French military without a systematic method of officer promotion. Under the prior system, most could buy rank without proof of military ability or training. Officers of lesser means, typically poor provincial nobles, were consigned to the lower ranks of the officer corps, possibly achieving captain after decades of honorable service. While the system benefited particularist interests, it hardly provided for a professional military. It also greatly contributed to the animus between members of the traditionalist nobility and the anoblis.[41]

To remedy the issue, the council constructed a system designed to ensure orderly promotion for all officers. It began with the creation of the rank of *cadet-gentilhomme*, designed as the lowest rank in the military. This provided an entry-level commission for the continuing education of officers with no experience outside the classroom. Cadets-gentilshommes would be the protégés of more-senior officers, benefiting from the experience and guidance of their mentors.[42]

Officers were required to spend a minimum of one year as a cadet, living with soldiers and noncommissioned officers to learn their trade and to benefit from their technical knowledge and skills. The Council of War attempted to curb rapid advancement without merit by instituting a fourteen-year service requirement for promotion to colonel and by empowering regimental councils. These councils consisted of a regiment's lieutenant colonel, major, and senior captain and had the power to veto promotions within the unit.[43] The construction of this promotion system was intended to bring equality to all officer candidates, eliminating the debate between upper and lower nobility and especially between these and the anoblis officers of more recent extraction.

Another area of privilege within the military was the length of time officers spent away from their units. Typically, general and senior officers served with their commands only in the spring and summer during peacetime, arguing that their estates and business ventures required constant attention, which would be lost if they spent more time with their units. Drill and training thus devolved to junior officers, who received little instruction themselves beyond petty tactics and parade-ground maneuvering.[44]

The council passed a measure in late spring 1776 addressing this issue. It required all officers to spend a minimum of six months per year with their units, training them and themselves. This included the transfer of command of the Neustria Regiment to Guibert.[45] With this and the other measures, the council hoped to produce an officer corps of innate skill, excellent education, and practical experience to lead the army to victory.

In mid-1776 Guibert's influence over the council waned as it turned from systemic to technical issues. The decade witnessed the waxing of Prussian doctrinal influence on the French army, particularly the minutiae of tactics and maneuvering. Provisional regulations in 1774 and 1775 prescribed detailed march and maneuver based on the Prussian example of parade-ground discipline and precision. The increased role of such theory in France led to the major doctrinal change under Saint-Germain. The council issued the new regulations on 1 June 1776. Rather than Guibert's flexible system of l'ordre mixte, these instructions looked instead to the work of Johann Ernst von Pirch. His work was the epitome of l'ordre mince, arguing for strict discipline in thin lines to reproduce the devastating volleys of the Prussian service. The 1776 Réglement included these elements, creating a deployment on lines of three ranks. Most significantly, it called for maneuver in open columns using Pirch's moving pivots. This was a reversal of the extant use of Guibert columns, which were closed rather than open.[46]

The 1776 Réglement, which Robert Quimby labels as basically "the last drill regulation of the Old Regime," remained in effect until 1788. That the Council of War did not adopt Guibert's constitution speaks volumes about the ongoing polemical debate between l'ordre mince and l'ordre profond. Few in the army needed persuasion of the efficacy of the Prussian system after Rossbach. Pirch's work had convinced many that the adoption of Prussian methods via l'ordre mince would prove superior to the more "French" l'ordre profond. These regulations remained stilted in their insistence on a particular theoretical system as opposed to the more generalist principles of Guibert's doctrine. They reflected perfectly the nervousness with which Guibert entered the council, fearing that Saint-Germain would waver in his insistence on a middle path in the polemical debate. Essentially, the "old man" had lost his nerve and submitted to the proponents of l'ordre mince, resulting in the 1776 Réglement. Nevertheless, these new methods also included elements of Guibert's doctrine by adopting the Gribeauval system for the artillery and deemphasizing the magazine-and-depot system, decreeing foraging on the march to be the proper method of supply.[47]

One of the council's minor changes, the plight of the soldier, proved to be its most controversial act. In his writings Guibert had expressed sympathy for the common man and soldier, which the council shared. But its members were also concerned with the high desertion rates that plagued all eighteenth-century armies. Corporal punishment had been introduced to curtail this and institute discipline in the ranks.⁴⁸ Yet French society increasingly viewed violent punishment as anachronistic. The spectacular and grotesque execution of Robert-François Damiens in 1757 offended nearly everyone, including Louis XV, who had ordered it. The sadistic impulses of the masses waned as the Enlightenment stressed understanding and sympathy over schadenfreude, making the Damiens affair a turning point in public and philosophe opinion.⁴⁹

On 25 March 1776 the Council of War issued a decree reforming the discipline of soldiers. It forbade the use of corporal punishment, specifically the beating of soldiers by officers and running the gauntlet, and required that all punishment be in the form of blows from the flat of a saber. This punishment was not intended to be as physically painful as running the gauntlet. Rather, it was intended to impart a measure of shame on the offending soldier to discourage future transgressions. Public punishment also served in this respect.⁵⁰

By late 1776, the majority of the council's reforms were in place. Guibert had found advancement for himself, including high office that would bring a large pension to himself and his family. More importantly, his efforts had played a central, if not complete, role in their accomplishments. He also sought to implement the elements of his system. His work with the council, particularly regarding the Invalides, education, and promotion, served to lay the foundation of social and political change that would produce his institutional doctrine. Guibert was the "primus motor" for these reforms. In particular, his analysis of the union of state, society, and the military in the *Essai* had provided the basis of the major work of the council. The council's reforms of the education and promotion systems rested on the foundation of Guibert's writings too, as Saint-Germain noted. The colonel provided much of the research and reform plans for the changes in education, promotion, and the Invalides. In addition, the cost-cutting measures matched his call for a more efficient army that would be less damaging to society and the populace. His insistence on a lighter and more operationally mobile army also prompted the transition to the Gribeauval system and away from magazines and depots.

Conversely, Guibert's most prominent advocacy, in the area of tactics and organization, actually suffered during the period. The new regulations were a step back from the 1769 *Instructions for Light Troops*, particularly in the rejection of closed columns of maneuver.

Instead, the army opted for a more Prussian-style open column of maneuver, which provided increased precision and discipline but limited flexibility. Perhaps ironically, Guibert's system now stood more on the side of l'ordre profond as Pirch and other Prussian advocates eschewed use of the column altogether. Together, these tactical reforms represented a transitional step toward an institutional army with a single doctrine.

More fundamentally, Guibert's personality and burning ambition worked against the full implementation of his system. Throughout the tenure of the council, he constantly agitated against Saint-Germain's character and lack of energy. The colonel expressed his loyalty to "the old man who shows me friendship" and swore to dedicate himself to "building up [Saint-Germain's] strength." Yet this occasionally turned to distaste: "he is ruining himself, he is dishonoring himself." In rare moments Guibert even appeared paranoid over his place in the government: "so you think," he wrote to Lespinasse, "that the comte de Saint-Germain does not tell me everything? So much the worse for him, if he is deceiving me. His business will go badly, and he will pay for the error of dividing his confidence."[51]

Guibert even went so far as to argue to her that he should be secretary of state for war rather than Saint-Germain, a dangerous ambition that could lead to public backlash. Lespinasse attempted to mediate his more extreme moods in her many missives. She also cautioned against his ambition and the public recognition that accompanied it: "I see you intoxicated by the praises and flatteries in which they enwrap you all day. That might be sufficient for your vanity, but your activity needs an answer from M. de Saint-Germain which might satisfy both your vanity and your ambition at the same time."[52]

During 1776, the War Ministry's attention began to turn away from reform. The rebellion of Great Britain's American colonies produced a transoceanic war that threatened to sap London's financial and military resources. Led by the military, elements within the government argued that France should intervene on behalf of the rebellious colonies. The question divided the government. Saint-Germain and Secretary of State for the Marine Antoine Raymond Jean Gualbert Gabriel de Sartine, comte d'Alby, argued for intervention to avenge French defeat in the Seven Years War. Turgot led the opposition, contending that support of a colonial rebellion would encourage French colonies to rebel in turn and that the costs would be ruinous.[53]

Guibert enthusiastically supported intervention, both on principle and to advance his own career. In February 1776 he addressed a memorandum to Saint-Germain offering his services in the event that France went to war. In the following months he issued several more memoranda and letters warning of the danger posed by the British to French and Spanish colonial possessions. As the debate raged, the Council of War largely set aside its reform work. Guibert advocated more intensely for intervention, hoping that he would be swept along to even greater glory. But the controversy caused by the council put an end to his ambitions.[54]

Despite the progressive notions of the young king and reformers within the Ministry of War, the reactionary element would not be denied its voice. As the Council of War implemented its changes, the more conservative nobility united behind Alexandre-Marie-Eléonor de Saint-Mauris, prince de Montbarey et du Saint-Empire. This group railed against the reforms, castigating the council for overturning centuries of French tradition and replacing it with Prussian militaristic technocracy.[55]

As a leading figure on the Council of War and author of a treatise on tactics containing much drawn from the Prussian service, Guibert became a target of this criticism. Led by Montbarey, the reactionaries compared Guibert and Saint-Germain to Maupeou. They argued that the changes had undercut the noble hierarchy, which formed the foundation of the military. The elimination of most aristocratic privilege, including the household regiments and purchase of commissions, came dangerously close to rendering the nobility obsolete within its one refuge of privilege.[56]

Although this argument resonated with many traditionalists, it remained out of favor within the government. The rising tide of revolution in America spurred Enlightenment notions of *liberté* and *égalité* in the minds of many Frenchmen, ideas that ran directly counter to those of noble privilege and hierarchy.[57] Public opinion largely supported the American rebels, limiting the options for the reactionaries. Guibert's reforms, and the fundamental arguments of his military constitution, fit more with the republicanism espoused by the American patriots than it did with French reactionary groups. This fired the imagination of the philosophes at court and prevented a direct attack from the traditionalists.

Guibert's first indication that his career aspirations were in danger came in late 1776, as France marshaled its forces for possible war against Britain to support the American colonies. His memoranda on the conflict went unanswered by the Ministry of War or the court. As France made the decision for war, Guibert offered his own service, eager to experience American republicanism firsthand. He also saw the opportunity for a brilliant career move, as his rise to fame had been accomplished only through combat and the resulting honors.[58]

Unknown to Guibert, the reactionaries had gathered at Versailles. His first letters requesting American service were greeted with polite responses but no action. As units began to mobilize, the colonel requested to accompany his own regiment to America. The request went unanswered, as did his subsequent pleas. Guibert never received orders to depart for America, apparently never realizing that his policies were the reason. By 1777, French supplies were fueling the rebellion's efforts, and French troops were not far behind. Guibert, however, had larger problems at Versailles.[59]

For months the reactionaries had sought an angle of attack palatable to the public. In a memorandum on the state of soldiers, Guibert complained to Saint-Germain that budgetary concerns limited the scope of reforms, thus reducing their effectiveness. This continued throughout the period and undoubtedly rankled the minister. As early as winter 1776, Guibert noted that he had become "the firebrand, the fire-ship, in M. de Saint-Germain's office." His ambition and outspoken nature led to public criticism, which only blossomed throughout the year. In late 1776 his opponents settled on an attack acceptable for public consumption by targeting the punishment decrees. Montbarey and his followers charged that Guibert had introduced Prussian elements into the French military constitution, undermining its very nature and turning the nation into a second Prussia. While the Prussian system had many admirers other than Guibert, the great majority of French soldiers and officers deeply resented the Prussians for their victory in the Seven Years War. In the subsequent years a strong revanchist element arose, seeking opportunity to return the favor to Prussia. The reactionaries seized on this argument, painting Guibert as a traitor to the French national character. Louis-Philippe, comte de Ségur, summarizes the argument: "Wanting to establish in their camps a German discipline incompatible with our morals, he subjected French soldiers to a humiliating punishment of blows from the flat of a saber; it was obeyed with repugnance and incompletely. I remember seeing in Lille grenadiers of a regiment of four battalions shedding tears of rage at the foot of their colors, and the duc de La Vauguyon, their colonel, mingling his tears with theirs."[60]

While all members of the council fell under attack, Guibert received the largest measure of criticism. Given his outspoken and contentious nature and his fast rise from provincial obscurity, the colonel presented the perfect target. His writings, particularly the incendiary introduction to the *Essai*, attacked the establishment's most fundamental principles. The tone of his writings especially rankled conservative and patriotic Frenchmen who resented any form of foreign influence.[61]

Most disastrously, Guibert received blame for uniting the French and Prussian military constitutions, thus harnessing the military to a system that had defeated it in the last war. His political opponents pounced, condemning him for the cardinal sin of diluting the national character through his reforms. They accused him of implementing the same rigid, Prussian discipline and formalism that Guibert actually had decried in his writings. They argued that his reforms of military punishment were demonstrably anti-French and degrading to soldiers. Conservative officers believed that corporal punishment was a vital ingredient in the proper education and training of a soldier.[62]

To many, Guibert had betrayed not only his national character but also the noble profession itself, eliminating the technique that elevated aristocratic officers above common men and replacing it with demeaning blows from a cavalry saber. After suffering a humiliating defeat at the hands of Frederick, revanchist officers could not abide anything perceived as Prussian. In fact, the word "Prussian" became an epithet in France and was frequently applied to Guibert and his reforms. His efforts to combine the best of the Prussian system with the best of the French had failed.[63]

For the eighteen months of Saint-Germain's ministry, the Council of War served as the most powerful advocate for reform in the French army, with Guibert as its loudest voice and recording secretary. Saint-Germain's administration also inaugurated a new generation of reformers like Gribeauval and Wimpffen. Nevertheless, the council soon began to show its flaws. The primary deficit lay in the nature of its members. Saint-Germain held no position beyond the prestige of an honorable career; his star had long since faded. Most of its members were younger, lower-ranking officers with little pull. Gribeauval, perhaps the most important technician in the army, proved to be interested in little more than the minutiae of artillery. Wimpffen, who would later direct the Revolution's army for a time, showed himself to be a moderate, unwilling to follow Guibert's strident calls for reform. The other members were nonentities, unable to muster a following within the army or at court. The council's inability to form a faction at court ultimately led to its downfall. Within the army, it represented the younger, reform-minded officers who sought an enlightened officer corps and a professional army. Their ideas ran counter to the entrenched interests of the particularist groups who sought to dominate reform to ensure their own success.

Moreover, Louis XVI shared the council's desire for change but rarely mustered the leadership to direct it. Reform of promotion and education angered the conservative nobility, who insisted on their innate ability of command. Adoption of "Prussian" punishment, blows from the flat of a saber, angered those who saw the measure as unnecessarily cruel. Guibert insisted on the rightness of his reforms but could not manage to convince anyone of their merits outside of his own faction. He was denied his request for service in the Americas, and greater political peril awaited. Louis succumbed to pressure and dismissed Saint-Germain, with Guibert and the council following shortly thereafter.[64]

Guibert's work on the Council of War under Saint-Germain laid the foundation for his official work within the Ministry of War that would later establish the institutional army. In particular, the ministry's reforms of officer education, promotion, and the Maison militaire du roi eliminated much of the wasteful spending and direction of the army, waste that had led to its humiliation in the Seven Years War. Guibert's dismissal temporarily checked his direct influence, but his advocacy for his military constitution and the implementation of institutional doctrine remained strong. In the next years he would attempt different avenues outside of the Ministry of War to see to its implementation.

CHAPTER 6

WAR, HOME, AND ABROAD

The failure of the Council of War to effect all of its reforms between 1775 and 1777 did not entirely stymie Guibert's ambitions. During this same period, he sought to advance them in a variety of other directions. The first among these was literary. He continued his burgeoning publishing career to much acclaim by entering essay contests sponsored by the Académie française. He also maintained his associations with the salons and the Republic of Letters.

But the military would always remain Guibert's primary interest and focus. Despite his setbacks in the Ministry of War in 1777, he remained confident of a role with the expeditionary force planned for America the following year. More importantly, the assembly of that army would prove a final test in the ongoing tactical debate, which Guibert hoped to help settle in his own favor. The culmination of both of these processes occurred at the Camp of Vaussieux, a series of exercises held in late 1778 on the Norman coast. Guibert attended, along with Mesnil-Durand and a host of the other luminaries of the French army. Vaussieux definitively proved the inefficacy of l'ordre profond to nearly everyone who attended or read the reports of the exercises. To cement this conclusion, Guibert wrote his own analysis of the camp, contained in his second great work of military theory, the *Défense du système de guerre moderne*, published in 1779.

The late 1770s proved a time of transition for Guibert. He had come close to achieving his reforms under Saint-Germain but ultimately failed. He also lost a close friend and experienced a setback in his literary career. Only Vaussieux and its outcomes, particularly Guibert's analysis of the camp and its results, would buoy his flagging spirit. The period would thus serve to remove him from a more active role in the Ministry of War and the court.

Guibert's service in the ministry encompassed two personal defeats for the young philosophe. These concerned his literary activities, particularly his aspirations as a panegyrist and essayist. The most significant, however, came in the death of his closest associate. As Guibert immersed himself in his work in the Council of War, the health of his correspondent and erstwhile lover Julie de Lespinasse started to fail in early 1776. For years she had taken opium to soothe her nerves, and its effects led to deteriorating health.[1]

Lespinasse's health worsened throughout the late winter and early spring. The marquis de Ségur posits a darker reason for the opium use. He records that she had a "severe attack," possibly of epilepsy, in the summer of 1775, which prompted her use of the drug, particularly to sleep. By early 1776, she took as many as four grains of opium, a dangerous amount. This he attributes to Guibert's marriage, which devastated Lespinasse: "this last phase of her life [was] nothing less than a long-drawn suicide, coldly premeditated and relentlessly accomplished."[2] Ségur's work tends to the melodramatic, particularly in its castigations of Guibert. But Lespinasse did suffer emotionally from his diverted attention, likely contributing to her health woes and resulting drug abuse.

Perhaps knowing she was dying, Lespinasse reached out to Guibert. He responded with uncharacteristic passion, particularly given his focus on his government work. "My friend, if I can still use the word, never has your condition left so painful and deep an impression on my mind," he wrote in early 1776. "It pursues me, it fills my thoughts and freezes them with terror. I spoke to you, I fell at your knees, I told you that I loved you, and you still lay dead."[3]

Time ran short for Lespinasse. In May she fell seriously ill. Guibert rushed to her side, joining d'Alembert in an impotent bedside vigil. Lespinasse soon banished Guibert from her presence, unwilling to have him witness her suffering. The two instead wrote letters of regret and sorrow, which d'Alembert relayed. "I have always loved you," Guibert confessed. "I loved you from the first moment I knew you. I have a secretary here waiting for me to dictate to him. What shall I dictate? That I love you, and that you are dying? That is all that fills my thoughts."[4] The sentiment exceeds the normal impassioned language of the time, even given Lespinasse's straits. No sexual liaison seems possible, particularly given d'Alembert's hovering attention, but the passion of their affair returned in full force.

Lespinasse returned Guibert's emotion in her last days. "Good-bye, my friend," she responded, "if I ever come back to life, I should like to spend it again in loving you, but there is no time left."

As Guibert anguished, she wrote: "My friend, I love you; that is a sedative which stupefies my pain.... Alas! I feel so sick of life, that I am ready to beg your pity and generosity to grant me that relief. It would put an end to a painful agony which will soon weigh heavy on your mind. Oh! My friend, let me owe repose to you; in virtue's name, be cruel once. I am sinking. Good-bye."[5]

Such missives continued for days as Guibert, d'Alembert, and her other friends and admirers hoped for a recovery. A return to health was not to be had. On 22 May 1776 at 2:00 A.M., Lespinasse succumbed to her illness and addictions. Guibert mourned her with an *Eloge* containing some of his most poignant words: "What darkness! What solitude! Dreadful emblem of my heart! Tomorrow the night that surrounds me will have passed, but the night that enfolds Eliza is eternal! Tomorrow the universe will waken again; Eliza alone will never waken. Eliza is no more! Who will enlighten my judgment, who will warm my imagination, who will spur me to glory, who will replace in me the profound sentiment with which she inspired me? What shall I do with my soul and with my life?"[6]

The loss of Lespinasse would have profound effects on Guibert's social life. Although he maintained a steady rotation between the leading salons, hers had remained his primary and preferred institution. Her circle, particularly d'Alembert, comprised his closest friends and social connections. The end of these shattered the group. D'Alembert retreated to an apartment under the Louvre, where he lived out the remainder of his life largely in solitary retreat.[7]

Meanwhile, Guibert worked to further his literary career. This effort increased his stature in the Republic of Letters but also made him enemies. His writing simply did not have the eloquence, wit, or charm of his contemporaries. Despite these literary deficiencies, the colonel devoted much of his energy to winning the essay contests sponsored by the Académie française. These were a staple of the academy and a favorite of readers across the Republic of Letters. The body sponsored questions and invited essays, occasionally elegies, in response. They were intended as a portion of the Enlightenment to inform the public and elaborate on political, social, and occasionally military theory.[8]

The essay contests elicited compositions from one of the most cantankerous figures of the later Enlightenment in France. Jean-François de la Harpe was born into poverty in Paris in 1739. Orphaned as a child, as a young man he developed a reputation for sharp criticism and literary skill. He began his career in the latter pursuit with a series of plays written and published between 1763 and 1765. The most successful of them, *Warwick*, achieved a court performance and Voltaire's attention. La Harpe decamped to Ferney for long stretches, apprenticing himself to the great philosophe and sharpening his rapier wit under the tutelage of the master of that skill.[9]

In 1768 la Harpe returned to Paris, where he found employment as a literary critic and writer. His acid tongue, unflinching manner, and aggressive style soon marked him as the premier literary critic in Paris, replacing Voltaire. For the remainder of the period, he published a variety of essays, elegies, plays, and longer writings. This included work on the *Correspondance littéraire, philosophique, et critique*, the social journal of record in France between 1747 and 1793.[10]

Guibert likely encountered la Harpe in the salons, although he did not record such a meeting. The two definitely tangled in the essay contests of 1775 and 1777. The academy sponsored elegies of Nicolas Catinat and Guillaume-François-Antoine, marquis de l'Hôpital, in 1775 and 1777 respectively. "La Harpe became Guibert's antagonist," noted near-contemporary historian Laure Junot, duchess d'Abrantès.[11] Their rivalry divided their supporters into feuding factions within the Republic of Letters. The members of Lespinasse's salon and later Necker's, including Condorcet, d'Alembert, and Diderot, supported Guibert. Deffand backed la Harpe, as did Voltaire: "[he] preferred [la Harpe's] elegy of Catinat; he did not even speak of Guibert's." La Harpe's elegy, with Voltaire's support, won the competition. Guibert had his revenge in 1777, when his elegy of l'Hôpital triumphed over la Harpe's.[12]

This rivalry did not distract Guibert from his major work with the military or in the Ministry of War. His literary pursuits remained a sideline, particularly those that did not have direct relevance to military reform. Even Lespinasse's death proved ephemeral in diverting his attention. In the late 1770s Guibert busied himself with the ministry and the looming crises over both the doctrinal debate and the war in America.

Guibert's work, both in the *Essai général de tactique* and in the Ministry of War, stoked the polemical debate within the French army. Since the invention of l'ordre profond by Jean-Charles, Chevalier Folard, support for the "French system" increasingly called for its adoption by the army. Jacques-François de Chastenet, marquis de Puységur, continued this trend throughout the period. Marshal

Broglie increasingly favored this approach during the 1770s, becoming the most visible practitioner advocating l'ordre profond. Yet he remained less doctrinaire than the theorists, particularly in his willingness to adapt elements of the proposed systems to battlefield exigencies. The opposing view, l'ordre mince, reached its ascendancy with the *Réglement* of 1776. The system allowed only open columns for deployment, aping the Prussian practice, and drawing from Pirch's system, emphasized precision in maneuver and rigid discipline.[13]

Guibert's constitution, presented in the *Essai général de tactique*, fell behind these two simply because it did not present a strong polemical argument. Its l'ordre mixte epitomized the best of both systems rather than championing one or the other. While he touted the benefits of the Prussian constitution, he also denigrated much of it, particularly its insistence on rigid discipline and formalistic maneuvers.[14]

Polemics swirled around the issue, as academic debates were wont in France. For Guibert, this meant his literary and military careers intersected, particularly with regard to his growing rivalry with another theorist, François-Jean de Graindorge d'Orgeville, baron de Mesnil-Durand. Mesnil-Durand emerged in the 1750s as a minor supporter of l'ordre profond. He published a number of pamphlets during the next three decades, all arguing for a modification of Folard's original system. Like Guibert, Mesnil-Durand served as an aide to the powerful and influential, including Broglie. By the 1770s, he had become the chief proponent of l'ordre profond.[15]

The debate drew directly on the growing personal rivalry between Guibert and Mesnil-Durand, which ballooned during the colonel's time in the Ministry of War. Perhaps as a response to Guibert's writings, Mesnil-Durand revised his system of l'ordre profond in a 1774 work titled *Fragments de tactique*. Drawing from his rival's example, he allowed for deployment and maneuver in small columns rather than unitary or dual columns. He also adopted Saxe's method of deploying a "cloud" of skirmishers ahead of an army to screen it from enemy fire. Such modifications would allow the main body to maneuver with the speed it required to close with the enemy and deliver the shock attack he held as the only appropriate doctrine for French soldiers. These became the basis of the 1774 *Réglement*, which adopted much of his system for official use.[16]

Despite these adaptations, Mesnil-Durand's system remained mired in the formalism of previous iterations of l'ordre profond. In particular, he retained deployment on the square, which nullified much of the speed gained from maneuver in smaller columns. Mesnil-Durand touted this formalism as the solution to the "fog of war" that blanketed the battlefield and prevented coordination between units after combat commenced.[17] His doctrine depended on formalism and central deployment as its chief tenets. The first flowed naturally from the second. He insisted that the army deploy from a central column, or in his later writings, from a pair of columns. This would allow for his complex system of deployment to place individual battalions where demanded by predetermined order and to provide the proper transition from march column to battle line. He acknowledged the inefficacy of a single column and desired the retention of the twin column, insisting that armies retain central deployment to keep his geometric system intact.[18]

Mesnil-Durand's salvo, directed at Guibert, pushed the debate between l'ordre profond and l'ordre mince to its apex. With the *Fragments*, all the major documents in the debate had been published. The theories of both sides remained in sharp contrast and bitter contention, particularly with regard to the basic doctrines of maneuver and attack. Mesnil-Durand also drew the distinction between the "French" system of l'ordre profond, relying on the supposed élan and indiscipline endemic to the "national character," and the Prussian l'ordre mince, hidebound and relying on the harsh discipline of the Germanic nature. Perhaps ironically, the 1776 *Réglement* represented a defeat not only for Guibert's hybrid l'ordre mixte but also for Mesnil-Durand's stringent l'ordre profond.[19]

As polemicists debated and the Council of War met its end, France's attention remained fixated on the conflict in the British colonies in North America. In the summer of 1776, the Continental Congress declared its independence on 2 July. The French eagerly sought an opportunity to profit from it. For much of the period after 1688, England had bested France in the colonial game. In each major war between the two powers, their forces fought over imperial possessions around the world. England generally triumphed in this arena, particularly after 1740, when the Royal Navy became the undisputed ruler of the seas. British amphibious efforts seized French colonies with relative ease in each conflict during the period, which is often called the Second Hundred Years War.[20] The most dramatic consequence of this imbalance was the loss of France's North American colonies in the 1760s, with Britain receiving New France and Spain taking the Louisiana Territory.

The outbreak of unrest in America provided a unique opportunity. Britain had never faced a major colonial rebellion, allowing it to spend relatively little money and military power to maintain order. Hostilities now could force London to focus its resources on North America and away from its other possessions, some formerly French, in the Caribbean and India. France stood to gain in these regions if the American rebellion required a major British military commitment. Moreover, if the American colonies could somehow hold off the British, that kingdom would lose valuable resources and markets as well as a great deal of prestige. France could capitalize on this loss, both in the degradation of British power and in France's own material and moral gain.[21]

Like Guibert, many presumed armed French involvement and planned accordingly. This belief flowed not only from the practical reasons noted but also because of the ideology of many of the rebel Americans. Some leading revolutionaries, including Thomas Jefferson and Benjamin Franklin, had spent extensive time in France, absorbing the teachings of the Enlightenment and participating in the Republic of Letters. In particular, the Americans adopted much of their criticism of irrational government from Voltaire, the notions of constitutional rule from Montesquieu, and the dream of a republic from Rousseau. Taken together, these produced an Enlightenment sentiment in the colonies that drove much of the ideology of the American Revolution.[22]

In France this ideology presented the possibility of America's becoming a test case for a republic. Numerous figures wrote of their excitement over this, including Guibert. As expected from his earlier writings, the colonel lauded the potential for producing a "free people" in America that would mirror the idyll of his writings.[23]

Yet Louis XVI did not wish to upset his government's reform efforts, particularly the financial measures that would be nullified by a shift to wartime spending. More fundamentally, his ministers waited to ensure that the colonists were worth supporting. The early years of the war produced only defeats in that regard as the British pushed George Washington's American forces south from New York into Pennsylvania and New Jersey.[24]

French reluctance evaporated in late 1777. An American force under Horatio Gates and Benedict Arnold met British general John Burgoyne's forces on their march from Canada to reinforce the royal position in New England. From mid-September to October, the two armies fought a series of engagements around Saratoga, culminating in a decisive battle on 7 October. The American forces defeated the British in a hard-fought contest resembling the great linear battles of Europe. This proved to the French not only that the colonists could defeat the British but also that they could win a battle fought with traditional tactics. Consequently, Louis's government began preparations to enter the war on the side of the Americans, cementing a treaty of alliance on 6 February 1778.[25]

To prepare for war, the army held a great training camp in late 1778. The polemical debate produced enough partisans of the various systems to warrant a test of their efficacy, even if Broglie's sympathy lay with l'ordre profond. More fundamentally, France prepared for large-scale entry into the war, which would perhaps include combat against the British or other European powers. Army-wide doctrine required training and experience for the officer corps to successfully command large bodies of troops. This could be gained only in the camp setting. The acknowledgement of this fact indicates the depth to which the advice of Guibert, as well as other philosophes, had been heeded for greater education and training.[26]

In early 1778 Broglie received orders from Secretary of State for War Alexandre-Marie-Eléonor de Saint-Mauris, prince de Montbarey et du Saint-Empire. Montbarey had replaced Saint-Germain in early 1778 and would oversee France's entry into the war in America. He ordered the marshal to gather forty infantry battalions, along with attached cavalry and artillery, under his command in Normandy around Bayeux. These forces deployed near Bayeux and the small village of Vaussieux, the latter lending its name to the maneuvers. Broglie's assignment was threefold: protect the coast from possible British amphibious action, prepare the army for an invasion of Britain, and settle the debate between l'ordre mince and l'ordre profond.[27]

Much of Broglie's correspondence relates to the second of the three tasks. Like Napoleon's famous Boulogne camp held nearly thirty years later, Broglie's Vaussieux exercises would threaten invasion and forge the army into a weapon to attempt such an expedition. If France could manage to find an opening in the British naval defense of the English Channel, an invasion would go forward. If no such opportunity presented itself, the army would constitute a force-in-being, requiring the British to assemble a comparable counterforce in southern England, denying these resources to the American theaters.[28]

Tactical and doctrinal issues remained a minor concern to Broglie. Much of his attention focused on the larger question of the invasion, particularly the organization and supply of his forces. A great deal of his correspondence addresses issues of food.[29] The marshal also dedicated a portion of his efforts to securing positions within the army for the minor nobles who sought such. He mediated many disputes between officers, addressed matters of justice, and appointed a number of nobles to the officer corps, usually to supernumerary positions.[30] This indicates the reality of one of Guibert's chief attacks on the military establishment during the Saint-Germain ministry, namely the bloated officer corps.[31] Too much of Broglie's attention focused on the appointment of supernumerary positions and settling disputes rather than on the needs of the troops or the impending exercises and possible invasion.

Montbarey supervised the camp from the court. His role would not be to settle the theoretical debate, in which he evinced little interest, but rather to coordinate with the other ministries to prepare for impending war with Britain. The majority of his letters to Broglie concern finance and organization, particularly missives to reduce costs.[32]

The camp itself was a limited affair, particularly when contrasted with the grand exercises held in Prussia every autumn. But it would prove the decisive event in the polemical debate. Broglie's chief concern was to implement the methods of the 1774 *Réglement*, which contained much of his and Mesnil-Durand's beliefs, rather than the 1776 document, which espoused Pirch's l'ordre mince. The marshal's views were not doctrinaire but nevertheless insisted on the preeminence of l'ordre profond. Therefore, Vaussieux would be a showcase of Mesnil-Durand's constitution and a vindication of Broglie's beliefs in the man and his system.[33]

Exercises opened in early September. "The first days of the month," Broglie reported to Montbarey, "were employed in establishing the troops in the Camp and exercising in observation of the Rules of Discipline explained in the Provisional Regulations." Battalions and then regiments trained individually, drilling in the maneuvers and tenets of Mesnil-Durand's system and presumably the 1776 *Réglement*, all to prove the effectiveness of the forms of l'ordre profond. In addition to preparing for the larger maneuvers to come, this training educated novice soldiers in battle drill, veterans in the new systems, and the entire army for potential deployment.[34]

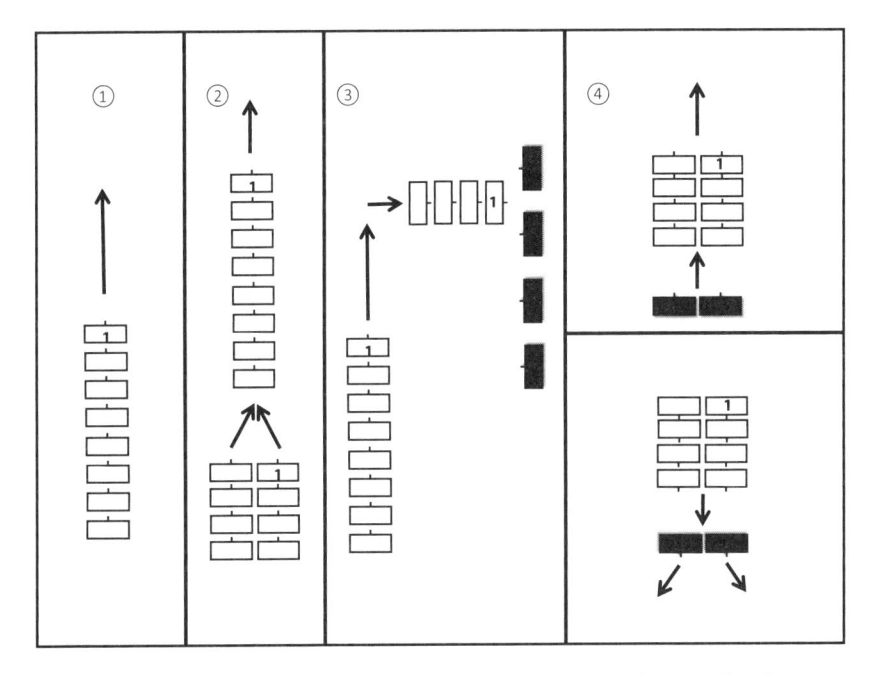

Camp of Vaussieux, maneuvers of 9 September 1778. (1) Broglie forms a march column and advances; (2) forms a single column of march from double columns; (3) marches a unitary column forward and deploys on the square to meet an enemy; and (4) concludes by marching a double column forward and performing an about-face to meet and disperse an enemy to the rear.

Following battalion and regimental drill, Broglie combined the forces of the camp into brigades and divisions for large-scale maneuvers. These began on 9 September. The marshal organized his thirty-two battalions into four divisions of two brigades each, placing four battalions into each brigade for the exercise. He formed these into columns of battalions in a single line, with half-intervals between each, and marched them forward.[35]

From this line, the army formed two columns of two brigades each and advanced. The columns formed by division and combined into a single column by division, continuing the advance. Broglie then declared the presence of an enemy to the right, whereupon the entire column wheeled right, with the first division advancing and the other three following behind. He ordered the first (leftmost) battalion of each regiment to halt in line while the remainder advanced against the enemy, which Broglie declared had deployed itself behind an obstacle to fire. Satisfied with the maneuvers, the marshal ordered his battalions to return to camp in double march columns. Along the route, he placed an enemy army on the attack, requiring his columns to about-face to meet and repulse the threat. During the following two days, the maneuvers were repeated and refined.[36]

On 12 September Broglie held his second maneuver. Marshal Jean-Baptiste-Donatien de Vimeur, comte de Rochambeau, received command of the brigade of Bassigny, which would maneuver using the methods of the 1776 *Réglement*. The opposing force, a division, would contest the maneuvers using Mesnil-Durand's ordre-profond system. Baron Wimpffen awarded the contest to Rochambeau, noting the inefficacy of the maneuvers using l'ordre profond against his more active movements.[37]

After a day of rest on the thirteenth, Broglie constructed a series of maneuvers in an attempt to correct a major issue with the previous exercises. In those the movements of each battalion did not conform to Mesnil-Durand's ideal, largely because the theorist did not provide for a battalion of alignment. During the maneuvers of 14 September, Broglie designated one battalion of each regiment for alignment, hoping to find a compromise solution to the problem of preexisting deployment plans versus deployment by exigency.[38]

The maneuvers began with practice in this deployment followed by marches in line and change of front while deployed in line for the remainder of the morning. Broglie then ordered the army to deploy in a quincunx by advancing the right battalion of each regiment one hundred paces, forming the checkerboard pattern, which then advanced behind a screen of hussars. The marshal then formed the army for combat, infantry advancing in a single line with bayonets fixed, before resuming the checkerboard by the same maneuver when an imagined obstacle called for fire instead of shock.[39]

The following day, 15 September, Broglie repeated the exercise, this time with an enemy present under the command of Louis-François-Jean Chabot. Under these circumstances, Broglie made extensive use of his chasseurs to harry the opposing troops and screen advances and retreats, likely drawing from his experiences during the Seven Years War. Broglie afterward pronounced his complete satisfaction with the exercise: "it was impossible to desire more precision in the very difficult movement, and it demanded the attention and intelligence of the troops." Rochambeau, commanding part of the opposition, arrived at a different conclusion, as he

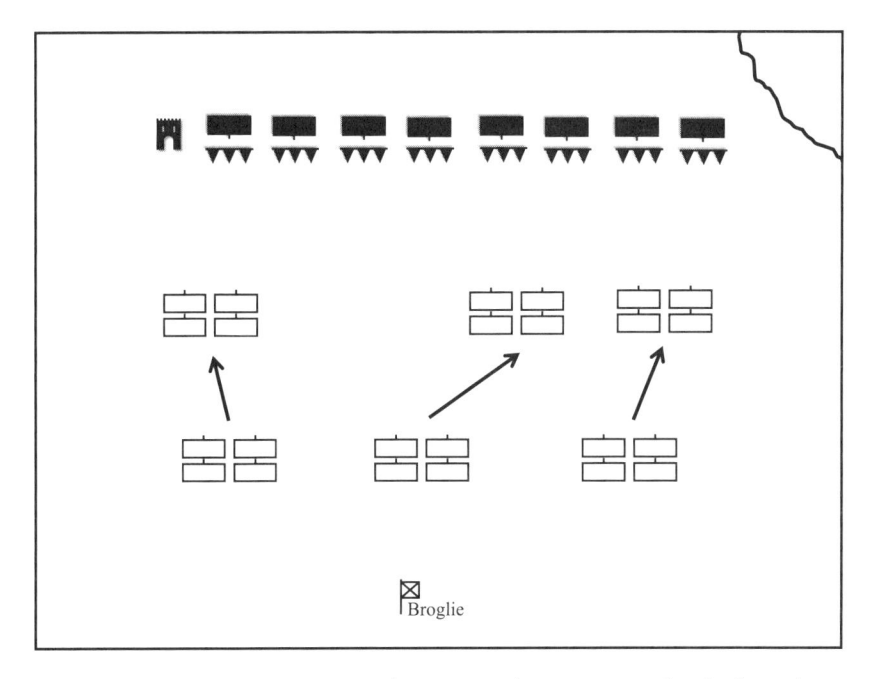

Camp of Vaussieux, maneuvers of 21 September 1778. Broglie deploys three major columns against an entrenched enemy, feinting on the left and carrying the right with a shock attack in Mesnil-Durand-style columns.

"marched rapidly" and confused Broglie's forces, placing his own forces in an unassailable position. After another day of rest on the sixteenth, Broglie ordered a repeat of the exercises of the previous two days. He formed the grenadiers and chasseurs of his own army into unique battalions, which he placed on his flanks. The maneuvers of the preceding days were then repeated to the same effect.[40]

Beginning on the twentieth, Broglie directed larger exercises with much of the forces under his command. That day he ordered five brigade columns to form on the field. This army then marched in double column by division, as the terrain proved too rough for march in columns by platoon. Following this, the two divisions of grenadiers and chasseurs attacked a fortified position.[41]

On 21 September Broglie again designed an attack on a fortified position. He arranged an enemy force to form near a village and march toward Caen, occupying a strong defensive position, with its left anchored on a ravine and its right on the village itself. For the attack, Broglie formed his own army into six columns. Following the prearranged plan, he directed two columns to make a feint against the enemy right, drawing its forces into the village. The other four columns then launched his principal attack, breaking the enemy "with the bayonet and the butt of the fusil." This assault dislodged the defenders, who retreated in good order. Broglie ordered a pursuit, with two columns on the left and four on the right. The remainder of the exercise that day consisted of his forces pursuing the fleeing enemy, which he commended for its swift action to prevent further damage.[42]

The next large exercise occurred on 24 September. This consisted of twelve major movements without an enemy present. Broglie put the army through its paces, paying particular attention to the formation of line from battalion columns. Once the troops deployed, he ordered advances and retreats in line per the parade-ground precision of Mesnil-Durand's system. The final large maneuver occurred on 28 September. Broglie formed the entire army for this exercise, including the cavalry and artillery, a rarity in eighteenth-century training camps. Like previous scenarios, he assigned an enemy force to act autonomously against his own units, which he arranged in four divisions deployed in line with cavalry on the flanks and artillery dispersed throughout. The first three maneuvers consisted of simple deployment and advance, including refusing his left flank and deploying several of its battalions in column. Broglie then allowed the enemy to attack. This occurred on the left flank, which prompted the marshal to re-fuse his right and advance his left, with cavalry leading and infantry attacking with the bayonet. Following this, Broglie reset both forces and proceeded with his march. The enemy again attacked, once again forcing his troops to resort to the bayonet. But the enemy commanders shifted from assault to fire, which forced Broglie's counterattacking columns to retreat under a withering hail.[43]

With the maneuver of 28 September, the camp largely accomplished its goals. The soldiers had drilled in both the 1776 maneuvers and the system of Mesnil-Durand, both in small units and as part of an entire army. The king ordered Broglie to disperse the forces assembled at Vaussieux by 1 October in preparation for action against Britain.[44]

Guibert's direct role in the exercises was minimal. The army was much less concerned with his work than it was Mesnil-Durand's, particularly as filtered through Broglie. Both theorists served as aides during Vaussieux, making it a de facto referendum on the mince-profond debate. Montbarey found little value in

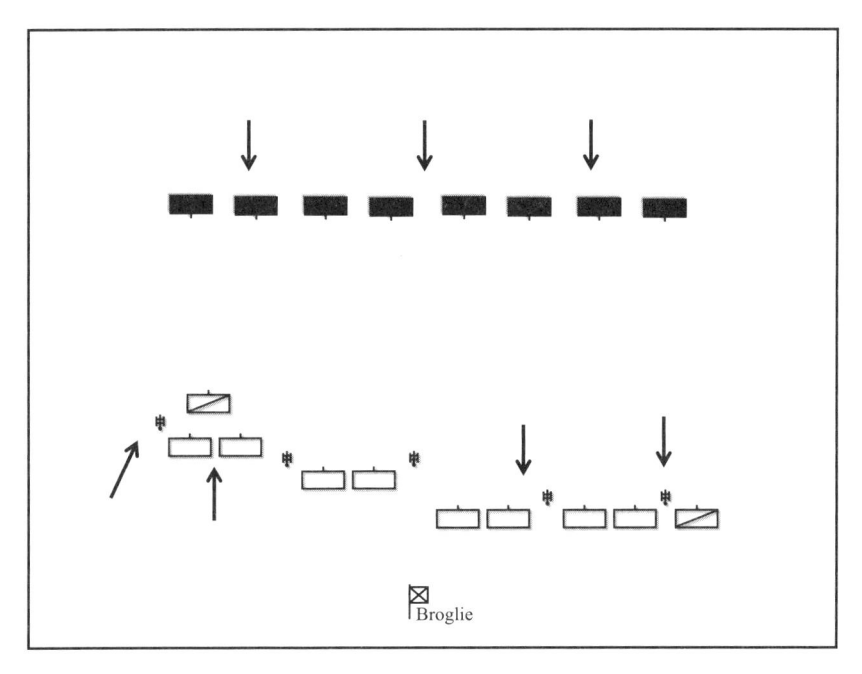

Camp of Vaussieux, maneuvers of 28 September 1778. Broglie executes the classic "oblique attack" attributed to Frederick II but likely drawn from Vegetius. The general refuses his right and pushes the left forward, defeating the advancing enemy.

the exercises, declaring them to be "sterile demonstrations, quite expensive, and not even producing definitive results on the new tactics; this was the occupation of the troops under the command of Marshal Broglie."[45]

Broglie concluded, "I have been content with the manner of our troops during all of the maneuvers." He maintained this stance throughout the camp and afterward, frequently writing to the king and Montbarey of his satisfaction with the maneuvers. Yet to most observers, Mesnil-Durand and Broglie were entirely discredited. Rochambeau's quick and decisive maneuvers stymied Broglie's columns, demonstrating their inherent ineffectiveness. Rochambeau himself offered a different analysis from his commander's: "The result of these unfortunate discussions was very unhappy for Broglie; I took leave of him at the end of the camp and I told him pathetically and with tears in my eyes [that he was wrong]; he seemed touched but would not be convinced."[46]

The Camp of Vaussieux, to most observers like Rochambeau and Wimpffen, proved the complete inutility of Mesnil-Durand's system and of l'ordre profond at large. It sparked a number of written responses, including Guibert's own. Ultimately, however, it would prove the end of the polemical debate. Jean Colin argues that the exercises convinced Broglie of the usefulness of the column, not the unitary or double formation of Mesnil-Durand, but rather the small maneuver column of Guibert's *Instruction for Light Troops*. The marshal would remain its protector through the period.[47]

In a larger sense Vaussieux pushed France away from either end of the polemical spectrum. The *Réglement* of 1776, heavily influenced by Pirch and l'ordre mince, remained in effect for another decade. Even so, nearly every theorist retreated from the radical positions of either side. The result was the search for a true l'ordre mixte, a system that could combine the best of the two. Guibert had already produced such a method, and many within the army looked to his work for its implementation over the next decade.[48]

Broglie lost at least a portion of his influence after Vaussieux.[49] Command in the coming war remained a divided prospect. Montbarey, in his role as secretary of state for war, theoretically commanded France's armed forces for the king, but he exercised little direct control. Much of the American war would be fought at sea, thus leaving the majority of its campaigning to the Department of the Marine, helmed by Antoine-Raymond-Jean Gualbert Gabriel de Sartine, comte d'Alby. The land contingent under Broglie never accomplished its mission of invading Britain. Portions departed for America under Rochambeau, who led them during the famous campaign that culminated in the victory at Yorktown in the autumn of 1781.[50]

Guibert repeatedly requested a position under Rochambeau but was denied. No definitive explanation for this has surfaced in Guibertian literature, as previously discussed. Guibert may have been denied service simply because of his junior status, both in the nobility and in the army. He was a colonel of relatively young age and low extraction in a military that valued lineage and rank as its highest virtues.[51]

More practically, the American expeditionary force was relatively small, consisting only of a few thousand soldiers, which limited the number of officers who could be attached even as supernumeraries. Guibert also was seen as a theorist only, despite his combat experience during the Seven Years War and on Corsica.

Dispatching a philosophe to the front in America likely would not profit the expedition. Guibert also seemed to have no lasting relationship with either Lafayette or Rochambeau, both of whom could conceivably have brought him on the mission. Most likely, his strongest connection was through his father, who continued to serve as a Manchurian in the *logis*, using his expertise at organization to continue the care and feeding of French troops stationed across the kingdom.[52]

At the conclusion of Vaussieux, Guibert penned his second work of military theory, *Défense du système de guerre moderne, ou réfutation complète du système de M[esnil-]D[urand]*.[53] As the name suggests, the majority of the book attacked Mesnil-Durand's tactical system, particularly as refined after 1774. This marks it not as a second part of the *Essai général de tactique*, as it is often presented, but rather Guibert's only entry into the polemical debate in the form of a polemic itself. The work also includes an in-depth discussion concerning the Camp of Vaussieux and his observations of the exercises. Most importantly, it offers a shift in Guibert's doctrine. The colonel here demurs from his prior advocacy of a citizen army in favor of a more professional force. He also explores the upper levels of warfare, particularly operations and strategy.

Guibert declares his intentions in the *avant-propos:*

> I am not the creator of any system. I have only, in my *Essai général de tactique*, widened and written known ideas. I have had no part in the Ordinances of maneuver [regulations] given during the peace. If in this work I demonstrate that the project of Mesnil-Durand is unacceptable, I intend to take from this success neither prizes nor glory, because I have only obtained them by collecting the opinions of most of the army and the principles of the King of Prussia. My ambition will be fulfilled if I pass on *un bon esprit* that has been well designed and conceived.[54]

This opening salvo inaugurated Guibert's systematic attack on Mesnil-Durand. He continues by arguing that the army in general misunderstood the lessons of Vaussieux, as it did not participate directly in the exercises and had received no clear report of them.[55]

Guibert offers his own report of Vaussieux, particularly the efficacy of l'ordre profond, in the first volume of the *Défense du système de guerre moderne*. That school, he argues, was misconceived from its beginnings by Folard, who took "an accidental formation" and made it the basis for his system, chaining the French army to the deep order.[56] Mesnil-Durand slightly improved on the system, Guibert continues, by stripping away the pike and improving the ponderous nature of Folard's formations. But the system remained "a bizarre assortment" of columns and lines, with cavalry and artillery scattered nonsensically throughout. L'ordre profond was fundamentally flawed in its inception, he concludes.[57]

Vaussieux, Guibert argues, demonstrated the inefficacy of Mesnil-Durand's system. The various maneuvers attempted by the army required a pedantic and complex organizational system. Following Mesnil-Durand, Broglie divided his battalions into two *"manches"* consisting of two companies, each with two platoons; these were divided into columns of four sections. Guibert found this to be *"une chose puérile,"* a silly thing, as it depended on exactly equal numbers in each formation and provided no permanent division, substituting temporary formations to deploy the army according to Mesnil-Durand's strictures.[58]

After the maneuvers began, Mesnil-Durand's system broke down repeatedly. Its insistence on central deployment required a number of processional movements from march column to battle order, all inviting counterattack from enemy forces. In particular, Guibert notes that the flanks of the deep formations proved dangerously exposed, particularly to cavalry. L'ordre profond offered no solution to this problem, indicating its systemic flaws. Guibert argues that the closed columns also proved exceptionally vulnerable to enemy fire, particularly when they became the target of concentrated artillery and infantry fire. More damningly, he finds that the complex and confusing deployment of the different subformations in the system required constant redressing of the battle formation, which came undone with the slightest movement even in simulated combat.[59]

The Vaussieux exercises condemned Mesnil-Durand's system completely, according to Guibert. Its insistence on formalistic and rigid deployments, a single formation, and dividing battle order from march order rendered it as ineffective as the Old Regime system of personal, feudalistic doctrine. In particular, the necessity of maneuvering in large columns,·whether single, double, or quadruple, proved a fatal flaw. Such formations only functioned properly on a parade ground, and then only if the column's front did not shift, as it often would in battle. "The need to always return to the state of the simple column for maneuver is found in many of the maneuvers of

Mesnil-Durand and is one of the most fatal complications resulting from his *ordre primitif*. That alone, in my opinion, makes his system, with respect to internal details, absolutely defective and inadmissible for war," Guibert concludes.[60]

More fundamentally, the chaos of battle and the irregularity of the battlefield rendered any single system, and especially one using a single formation, inherently unworkable. Instead, Guibert insists, the French army should adopt the system already presented in the *Essai général de tactique*. In particular, his Guibert columns would solve the problems of maneuver and deployment inherent in the complex systems of l'ordre profond. They also would provide the opportunity for a large army to articulate itself tactically to surmount battlefield obstacles and enemy action if and when necessary. Guibert's own system was flexible, he argues, in sharp contrast to the rigid formalism of Mesnil-Durand's.[61]

Following his lengthy discussion of Vaussieux, Guibert turns next to a treatise on the nature of the "French national character." This point proved vital to the polemical debate. Proponents of l'ordre profond had argued that élan was the primary virtue of the French national character, particularly when expressed in the bayonet-wielding assault column. This contrasted with the Prussian character, which lent itself to rigid and often brutal discipline embodied in the thin battle line delivering fire. Because the French soldier did not take to harsh discipline, so went this argument, his character was better harnessed in l'ordre profond.[62]

Guibert disputes this notion. He notes that French soldiers did demonstrate élan, as well as valor and courage, in numerous battles throughout history. Yet he argues that these characteristics were hardly confined to one people and appeared in all militaries. Arguing that France was unique in this respect was simply "the fumes of national vanity." The argument for the primacy of élan could even be harmful, he notes. Guibert provides as support the classic examples of the Battles of Crécy, Poitiers, and Agincourt, where French forces charged valiantly into English longbow formations and were duly slaughtered.[63] More recently, he draws from his own experience to cite the Battle of Minden, where a mere 6,000 Prussian infantry threw back seventy-two squadrons of French cavalry with disciplined fire. He concludes that national character must remain an element of any doctrinal system, but that too great an emphasis on it would lead to a malformed system, as it had with l'ordre profond.[64]

In the second volume of *Défense du système de guerre moderne*, Guibert refines his extant doctrinal system. In particular, he develops the operational and strategic levels of war in relation to his system. The last point proved important in the larger development of military theory and terminology. Previously, strategy had been divided into tactics and "grand tactics," which encompassed every aspect of war from operations to grand strategy but generally referred to the modern concept of operations.[65] Guibert, though, notes the need for higher levels of analysis. He coins the term "*stratégique*" to encompass this higher level, referring to it as "the tactics of armies." It represents the movement of armies on campaign; their origins, discipline, composition, and training; or the operational level of war with some of the strategic. Much of the second volume concerns this newly identified nuance in the levels of war. As with the *Essai général de tactique*, he notes that the roots of effective stratégique are laid in the training camp and the skills of fortification and forage. These enable an army to maintain its dispersed nature in divisions, which he also retains from his previous work.[66]

Because of his increased emphasis on the operational level of war, Guibert reiterates his missives that the army be well led by an "homme de génie." He lauds Henri de la Tour d'Auvergne, vicomte de Turenne, for his campaigns against Raimondo, graf Montecuccoli, during the late sixteenth century. Guibert argues that Turenne demonstrated proper stratégique in his campaigns, forming his forces into a net to trap Montecuccoli and confine him to an inferior position. This would have resulted in a decisive battle had Turenne lived to press the advantage.[67]

Guibert's analysis in this regard again shows his debt to Bourcet's operational principles. His analysis includes much of Bourcet's plan of many branches, as had his prior work in the *Essai*. Little of this had changed significantly, particularly as the purpose of *Défense du système de guerre moderne* was to address tactical, not operational and strategic, issues.[68]

Défense du système de guerre moderne represents both continuity and change in Guibert's political thought. In its closing sections, he returns to the issues of military, politics, and society that had played such a prominent role in the *Essai*. He renews his call for reform to produce discipline, professionalism, and virtue in all three areas. Yet as a veteran of public service and an erstwhile member of the establishment, Guibert tempers his prior condemnations of French society and politics. "When I wrote my previous work," he notes, "I was twenty years old, more or less. The vapors of modern philosophy clouded my head and obfuscated my judgment. It is so simple, at the age where one does not think carefully, at the age where one uses . . . the whole spirit of his soul to indulge in illusions of that which he believes will improve and grow [the state]!" In this vein he refutes his previous assertion that a citizen militia filled a necessary role in national defense and a well-formed society. He reiterates his previous doctrine of a small, professional army fighting limited wars according to a "fixed plan of aggrandizement." Popular participation, even in a limited militia role, now appears completely anathema to Guibert.[69]

This shift undoubtedly occurred as he grew more mature, both in his political involvement and in his philosophy. As a young officer outside the Parisian establishment, he had little to lose by offering a scathing indictment of the system in his earlier work. But now as a seasoned military and political veteran, he owed his position, popularity, and income to the state. Moreover, his contacts with more moderate and even conservative reformers may have served to moderate his stance. Men like Wimpffen counseled military reform with the same zeal as Guibert but with less far-reaching social and political implications. In *Défense du système de guerre moderne*, Guibert perhaps comes closest to resembling the other reformers of his day in playing down the social and political reforms to emphasize military doctrine.

Unlike the argument in the *Essai*, the need for discipline trumps the regeneration of society in *Défense du système de guerre moderne*. Guibert's desire to reduce the destructiveness and ramifications of war overcame his advocacy of a disciplined and virtuous society. While the social elements remained in his doctrine, he severs the direct link between society and the army. No longer would the citizen militia form a keystone of his constitution. Instead, the professional army would accomplish the state's military goals.

This presents an intriguing historiographical debate. As noted, the *Essai* received wide publication, not only in France but also across the world. In particular, the incendiary political and social critiques of the "Discours préliminaire" resonated in the Republic of Letters and those who would later perpetrate the Revolution. Guibert's refutation of this argument divided scholars on its intent and implications for his legacy. Matti Lauerma provides the standard argument, claiming that Guibert's political and social thought were something of a lark, that the *Essai* carries his true meaning as the "prophet of the Revolution."[70] R. R. Palmer presents a competing view, one worth quoting in full:

> Guibert, in both books, glimpsed the difference between limited and unlimited war, or between the clashes of professional soldiers and the destructive struggles of peoples. He saw the close relation between warfare and the structure of government. His inconsistency was not logical but moral, an inconsistency of attitude, not of analysis. At twenty-nine, he looked upon the ideas of national armies and blitzkrieg strategy with favor. At thirty-five he looked upon these same ideas with disapproval. At neither time did he show much practical foresight, as distinguished from lucky predictions, or any sense that the ideas that he favored in 1772 and rejected in 1779 would become realities for the generation then alive.[71]

Palmer's analysis pinpoints the nature of Guibert's political and social analysis during the decade. Unlike his military theory, Guibert never expected his political and social reforms to be taken as more than philosophical musings. He states this directly in the *Essai:* the "vigorous people" of his Utopian ideology "do not rest in Europe in any nation" and would not appear.[72] The Vegetian social reforms of both works are thus a thought exercise rather than instructions, as his military constitution was intended.

Guibert first published *Défense du système de guerre moderne* in 1779 to little acclaim and readership. Unlike his prior work, it proved to be too technical and polemical to win over the salons. The Camp at Vaussieux would also herald the end of his direct service to the Ministry of War for nearly a decade.[73]

Guibert's service in the government and the period immediately afterward illustrates a fundamental flaw in his personality. Unlike his father, Guibert demonstrated an almost complete inability to navigate the tricky political waters at court. This was most evident in his long fallout with the Broglies. By all indications, the Guibert and Broglie families enjoyed a mutually profitable relationship. Charles Guibert served under Broglie during the Seven Years War and after. Guibert himself likely met the marshal at an early age, a relationship that likely led to his positioning with the Regiment d'Auvergne and with the Corsican Legion. His return to the metropole and debut in

Paris society also seemed to have come as an indirect result of powerful connections within the government and at court.

The inability of Guibert to play court politics directly led to his downfall from the Council of War. He never managed to form the connections necessary to shield him from blowback as his father had done. Moreover, the colonel's own zeal alienated his few court connections. The Vaussieux incident severed the ties between him and the Broglie family. "Guibert was too vain," his childhood friend Dumouriez recorded, "to pardon the Marshal de Broglie, to whom he owed everything, for his opinion; and in an answer to Mesnil-Durand, he accordingly attacked his benefactor in an epigram: this was inexcusable."[74] Guibert never learned to place personal advancement or discretion over his desire for reform, much to his detriment on multiple occasions.

The latter half of the 1770s greatly slowed Guibert's meteoric ascent from the first half of the decade. Lespinasse's death deprived him not only of a friend and erstwhile lover but also of his chief networking advocate. His writing career stalled, particularly as the venomous criticism of la Harpe illuminated the flaws in his talent in that field. But Guibert's influence on the French army and its theory was not entirely checked by these setbacks. He strongly advocated participation in the War of American Independence, composing a number of memoranda on the topic and remitting them to the Ministry of War. He would not see service in that conflict, much to his chagrin. He continued advocating his ordre mixte as the polemical debate continued throughout the decade. The Camp of Vaussieux finally demonstrated the superiority of a more flexible system like Guibert's over Mesnil-Durand's ordre profond, much to the chagrin of its commander, Marshal Broglie.

While Guibert lost much of his official influence after Vaussieux, he continued to refine his theory and the doctrine that it produced. His *Défense du système de guerre moderne* argues that his system proved superior to Mesnil-Durand's at the camp. To many within the army, this argument proved decisive and ended the polemical debate in favor of l'ordre mixte over the rigid systems of l'ordre mince and l'ordre profond. Guibert returned to his estate at Courcelles after the camp's conclusion, ill and disillusioned.[75] Yet even as he lost official power within the Ministry of War, his doctrine would continue to shape the progress of the military toward the implementation of an institutional army.

CHAPTER 7

Commencement d'une vie nouvelle

In the years after the Camp of Vaussieux, Guibert settled into a steady and low-profile routine. After recovering from illness, he returned to Paris to resurrect his public image. Many of the paths he had taken to reach the heights of power still remained open, but others had closed. Vaussieux led to a breakdown in the close friendship of the Guibert and Broglie families. The colonel's personality and reforming spirit had burnt most of his other bridges within the military. His reforms had alienated conservatives, and the "Prussian" nature of his military constitution had turned away many of his fellow reformers. Most importantly, he had lost his staunchest social partner with the death of Lespinasse and the closure of her salon. Bereft of the avenues that had launched him to fame, Guibert fell back on his network in Paris.

The majority of Guibert's energy in the decade was therefore devoted to his literary pursuits, the "commencement d'une vie nouvelle" (commencement of a new life).[1] He composed a sort of sequel to his travelogue from his German voyage in 1773 as he toured Prussia, inspecting garrisons and fortresses. Other publications included essays submitted to the Académie française for contests during the late 1770s. He also busied himself with the composition of two plays, neither of which achieved publication or production.

Debate continued, particularly with regard to the legacy of Guibert's time in the Ministry of War. Tactical disputes did not recur during these years, having been largely settled at Vaussieux. But deeper social and political issues came to the fore. In particular, the debate over the nature of officer promotion and venality became the central topic, culminating in the infamous "Ségur Decree" of 1781.

Guibert did not directly participate in Ségur's administration, remaining a political exile. This allowed him time to continue his literary pursuits, write several unpublished works on France and its history, and travel the countryside. He also reforged his social networks, establishing connections with a new generation of salonnières and philosophes. Together, this represented his "new life."

Guibert faced a starkly different social spectrum on his return to private life in 1779. Lespinasse's death had left a large gap in the Parisian social scene. The deaths of Rousseau and Voltaire in 1778 also signaled a shift in generation within the Enlightenment. All three had tended to refrain from political activism, preferring literary and philosophical pursuits. They often discussed politics but rarely acted in that arena, whether in print or physical association. Most famously, Voltaire lauded the Maupeou "revolution," claiming that the government's actions were necessary to prevent despotism by the parlements.[2]

To literary historian Robert Darnton, this wave of deaths marked the passing of the Enlightenment's last great writers. "With the death of the old Bolsheviks," he declares, "the Enlightenment passed into the hands of nonentities like [Jean-Baptiste-Antoine] Suard: it lost its fire and became a tranquil diffusion of light, a comfortable ascent toward progress." These heirs to Voltaire and Rousseau lacked their predecessors' ability, which caused the Enlightenment to fall to Grub Street. Men of little talent like Jean-Paul Marat and Jacques-Pierre Brissot, scribbling furiously, churned out reams of vulgar literature to advance their own positions and, most importantly, to make money.[3]

Rather than excelling at literature, this generation was much more political. First among their favored salons was that of Suzanne Necker, "the antechamber of the Revolution." Her husband, Jacques Necker, was generally recognized as the chief economist of France, both for his theory and for his ties to the Geneva banking community. He served as controller general of finances from 1777 to 1781, reversing many of Turgot's physiocratic policies in favor of shifting France to a more market-based economic system.[4]

Like Guibert, Necker fell from power after being attacked by conservatives at court and spent the majority of the 1780s out of public service. This came in large part because of the release of a vital document in the decade before the Revolution, Necker's *Compte rendu au roi*, penned in 1781. For the first time in the kingdom's history, this accounting publicized the budget, including expenditures and crown revenues. Historiographical opinion sharply divides on Necker's motives and the nature of the document, which shows a budget surplus of approximately ten million British pounds, allegedly due to the cost-cutting measures of the previous two decades. Given the financial collapse of the state only years later, this accounting rings patently false. Necker likely excluded extraordinary debts from his numbers, including those incurred from the massive spending efforts necessary to fund the American expedition.[5]

On the surface, Necker's motivations appear clear: he intended to project governmental financial strength, likely to ensure France's continuing access to international credit. But he had deeper intentions. The open release of the document galvanized public opinion. It fed the Enlightenment desire for knowledge and definition, specifically of crown finances. But it also questioned Necker's honesty and competence, as the government had been speaking for years about the mounting deficits, and the American war demonstrably cost a large amount. Most immediately, the *Compte rendu au roi* solidified an opposition group, bringing the physiocrats and more conservative nobles together against the financier. Like Guibert, Necker was unceremoniously removed from office shortly after the publication of the document.[6]

Necker spent the majority of the 1780s participating in his wife's salon. Suzanne Necker established a reputation as a leading salonnière in the 1760s, contemporary to Lespinasse. At the death of the latter in 1776, Necker inherited many of her attendees, most prominently Diderot and d'Alembert, when the latter ventured from the Louvre. She also drew the attendance of other leading salonnières, including Marie Thérèse Rodet Geoffrin and the marquise du Deffand.[7]

Guibert had been a welcome visitor at Necker's salon since his entrance into Paris in 1771. After 1780 he made it the center for his social life, much as he had done with Lespinasse's salon before her death. As he had done before, he mingled with the assembled philosophes and shared his work with them.[8]

Among this new group, Suard and his wife, Amélie, became Guibert's closest friends. "I had much good feeling [*amitié*] for Guibert," remarked Amélie Suard. Her husband was a lesser philosophe brought up in the salon of Geoffrin. He attached himself to the Encyclopedists, particularly d'Alembert, in the late 1760s and early 1770s. This led, perhaps through the intervention of Lespinasse, to his elevation to Seat Twenty-Six of the Académie française in 1772. In 1774 Louis XV named Suard censor of theatrical materials. He produced no work of note, preferring instead to confine his talents to the salons.[9]

Suard's greatest coup came in his marriage to Amélie Panckoucke in 1766. Unlike him, her literary talents marked her as one of the better authors of the age, particularly of correspondence. Like her husband, she joined the salon culture in the 1760s and remained a leading figure throughout the late Old Regime. Many of her letters prove invaluable in characterizing the period, particularly after the deaths of many of the great Enlightenment figures from midcentury.[10]

Guibert met the Suards early in his social activities. Only after Vaussieux did their friendship deepen, however. He spent much of his time in Paris with them, both at Necker's salon and at the other institutions of Parisian society. In particular, his connection to Amélie proved the strongest of his post-Vaussieux relationships. The two had been close friends from his earliest days in Paris. Though little evidence exists of a romantic attachment between them, Guibert's most recent biographer unearthed a series of letters between the two that may indicate a liaison. In this correspondence Amélie expresses a great interest in Guibert's romance with Lespinasse. The intimate nature of the letters hints at a relationship deeper than friendship, but further evidence is needed to conclude an affair.[11]

Guibert's romantic activities seem to have waned after Lespinasse's death or perhaps his marriage. His first mistress, Jeanne Thiroux de Montsauge, also remained in France. Yet without Lespinasse's chronicles, evidence of a continuing affair remains inconclusive at best.[12] Guibert's wife, Alexandrine, remained a constant, if quiet, presence in Paris and on the couple's estate at Courcelles. Unlike Lespinasse, she never evinced any jealousy of Guibert and his possible affairs. The couple welcomed their only child, a daughter named Appolline-Charlotte-Adélaïde, on 15 December 1776. No record exists of the nature of Guibert's relationship with Appolline, although he died before she reached adulthood.[13]

Guibert's ambition led to his making enemies among Parisian society in addition to those within the army. Early in his career, he had run afoul of Deffand, salonnière and sometime mentor to Lespinasse. Before the advent of the salons of Lespinasse, Geoffrin, and Necker, that of Deffand virtually ruled the Parisian social scene. An older woman by the 1770s, she maintained her salon and expected the courtesy of visits by ambitious newcomers. Guibert apparently failed to pay her proper respect: "This M. de Guibert has not bothered to make my acquaintance, although I have given very heartfelt praise to his *Connétable*," she complained to Voltaire.[14]

Walpole, Deffand's constant correspondent and sometime lover, shared her low opinion of the young man: "I have just read Guibert's discourse; I put it at a mediocre hit. The subject demands a person of profundity, and the gentleman is not profound. The comparisons are puerile. . . . I enjoy the second part better, apparently because I hear of it less." He perhaps adopted Deffand's tone of enmity toward Guibert when concluding, "I do not like the name of Guibert."[15] An anti-Guibert sentiment coalesced around Deffand and Walpole, spreading through society as the colonel's prominence increased. His criticism indicates the deficit in Guibert's writing abilities and the formation of an opposition party within society.

Guibert's ouster from the Ministry of War left him without a significant military assignment. He was promoted to brigadier in December 1781, but his regiment required little of him beyond periodic visits. Louis XVI wrote of a half-considered plan to dispatch Guibert to the Porte as a military consultant and ambassador at the request of the sultan. Nothing appears to have come of the project, likely because Franco-Ottoman relations had waned significantly during the period.[16]

Guibert's situation changed in 1783 after his father received appointment as governor of the Invalides. The hospital had evolved from the days of Louis XIV into a thriving community of over 30,000 residents. As governor, Charles oversaw its administration and the regiments attached to it. While Saint-Germain had attempted to remove most of these units, many still remained stationed in France's border fortresses. Charles assigned his son as his official inspector of these regiments. For the next four years, Guibert undertook periodic journeys to the kingdom's frontiers to conduct the inspections.[17]

Like he had on his journey to Germany in 1773, Guibert kept an extensive journal of his voyages. Traveling stimulated his interest in science and the idyll of the countryside, which had also figured prominently in the earlier voyage.[18] In particular, Guibert enjoyed the solitude of his journeys. "I regret the soft solitude with which I am used to travelling," he recorded when joined by a companion. Also like his 1773 trip, Guibert's account of his later voyages contains much analysis and criticism of military institutions. In particular, he almost universally denigrates the quality of the troops attached to the Invalides garrisons, finding them improperly equipped, trained, and situated. As always, this drew him back to his advocacy for an improved social and military constitution to correct the situation.[19]

Ultimately, Guibert evinced a profound ennui and dissatisfaction with both his work and his station. He enjoyed the time afforded by his work and travel to continue his projects, yet he longed to return to the Ministry of War. He notes: "I see more and more that I am too old to travel; I do not have before me the fullness of days that made me productive. My horizon is closer to my head and what I consume cannot be replaced."[20]

While he had drafted many works early in his life, only after 1778 did Guibert have the freedom to devote serious attention to them. In the earlier years of the decade, he concentrated on theatrical and literary compositions. Guibert wrote two historical tragedies in addition to *Connétable de Bourbon*. The first, *Les Gracques*, was probably drafted in 1774. It tells the story of Tiberius and Gaius Gracchus, Roman tribunes who attempted collectivist reforms during the late Roman Republican period. To Enlightenment thinkers, the Gracchi were prototypical republicans who fought for liberty and freedom. In the play Guibert constructs an eloquent argument against the tyranny of a centralized government. He first presented the work in the salons, where it was received with little acclaim. In 1775 the Guerre des farines erupted across Paris, and the antityranny message of *Les Gracques* afterward resonated with the philosophes, earning it a small measure of public acclaim.[21]

However, *Les Gracques* quickly lapsed into obscurity, and Guibert only returned to its editing in his spare time in the late 1770s. His revisions led to its recirculation, at least within the salons, before it reached a wider audience in 1780. That August the *Correspondance littéraire* remarked: "M. de Guibert's piece is historical, like a drama by Shakespeare. In this work, there is much neglected verse, but [also] a grand elevation of sentiment, ideas, and passages of the most sublime eloquence."[22]

In 1777 Guibert drafted his third tragedy, *Anne de Boleyn*. It focuses on the relationship between King Henry VIII of England and his mistress, Anne Boleyn. Portrayed as a tyrant, Henry courts the young Anne, who is not unreceptive to his attentions. Her brother,

Alfred, warns Anne of Henry's legendary temper and bouts of tyranny. She is torn between Henry's charm and Alfred's pleading, forming the central conflict of the work. Alfred's concern is not only that of a brother for his sister but also that of a romantic attachment. While the incestuous theme is heavily concealed, it nevertheless runs through the entire work. Like *Connétable*, *Anne de Boleyn* is not well written but serves as a thinly veiled analogy for events in Guibert's own life.[23]

Most modern scholars agree that *Anne de Boleyn* is a dramatization of the early life of Guibert's deceased mistress, Julie de Lespinasse. A social orphan by virtue of her bastard birth, she led an unhappy existence at the home of Gaspard de Vichy in Chamrond. The relationship between Lespinasse, Gaspard, and his wife mirrored that of Henry, Anne, and Alfred. While history has recorded no evidence of an incestuous relationship at Chamrond, the distaste with which Guibert wrote indicates a certain level of personal involvement absent from many of his other writings.[24]

After Vaussieux Guibert circulated both works among friends, who offered their approval. Despite this, he never sought to have either work performed on stage, in all probability due to the failure of *Connétable de Bourbon* in December 1775 and the resulting literary backlash. Leading this charge was la Harpe, prominent author and cynic, with whom Guibert had a public rivalry dating from the first editions of the *Essai général de tactique*. La Harpe was the better writer by any measure, but Guibert enjoyed the attention and patronage of a wider range of important people, many of whom lay outside of traditional literary circles. La Harpe panned every one of the brigadier's forays into literature, remarking that he was a "man of spirit, a distinguished military man, but a mediocre writer and a bad poet."[25]

In addition to his theatrical works, Guibert drafted a number of histories. Immediately following the *Essai*, he sought to construct a military and political history of France. Stymied by the large scope of the topic, he narrowed his focus to what became a "Histoire de la constitution militaire de France." He researched extensively, spending much time at the Bibliothèque nationale and the Bibliothèque du roi. He also frequented the Bibliothèque mazarine, the libraries of Saint Victor and Saint-Germain-des-Prés Abbeys, Sainte Geneviève, and the University of Paris. Continuing the theme of the *Essai*, Guibert hoped to produce a history that would illustrate the need for political and administrative reform within the kingdom.[26]

He never finished the study, perhaps due to its scope or having moved on to other projects. But its draft reveals much about Guibert's thought in the mid-1780s. His desire for definition of France's military constitution remained strong. The work purports to be "a history of the conception of my plan, or, if one wishes, the history of my thought." It provides the most penetrating self-analysis in Guibert's writings. He notes: "I saw my military career lacking the avenues that had been closed before me. I let myself go, I wrote."[27] For the first time, he openly acknowledged the setbacks of the prior decade and his relative isolation since 1778. This defeat, combined with his lack of influence to implement his work, rankled Guibert. It also produced a remarkable moment of self-reflection:

> Who am I? A military citizen, a man who from his earliest youth developed himself to the study and love of truth, a man who believes that his country must use its talents in all respects, a man who does not regard virtue when it is not accompanied by the ardor of good. Who am I! To you among my comrades in arms who fought war and [wrote on theory,] only your votes do I recognize as my judges; I am your organ and your representative. I am a man who, for twenty years, collected your words and who has on you the advantage of having deepened and developed what you said or thought a thousand times.[28]

His passion for reform continued despite his relative exile.

Guibert also found time to dabble in fiction. Suzanne Necker recorded an intriguing work presented by the philosophe, likely at her salon. Guibert told the futuristic story of the period after the reign of Louis XXIX, around the year 1980. France had fallen into ruin, losing its colonies and ruled by a craven king, Constantine. Holland had been submerged, Britain had fallen into chaos, and only America stood as a bastion of freedom and liberty. France needed to call on its American cousins to restore its former glory. "Guibert, in reading this piece, gave us a very strong emotion that uniquely [illustrated] the élan of his soul," Necker remarked.[29]

During his time at Paris, Guibert began another association that would prove important to his legacy. Germaine Necker, daughter of the minister and the salonnière, came of age in her mother's salon. A woman of towering intellect and notable wit, she proved a worthy heiress to her mother. Like many other patrons, Guibert was taken by Germaine, who reminded him of Lespinasse, with her bright, inquiring mind and social graces more than offsetting her lack of physical beauty. The young Necker found much in Guibert that resembled both her father and her ideal man. As a result, the two developed a close relationship. "His profound admiration for my father, and his veneration for my mother, captivated my interest," she wrote. Guibert returned the attention, and their relationship may have turned romantic.[30]

In January 1786 Germaine married Erik Magnus Staël von Holstein, ambassador of Sweden to the French court. Staël grew increasingly jealous of Guibert's relationship with his wife, culminating in a series of accusations that the two were having an affair. Guibert offered vociferous denials, to which Germaine added her own: "M. de Guibert is certainly one of the men that I love and respect most. He is certainly one to whom I owe most for his profound attachment to me at all times. I do not know exactly where his feelings for me begin and end. But I am certain of the perfection of his behavior towards me. . . . I repeat once again that I do not believe M. de Guibert to be in love with me. . . . [W]hat is certain is that all I have for him are feelings of the most tender friendship."[31]

Staël seemed to have been satisfied by the explanation, yet the truth of the relationship between his wife and the brigadier may never be known. Guibert proved a notorious coquet, and Necker was exactly the kind of woman he favored, a new Lespinasse without her extremes of passion. She was undoubtedly attracted to Guibert, and he would provide inspiration for elements of her famous works.[32]

Despite his quasi exile, Guibert remained a military man first and a social and literary figure second. During his long tenure outside the Ministry of War, great changes took place within it. Philippe-Henri, marquis de Ségur, replaced Montbarey as secretary of state for war in 1781.[33] Unlike his fellow reactionaries, Ségur proved to be an advocate of limited change. He instituted a series of reforms not unlike those of Guibert, including the preservation of Saint-Germain's education system based on provincial schools. He also continued his predecessors' cost-cutting measures, further reducing military expenditures and supernumerary positions. Ségur established a standing council that would function as a guiding body for the French military, fulfilling the desire of Guibert and others for a permanent general staff.[34]

To ensure the timely promotion of meritorious officers, Ségur created a dual-track system of advancement. Members of the upper nobility could quickly advance through the lower ranks of the officer corps but not to the rank of colonel without a long term of service. Members of the lower nobility took a slower route through the lesser ranks but were assured regular promotion for meritorious service. Most importantly, he retained the abolition of venality, eliminating the most significant barrier for the advancement of impoverished rural nobles.[35]

Ségur's most significant reform came on 22 May 1781, when the Department of War issued an edict requiring all officer candidates to demonstrate four degrees of nobility. The infamous Ségur Decree, as it became known, has been the object of much historiographical debate. The liberal philosophes who led the Revolution derided it as a desperate attempt to entrench aristocratic privilege at the expense of talent and merit.[36] Guibert's role in the debate provides a glimpse into the questions surrounding the decree. He evinced no opposition to it, and the brigadier's various educational reforms, published later, indicate his approval of the plan. This leads to a question that has vexed many historians: namely, how could a committed military reformer support such a reactionary measure?

The answer lies in the nature of the decree itself. The traditional picture, sprung from revolutionary rhetoric and adopted by many historians, is that it represented the most obvious measure in the "Aristocratic Reaction." This argument contends that in the decades before the Revolution, the nobles of France used their political and social positions to suppress the rising bourgeoisie. Measures like the Ségur Decree were intended to exclude wealthy members of the bourgeoisie from purchasing commissions and undermining aristocratic control of the army. This mirrored similar reactions in the political realm, where measures were taken to prevent bourgeois purchase of political office and the attached noble patents.[37]

Several problems emerge from this analysis. Most obviously, it presupposes a unified nobility combatting a unified bourgeoisie. In reality, neither existed. The term "bourgeoisie" can be applied to a large portion of French society, ranging from wealthy merchants to urban artisans.[38] These groups held little in common beyond the growing belief that the government should be reformed. The notion of a unified nobility also proves false. The nobility during the late Old Regime was as fragmented a group as the bourgeoisie, ranging from members of the royal family to impoverished rural nobles with little more than a family name to their credit.[39]

At the bottom of the noble class were the anoblis, or families of questionable nobility. Most often, these were members of the bourgeoisie who had purchased a noble patent but had not been accepted by aristocratic society. They occupied an uncertain position in the French social structure. While technically nobility, they enjoyed few of the same privileges. Often, they lived bourgeois lifestyles, with only a nebulous title to distinguish them from their bourgeois bretheren.[40]

The true power of the anoblis, and thus their ability to disrupt the status quo, lay in the financial system of the kingdom. Eighteenth-century France developed a complex economic system to fund its government. Nobles were expected to render military service, for which they would be compensated, though this rarely provided for a comfortable lifestyle. Throughout the eighteenth century, revenues from feudal dues declined, leading to a financial crisis for the nobility. The state, experiencing its own financial crisis, then turned to the rising bourgeoisie. Louis XIV inaugurated the system whereby wealthy subjects could purchase a noble patent for an exorbitant sum; for an additional fee, they could pass the title to their heirs. This buttressed the economic health of the kingdom, although war debts continued to drag it toward bankruptcy.[41]

Reacting to this shift, the established aristocracy attempted to profit by it. Eighteenth-century French nobles achieved status by purchasing government offices, including army positions. Common families raised themselves to nobility through the same system. Yet members of both groups often lacked the financial resources to purchase increasingly costly patents and positions. To provide a supply to meet this demand, the state developed a system of credit whereby impoverished nobles and bourgeoisie received royal pensions to purchase their offices, essentially buying them on credit. This system of defraying the cost of social and political advancement to creditors enabled the state and society to continue operation despite crushing debts. Throughout the government, existing offices were duplicated and new offices created to meet the demand. Few of these performed a concrete bureaucratic function; most existed only on paper. This occurred prominently in the army, where it led to a huge expansion in the number of officers. Most were anoblis and occupied supernumerary positions, demanding rapid promotion and light service.[42]

The Ségur Decree was not intended to bar meritorious commoners from officer positions. Commoners promoted from the ranks by merit, called *roturiers*, were rare in the French army. The vast majority served as junior officers, and then only after years or decades of enlisted service. To pass an army-wide regulation against their advancement would have proven superfluous. The almost complete lack of outcry against the Ségur Decree until the beginning of the Revolution thus undermines the argument for it as an example of class struggle between the nobility and the bourgeoisie.[43]

The proliferation of offices and the introduction of bourgeois officers inflamed both conservatives and radical reformers within the army, provoking a series of calls for reform. The Ségur Decree represented the culmination of this effort, aimed as it was at the lowest levels of the nobility, the anoblis, who occupied the newly purchased and often supernumerary positions. Both reform groups desired their absence from the military. Conservatives counseled an army led by nobles of ancient bloodline, believing that the skill of command lay in the tradition of familial service. They argued that their system did promote by merit—that of noble heritage and genetic ability. Newly minted aristocrats simply lacked the requisite skill to command troops.[44]

Radicals, including Guibert, advocated an army thoroughly professional and educated in its training and methods. They demanded a technical education for officers, which many anoblis lacked. In addition, these parvenus rarely displayed the abilities, education, or motivation to command soldiers. They occupied their positions in absentia, demanded rapid promotion, and provided little of value on the battlefield. As noted, the storied units of the Maison militaire du roi, ostensibly the elite of the army, contained so many supernumerary officers that they could not be deployed during the Seven Years War.[45]

Therefore, the Ségur Decree was not a reactionary measure designed to promote officers via birth rather than merit. Instead, it was designed to produce a skilled, disciplined, merit-based army. Whether merit came from birth or education remained a point of contention between conservatives and radicals, but both groups were united against the anoblis. This explains Guibert's support for the decree. He constantly lobbied for a professional, disciplined, and streamlined army. The anoblis incursion ran directly counter to these virtues. Rather than an abrogation of Guibert's reform spirit, his support of the Ségur Decree represented its fulfillment.

During this debate, Guibert continued his literary and social activity. His crowning achievement in the Republic of Letters came in early 1786, following the death of famed poet and orator Antoine-Leonard Thomas, an associate from his early salon days, in September 1785. His death left vacant the Thirtieth Seat in the Académie française. Founded in 1635 by Louis XIII, the academy was intended to provide patronage and prestige for the kingdom's best artists, writers, and cultural figures. By the late eighteenth century, its status as the apex of French culture had diminished somewhat, particularly as the literary market arose and capitalistic enterprise began to replace royal patronage.[46] Nevertheless, appointment to a seat in the Académie française remained a significant accomplishment for a writer of the period.

La Harpe's acerbic criticisms notwithstanding, many of Guibert's friends and associates had already pursued public recognition for him prior to Thomas's death. Suzanne Necker and Amélie Suard launched a campaign to have him elected to the academy. Nothing came of this initial effort. After Thomas's death, Necker and Suard expanded their campaign, drawing on their extensive social connections to win Guibert's appointment to the vacant seat. The brigadier tentatively joined the effort, soliciting votes from academy members. He studiously avoided la Harpe, who had occupied Seat Twenty-One since 1776 and now led the opposition to Guibert's appointment.[47] Despite this resistance, the campaign soon paid dividends.

The exact reasons for Guibert's elevation remain unknown. Since his dismissal from the Council of War in 1777, he stood as something of a pariah at court. Yet he retained his status as a popular, if somewhat tarnished, figure. The dearth of "great men" in the academy also may have provided justification. With the deaths of Voltaire and Rousseau in 1778, France had lost the leaders of the Enlightenment and its greatest writers and cultural figures. Although many men of skill like la Harpe, Grimm, and Diderot still wrote, a sense of loss permeated French society. After 1775, salons became less a place for polite conversation and literature and more self-consciously political. Increasing numbers of disaffected bourgeoisie and lower nobles infiltrated their ranks, giving birth to many of the movements that would coalesce into the Revolution. In many ways Guibert's appointment served not as a particular acknowledgment of his literary skill, but rather of his social status and his contributions.[48]

On 13 February 1786 Guibert received induction to Seat Thirty of the Académie française. "Never do we remember," remarked the *Correspondance Littéraire*, "having seen a public sitting of the

Académie française more brilliant, or more numerous, than that of Monday the Thirteenth, 1786, for the reception of the comte de Guibert." The academicians held a lavish ceremony, as was tradition, including a banquet and a reading of the inductee's works. Over one hundred attended, including Guibert's parents; Germaine de Staël; the wife of François-Félix-Dorothée des Balbes de Berton, comte de Crillon; and Marshals Charles-Eugène-Gabriel de la Croix, marquis de Castries, and Ségur.[49]

First, a selection of Thomas's works received a reading to acknowledge the departed member's legacy. Following this, Guibert himself rose to speak. His remarks ran several minutes and displayed an uncharacteristic humility and modesty. He thanked his benefactors, recognizing their efforts in achieving the appointment. Afterward, Jean-François, marquis de Saint-Lambert, spoke, attesting to Guibert's literary and military merits before closing the ceremony.[50]

The ensuing celebration, and indeed the appointment itself, seemed to have embarrassed Guibert. This stood in stark contrast to his military and political activity. Despite setbacks in those areas, he never ceased pursuit of his military reforms and his own political advancement. One scholar suggests that Guibert's curious humility was due to his own knowledge that he was a mediocre writer and did not deserve membership in the academy based on literary merit alone.[51]

It is perhaps significant that the nomination occurred after Guibert's greatest setbacks, namely the dissolution of the Council of War and the failure of the *Connétable de Bourbon*. The latter contributed the most to his reticence. Charles Guibert also did not approve of his son's literary career, perhaps hampering its advance. Although Guibert kept producing literary works after the *Connétable de Bourbon* disaster, he never sought to make them public beyond the closed circle of the salons. Indeed, he even refused permission on numerous occasions for various productions of *Les Gracques*, which would remain in vogue throughout the latter half of the 1780s.[52]

Despite his many setbacks, Guibert's nomination to the Académie française indicated his position within the upper level of the Republic of Letters, which would continue after his untimely death in 1790. The formation of his legacy in the years after his death cemented his position as a leading member of the French Enlightenment. Madame Junot refers to him as "the famous comte de Guibert . . . , a man of the most remarkable ésprit and manners," in her works composed afterward.[53]

Although his writings were better than average, Guibert's talents clearly were not literary. He lacked the biting wit and jaundiced eye of the Enlightenment philosophes, preferring instead a proto-Romantic idealism and flowery prose.[54] Most importantly, Guibert was a man of abounding pride and ambition. He could stand his military works being criticized because he knew that his was the superior constitution. His political writings were drawn from his military thought and could be similarly defended. His literary writings, however, could not. While taking great pride in them, Guibert knew that they were not academy quality, or even appealing to a wide popular audience.

Additionally, his military writings always had an audience, as Guibert led the schools of l'ordre mince and the fledgling l'ordre mixte. His literary works had no such backing beyond his personal friends. While Guibert could be given to romantic ideals and flights of fancy, he was above all a pragmatist. When the *Connétable de Bourbon* failed, it harmed his reputation and pride in a way that the dissolution of the Council of War did not. A similar failure of another literary work could have doomed him to the sidelines of literary Paris, which would have upset his life's ambition of fame and recognition.

Shortly after his induction to the academy, three deaths struck Guibert. The first two were his parents: his father died in 1786, his mother the year after. Bereft of his family connections and support network, Guibert devoted himself to his work. On 18 August 1786 his military hero, Frederick II of Prussia, died, ending a long and illustrious reign. Guibert composed an elegy to the dead king, publishing it shortly after his mother's death. Essentially a panegyric, the elegy lauds Frederick's military system but faults the king for failing to properly care for his soldiers.[55] It was published the following year and made the rounds in the salons.

Guibert's period of exile represented the most significant check on his political ambitions. In the years after the Camp of Vaussieux, he dedicated himself to personal pursuits and a limited social engagement. He continued to act in the salons and the Republic of Letters but largely retreated from the public view.

His literary activity, particularly during this time, proved vital to his personal legacy and to that of the later Enlightenment at large. Voltaire and Rousseau died in the 1770s, and with them perished a sense of optimism and hope, particularly as the French state continued its long slide into financial insolvency and revolution. Robert Darnton has characterized this period, particularly during the 1780s, as a lesser Enlightenment, peopled with writers like Jacques-Pierre Brissot, a "failed philosophe" of little literary talent. To Darnton, such men did not match the skill or influence of their predecessors, leading to a waning of the Enlightenment before the Revolution.[56]

These years determined Guibert's role in the Enlightenment as well as his legacy. Following the Darnton historiography, Guibert would either establish himself as a great author like Rousseau or a lesser writer like Brissot. The *Essai général de tactique* arguably moved him automatically into the former category. Yet contemporary criticism and his lack of strong subsequent works, particularly during his time of limited distraction during the 1780s, arguably pushes him toward the latter.

Guibert's cloistering ended with his appointment to the Académie française in 1786, the highest honor for a philosophe and man of letters in contemporary France. While detractors mocked him for his weak prose, his work captured the attention of the literary public and the crown. This elevation, along with the monumental influence of his military writings, marked Guibert as one of the leaders of the Enlightenment. Rousseau and Voltaire may have died during the prior decade, but Guibert carried a measure of their skill and ideals into a new generation. He also partnered with fellow reformers like Turgot and Necker to seek changes through informal channels. Despite his loss of political power, the brigadier's social and personal life continued as the Revolution neared. He would receive the opportunity to once again rejoin the Ministry of War to implement his military constitution and remake French doctrine in his image.

CHAPTER 8

GUIBERT'S REVOLUTION

Despite the traditional start date of 1789, the events that produced the French Revolution began in 1787. Often termed the "Prerevolution" and increasingly considered the progenitor of the Revolution itself, these years marked the Noble Revolt, whereby the kingdom's aristocracy rose against the crown and demanded power and influence. Louis XVI, never a strong monarch, convened an assembly of notables to address the impending financial failure of the state and the deeper social and political issues.

At the same time, the need for reform once again prompted Guibert's return to power. Secretary of State for War Philippe-Henri, marquis de Ségur, reconvened the Council of War in response to the Prussian invasion of the Dutch Republic.[1] He gave the brigadier complete control of the military-reform process, which Guibert used to implement his doctrinal system to professionalize the army, centralizing its command and modernizing its tactics. Despite the replacement of Ségur in late 1787 by Louis-Marie-Athanase de Loménie, comte de Brienne, the council produced provisional regulations in 1788 that enshrined Guibert's reforms in law.

As Guibert toiled on the Council of War, he also determined to implement his political ideology via the Estates-General. The insoluble nature of the financial crisis required more than an assembly of notables—it required constitutional reform. That could only happen through the Estates-General, which was called into session in early 1789. Guibert stood for election, but reactionaries sunk his candidacy. He thereupon returned to the Ministry of War, where the same reactionaries drove him from power later in the year.

For the next twelve months, Guibert produced a flurry of political writings that would define his political legacy. He critiqued many elements of the budding Revolution, chiefly the populist violence of July and October 1789. He also revamped his political and social constitution in his political magnum opus, *De la force publique*. Together, these works involved Guibert in the early Revolution in a theoretical manner. Yet he would die in the spring of 1790, before the Revolution turned on itself in bloodshed through the Terror, prematurely ending his life but allowing his influence to remain on the French army.

By the 1780s, France's economic crisis deepened to dangerous levels. The backward nature of the kingdom's political economy was not due simply to extant financial and economic systems. Rather, it proved deeply ingrained in a psychology and sociology rooted in centuries of rural, agricultural orientation. Trade, manufacturing, and even banking were foreign ideals to the majority of French subjects, even by the 1780s. A large rural population resisted any change from a way of life that had deviated little since the Roman conquest of Gaul.

Throughout the 1780s, a variety of reform-minded ministers strove to rectify the increasingly dangerous fiscal shortfalls of the state. Generations of war spending and the changing financial landscape of international trade and credit markets threatened to shatter the French state and society along its longstanding fault lines. But many groups resisted change. As James Collins argues, no single group had any interest in, nor would profit from, the collapse of the state or society. Yet each group maintained its corporate interests and goals, often at the expense of the others. Noble, *parlementaire*, bourgeoisie, and commoner all clashed over the nature of reforms, neutering various efforts or preventing them altogether.[2]

Thus, a complex web of fissures crossed the French state and its society. Wedges driven into them throughout the 1770s and 1780s caused vast gaps to appear. Each group entrenched itself to prevent losing power or prestige. The crown proved largely impotent, particularly after Louis XVI reversed Maupeou's policies in 1774. Increasingly, various groups called for a meeting of the Estates-General. This body had last met in the early 1600s and represented a semimythical legislative element completely absent from the French political system. Each group, most prominently the upper nobility and the parlementaires, called for the meeting to rectify the situation and better define the workings of the French government.[3]

These threads all combined in early 1787, when Controller General Charles-Alexandre, vicomte de Calonne, attempted to close the mounting deficit with increased taxes. Yet the inefficient system yielded little revenue. Moreover, Calonne came under increasing criticism from the various interest groups as his reforms proved ineffective. His scheme to replace the royal corvée with a cash payment, coupled with a return to Turgot's efforts to liberalize the grain trade, were the last straw. Opposition mounted, and an exasperated Calonne followed the call of different opposition groups, not for convening the Estates-General, but rather for summoning of an assembly of notables. Such groups met periodically throughout the Old Regime and were composed of the leading nobles of the realm, gathered to advise the crown on issues of particular delicacy. Louis assented to the meeting, and the group assembled in early 1787. It consisted of 144 members, including seven *princes du sang*, fourteen senior bishops, and a collection of high nobles, bureaucrats, parlementaires, and leaders from the kingdom's major cities.[4]

Presided over by Calonne, the Assembly of Notables convened on 22 February 1787 at Versailles, tasked by Louis with solving the state's vexing problems. For the next three weeks, Calonne revealed France's dire financial straits and demanded action on his proposed reforms. Opposition solidified around Etienne-Charles de Loménie de Brienne, archbishop of Toulouse. Backed by the majority of the Notables, he demanded that the controller general demur from his reforms, particularly regarding the grain trade.[5]

Throughout March and early April, opposition hardened behind Brienne's leadership. Calonne's insistence on the immediate payment of Church debts threatened clerical autonomy as much as his physiocratic reforms attacked the agricultural foundations of the French economy and nobility. The question of state bankruptcy rose in the discussions, although no one in the assembly was prepared to take that radical step. Instead, Brienne usurped authority from the controller general via missives to the king, the queen, and other members of the Council of State. On 8 April the king recalled Calonne. For weeks, Louis vacillated on nominating a suitable replacement. Finally, on 1 May he named Brienne head of the Royal Council of Finance, thus making the archbishop the de-facto minister of finance.[6]

Brienne enjoyed widespread support at his ascent, particularly from the queen and the Assembly of Notables. His position, like Choiseul's two decades prior, resembled a prime minister more than a simple finance guru. For the next fifteen months, Brienne wielded near-absolute power in his efforts to enact change. Ironically, his reforms were those proposed by Calonne: liberalization of the grain trade, commutation of the corvée, and increased taxes. As with his predecessor, the assembly protested against Brienne. But the archbishop possessed the backing of both the crown and a large group of nobles and notables. This enabled him to act increasingly despotically, culminating in a series of *lits de justice* in the summer of 1788 and the exile of the parlement of Paris.[7]

For the Ministry of War, Brienne's power grab meant attention shifted away from Ségur's ongoing reforms. Aware of the tumult within the government, Guibert communicated a series of memoranda to Ségur proposing a new Council of War. The minister assented to this, after which the brigadier informally joined his staff.[8]

In early 1787 Guibert drafted a memorandum in Ségur's name, addressed to the personnel of the Ministry of War, that asserted the need to reduce costs substantially. Drawing from his constitution, he advocated reducing the number of fortifications, supernumerary officers, and unnecessary units supported by France. He called for the reform of the medical and educational services, streamlining them to reduce costs. Guibert also demanded the immediate implementation of permanent divisions, a change that had lagged since his previous tenure on the War Council. In the spring Ségur presented the memorandum to the king with only minor changes.[9]

At first the reforms proposed by Guibert went largely ignored, as an international crisis threatened France's martial prowess and diplomatic honor. In 1785 France had inked an alliance with the United Provinces. The politics of that state were divided between the burghers of the provinces, who desired a continuation of autonomous rule, and the stadtholder, William V, prince of Orange-Nassau, who sought hegemony over the provinces. In 1786 a group of burghers known as the Patriot Party sought to reduce William's influence. To embarrass the stadtholder, they denied his wife, Frederika Sophia Wilhelmina, princess of Orange, entry to The Hague in June 1787. Wilhelmina called on her husband for support, yet his power was not sufficient to attack the Patriot Party directly. But her brother, the newly crowned King Frederick William II of Prussia, determined to intervene. He dispatched an army of 20,000 men in September to restore order in the United Provinces. This force crossed the border on 12 September and fought its way toward Amsterdam, the headquarters of the Patriot Party.[10]

At this point France's foreign policy stood poised on the edge of a knife. William harbored British sympathies, not unusual for a member of the House of Orange. The alliance between Prussia and Britain from the Seven Years War kept open those diplomatic channels, and the latter threatened general war if France interfered in the Dutch crisis. The kingdom could ill afford another conflict, even after London had been chastened in the War of American Independence. Yet France's alliance with the United Provinces required immediate intervention, particularly to stop the Prussian invasion.[11]

The disorder of the government, paralyzed by both the Assembly of Notables and the financial crisis, meant that intervention was impractical. The army agitated for action, particularly after the crisis bloomed in July. This protest was led by Ségur and Charles Eugène Gabriel de la Croix, marquis de Castries, one of the army's senior marshals. They had proposed placing French soldiers on the Meuse River to block the Prussian invasion in August. Brienne vetoed this action, though, leading to the resignation of both the marshal and the secretary of state for war in late August. The Prussian expeditionary force, thus unimpeded, destroyed the Patriot Party by October, securing William's power and ending the crisis.[12]

The Dutch crisis proved devastating for French prestige. The kingdom's financial straits had become public knowledge, particularly during the early days of the Assembly of Notables. That it prevented military intervention indicated the depths of economic depravity in Europe's oldest monarchy. The Dutch crisis humiliated France, particularly its army. Ségur's reforms promised an army capable of restoring the kingdom's prestige. Yet in 1787 it could not interfere in a minor Continental dispute, much less hope to triumph in a major war. Morale collapsed, not only within the army but also across the kingdom.[13]

For Guibert, this meant change within the War Department. Ségur's resignation required a new secretary of state. In the autumn of 1787, Brienne secured the position for his brother, Louis-Marie-Anthanase de Loménie, comte de Brienne. Guibert and the comte de Brienne were long acquainted, having been members of Lespinasse's salon. The brigadier presented his reform plan to the new minister, who passed it to his brother and to the king. After some initial concerns expressed by the crown, the Council of War was permanently created on 9 October 1787.[14] In a long memorandum to the new body, Louis ordered it to address the following, in order of precedence:

Constitution of the Troops, including the Maison du Roi
Addressing details of soldiers—manning, recruitment, etc.
Armament, dress, and equipment
Manning, especially in peacetime
Provincial troops, annual camps, and other training
Life, forage, and hospitals
Artillery and engineers
The Invalides
The military orders, especially the Order of Saint Louis
The *Maréchaussée*
Police and discipline
Crimes and punishments
Revisions of *Réglement*
The creation of definitive service ordinances for troops on campaign and in peacetime
Building a Bureau de Guerre
Ensuring compatibility between departments
Developing a General Code for the army and the Council of War[15]

Army regulations lay at the bottom of the list, but Louis requested that the council produce a new code shortly so that it could be implemented immediately. Unlike in Saint-Germain's War Council, Guibert drove the debate and reforms of the Brienne ministry. The comte's brother and the king followed the minister; thus for all intents and purposes, Guibert had complete control over the French army.[16]

Guibert's first step was to populate the War Council, which he began by naming himself its reporter and editor. He appointed as members lieutenant generals Louis Pierre de Chastenet, comte de Puységur, his old nemesis of theory; Jean-Baptiste Vaquette de Gribeauval; Adrien Louis de Bonnières de Souastre, duc de Guines; Arnail-François, comte de Jaucourt; Valentin Ladislas, comte d'Esterhazy; Antoine-François, comte de Fourcroy; Jean-François, marquis de Saint-Lambert; and Jean-Thérèse-Louis de Beaumont, marquis d'Autichamp. Brienne served as the council's president and Gribeauval its vice president.[17]

Like the earlier council on which he served, Guibert's faced three challenges: address the vexing issue of nobility, including education and promotion; reduce the army's expenditures, to fulfil the now-vain hope of averting financial disaster; and answer the lingering questions of doctrine and tactics. Ségur's ministry had worked on these issues, particularly the first, but they remained unresolved.[18]

With regard to the primary questions surrounding nobility and manning, Guibert drew on his prior writings. He always had counseled a smaller, professional military and warned against a popular army or militia. His work in the 1780s in the *Défense* and on the War Council cemented this ideology. He joined his fellow aristocrats in supporting the Ségur Decree, hoping to eliminate anoblis parvenus from the ranks of the army in favor of professional officers, as his service on the council had and would again demonstrate. Above all, he sought "the establishment of the most great uniformity in the constitution of all the [army]."[19]

The War Council undertook its work with Guibert's customary vigor. Its first task was the thorny issue of nobility and officer promotion. While Ségur's promotion system and nobility requirements remained in place, the increasingly contentious debate about aristocratic privilege had gained momentum. The council left the Ségur Decree in place but made significant alterations to the system of advancement. On 17 March 1788 it issued the "Ordinance of Regulations on the Hierarchy and on Military Promotions and Nominations." This directive eliminated the position of colonel en second and replaced it with major en second, which required five years' service before attainment.[20] It also eliminated the rank of brigadier, promoting all current brigadiers to maréchal de camp; Guibert was included in this group and received the intendant promotion. The council issued a similar ordinance on 17 June implementing the same measures for cavalry units.[21]

The next attack came against extraneous units. On 30 September 1787 the council issued a memorandum suppressing the *compagnie des chevaux-légers de la garde* and the *gendarmes de la garde*. On 2 March 1788 the *gendarmerie de la France* and the *gendarmerie du roi et des princes* were similarly suppressed. Following these reductions, the Maison du roi consisted of one regiment of cavalry, six battalions of royal guards, four battalions of Swiss Guard, and some small detachments.[22]

On 9 October 1787 the Council of War ordered the École militaire closed. The act went into effect on 1 April 1788, with the cadets returned to the regional schools. A memorandum issued on 20 June forbade the recruitment of criminals or men of low character and increased the medical standard for service. Taken together, these measures were intended to improve both the education of officers and the quality of their men as well as to promote equality at all levels.[23]

Finally, on 17 March 1788 the council issued an ordinance that significantly altered the structure of the French army. It disposed of the traditional organization by provinces and created divisions stationed in one of seventeen new "provinces," or military zones.[24] The three zones on the northeastern frontier of the kingdom, those most vulnerable to enemy incursion, were commanded by a marshal; all others were assigned a lieutenant general. Each commander exerted authority over all troops in his district with the exception of the Maison du roi. All infantry and cavalry were organized into brigades commanded by maréchaux de camp; brigades were loosely organized into twenty-one divisions, each commanded by a lieutenant general. Artillery remained separate but subject to the district commander. Royal inspectors were assigned to each division. Guibert won appointment as inspector of infantry for the Nineteenth Division and resigned his command of the Regiment of Neustria. These inspectors also served as de-facto brigadiers, receiving command of a brigade during army-wide exercises and times of war.[25]

Establishing these military zones served a dual purpose. The system's primary role was to better organize the army in peacetime and for war. Placing a general in charge of each region on a permanent basis allowed for systematic training and exercise over several years rather than the existing regime of haphazard training within the regiment and infrequent camps. All officers, except the provincial commanders, rotated between provinces every two, three, or six months, using their education and experiences in the instruction of each unit in turn under their command. This provided cross-training, and more importantly, developed an institutionalized army rather than one subject to the doctrinal whims of a commanding officer. The second purpose of the provincial system related to the use of the army in large-scale exercise and in war. In either circumstance the brigades assigned to each province would be grouped into divisions that would form one or two armies. According to the council's directive, "neither the number of divisions nor the number of battalions and squadrons [in each division] needed to be determined in advance. One division could be composed entirely of infantry, another entirely of cavalry," and a third of both.[26] This flexible system allowed for the creation of an army from existing brigades organized into divisions according to their provincial location. It also provided the command, logistical, and training structure necessary to utilize the division system advocated in Guibert's writings and used during the Seven Years War, not as an ad-hoc practice, but as an institutional doctrine.

These changes radically altered the fundamental structure of the French army. No longer did it cling to its traditional provincial and regimental organization. Thus, Guibert's reforms created the basis for the permanent division system, which elevated the basic unit of strategy from the regiment to the division. The War Council itself provided a general staff that would direct these divisions to meet any threat to the kingdom.[27]

The council next turned its attentions to technical matters. Tactics of the period were heavily influenced by the writings of Friedrich Christof von Saldern, a general of great experience in the Prussian service. His *Eléments de la tactique de l'infanterie* of 1783 circulated widely in France after its publication. It revealed that the technically precise and ponderous tactics and maneuvers that formed the basis of Pirch's system, and therefore of the French regulations in force since 1776, had fallen out of favor in Prussia, replaced by a more flexible system that resembled the 1769 *Instruction for Light Troops*, authored by Guibert. This shift discredited l'ordre mince and the 1776 regulations, requiring their replacement.[28]

The first response of the council was to task Puységur and Guines with drawing up new regulations to replace those of 1776. Guines shared Puységur's penchant for l'ordre profond, a bias reflected in their provisional regulations of 1787, essentially returning to those of 1774. Such guidelines proved improper for a post-polemical-debate doctrine; as a result, on 20 May 1788 the council issued a second provisional set of regulations, with follow-up clarifications on 1 July and 12 August. The last unofficial doctrinal pronouncement of the Old Regime, they largely returned to the 1769 prototype established by Guibert and his father. The document called for a march step of 76 paces and a double of 110, echoing an argument put forth by Saldern. Kneeling fire was the preferred method, but soldiers were allowed the *billebaude,* or fire at will, within the first two ranks.[29]

These measures strongly reflected Saldern's influence, particularly their precision and ponderousness. While the Prussian service had retreated from its insistence on both, it retained elements of them in its tactics, as Saldern relayed. The new guidelines ran squarely counter to Guibert's pronouncements, particularly the notion of kneeling to fire. But as both Colin and Quimby noted, the regulations were conceived as provisional, to be revisited after proper testing in camps.[30]

Despite Guibert's defeat, his influence reigned in the most important reforms of the 1788 regulations. They prescribed the use of Guibert columns for march, maneuver, and deployment. His intervals and formations were maintained, both from his ministerial work in 1769 and the *Essai général de tactique.* In addition, the evolutions and maneuvers now instituted were greatly simplified, stripped of much of the parade-ground precision that had been present since Broglie's heyday.[31]

In addition, the new regulations eliminated all forms of corporal punishment, replacing them with the infamous blows from the flat of a sabre. Regiments were required to maintain an elementary school for officers and to create a *police occulte* to prevent desertion. Each regiment was equipped with a bakery and portable granaries, theoretically eliminating the need for magazines and allowing war to nourish war. The regulations also gathered all food supply under a *directoire des subsistances,* created a *directoire de l'habillement et de l'équipement,* and improved both the medical and veterans' service by streamlining them and providing increased funding and services for both.[32]

Not intended as permanent, the 1788 *Réglement* never received due attention to test their mandates, particularly concerning organization and fire systems. Instead, they became the prototype of later, post–Old Regime doctrine, particularly Guibert's contributions. They created the institutional army in theory, lacking only the implementation to make it a reality.

These changes, as previous reforms had been, proved contentious within the army. As had become tradition, camps were planned to test out the new tactical systems. The most significant of these occurred at Metz and Saint-Omer in late 1788. The exercises at Saint-Omer opened in September in the far north of the kingdom on the Pas-de-Calais, not coincidentally a prime position for intervention in the Dutch Republic. An army of 30,000 soldiers assembled, including the Swiss regiments of Sansade and Diesbach. The various units drilled in the new tactics, which detractors found to be excessively Prussian. This launched yet more criticism, spilling out from the military into society at large, as it had in 1777.[33]

At the same time, a separate camp convened at Metz on the eastern frontier of the kingdom. Like at Vaussieux, Victor-François, duc de Broglie, commanded the proceedings. Unlike Vaussieux, the Metz exercises made use of exigencies in its maneuvers, particularly deployment from battle to march order, which now occurred definitively by practicality and not by precedence.[34] The camp also streamlined the details of administration and practice of divisions, including exercises with their maréchaux de camp serving administrative duties.[35]

These camps indicated that technical opposition to Guibert's constitution had largely ended. The army accepted his tactical and organizational doctrine, even if it largely rejected his wider social and political ideas. Above all, as the official record notes, units were to move not with parade-ground precision, Prussian discipline, or noble precedence, but rather "in the most economic manner possible."[36]

Despite this success, Guibert and the rest of the council soon became subject to forces far beyond their control. By the summer of 1788, Brienne had come under increasing criticism from nearly every group in the government and society for his despotic turn. The return of Jacques Necker to head government finance the previous year could not quell the uprising. Faced with a bankrupt government and failed reforms, Brienne resigned on 25 August; his brother followed in November. Puységur won appointment to replace the comte de Brienne, but opposition continued from reactionaries throughout the kingdom. They resurrected the epithet of "Prussian" for Guibert, painting him as a member of the very noble group whose privileges he had assailed. The remaining conservatives, desperate to retain their hold on power within the military, also attacked Guibert.[37]

His last desperate measures having failed, Louis XVI reconvened the Assembly of Notables. Their advice now followed that pursued by the parlementaires: convene the Estates-General. The king vacillated, as he often did, throughout the summer and autumn. Finally, in late 1788 he ordered the meeting. His government sent dispatches across the kingdom, soliciting the traditional *cahiers des doléances* to provide an agenda for the meeting and to organize elections for delegates.[38]

The Estates-General held unprecedented hope for the kingdom, as nearly every group expected the meeting not only to solve the financial crisis but also to recreate the state by giving it a legislative body and an enumerated constitution. But the contentious and polemical nature of French society and politics doomed the proceedings before their beginning. Many of the nobles only assented to the meeting believing that they could dominate the proceedings, as they traditionally held not only their own Second Estate vote but also that of the First Estate, which caucused with the aristocracy because of a high-born minority entrenched in its upper echelons. In contrast, the Third Estate amalgamated many who desired an equal voice, most prominently the parlementaires and bourgeoisie, who had long fought for limits on the monarchy and for an increase in their own power.[39]

Throughout the winter and spring of 1788–89, both sides debated, often in public and in print, the merits of the traditional system of vote by estate. The Second Estate supported this method, which would allow it to dominate the proceedings. Guibert himself equivocated on the point, pointing out that vote by estate would "without doubt form a Nation" but noting too that domination by a particular interest group, especially the nobility, would hamstring the ability of other groups to achieve an equal voice. The Estates-General had not convened since the early seventeenth century, and French society had undergone a considerable transformation since that time. As much as the financial crisis, the Enlightenment influenced the Estates-General, chiefly the call for a defined, rational, and above all representative government.[40]

The Third Estate thus demanded two revisions to the meeting: vote by head and the doubling of the Third. The first change would neutralize the advantage of the nobility, which also controlled the First Estate, to win all votes by a simple two-to-one majority; vote by head would prove to make the meeting representational. Not secure in that mechanism, doubling the Third Estate's delegates from the traditional three hundred to six hundred would allow them to overrule the other two estates and thus have an equal, if not greater, voice in the proceedings.[41]

These arguments appeared in print, especially in the *cahiers des doléances*, and continued through the new year.[42] In January 1789 Louis assented to both vote by head and the doubling of the Third Estate after threats of domestic violence, particularly in Dauphiné. Throughout the late winter and spring, elections occurred all across the kingdom to produce the delegates for the new Estates-General. Learning of this, Guibert determined to stand for election as a member of the Second Estate.[43]

As Guibert's marital estate, Courcelles, was located in Berry, he journeyed to the provincial capital of Bourges to stand for election. The officer arrived at Bourges on 15 March and delivered an address that was well received by the local bourgeoisie, who apparently sought to influence the election for the Second Estate. The elections took place three days later in the church of Carmes. Claude-Louis, comte de la Châtre, presided over the meeting of the First Estate. La Châtre opened the proceedings and gave the podium to Guibert, who began to address the assembled nobles. They refused to maintain decorum, though, hurling insults at the officer and accusing him of being a traitor to his country vis-à-vis the "Prussian" punishment reforms. After an intense shouting match, la Châtre ordered the meeting hall cleared.[44]

Over the next two days, an intense debate raged at Bourges. The local aristocracy remained opposed to Guibert. Minor nobles accused Guibert of being a member of the upper nobility and caring only for the preservation of traditional privilege, which he had demonstrated by supporting the Ségur Decree. Members of the upper nobility accused him of betraying French values. Both noted that Guibert was only a member of the Berry nobility through marriage and thus should not stand for election. The local bourgeoisie supported him, which may have further harmed his standing with the aristocrats. Guibert addressed a letter to the assembly and pled his case in person at the Hôtel de Ville. La Châtre and Armand Joseph de Béthune, duc de Chârost, argued his case as well. Their intervention proved to no avail, though, and the nobles refused to hear Guibert. Defeated, he departed Bourges for Paris on 21 March.[45]

Shortly afterward, Guibert and the remainder of the Council of War were deprived of any decision-making power.[46] These twin failures cut him loose from any major responsibility. His military work had been accomplished, either by his own hand or his successors in the army, but larger matters loomed on the eve of the Revolution. For the next year, Guibert again took to his pen to advocate political and social reforms, which had largely been stymied by Old Regime beneficiaries far too entrenched to allow wholesale change. Nobles who benefited from privilege in the army and society were loath to cede their positions. Parlements and the crown, for their part, refused to compromise on an equitable reform of the government.

This situation changed in 1789 with the outbreak of the Revolution. The Old Regime's political and social institutions were swept away, replaced by a bourgeois republic. As the new National Assembly struggled with writing a constitution throughout 1789 and early 1790, Guibert produced a flurry of political writings detailing his own thoughts on the matter. He wrote furiously, producing a number of political pamphlets defending his work and espousing revolutionary ideals. He began by publishing the *Précis de ce qui s'est passé à mon égard à l'Assemblée du Berry*, a description of the events at Bourges. This won him a small following among the moderate nobles of Paris, who sympathized with his plight. Yet Guibert destroyed that goodwill with his next publication, entitled *Projet de discours d'un citoyen aux trois Ordres de l'Assemblée de Berry*. In this work he argues that the king could not make laws without the people's consent, which required a permanent Estates-General.[47]

The backlash was swift and decisive.[48] Having upset the reactionaries with his reforms and the revolutionaries with his "Prussianism," Guibert now alienated his few remaining supporters. While moderates would defend his reforms, *Projet de discours* was far too radical for their tastes. King Louis reportedly flew into a rage on being informed that one of his highest-ranking military officers had publically undermined the crown. In July representatives of four regiments stationed at Rennes issued a statement repudiating blows from the flat of a saber and demanding Guibert's resignation from the War Council. The king acted on this report, replacing Guibert with Mathieu Dumas.[49]

Guibert continued to write, however, producing some of his finest political works. In late 1789 he produced the *Mémoire adressé au public et à l'armée sur les opérations du Conseil de la Guerre*. In it he apologizes for the offense taken to his reforms but insists that they were necessary to mend the French military constitution. He also refutes the claims that were circulating within the army that he had mistreated his own regiment.[50]

The most important of Guibert's works during this period was *De la force publique,* an essay often considered his political magnum opus. Guibert argues strenuously for discipline, skill, and ability in governance. He again counsels a strong guiding hand for the military to maintain its professionalism, discipline, and training. But he shifts from a similar unitary command of the nation's political system. By 1790, Guibert believed that the national government should have strict limitations. The powers of the army, executive, municipalities, and legislature should all be sharply defined, with a constitutionally implemented system of checks and balances to prevent any one group from exercising undue power over the others.[51]

As the title suggests, Guibert concerns himself with the correlation between military and political power. He had watched with consternation from his Parisian home as command and control in the royal army disintegrated in 1789. The precedent set by the storming of the Bastille, where members of the Royal Guard participated alongside the mob, ran squarely counter to the detached, professional army that he had long advocated. The army required a strong guiding hand to prevent such mutinies. Yet he no longer trusted the monarchy with such a task. Following the lead of the revolutionaries, he argues for a constitutional monarchy. Much like Montesquieu decades before, Guibert writes of the need for a "middle institution" to moderate the crown's influence on the citizenry. Unlike Montesquieu, he already had such an institution: the National Assembly.[52]

Guibert seizes on the thread of the developing Bourgeois Constitution to insert his own commentary in *De la force publique*. He envisions two active forces in France's political arena, the executive and the legislature, and determines that they should be coequal branches of government. In addition, local autonomy must be maintained to prevent the complete domination of the state by the central government. Guibert tasks the various municipalities of the kingdom with this effort. To that end, each body would require a measure of military backing in order to assure its own position and prevent usurpation by the other. Guibert argues that this "public force," or rather a balance of such forces, would prevent tyranny, allow for an ordered state, and work to the benefit of all citizens.[53]

Guibert divides the public armed forces into four sectors: the line army, the *maréchaussée*, the police, and the militia. The first of these was the most important, as the army was the only force that his system allows outside the borders of the kingdom. It would operate under the purview of the crown, as Guibert believes that only the king has the moral superiority, ability, and skill of command. But the army's budget was left to the legislature in an American-style check and balance, preventing abuse by either the executive or the legislature.[54]

A remarkable passage from the work touches on the prickly issues of the army, politics, and society. Many others had called for an army of citizen-soldiers, motivated by love of *la patrie*, to replace the old, aristocratic line army. Guibert firmly rejects this notion:

> The principles that serve at the base of discipline, and the prejudices that compose the military spirit, are necessarily and by their nature in opposition to all the principles of the civic spirit ["l'esprit citoyen"]. Soldiers must have [a] thirst for war and citizens [a] love of peace. Equality and liberty are the rights of the citizen. Subordination and passive obedience are the duties of soldiers. Soldiers can have neither the same tribunals, nor the same sentences, nor the same objects of emulation as citizens. Soldiers must have esprit de corps and professionalism. Citizens must only have public and national spirit ["l'esprit public et national"]. It is perhaps impossible to make [of] citizens soldiers.[55]

This serves two purposes. For Guibert, it highlights the need for a professional army detached from society. Many revolutionaries calling for citizen-soldiers believed that élan and patriotism would suffice as an army's cardinal virtues. Having served in the military, though, Guibert knew the need for discipline above élan. As he notes, freedom is the virtue of the citizen, while discipline and obedience are those of the soldier. The two necessarily conflict, and no army founded on the principle of freedom could expect its soldiers to obey their commanders. Military service by its very nature implies an abrogation of the freedoms guaranteed by the "Declaration of the Rights of Man and the Citizen" and espoused by the Revolution.[56]

Furthermore, Guibert insists that soldiers not be required to swear an oath of loyalty to the government or to participate as active citizens. He argues that the oath of loyalty to the army was the same as one to the nation, as the former existed only to serve the latter. In terms of political participation, Guibert believes that a soldier's first duty is to the army. After a man has served a lengthy period, at least twenty-four years, he might win the right to participate in the government as an active citizen. This measure serves to further divorce the army from society, granting it a singular purpose of winning France's wars and preventing it from interfering in the political process, as it had most famously at the Bastille.[57]

While the line army forms the central body of the public force, Guibert creates others to balance its effects. First, he forbids it from acting within the kingdom's borders, realizing full well the danger of Caesarism. He then begins the process of creating other organizations to preserve law and order, the two most important of these being the maréchaussée and the police force. The former was constituted from the old maréchaussée, which had been tasked with policing the kingdom. It traditionally had been underfunded and understaffed, which Guibert proposes to rectify. In addition, it would be expanded to include cavalry units, enabling it to patrol and secure the countryside. Most importantly, the maréchaussée would fall under the command of the legislature, which also set its budget. While it would not be a military force per se, its paramilitary nature would serve to deter an ambitious monarch from using the army against his own subjects.[58]

The companion to the maréchaussée was the police, another paramilitary law-enforcement organization. Policemen would serve in towns, securing peace and protecting the citizenry from crime. They would operate under the aegis of their respective municipality, which would be responsible for their outfitting, funding, and operation. In Guibert's system the police would serve as a similar deterrent to an aggressive crown or legislature in defending regional autonomy.[59]

The fourth element of Guibert's public force is the militia. He envisions this body as a local force raised, equipped, and trained by municipalities but funded by the central government. As in previous works, he firmly rejects the notion of using the militia as a ready reserve, as most units would not suffice qualitatively for field duty. Instead, the militia would function as a last line of defense in the event of invasion or military disaster. In times of national emergency, it would be raised to defend the homeland. Guibert refuses to allow militia units to travel outside their native regions, believing that discipline would last only if its members were fighting to protect their homes. Only in extreme circumstances could such units be used in conjunction with the regular army to suppress a rebellious town or province. The defense of the kingdom would remain the army's responsibility, while the militia would serve only in the event of a catastrophe that rendered the army powerless to prevent invasion.[60]

The most portentous passages of *De la force publique* addresses the true union of society, politics, and the army. While Guibert always had counseled a judicious union, he here expressly forbids a true combination in what a modern analyst would refer to as total war. "I repeat," he argues, "that the change [to national war] will be very destructive to those who count the blood and misfortune of men for something."[61]

Throughout his works, Guibert anticipated the triad of politics, society, and the military that the Revolutionary government was only beginning to assemble at the time of his death in 1790. His reforms were designed to regenerate society from root to branch, creating a disciplined, professional, rational, and practical constitution for all citizens. He intended to reduce the destructiveness of war by the creation of a small, highly skilled, and professional army.

In his early years Guibert sought an army of citizen-soldiers for this end. By the later years of his life, he had foreseen the destructiveness inherent when society and warfare intertwined and so refuted the citizen army. His work in the Ministry of War largely produced a professional, adaptable, and mobile army, laying the foundations for the military success of the Revolution and Napoleon. Yet he never achieved the commensurate reforms of politics and society. These would come during the later Revolution, which Guibert would not see. His last work explored the political implications of the early Revolution on the French army and society, concluding that only an American-style system of checks and balances could prevent the unleashing of the political-social-military complex that was just beginning to form. Rather than heed his warnings, the Revolution seized on his ideas and created a centralized state that could fully harness its considerable resources for the purpose of war with his reformed army. Unleashing this force, especially under Napoleon, provided the destruction that Guibert abhorred.

His intense activity on the War Council and his political writings wore on Guibert's health. He always had battled fevers, but the strain of the Revolution proved too much. Guibert fell seriously ill in early 1790. Like his erstwhile mistress Julie de Lespinasse, he spent his final days bedridden in Paris, surrounded by friends. On 6 May Guibert succumbed to his fever. His dying words echoed his final years' work and foretold his legacy: "I will be known, I will have justice!"[62]

Guibert's second stint in the Ministry of War proved the turning point, both for his career and for the French army. Through the War Council's efforts, Guibert finally created the institutional army he long advocated. Ségur's reforms laid the foundation for these changes, building on the work of his predecessors. Guibert laid his doctrinal system over the social and structural changes of that minister. He recreated the army's educational and training systems and drastically reduced costs through many measures. He created an operational organization plan based not on venal regiments assembling in wartime, but rather on territorial divisions forming operational divisions for peacetime exercises or for war. While Guibert's tactical reforms were largely set aside by the council, their germ remained to become the basis of the French regulations of the future.

Despite these successes in the Ministry of War, the Revolution sped at a pace that left Guibert behind. Prior criticism returned, particularly the anti-French tirades of the 1770s, which prevented his participation in the Estates-General and may have contributed to the stresses that shortened his life. He was removed from the Council of War at a crucial step in the reforms, stymieing his final attempt at full implementation of his system. Thereafter, he took to his pen during his last year, furiously producing pamphlets and essays on the nature of politics, society, and the military that would prove prescient in the following decade of revolutionary chaos. Guibert died in early 1790, having laid the foundation for an army with institutional doctrine, one composed largely of his theory. But it remained for his successors to implement them. The next ten years would see this occur, as the French army developed into the Grande Armée that would conquer the Continent.

CHAPTER 9

THE FATHER OF THE GRANDE ARMÉE

The era of the French Revolution and Napoleon imparted few revolutionary changes in the French army, as very little of its doctrine, organization, or practice changed radically. Yet the revolutionary view remains seductive to historians. Its origins lie in the propaganda of the period and its scholars. French leaders, especially during the Terror, had to portray their movement as a radical departure from past traditions and systems to maintain its momentum.[1] Their Napoleonic heirs adopted a similar policy, acknowledging the Revolution's contributions via the *Réglement* of 1791 but failing to acknowledge the contributions of the Old Regime. Nationalist French historians inherited and elaborated this view, often in times of national crisis.[2]

In reality, nearly every element of the Grande Armée evolved from its Old Regime predecessors rather than being innovated by the Revolution or Napoleon. As noted, this process began with the adoption of the socket bayonet in 1698, which united shock and fire in an infantry weapon. Institutional doctrine, and the foundation of the institutional army, began with the adoption of the cadenced step in 1755. Guibert columns appeared in 1769, providing the basis for maneuver and tactics.

Polemical debate remained to determine the exact nature of the nascent doctrine and army. Refining tactical systems and practices occupied much of the late Old Regime's army. At the fore of this effort stood Guibert. His theories in the *Essai général de tactique* provided the lens that focused the Old Regime reforms into a coherent doctrine and constitution. His work on the Council of War from 1775 to 1777 and again from 1787 to 1789 enshrined this system in doctrine, chiefly the provisional *Réglement* of 1788.

Guibert's death in 1790 deprived him of the opportunity to witness his reconstituted army in action as war broke out in 1792 and continued almost without pause until 1807, at which time the Grande Armée became diluted through geographic dispersion and inclusion of non-French units. Regardless, the *Réglement* of 1791 provided the foundation for success during that period. Guibert's doctrine and system forged the institutional army that the Revolutionary and Napoleonic governments used to conquer much of Europe by 1807.

As noted, Old Regime armies suffered from traditionalism and pedantic processionalism in their tactics and grand tactics. Units deployed not due to the battlefield situation or terrain, but rather by precedence. Due to either service rivalry or the lack of overarching army doctrine, infantry, light infantry, cavalry, and artillery often failed to coordinate their roles on the battlefield. Combined with simplistic, rigid tactics, the French army failed to perform better than its opponents during the wars of the mid-eighteenth century.

The process of implementing Guibert's doctrine occurred in fits and starts, both during the Old Regime and during the Revolutionary and Napoleonic eras that followed. Guibert's dynamic, practical, and articulated system of tactics received its implementation early in the period and provides the clearest example of his influence on the army as well as its backbone. His recommendations in other areas proved more difficult to enact, and many elements of his doctrine were not achieved until the rise of Napoleon and his empire.

These changes began in October 1789, when the Constituent Assembly replaced the War Council, and the entire War Department for that matter, with the Military Committee. Over the next two years, the government shaped this organization to be the governing body of the military, with Louis XVI as its commander in chief and the assembly providing its funding. As part of this process, the Military Committee determined to provide new and permanent regulations for the army. Throughout 1791 it labored to produce a new system of rules and guidelines, which became the official regulations on 1 August.[3] These remained in force throughout the period, providing the Guibertian foundation for the Revolution's tactics.

The *Réglement* of 1791 adopted much of Guibert's institutional doctrine, particularly as channeled through the provisional regulations of 1788. Unlike prior réglements, those of 1791 did not restrict the French army to either l'ordre profond or l'ordre mince as its primary formation. Rather, they allowed both column and line for common use as well as within the same operational formation. This was the formal implementation of Guibert's l'ordre mixte, which gave military commanders exactly the tactical and organizational flexibility he had championed throughout his career.[4]

According to the regulations, maneuver would occur via both open and closed columns. The open column deployed according to well-established practice. Closed columns remained the chief method of deployment, given their ease of control compared to open formations. Those advocated by the 1791 *Réglement* were Guibert columns, constructed and maneuvered according to the instructions of Guibert's system.[5]

The new system differed from Guibert's doctrine in some small details. It provided for two battalions per regiment, which consisted of four divisions of two companies each, with one additional company of grenadiers per regiment. This differed from Guibert's insistence on a regiment divided into threes, thus providing for a left, right, and center. Most importantly, the regulations required deployment of the grenadier company ahead of the remaining troops, hearkening back to pre-Guibertian processional deployments by precedence. The evolutions likewise proved more processional than functional, particularly with regard to the shift from column to line.[6] Such elements abrogated the spirit of Guibert's system.

As a result, commanders after 1815 railed against the restrictions of the 1791 regulations, specifically the processional elements. Laurent, marquis de Gouvion Saint-Cyr, particularly attacked the regulations, arguing that their maneuvers were impossible when facing an enemy. Mathieu Dumas, Jean-Jacques-Germain Pelet-Clozeau, and Charles-Antoine-Louis Alexis Morand also have noted the absence of functional doctrine in the minutiae of maneuver in retrospectives written in the 1820s and beyond.[7]

Yet like the 1788 regulations, those of 1791 were intended to be refined in the field through practice and testing. Postwar critiques indicate Guibert's conceptual influence on the regulations and the French army of 1792–1815. This extended beyond the elements officially adopted in 1791 to a deeper conceptual level. François Roguet presents the most salient analysis of the subject: "the Regulations are perhaps only the grammar of tacticians, who then must be on the field and before the enemy; the enemy formations give them their regulations."[8] The use of l'ordre mixte and Guibert columns were the two most direct tactical influences from Guibert's work that gave the regulations the spirit of his system. The organization and tactics instituted therein thus provided the grammar by which officers educated their troops and fought as part of the larger army. Once they learned that grammar, commanders innovated within the system to meet exigencies and battle conditions. Such innovations gave the Revolution's military a flexibility of use that no Old Regime army possessed, forming a primary contribution to its success.

This reveals Guibert's most salient contribution to the 1791 regulations and to the Grande Armée that would result from them. His work and career provided much of the substance of the reforms that would be implemented, but the spirit of his system remained the overriding change. His encouragement of commanders and theorists to look outside of individual polemical methods to find practical and utile doctrine became the foundation of the regulations and French doctrine after 1791.

The army's transition during the Revolution raises many questions as to the exact usage of Guibert's tactical system. Trained in Old Regime regulations and training camps in the 1770s and 1780s, the royal army met its demise during the early days of the Revolution. The traditional narrative dictates that discipline and professionalism all but disappeared between 1789 and 1793, replaced by hordes of National Guardsmen, *fédérés*, and sans-culottes carrying the fight to the enemy at the point of their bayonets.[9] Although the royal army did collapse, discipline and professionalism hardly disappeared. Veterans who continued to serve formed the professional core of the Revolutionary army. The early Revolution struggled first with manpower and then with the integration of the citizenry, with some failures of discipline to be expected. But its army generally performed well. John Lynn's superb study of the Armée du Nord illustrates that this force employed nearly every possible tactical formation in battle between 1792 and 1794. Primary sources support this analysis.[10] And the French army as a whole gained experience as the wars continued, allowing for increasing levels of tactical nuance.

From 1802 to 1805, Napoleon Bonaparte consolidated his power and created the Grande Armée. This process largely occurred at the camps of Boulogne along the English Channel, where he devoted over two years to inducting conscripts, drilling, and organizing corps d'armée. The period of peace was interrupted only by occasional skirmishes with British forces. "Three years in camps had had an excellent result on our troops," Jean-Baptiste-Antoine, baron de Marbot, reported. "Never had France possessed an army so well-trained, of such good material, so eager for fighting and fame.

Never had a general had under his hand forces so powerful, both materially and intellectually, with such capacity for using them."[11] Most importantly, never had France had an army intensively trained in Guibert's doctrine. This allowed Napoleon and his subordinates to craft the finest French fighting force since the armies of Louis XIV marched into the Spanish Netherlands.

This argument runs counter to prevailing trends in the historiography of the period. One historian has argued that the French triumphed, particularly during the Revolutionary period, simply because of manpower superiority. Another contends that Guibert, or the French army using his methods, developed a specific tactical formation known as l'ordre mixte that proved superior to those of the nation's enemies.[12] While each of these elements did contribute to success during the period, the chief element of the French army's dominance lay in the implementation of Guibert's system, as the following examples illustrate.

While it remains clear that the French army enjoyed superiority in manpower and morale, these advantages are often overstated. Although the nation held an overall superiority in manpower over any single foe, this often existed only on paper. Contrary to the arguments of T. C. W. Blanning, the French rarely enjoyed a superiority in numbers that ranked as decisive or was proportionally greater than typical Old Regime battles.[13] In addition, quantity did not guarantee victory. For example, the Armée de Sambre-et-Meuse enjoyed a slight manpower advantage of 65,000 to 55,000 at the First Battle of Fleurus on 16 June 1794 but lost that fight; a similar disposition of 70,000 French troops to 55,000 Austrians at the Second Battle of Fleurus on 26 June yielded victory.[14] Bonaparte experienced a manpower deficit throughout his First Italian Campaign; the fact that he was able to maneuver more troops into battle for local numerical superiority is a tribute to his operational skill, not an advantage in manpower. While it undoubtedly contributed to the French army's successes, particularly on the strategic level, manpower cannot solely account for victory.[15]

Similarly, the leading works on the tactics of the period argue that French armies employed formations that combined line and column, l'ordre mixte, on the battlefield. Guibert is often credited as the theoretical father of this formation, which ostensibly led to French success. Although his tactical system did not specify the exact formation to be used by units deployed in "mixed order," his advocacy of the combination of line and column on the battlefield proved monumental. Guibert's system rendered moot the entire debate of line or column. The flexibility of his organization and tactics allowed a commander to utilize any formation to maximize fire or shock. Moreover, units could make use of several formations and methods within a single engagement. While the default formation appeared to be the line using fire, this did not preclude the use of column, shock, squares, or open order as demanded by the situation or the terrain. Fire could be delivered from lines, columns, squares, and open order. Shock could be effected with columns, lines, and occasionally open order. The false dichotomies introduced by Guibert's contemporaries and in the historiographical "line or column" debate held little traction on the actual practice of battle.[16]

Guibert combined tactical formations, uses, and organization in his system, thus liberating the military from its reliance on any single tactical system. He utilized the best of each, detailing a variety of formations for his tactical doctrine, which allowed battalions or any other unit to fight in line, column, or open order as required by the exigencies of battle. He created not a tactical system per se, but rather a tactical doctrine that combined the best elements of existing systems to produce an organic doctrine adaptable to any battlefield situation.

Despite often having little to no time to properly train and drill soldiers, the armies of the French Republic and Napoleonic Empire fought in line, column, square, and open order, using both fire and shock. These forces often utilized multiple elements in the same battle, displaying a significant tactical flexibility from their earliest deployments in 1792 to their great victories from 1805 to 1807, as examples illustrate.

As Guibert had desired, l'ordre mince remained the basic tactical formation during the French Wars. Neerwinden, fought on 18 March 1793, illustrates the basic linear deployment using fire: the Armée du Nord "divided into two columns [and] deployed in three lines . . . , fire engaged from one end to the other," to defend against an Austrian attack. This sort of linear formation increased the volume of fire and controlled a wider portion of the field. Almost every battle during the period saw the use of l'ordre mince in some form.[17]

The French armies also widely used columns during the period. In particular, the Guibert column became the standard formation for march and deployment. These nimble columns provided a much superior system to the Old Regime's ponderous march columns and battle order. They also combined with a "French character" that emphasized élan to produce a powerful force on the battlefield. A prototypical use occurred late in the War of the First Coalition when General Michel Ney divided his force into three columns. He directed each at a weak point in the Austrian lines near Mainz on 4 June 1796, and each of the mobile formations achieved its goal. Many other such occurrences can be found in the records of the period, including early in the Revolution, a time, many authors have argued, when disciplined tactics were all but absent.[18]

While the line and column proved the basic tactical formations of the period, French commanders used the grammar provided by the Guibertian regulations to innovate their own formations, most notably the infantry square. This developed during the period and received its most famous use at the Battle of Auerstadt on 14 October 1806. Moving south with the Third Division, commanded by General Charles-Ètienne Gudin, Marshal Nicolas Davout encountered unexpectedly heavy resistance from Prussian units deployed in line. Gudin formed his division into large squares, likely regiment sized, to defend against Prussian infantry and cavalry attacks. Generals Louis Friant and Charles Morand arrived in sequence to reinforce Gudin, deploying to his left in squares to resist Prussian attacks; they formed lines and columns to counterattack only after the initial danger had passed. Other examples illustrate deployment in squares, including early in the Revolutionary Wars.[19]

In addition to closed formations, French armies learned to make use of open order. As Guibert had desired, large numbers of specialist light troops were not used by the armies of the period. Such forces did play a vital role, but the true innovation came with the adoption of Guibert's suggestion that line infantry be trained to deploy in open order and to skirmish. This was often referred to as deployment *en tirailleur* and occurred frequently on both the offensive and the defensive.[20]

These examples illustrate the dynamic and flexible nature of French tactics and organization during the period from 1792 to 1807. Gone were the ponderous and traditionalist formations of the Old Regime, replaced by Guibertian doctrine. The *Réglement* of 1791 rewrote the grammar of army doctrine, and the officers of the French Wars refined it through practice, particularly before 1796. They discovered and shaped a dynamic system in which any formation could be used to meet battlefield needs. This was the true implementation of Guibert's l'ordre mixte: a doctrine rather than a dogmatic set of hidebound formations.

The development of this tactical flexibility created a foundation on which operational doctrine could be built. The union of the march and maneuver columns in the Guibert column at the grand tactical level provided a new mobility and flexibility. This translated up to the operational level, where marches became free of preordained orders. Instead, commanders used their discretion to match an exigency and create new and dynamic operational-level warfare.

The key element of this process occurred with the adoption of another Guibert-touted innovation, the combined-arms division. These first appeared on an ad-hoc basis around 1793, as generals began to divide their armies into separate "wings," usually a left, right, and center. For example, at the Battle of the Roer on 2 October 1794, Jean-Baptiste Jourdan dispersed his forces by wings to attack the largely stationary Austrians on multiple fronts simultaneously, probing for a weak point. This method proved successful, and the Austrians retreated from their position.[21]

This "impulse system of grand tactics," as Nosworthy dubs it, would evolve throughout the period. Gradually, French armies became more dispersed into wings. These became more formalized, crystallizing into combined-arms divisions around 1793. This made possible operations on multiple axes rather than the unitary march axis of long practice. As Bourcet had predicted and Guibert had echoed, their adoption provided an operational flexibility to match that found in tactics and strategy.[22]

Operational-level warfare did not achieve its fruition during the Revolution. The fractured nature of the state and constant changes of government often robbed generals of their commands, preventing significant innovation beyond the tactical level. More importantly, although the Revolutionary army possessed excellent leaders, none was able to fully recognize the potential for operational warfare granted by the new system.[23]

Napoleon Bonaparte would first realize this and bring it to its apex in the Grande Armée. He first illustrated this ability during the First Italian Campaign (1796–97), when faced with the numerical inferiority and less-than-ideal supply and morale conditions. Bonaparte overcame these challenges by creating combined-arms divisions and placing each under a seasoned general. Using their already established Guibertian doctrine on the tactical and strategic level, these divisions dispersed to various points throughout late 1796 and early 1797 to counter Austrian advances. When enemy armies met one division, the others joined rapidly, and Bonaparte defeated each adversary with local numerical superiority obtained through the French system's increased march speed and enhanced organization. The union of Guibertian doctrine and Napoleonic operational genius proved victorious, not only in Italy but also across Europe, bringing the War of the First Coalition to an end.[24]

Bonaparte's first command illustrated the foundations of his art of war. He made no alterations at the tactical level, as they had already been implemented via the 1791 *Réglement*. Rather, like his fellow officers during the Revolution, he pushed the evolution of the extant system, further refining and improving it. Only Bonaparte, however, was able to effect enormous change on the entire French army, as only he rose to power in 1799 and ruled France for the next fifteen years. He would use this period, particularly the lapse in conflict between 1802 and 1805, to remake the army at the operational level, forging it into his Grande Armée.

Bonaparte's key innovation was the development of the corps d'armée. He borrowed the idea and function of the division system for these units, typically composed of two or more infantry divisions, several cavalry squadrons, and attachments of artillery and light infantry. Each corps generally contained at least 10,000 men, with a size of 20,000 or more common. Bonaparte originally created eight numbered corps d'armée by 1805 and assigned command of each to a marshal or a senior general supported by a large staff. They would be permanent organizations with no territorial origin.[25]

Napoleon envisioned his corps within a larger battle plan that became known as the *bataillon carré*. This required at least five corps to deploy in a diamond pattern, with one leading, one following, one on each operational flank, forming the four points of the diamond, with at least one in the center; each would be no more than a day's march from its diagonal neighbors. This formation was largely a paper idea and even a jest of the emperor's, but it represented the ideology that underlay the organizational system. The corps was an autonomous, all-arms force designed to fight on its own, even for a protracted period of time. They could be dispersed widely by contemporary standards but still be well within supporting distance of each other. This allowed Napoleon to throw a wide operational net, locate the enemy, and collapse his nimble corps on his opponent's weak flanks and rear. As a result, the Grande Armée was far more maneuverable and effective at the operational level than the armies it faced.[26]

Napoleon made use of this army in the great campaigns from 1805 to 1807. Most famously, he created a textbook bataillon carré in the 1806 campaign against Prussia. Following the conquest of Austria the previous year, Napoleon stationed the army across southern Germany. When Prussia moved its own army south, the French commander mobilized his corps for a march north. By early October, he had created his bataillon carré. The I and III Corps of Jean-Baptiste Bernadotte and Davout led the march, with Napoleon in the center approximately fifteen miles to the southwest. To his left was Jean Lannes's V Corps and to his right, Nicolas Soult's IV Corps and Ney's VI Corps. In support was Pierre Augereau's VII Corps to the south. This deployment created the idealized diamond formation and functioned exactly as its creator intended. Over the next few days, the emperor marched his corps north. The van bypassed the Prussian army near Jena, with the western flank first encountering enemy forces. With that contact on late 13 October, Napoleon pivoted the entire formation to make Lannes's position the new van and collapsing the other corps to support it, resulting in the Battle of Jena the following day. Davout fought his own engagement simultaneously at Auerstadt, and both decisively defeated the Prussians.[27] Only in Napoleon did Guibert's doctrine achieve its fullest operational possibilities, transcending even what Guibert thought possible.

A flexible army thus constituted, Guibert had argued, required a structured leadership. It needed to be capable of handling the complexities of both his tactical system and the budding operational and strategic elements of his doctrine. To this end, he proposed the creation of what is now called a general staff. These reforms became the basis of the organization of the French army during the Revolutionary period. With Guibert's dismissal in 1789 and death in 1790, his work fell to others to accomplish. Baron Wimpffen continued the reform as a member of the Comité militaire, the committee created as the direct successor to Guibert's Council of War. Change in government brought new ministers, and Lazare Carnot, the "architect of victory," used his position within the various Revolutionary governments to continue and extend the reforms.

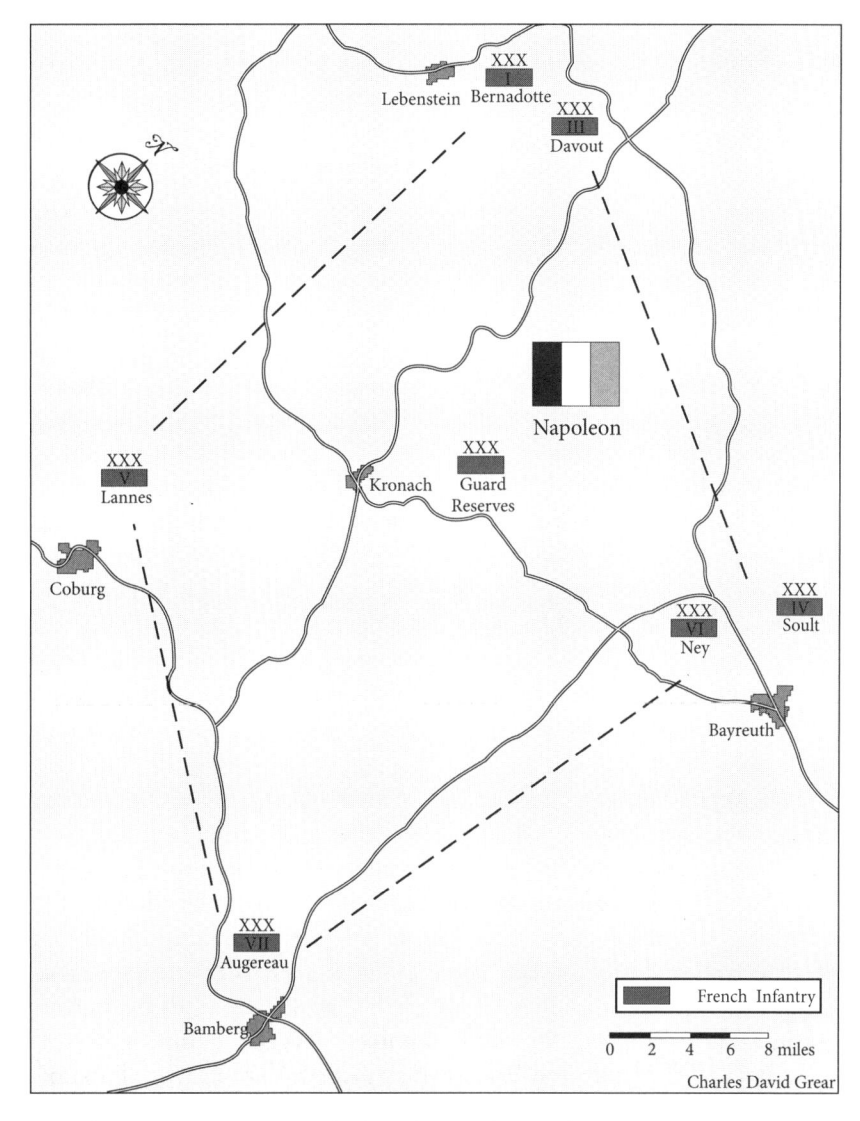

Napoleon's *bataillon carré* deployed in early October 1806, centered on Kronach and en route to the Battles of Jena and Auerstadt. Map by Charles David Grear. Copyright © 2016 University of Oklahoma Press.

Under Carnot, the general staff became a functional strategic body. Various departments within the staff, like logistics, developed their own organization and bureaucracy. Division staffs multiplied, adding educated and skilled officers to oversee their operations. Army commanders added their own staffs as planning and advisory bodies, but these remained on a mostly ad-hoc basis. Carnot retained Guibert's permanent divisions, each comprising two infantry brigades, one cavalry brigade, and one artillery company.[28]

Organizational reform required similar changes in the army's logistics. Guibert constantly wrote of the need to ameliorate the effects of warfare on civilians. Reforms of the army's supply provided a significant part of this effort. Guibert counseled that an army should live at the expense of its enemies, that "war should nourish war." Yet he protested vehemently against pillage and looting. Rather, he preferred orderly requisitions from occupied states, paid for by the French government if possible. This would eliminate the privations that armies visited on an occupied populace, which Guibert often lamented, and also serve to maintain discipline within the ranks. As such, he advocated the nationalization of all supply, which previously was maintained by private contractors paid by the government. This system had been rife with abuse, and much of the funding simply disappeared. Guibert's nationalization program eliminated this risk, bringing all supply under the auspices of the staff bureaucracy. This also prevented contact between profit-seeking contractors and soldiers, who could prove unscrupulous themselves.[29]

Despite some innovations, the armies of the Revolution often struggled with logistics. Bonaparte famously lamented the poor state of supply in the Army of Italy on his arrival in spring 1796.[30] The various Revolutionary governments never developed the kind of centralized logistical system that Guibert desired, relying instead on local efforts. But the armies were hardly the rapacious hordes of legend. Louis Joseph Bricard, who served with numerous commands from 1792 to 1802, reported several instances of soldiers being hanged for looting, both as punishment and as an example to their comrades. While he notes that discipline occasionally broke down in times of extreme privation, officers generally maintained order via regular purchase and requisition.[31] Several factors contributed to this development. Chiefly, they hoped to retain the cohesion of the army, which would allow it to survive forays into enemy territory. More fundamentally, France conquered large swaths of new territory starting in 1794. Indiscriminate pillage reflected poorly on the Revolution, which hoped to befriend, if not outright subjugate, conquered states. Discipline on the march aided these political goals, as Guibert had insisted. A proponent of a professional army, he acutely felt the need to maintain a cohesive army free of desertion and insubordination. These elements proved a foundational element of his Enlightenment theory, reducing individualistic chaos in favor of a functional system at the basic levels. Discipline also ameliorated the destructiveness of war: civilians suffered less when soldiers maintained orderly requisitions and refrained from looting or deserting.[32]

Discipline remained a signal effort of Guibert's doctrine, representing one of its foundational pillars. Only well-ordered troops could perform with the tactical finesse required by his system, maintaining march order when in enemy country and refraining from pillage or desertion. More fundamentally, disciplined troops were the outward sign of a disciplined military, which in turn reflected a disciplined society. Guibert desired such a society, in which all people lived by the rational and scientific ideals of the Enlightenment. As such, he desired that soldiers be drilled rigorously and trained in the various elements of his doctrine. After the completion of this basic training, larger units would gather to conduct exercises on the brigade and division levels. This formed the "school of the officer," whereby officers would learn the finer points of command. Guibert had participated in such exercises in France, Prussia, and Austria and insisted on their inclusion in developing the discipline and professionalism of the army.[33]

But attaining such order and control proved difficult in the early days of the Revolution. The collapse of the royal army eliminated much of the veteran, professional core of the French military. Although elements remained, the majority of troops were now inexperienced volunteers, National Guardsmen, and a bewildering array of other units called *fédérés*. For much of 1792–93, this ragtag force struggled against its more professional enemies. In 1793, however, the government began to devote more resources and energy to the failing army. Too often, undisciplined citizen-soldiers fled from the enemy, deserted, or shirked their duties; some even resorted to expelling or murdering their officers. While these incidents were not widespread and are often sensationalized, their corrosive effects on discipline, morale, and professionalism were acutely felt by all within the command structure. Led by Carnot, the Directory centralized command of the army and reemphasized discipline—élan no longer remained the basis for military victory. If possible, soldiers trained more extensively in depots near the front before being deployed; if not, they trained on the march. If at all possible, units and entire armies conducted large-scale maneuvers to familiarize soldiers and officers with the newly developing operational art.[34]

The discipline of the officer corps also underwent a significant overhaul. The army's experiment with the election of officers failed when soldiers repeatedly elected men who would coddle them rather than lead them. By 1794, Paris had adopted a hybrid system of election from a pool of preselected candidates, ostensibly based on merit, which enabled army command, led by Carnot, to ensure that competent officers filled vacant posts. While offering this paean to democracy, the army of the Revolution had realized what Guibert constantly preached: the need for discipline trumped all other considerations, as an army without discipline could not function. While political considerations undoubtedly played a significant role, particularly during the Terror, the Revolution's officer corps proved far more accessible to nomination and promotion than had the Old Regime's.[35] By 1794, the officer corps closely resembled the disciplined, professional model sought by Guibert.

Discipline within the army required the new government to address the difficult social issues raised by the Revolution. Guibert eloquently described the problem: "the principles that serve at the base of discipline, and the prejudices that compose the military spirit, are necessarily and by their nature opposed to all the principles of the civic spirit."[36] Revolutionary leaders attempted to form a democratic army, where men served for the nation and elected good men to lead them. But this system soon broke down over the very issue Guibert had noted: military discipline and democratic ideals were, and remain, mutually exclusive.

The issue of discipline offers a glimpse of the underlying social changes within the army of the Revolution. The social makeup of the military underwent a significant shift during the period, representing the only truly revolutionary change from the Old Regime. This affected both the officer corps and the common soldier, the former radically and the latter fundamentally.

The army of the Old Regime had relied on the nobility to fill its command corps. At least 90 percent of officers came from the aristocracy, most from families with long lineage. Tradition, utility, and social pressure demanded this ratio. Many officers were holdovers from the Old Regime, and in fact most had some experience as officers or soldiers in the royal army. But the Revolution eroded the entire aristocratic layer of the officer corps, including the thousands of supernumeraries that Guibert had railed against in his writings and during his time on the Council of War. Officers instead were promoted based on merit, which included education, knowledge of the army's doctrine, and command ability, all of which formed the attributes of a military leader as detailed in Guibert's system.[37]

One of the first tasks the Revolutionary army set for itself was to reverse the trend of an aristocrat-dominated officer corps. Nobility was eliminated as part of the August 1789 reforms, necessarily removing it as a perquisite for becoming a military officer. Replacing it was a system of promotion by merit. Soldiers now rose to high positions, most notably the men who would become Napoleon's marshals, many of whom were mere enlisted personnel before 1789. These men would lead the army in its victories and defeats during the early Revolution. Attrition and oversight revealed most of the poor officers for removal, streamlining the entire command corps.[38]

By 1794, this process provided the most dynamic, skilled, and experienced officer corps in Europe. Its members possessed the education necessary to grasp the fundamentals of warfare, directing their units in the conduct of Guibert's doctrine. They were largely charismatic and skilled, possessing the coup d'oeil necessary to win more battles than they lost. Many resembled Guibert's "homme de génie," who could lead men to victory using his doctrine.[39] Jourdan, Lazare Hoche, Morand, and André Masséna among many others rose through the ranks to become victorious commanders.

This revolutionary change in the social nature of the army extended beyond the officers to the enlisted men. The army of the Old Regime was manned in a variety of ways, chiefly through recruitment. The Revolution began with this method, producing the Volunteers of 1791, 1792, and a variety of other paramilitary organizations like the National Guard. Volunteers alone proved unable to meet the required manpower, particularly in 1793 as the First Coalition formed. This forced leaders to turn to conscription, harnessing the manpower resources of the most populous state in western Europe. But such practices did not represent a significant change from the Old Regime. Kings had long used forms of conscription, chiefly the summoning of the militia, for raising troops. Yet the ideology experienced a significant shift. No longer were soldiers the dregs of society, removed from the streets and sent to struggle with the king's enemies. Soldiers of the Revolution were citizens first, throwing themselves at the enemy to preserve *liberté, égalité,* and *fraternité*. While this notion appears idealistic in the extreme, its effects on morale and unit cohesion were demonstrable. Just as officers were free to rise through the ranks in a pseudodemocratic process, so too were soldiers viewed differently. They had become emblems of the nation rather than embarrassing undesireables banned from public parks. The end of aristocratic restraints enabled those of skill to rise, bettering the army from top to bottom and vice versa.[40]

Guibert touched on many of these elements in his writings. The most famous passage from the *Essai* calls for a disciplined army of citizen-soldiers fighting for their nation, though it is often taken out of context and is not a call by a "prophet of the Revolution" for "total war."[41] Guibert later refuted this argument, asserting that only a professional, long-service army could provide the protection he so desired from destruction. Rather than a specific prescription for his doctrine, he presents the citizen-soldier as a Utopian model. His subsequent writings illustrated the need for discipline and professionalism above republican virtues. Yet few paid heed to this revision, and the call for a citizen army remained attributed to Guibert's doctrine after his death.

Historian Beatrice Heuser falls prey to this misconception in her analysis of the subject. She declares that "Guibert . . . wanted to develop an army of citizen-soldiers" and had "prophesied and wished for something like the *levée-en-masse*" in the *Essai*. Only later did he slightly moderate his message, moving from a call for a French republic to an affirmation of the monarchy and its "monopolizing the right to a standing army" in his later writings.[42] Like many of Guibert's contemporaries, Heuser misses the point of his advocacy of a "vigorous people" in the *Essai*. The passage calls not for a citizen army, but rather a citizen militia to defend the state's borders as a method of last resort. Guibert carefully bounds the use of the militia to such a circumstance and not as part of the regular military. Instead of a citizen army, Guibert advocates a highly disciplined and professional army that would reflect the discipline of the state and of society. The end result of the social shift of the Revolution, which Guibert had anticipated, was a highly skilled, educated, disciplined, and professional army as demonstrated in the

Essai. Ironically, it would spew the very destruction he had predicted across Europe.

Napoleon added few elements to the system inherited from the Revolutionary governments, but the changes he made were significant. Most importantly, his arrival heralded the missing element from each area: the homme de génie, not just at the head of the military but also as the political leader of the state. He swept away the chaos and frequent changes at the head of the French state and centralized all power, political and military, in himself. He adapted his own staff system to the extant one in Paris, creating a powerful bureau to plan, strategize, and supply his campaigns. Napoleon bureaucratized much of the War Department, solving many of the issues of supply and command that had plagued the Revolutionary armies. He centralized doctrine, both Guibert's at the tactical and organizational levels and his own at the operational and strategic levels. Finally, he promoted a number of generals, lesser hommes de génie, to command his corps and armies as his subordinates.[43] Together, these measures forged the state that would build the Grande Armée.

Napoleon's most important effort came in the area of logistics. As Guibert had noted, a nation required a closely controlled supply system in order to ensure timely delivery and to avoid the chaos of pillage. The Revolutionary governments had failed in this effort, largely because entrenched private interests maintained an iron grip on the logistical system. Napoleon broke this in 1799 almost immediately after his seizure of power. He created the Intendance, a supply bureau, over the next few years, manning it with technocrats well versed in accounting and supply. His goal was to create a centralized supply system, with all of the army's needs being met through predetermined logistics or advanced requisitions.[44]

The Intendance functioned chiefly as an oversight body. While some central supply accompanied armies from France, the vast majority originated with requisitions. Unlike the pillage of prior eras, however, Napoleon's requisition system functioned relatively smoothly. Officers were dispatched from the Intendance to negotiate supply purchases from areas along a march route, whether in enemy or friendly territory. Those supplies would be aggregated for the army's use on its arrival. Crucially, Napoleon eliminated much of the corruption of the previous system by nationalizing the requisitions system. Much of the money used for logistics before 1799 had disappeared into the pockets of contractors. While officers still skimmed some funds, the logistical system of the French army greatly improved as a result of the Intendance. This prevented the drop in morale that inevitably followed a lack of supplies and all but eliminated the chaos that could result, and indeed often had over the past decade.[45]

With this alteration, Napoleon forged his Grande Armée. Peace in 1802 brought time to consolidate his rule, both over the state and within the military. Most importantly, he used the period to remake the army, building on the foundation laid by Guibert and refined during the Revolution. At the camp of Boulogne from 1802 to 1805, he crafted his greatest weapon, drilling his soldiers endlessly, providing the discipline and training required; elevating and educating his marshals and generals, finding men like himself to command his corps; and designing the corps system to match their and his own genius. When war broke out again in 1805, the Grande Armée was prepared. It tore across Germany to meet the Austrian army in 1805, taking much of that force captive without great resistance at Ulm. Shortly thereafter, Napoleon crushed the Russian army at Austerlitz. The following two years saw the Grande Armée defeat the Prussians at Jena and Auerstadt and the Russians again at Friedland. These great victories signaled the defeat of the great Continental powers and the apotheosis of the "Dieu de la Guerre," holding the sword of the Grande Armée forged by Guibert, the "prophet of war," and by Revolutionary practice.[46]

The French army did not undergo a revolution in tactics to develop this system. Following its defeat in the Seven Years War, it experienced a period of intense self-examination and reform. A variety of politicians, ministers, theorists, and practitioners contributed to this change, which generally followed an evolutionary line from Choiseul through the Revolution to Napoleon. The intense debates of the period provided fertile ground for this evolutionary process. Yet they ranged widely across all areas of military theory and required focusing. Guibert provided this focus, beginning in 1771 with the publication of the *Essai général de tactique*, by elaborating a coherent doctrine for the first time in recent French history. His subsequent work while on the Council of War (1775–77, 1787–89) enshrined that doctrine in the army via the provisional regulations of 1788, which became the famous *Réglement* of 1791.

The Revolution brought massive social and political upheaval, and its armies struggled with the new doctrine, particularly in the years before 1794. But a core of Old Regime professional soldiers remained to form the foundation of the Revolution's armies. They melded Guibert's doctrine with the new social paradigms in France, creating a professional, adaptable, and motivated army led by hommes de génie. This force defeated its enemies at nearly every turn like "the north wind bending the reeds," expanding French control into the Rhineland, Italy, and North Africa.

The armies of the Revolution marked a step toward the fulfillment of Guibert's doctrine, which would reach its culmination in the Grande Armée of 1805–1807. Given the lapse of hostilities between 1802 and 1805, Napoleon honed his army to a razor-sharp readiness and preparation, fully training it in Guibert's system and giving it a flexible organization and leadership. With the declaration of war in 1805, Napoleon unleashed his Grande Armée on the combined powers of Europe, defeating Austria, Russia, Prussia, and Russia again in turn. His victories at Ulm, Austerlitz, Jena-Auerstadt, and Friedland signaled the triumph of the French doctrine over other European systems. After these signal victories, the Grande Armée dispersed across Europe and became increasingly less French and more multinational. While the French forces often benefited from greater manpower and morale as well as Napoleon's superior leadership and organization, it was ultimately Guibert's doctrine, itself the product of an evolutionary process begun in the Old Regime, that proved decisive in the French Wars of 1792–1807.

CHAPTER 10

Legacy

In 1743 the southern French town of Montauban produced perhaps its most important citizen: Jacques-Antoine-Hippolyte de Guibert. Guibert's early life provided the foundation for his career in the army, particularly under the tutelage of his father. Charles-Benoît Guibert worked in the Ministry of War during these years, allowing his son to witness the debates and reform efforts of that time. Coming during the War of Austrian Succession, Guibert's education included the military practices and theory of Frederick the Great's Prussia. He also witnessed the increasing fracturing of the French state and society, particularly the growing dislocation of the nobility and the nascent financial crisis as the state's debt expanded. Most importantly, he was steeped in both military and Enlightenment theory. Yet he remained a youth of little experience of warfare. Only in France's great midcentury conflict would Guibert gain the training and education he required to embark on his crusade to reform his nation's army and create an institutional doctrine.

By all accounts, Guibert was a precocious youth who naturally took to science and mathematics, which naturally for that era led him to the military. He served meritoriously during the Seven Years War and the Corsican War (1768–70), entering his adult life on the field of battle. On his return to the Continent, Guibert quickly developed his mature character, which would prove essential to his success. His close association with his father had benefited him immensely; Charles was renowned as intelligent, hardworking, and possessing a mind for minutiae. Guibert inherited these qualities and added an exceptional memory as well as an ability to read both rapidly and carefully.[1]

Guibert's legacy is complex. No man better typified the late Old Regime: he was promising, youthful, passionate, but ultimately doomed to failure. In Lespinasse's words: "There is a man whom nature has destined to be great, and not to be happy. Diderot has said that nature, when she creates a man of genius, shakes her torch over his head, saying, 'Be a great man, and be miserable.' Those, I think, are the words she uttered on the day of your birth."[2] Guibert's dying words indicate his agreement with this statement; posterity has borne out his wish. Guibert was a central figure in French politics, military reform, literature, theater, and society. From his entry into Paris in 1771 until his death in 1790, he exerted a significant influence on French letters, society, and military theory.

Guibert was heir to an evolutionary process of military reform that had commenced with the adoption of the socket bayonet in 1698 and continued through the early half of the eighteenth century. France defeated a number of foes during that period, prompting little change in its military. Only by the 1750s did the state begin to develop elements of an institutional army, chiefly the cadenced step in 1754, to match that of Prussia and the other nations of Europe.

The ministry of Etienne-François, duc de Choiseul, who served as secretary of state for war in the 1760s in the wake of the disastrous defeat of the French army at Rossbach in 1757, inaugurated the era of great reform. Choiseul attempted to create a more professional army by removing its feudal elements, binding regiments and officers to the state rather than the nobility. Charles-Benoît Guibert served as the minister's aide during this process; his son in turn served as Charles's aide and later advisor. Having personally witnessed the defeat at Rossbach and the earliest efforts at reform, the younger Guibert joined Choiseul's crusade to improve the army. The most significant event of Choiseul's ministry occurred in 1769, when Guibert authored the *Instruction for Light Troops*, which contained many nascent elements of his doctrine. Most prominently, this work prescribed the use of small columns of maneuver to break up the processional movements of past practice. These became known as Guibert columns, which proved to be one of the most significant organizational reforms of the century.[3]

Because of his efforts, Choiseul fell from power in 1770, pushed out by reactionary elements at court and in the army. Guibert, thus freed from professional service to his father, took to his pen to revive the process. This would lead to his most important efforts, producing enumerated theory and doctrine for the French army.

Following Choiseul, official reform languished while theoretical reform projects abounded. Throughout the kingdom, military practitioners and philosophers alike crafted elaborate schemes to effect the regeneration of the army. Many of these received attention at court, in the army, and especially in the salons. Public interest sparked a contentious debate between schools of reformers. The "French" school preached traditional attacks of cold steel in dense columns, believing that the natural impetuosity of the French soldier belied a more professional approach. The "Prussian" school advocated wholesale adoption of linear firepower tactics, harsh discipline, and mechanistic drill. The latter noted that the Prussians had handily defeated the French at Rossbach, where each army used its respective system, proving their way of war to be superior. The French school responded by charging that this pro-Prussian approach would dilute the army's national character.[4]

Yet deeper issues lurked beneath the technical reforms. Before 1740, France's budget was probably balanced or very nearly so. After the great midcentury wars, the state teetered on the edge of bankruptcy. As the army represented its single largest expenditure, the government's lack of funds created necessary impediments to any reform. In addition, particularist groups fought to elevate their own interests, often at the expense of kingdom-wide reforms.

These concerns joined with the growing Enlightenment to further complicate the process of reform. That philosophical movement sought definition according to rational principles as one of its primary virtues. French society and government traditionally operated through custom rather than any enumerated policy or rule; for example, the "constitution" of France was its governing traditions rather than a written document. Beginning in the sixteenth century, philosophers began to define and describe scientific processes for civilization, including in government and society. The jumbled nature of both in France aided as well as hampered military reform. Enlightenment philosophes like Montesquieu created theoretical systems to govern various aspects of French life, including the government and the military, which provided a blueprint for change. Yet the search for definition furthered the dislocation of French society, particularly debates about traditional privilege.

France would not fight a major war between 1763 and 1792, allowing the theoretical debate in the military to rage for decades. Army command vacillated between the two positions, adopting elements of the French school under Secretaries of State for War Monteynard (1770–74), Montbarey (1778–80), and Ségur (1780–87).

Secretaries Saint-Germain (1775–77), Brienne (1787), and Puységur (1787–89) used elements of the Prussian school in their attempts to impose reform from within the Ministry of War.[5]

Contemporaries argued that this period represented a low point in the army's history, and many studies gloss or pass over it entirely. Ostensibly, the theoretical debate and frequent changes in doctrine led to stagnation and decay.[6] In reality, these three decades were some of the most remarkable in the history of the French military. Great change occurred not despite the contentious theoretical wrangling, but because of it. The oscillation between schools allowed the army to test various elements of each system, adopting those that proved effective and rejecting those that did not. On the surface of the debate, each school contained proponents who refused to compromise and often used their positions to subvert the opposing argument, a common tactic throughout French government. Yet this opened the door for true change.

In 1772 Guibert produced the *Essai général de tactique*, which proposed a new "military constitution" for France.[7] It called for an army based not on arcane tactical practices or parade-ground precision, but rather on mobility, flexibility, maneuverability, and professionalism. He melded the best of the French and Prussian tactical schools, using both column and line in a flexible and pragmatic tactical doctrine he called "l'ordre mixte." This system epitomized the military wisdom of his day, creating a system that would reform the army into an organization able to adapt to any battlefield situation and overcome its enemies. It provided a tactical manual, operational and strategic guidance, organizational reforms, logistical precepts, reformed social dynamics, and training methods while calling for professional, intelligent, and dynamic "hommes de génie" for its leaders. Guibert's military constitution represented a new doctrine for the French army and for Europe.

After the publication of the *Essai général de tactique*, Guibert became the chief figure in the reform debates. His strident advocacy for change landed him a position in the government. From 1775 to 1777 and again from 1787 to 1789, Guibert served on the Council of War within the War Department. To create a military system based on his constitution, he strove to implement the concepts of the *Essai*. The result would be the *Réglement* of 1791, which created the foundation for the success of the Revolutionary armies and remained the basic military manual of France until the 1830s.[8]

Guibert's system marked a significant shift in the nature of doctrine. Prior to this, military doctrine largely remained the province of specific commanders. Frederick II of Prussia, the most famous general of the eighteenth century, enumerated his own methods of discipline and *Bewegungskrieg* for his army. With it, he defeated most of his enemies, including the French at Rossbach. His doctrine proved successful for a variety of reasons, chiefly his personal control of the army and the state as well as his unique military ability. For every Frederick, however, contemporary armies contained several commanders like Charles de Rohan, prince de Soubise, the Prussian's opponent at Rossbach. Soubise and most other commanders of the time attempted to define their own doctrines and led their forces to disaster.[9] Armies without a leader of Frederick's ability generally proved unsuccessful in winning lasting victories, largely because they had no defining doctrine that lasted beyond their commanders' tenure.

Beginning in the early eighteenth century, a slew of French theoreticians attempted to define an overarching doctrine for the French army. Men like Jean Charles, chevalier Folard, and François-Jean de Graindorge d'Orgevill, baron de Mesnil-Durand, composed lengthy treatises on the subject. All tried to enumerate a systemic doctrine, but most were too wedded to their own rigid ideas to effect real and lasting change. Folard and Mesnil-Durand, for example, insisted on the complete adaptation of their own tactical systems, variations of l'ordre profond, which called for massive blocks of men to fight in column using cold steel rather than firepower. Their doctrines contained little beyond these tactical systems, failing to address organization, strategy, or logistics. Other theorists like Maurice de Saxe wrote works of military theory but failed to produce a coherent system. Instead, they enumerated maxims for individual commanders to follow. While valuable, none of these works could provide comprehensive military reform.[10]

Guibert's system proved different. No other theorist produced a coherent doctrine, and none attempted one on the same scale. Rather than a specific tactical system, Guibert produced a systematic military constitution that was adaptable to any situation, precisely because he enumerated a doctrine that addressed the army from top to bottom. He also based his military establishment on institutional rather than personal doctrine. Regardless of commander, the French army would possess a system that guided it from its highest rank to its newest recruit.[11]

Nearly the entire evolutionary process of France's military development from the royal army to those Napoleon used to conquer Europe passed through Guibert. He expanded on the ideas of the reformers that came before him, including those of Folard and Mesnil-Durand, the French and Prussian schools, and practitioners like Frederick. He removed those elements that did not prove successful, like the Prussians' slavish adherence to precision or Folard's dense formations, and retained only those that functioned well, like Saxe's logistical ideology.[12] The reform debate of the eighteenth century thus concentrated through Guibert. He was not a bottleneck in this process but rather a lens, focusing the reform efforts into a lasting doctrine that would govern the French army for decades and lead directly to the great victories of 1792–1807.

The Revolution brought massive social and political upheaval, and its military struggled with the new doctrine, particularly in the years before 1794. But a core of professional soldiers from the royal army remained to form the nucleus of these armies. They melded Guibert's doctrine and the new social paradigms of the Revolution, creating a professional, adaptable, and motivated army led by hommes de génie like Lazare Carnot, André Masséna, and Bonaparte. These forces defeated their enemies at nearly every turn, expanding French control into the Rhineland, Italy, and North Africa.

The armies of the Revolution marked a step toward the fulfillment of Guibert's doctrine, which would reach its culmination in the Grande Armée of 1805–1807. Bonaparte's génie drove the French military and state to hegemonic heights, conquering much of central Europe and extending control beyond, both east and west. Like the men of the Revolution, Bonaparte innovated little. He preferred to retain the institutional army established by the 1791 *Réglement*, itself a creation of the Old Regime. While the armies of the period, particularly of the Revolution, often benefited from superior manpower and morale, Guibert's institutional doctrine ultimately proved decisive.

Guibert's legacy exists largely because of the unceasing labor of his widow. In the years after her husband's death, Alexandrine Guibert worked tirelessly to ensure his legacy. She became active in the Revolution, associating with several of its leading members, and used this influence to tout Guibert's memory and to publish his writings. She worked closely with several family friends to edit and publish Guibert's works. These included François-Emmanuel

Toulongeon, who published Guibert's *Journal d'un voyage en Allemagne*, prefaced by a lengthy biography, in 1803.[13]

She also arranged for the publication of Guibert's correspondence with Julie de Lespinasse, which first appeared in 1809. Edited by Alexandrine's close friend Bertrand Barère, the correspondence gained immense popularity during the romantic era of the early nineteenth century. She may also have spread rumors of Guibert's affairs with Germaine de Staël and Amélie Suard to increase his popularity and the readership of his works.[14] In 1804 Napoleon awarded Alexandrine a state pension, remarking on the importance of her husband's works for his own military. Before her death in 1826, she donated Guibert's papers to the Archives de la Guerre, where the majority now reside.

On 12 April 1795 their daughter, Appolline-Charlotte, married François-René Vallet de Villeneuve, who later served as Louis Bonaparte's chamberlain. In 1808 Villeneuve was elevated to comte and relocated the family to his hereditary estate at Chenonceaux. In 1814 he petitioned Louis XVIII to alter the family name to Villeneuve-Guibert, which the king granted. Appolline died in 1852; François in 1863. The family continued to promote Guibert's interests, including the definitive publication of his correspondence with Lespinasse in 1929 by the comte de Villeneuve-Guibert.[15]

Guibert's military contributions remain the most important aspect of his legacy. These began immediately after his death, when the Revolutionary government resumed the task of military reform. On 1 August 1791 the National Assembly issued new regulations, which saw Guibert's doctrinal system accepted by the French army. "It was the culmination of all the intellectual fermentation of the French army during the century, fixing tactics after the many variations of preceding regulations upon the intermediate ground represented by the tactics of Guibert." The military formally adopted l'ordre mixte—line for attack, column for maneuver—and dispensed with the former system of formalistic evolutions and deployment, taking instead his simple evolutions and articulated deployment. In short, it adopted most of Guibert's tactical and operational reforms.[16]

Closely tied to his military work was Guibert's political legacy. His two political ventures were as the lead reformer in the Department of War. Along with his fellow reformers, Guibert implemented large parts of his military constitution while in government. After his first stint under Saint-Germain, many of his changes were overturned. Significant portions remained, however, the most important being the reform of the Ecole militaire and the officer-education system, which remained largely intact. The young, ambitious, and highly skilled officers of the Revolution were products of this system, including Bonaparte.[17] Guibert's work under Ségur and Brienne proved more fruitful. Although his reforms were initially reversed, the Revolutionary governments eventually implemented most of them.

Guibert's political theory paints an enigmatic picture. His earliest such writings, contained in the "Discours préliminaire" of the *Essai général de tactique*, argued for a protorepublican military formed of citizen-soldiers. He touted a reforming crusade, although he felt that no government in Europe could fully reform to his standards. As he aged and attained more power and influence, his political opinions moderated. In the *Défense* he repudiated the idea of citizen-soldiers, calling instead for a professional army. His later political writings, composed after his second departure from power, reflected a reform spirit that espoused the ideals of the moderate Revolutionaries. He argued for a constitutional monarchy with a severely limited executive. Crucially, Guibert placed control of the military with the legislative branch, which he envisioned as a permanent session of the Estates-General.[18]

These writings provide an opportunity for a fascinating counterfactual: how Guibert would have responded to the Revolution. On the surface it would appear that he would have emigrated with his fellow nobles as the Revolution spun out of their control. His oldest friend, Charles-François du Périer Dumouriez, who was like Guibert in many respects, fled after attempting to gain power for himself. Given his penchant for political action and his desire to attain fame, it is more likely that Guibert would have remained in France during the early Revolution, as Ethel Groffier contends. Whether he would have survived the Terror is another matter, but speculation can produce a possible answer. A disciple of Guibert's, Carnot parlayed his military experience and reforming nature into positions with every government from the Legislative Assembly to Napoleon. As the "organizer of victory," he used Guibert's methods to shuttle massive numbers of French troops between as many as eleven separate theaters, holding off the combined might of Britain, Austria, Prussia, and Russia. Carnot's experience suggests that Guibert's status as the architect of the French military would have preserved him from the guillotine and perhaps elevated him to a position of honor. While he had little battlefield experience, it is not inconceivable that he would have been named an honorary marshal by Napoleon, though it is perhaps unlikely.[19] Guibert's fiery and contentious personality produced enemies throughout his life and career, and he may have angered too many within the government to survive the Terror or the numerous purges in the years before and after.

Guibert's literary legacy cannot be considered on par with his military or political reputation. His writings, including poetry, prose, and theatrical works, were mediocre by the elevated standards of his day. His contemporaries recognized the genius in his works, but the overall quality bordered on mediocre. His play *Les Gracques* gained a temporary popularity in 1790, when it was performed by the Comédie française. The popularity of his theatrical works, however, ended there; no further performances are recorded. Guibert's poetry was of no wide acclaim, even within his circle of friends. Without his admission to the Académie française, he would simply be remembered as an essayist who dabbled in literature. His seat at the academy, however, elevated Guibert the literary figure to a higher plane. While the academy acknowledged the quality of his military writings, his literary work certainly figured into their nomination. His literary peers, with the notable exception of Jean-François la Harpe, believed that Guibert's literary work was worthy of recognition.

A large measure of Guibert's legacy comes from his social, or rather his romantic, interactions. The publication of his correspondence with Lespinasse sparked a historiographical debate within Guibert studies. While the letters reveal his innermost thoughts on a variety of issues, his treatment of her has offended many scholars. Guibert's motives, while obscure, seemed never to include marriage or a serious relationship with Lespinasse. This makes for a fascinating tragic episode but also paints Guibert as something of a Machiavellian schemer who was only using her social connections.[20]

The relationship with Lespinasse and its resulting correspondence reveal an early sense of the romantic in Guibert's works.[21] He never developed the cynical, rationalistic nature of his Enlightenment counterparts. Rather, he was given to intense flights of Romantic, and perhaps naïve, fancy. His travel journals suggest a deep and abiding love of nature and the common man, both of which ran counter to the colder, rationalistic thought of his time. These attributes were, however, hallmarks of the Romantic movement that would take hold in the following decades. While Guibert probably had no influence on the development of Romanticism, his works anticipated the movement by several decades, much like those of Rousseau and Françoise de Graffigny.

In the end, Guibert's life and legacy were a resounding success. He rose from provincial obscurity to the heights of society and power in Paris. His military writings laid the foundation for the Revolutionary and Napoleonic armies that conquered nearly all of France's enemies for a time. The principles of his military constitution, adopted by Napoleon and his enemies alike, remained the foundation for linear warfare for decades into the nineteenth century. Forays into literature, while not as spectacular, nevertheless landed Guibert a seat in the Académie française. His political activity and ceaseless advocacy of reform ensured the implementation of his military constitution. And his relationship with Lespinasse provided an important romantic and social tie. For these reasons, Jacques-Antoine-Hippolyte de Guibert was one of the foremost figures of the later Enlightenment.

Notes

Introduction

1. See Hassall, *Louis XIV and the Zenith of the French Monarchy*; Lynn, *Wars of Louis XIV*; and Wolf, *Louis XIV*.
2. Szabo, *Seven Years War*, 94–98.
3. Ibid., 254–61, 352–54.
4. Anglophone surveys of the life and reign of Louis XV are scant in modern historiography. See Antoine, *Louis XV*; and Gooch, *Louis XV*.
5. Contemporary works illustrate these themes. See, for example, Montesquieu, *De l'esprit des lois*; Voltaire, *Henriade*; Voltaire, *Siècle de Louis XIV*; and Doyle, *Jansenism*. John McManners, addresses the issue of bourgeois attacks on the government from the perspective of Jansenism in *Church and Society in Eighteenth-Century France*.
6. Ponte Nuovo crushed the remaining Corsican resistance and ended major combat. To French writers, including Voltaire, it remained an enduring symbol of Republican élan combatting absolutist "tyranny." See Voltaire, *Précis du siècle de Louis XV* (1792), in *Œuvres complètes*, 1:190–530.
7. Guibert, *Essai général de tactique*.
8. A translation of the 1791 *Réglement* is Lacroix, *Rules and Regulations*.
9. Much of this criticism originates in the rhetoric of the subsequent French Revolution. Revolutionary leaders, especially during the Terror, had to portray their movement as a radical departure from past traditions and systems to maintain its momentum. Their Napoleonic heirs adopted a similar policy, acknowledging their debt to the Revolution but rarely looking beyond to the Old Regime. Nationalist French historians inherited and have elaborated this view, often in times of national crisis. See Michelet, *Histoire de la révolution française*; Sorel, *L'Europe et la révolution française*; Sorel, *Napoleon and the French Revolution*; Bertaud, *Army of the French Revolution*; Jaurès, *Histoire socialiste de la révolution française*; Mathiez, *La victoire en l'an II*; and Soboul, *Les soldats de l'an II*. James Collins presents an intriguing thesis that argues that the Old Regime actually died in 1750 and the period between then and 1789 marked the efforts of the French government to resuscitate its corpse. See *State in Early Modern France*.
10. For general works on the subject, see Gay, *Age of Enlightenment*; Outram, *Enlightenment*; and Roche, *France in the Enlightenment*.
11. Lacroix, *Rules and Regulations*.
12. Guibert, *Essai général de tactique*, 1:lxxviii.
13. Darnton, *Literary Underground*.
14. Toulongeon, "Notice historique de Jacques-Antoine-Hippolyte Guibert."

15. Lespinasse, *Lettres . . . écrites depuis l'année 1773*. See also Barère, *Mémoirs*, 1:149, 403; Abrantès, *Memoirs*, 2:366–67.
16. Bardin, *Notice historique sur Guibert*; Forestié, *Biographie du comte de Guibert*. See also "Jacques-Antoine-Hippolyte, comte de Guibert," in *Biographie universelle*, 28:86–90.
17. Jomini, *Précis sur l'art de guerre*; Clausewitz, *On War*.
18. See, for example, Lespinasse, *Letters of Mlle. Julie de Lespinasse*.
19. P. Ségur, *Julie de Lespinasse*. For other works on Lespinasse that take this tack, see Jebb, *Star of the Salons*; Lacoutre and Aragon, *Julie de Lespinasse*; and Royde-Smith, *Double Heart*. Henry Brougham provides a rare portrayal of Lespinasse that is neither flattering nor sympathetic; he reverses the standard view of her as a dupe of Guibert's and suggests instead that she ensnared both he and Jean le Rond d'Alembert in a web of deceit and unrequited romance. See *Lives of the Philosophers of the time of George III*, 434–36.
20. Delbrück, *History of the Art of War*. Delbrück, a civilian historian, largely inaugurated the field of military history among scholars and general readers, expanding it beyond its professional origins within military institutions.
21. Colin, *L'infanterie au XVIIIe siècle*; Colin, *L'éducation militaire de Napoléon*; Latreille, *L'œuvre militaire de la révolution*.
22. Wilkinson, *Defense of Piedmont*; Wilkinson, *French Army before Napoleon*; Wilkinson, *Rise of General Bonaparte*.
23. Paret, *Makers of Modern Strategy: Military Thought from Machiavelli to Hitler*; Paret, *Makers of Modern Strategy: Military Thought from Machiavelli to the Nuclear Age*; R. Palmer, "Frederick the Great, Guibert, Bülow."
24. *L'ordre mince*, literally "the thin order," called for armies to deploy on few ranks, usually three or even two, to maximize their firepower, which its supporters saw as the primary virtue of contemporary armies. In contrast, *l'ordre profond*, "deep order," argued for deployment in narrow, deep columns to maximize shock, which was its primary virtue.
25. Quimby, *Background of Napoleonic Warfare*.
26. Lauerma, *Guibert*.
27. The Ségur Decree, passed 22 May 1781, required four degrees, or preceding generations, of nobility for promotion within the officer corps. See Bien et al., *Caste, Class, and Profession in Old Regime France*.
28. Bien, "Army in the French Enlightenment"; Bien et al., *Caste, Class, and Profession in Old Regime France*; Bien, "Military Education in 18th Century France"; Bien and Godneff, "Les offices, les corps et le crédit d'état"; Bien and Rovet, "La réaction aristocratique avant 1789." These works refute those in the vein of Samuel P. Huntington's *The Soldier and the State*, which argues that Guibert only imperfectly glimpsed a professional military structure later perfected in the Prusso-German tradition.
29. Poirier, *Les voix de la stratégie*.
30. Charnay, *Guibert ou le soldat philosophe*.
31. Habermas, *Structural Transformation of the Public Sphere*.

32. Goodman, *Republic of Letters*; Roche, *France in the Enlightenment*; Gay, *Enlightenment*; Chartier, *Cultural Origins of the French Revolution*.
33. Groffier, *Le stratège des lumières*.
34. The operational level lies between tactics and strategy. It is best described as the methods for implementing strategy en route to the battlefield. It was first elaborated by Soviet theorists in the mid-twentieth century and spread to the West through their publications. See Savkin, *Basic Principles of Operational Art and Tactics*.
35. Blaufarb, *French Army*; Blaufarb, "Noble Privilege and Absolutist State Building"; Osman, "Ancient Warriors on Modern Soil"; Osman, "Patriotism as Power."
36. Heuser, *Evolution of Strategy*; Heuser, "Guibert: Prophet of Total War?"; Telp, *Evolution of Operational Art*; R. Palmer, "Frederick the Great, Guibert, Bülow."
37. Muir, *Tactics and the Experience of Battle*; Rothenberg, *Art of Warfare in the Age of Napoleon*; Griffith, *Art of War of Revolutionary France*; Ross, *From Flintlock to Rifle*; Nosworthy, *Anatomy of Victory*; Nosworthy, *With Musket, Cannon, and Sword*; Bertaud, *Army of the French Revolution*; S. Scott, *Response of the Royal Army*; Lynn, *Bayonets of the Republic*; Elting, *Swords around a Throne*.
38. Guibert, *Considérations militaires et patriotiques*; *Défense du système de guerre moderne*; *Eloge du Maréchal de Catinat*; *Eloge du roi de Prusse*; *Eloge historique de Michel de l'Hôpital*; and *Essai général de tactique*.
39. The standard collection of Guibert's personal correspondence remains Lespinasse, *Love Letters*. See also Lespinasse, *Lettres . . . écrites depuis l'année 1773*. His official papers are found in Service Historique—Armée de Terre, Vincennes, France (hereafter SHAT), 1 M 1790–94.
40. Dumouriez, *Life*; Staël-Holstein, *Mémoires*.
41. This approach likely originates with a famous quote from Frederick II to Voltaire, stating that "this Guibert desires glory by all paths: the applause of armies, the theatre, and women; this is a sure path to immortality." Frederick to Voltaire, 27 July [1775], Voltaire, *Œuvres complètes*, 52:307.

Chapter 1

1. Rogers, *Military Revolution Debate*, is the authoritative work on the subject. Knox and Murray, *Dynamics of Military Revolution*, is also useful.
2. See De Vries, *Guns and Men in Medieval Europe*; De Vries, *Infantry Warfare in the Early Fourteenth Century*; and Delbrück, *Medieval Warfare*.
3. De Vries, *Guns and Men in Medieval Europe*; De Vries, *Infantry Warfare in the Early Fourteenth Century*; Delbrück, *Medieval Warfare*. See also Black, *European Warfare*; Mallet and Shaw, *Italian Wars*; and especially Parker, *Military Revolution*.
4. Lynn, "Evolution of Army Style."

5. See Duffy, *Military Experience in the Age of Reason*, 3–34, 89–136; Nosworthy, *Anatomy of Victory*, 3–46.
6. Childs, *Warfare in the Seventeenth Century*, 73–76; Geoffrey Parker, *The Army of Flanders and the Spanish Road, 1567–1659: The Logistics of Spanish Victory and defeat in the Low Countries' Wars* (New York: Cambridge University Press, 1972).
7. Childs, *Warfare in the Seventeenth Century*, 73–76; Duffy, *Fire and Stone*; Nosworthy, *Anatomy of Victory*, 67–68, 80–84.
8. "Division" in contemporary lexicon referred to a half-regiment or half-platoon, particularly when the larger unit had no regular subordinate units or more than three. The term remained in common usage until after the Napoleonic period, causing no small confusion to modern readers of contemporary military theory. See Nosworthy, *Anatomy of Victory*, 147–62, 329–42.
9. See ibid., 65–78, 99–120.
10. Mousnier, *Institutions of France under the Absolute Monarchy*, remains the standard in the field of the French state and the role of the nobility. Corvisier, *Armies and Societies in Europe*, provides much of the same analysis through the lens of the French army. See also Collins, *State in Early Modern France*; Dewald, *Aristocratic Experience*; Dewald, *French Nobility in the Eighteenth Century*; and Kettering, *French Society*.
11. Corvisier, *Armies and Societies in Europe*, 121–98.
12. Nosworthy, *Anatomy of Victory*, 143–238; Colin, *L'infanterie au XVIIIe siècle*, 2–71.
13. Nobles considered service in the depot to be onerous, resulting in the absence of commanding officers. In peacetime the higher officers of a regiment spent as little as three weeks per year with their units, usually conducting them in a paradeground display for the king or another high official. This devolved training to junior officers, many of whom had little training and education themselves. As a result, venal regiments proved largely resistant to training. See Colin, *L'infanterie au XVIIIe siècle*, 27–72; and Guibert to Lespinasse, [Mar.] 1776, Lespinasse, *Love Letters*, 508.
14. Colin, *L'infanterie au XVIIIe siècle*, 27–72.
15. Nosworthy, *Anatomy of Victory*, 65–78, 199–222.
16. See Eckberg, *Failure of Louis XIV's Dutch War*; and Lynn, *Wars of Louis XIV*.
17. Lynn, "Evolution of Army Style," 517–19.
18. "Musket" refers to a muzzle-loaded weapon with a smooth bore. It was longer and heavier than the arquebus that it replaced, requiring two hands to hold while firing. Early muskets used a match or a friction wheel to provide the spark to ignite the explosive powder that expelled the ball. This mechanism proved prone to mechanical error and led to a high rate of misfire and weapon failure. The fusil, or flintlock musket, first appeared in the late seventeenth century. It used a striker to spark a flint to produce the explosion. This proved more effective and

less prone to failure than earlier methods, allowing the fusil to largely replace all other types of firearms by the mid-eighteenth century. See Nosworthy, *Anatomy of Victory*, 29–46.
19. Colin, *L'infanterie au XVIIIe siècle*, 27–72; Nosworthy, *Anatomy of Victory*, 29–46.
20. Folard, *Histoire de Polybe*; Folard, *Nouvelles découvertes sur la guerre*; and Folard, *Traité de la colonne*.
21. Jean Colin finds that Folard created ordre profond "it seems." *L'infanterie au XVIIIe siècle*, 27–40.
22. Quimby, *Background of Napoleonic Warfare*, 26–40, 290.
23. See ibid., 26–40; and Colin, *L'infanterie au XVIIIe siècle*, 27–40.
24. Nosworthy, *Anatomy of Victory*, 183–98; Rothenberg, *Art of Warfare in the Age of Napoleon*, 11–30. See also Louis Drummond, comte de Melfort, "Tactique et manœuvres des Prussiens," SHAT, 1 M 1793, 11.
25. On Frederick William I, see Ergang, *Potsdam Führer*. For a general overview of the war, see Browning, *War of the Austrian Succession*. For a survey of the Prussian wars of the period, see Showalter, *Wars of Frederick the Great*. For biographies of Frederick II, with particular regard to his military career, see Asprey, *Frederick the Great*; Duffy, *Military Life of Frederick the Great*; and Schieder, *Frederick the Great*.
26. Colin, *L'infanterie au XVIIIe siècle*, 13–71; Quimby, *Background of Napoleonic Warfare*, 7–25; Nosworthy, *Anatomy of Victory*, 183–98, 243–60; R. Palmer, "Frederick the Great, Guibert, Bülow."
27. Lynn, "Evolution of Army Style," 515–17; J. Puységur, *Art de la guerre par principes et par règles*; Folard, *Histoire de Polybe*; Folard, *Nouvelles découvertes sur la guerre*; Folard, *Traité de la colonne*. Folard's works were originally distributed, many without official publication, in 1727–30, 1724, and 1727, respectively.
28. J. Puységur, *Art de la guerre par principes et par règles*. Robert Quimby particularly emphasizes the rigid and processional nature of Puységur's system in *Background of Napoleonic Warfare*, 16–25.
29. Colin, *L'infanterie au XVIIIe siècle*, 40–72; Quimby, *Background of Napoleonic Warfare*, 80–105.
30. Colin, *L'infanterie au XVIIIe siècle*, 40–72; Quimby, *Background of Napoleonic Warfare*, 80–105. See also Nosworthy, *Anatomy of Victory*, 261–80.
31. Colin, *L'infanterie au XVIIIe siècle*, 3–72.
32. Ibid. See also Nosworthy, *Anatomy of Victory*, 261–80; and Nosworthy, *With Musket, Cannon, and Sword*, 85–89.
33. Colin, *L'infanterie au XVIIIe siècle*, 3–72. See also Nosworthy, *Anatomy of Victory*, 261–80; and Nosworthy, *With Musket, Cannon, and Sword*, 85–89.
34. Carlyle, *Friedrich the Second*, 7:140; Saxe, *Mes rêveries*, 20–57, 86–100; Duffy, *Military Experience in the Age of Reason*, 268–79.
35. Duffy, *Military Experience in the Age of Reason*, 33–58, 97–100.
36. Ibid., 33–57.
37. Montbarey, *Mémoires autographes*, 3:287–88.

38. See Mousnier, *Institutions of France under the Absolute Monarchy*, particularly 1:112–213. One example of such a group occurred midcentury with the rise of the Jansenists. Originally oriented toward a religious belief, the Jansenists became much more diffuse and political in their advocacy. They migrated to the *parlements*, where they argued strenuously for *parlementaire* power and against the perceived tyranny of the crown, though ultimately seeking their own advancement. See Doyle, *Jansenism*, 68–90; McManners, *Church and Society in Eighteenth-Century France*, 481–564; and especially Van Kley, *Jansenists and the Expulsion of the Jesuits*.

39. See Egret, *Louis XV et l'opposition parlementaire*; le Roy Ladurie, *Ancien Régime*; Roche, *France in the Enlightenment*, 449–84.

40. See Collins, *State in Early Modern France*, 79–124, 176–215 (esp.). The War of Polish Succession occurred between 1733 and 1738, pitting France, Spain, and Sardinia, supporting Stanislaw Leszczynski for the throne of Poland, against Russia, Austria, Saxony, and Prussia, supporting Augustus. For the only English-language academic treatment of this conflict, see Sutton, *King's Honor and the King's Cardinal*.

41. Numerous works address the crisis of state during the late ancien régime. Swann and Félix, *Crisis of the Absolute Monarchy*, provides a recent survey of the field. Tocqueville, *L'ancien régime et la Révolution*, arguably begins the historiography of the subject. In *The State in Early Modern France*, James Collins argues that the Old Regime ended in 1750, a contentious but important argument as it provides for a much earlier beginning to French Revolutionary historiography. The superior surveys on the period remain Doyle, *Origins of the French Revolution*; and Lefebvre, *Coming of the French Revolution*.

42. Rowlands, *Financial Decline of a Great Power*, 198; Collins, *State in Early Modern France*, 216–56. While Rowlands's work concentrates on the period before 1715, he projects his analysis to 1789, including the citation of an archival source with the noted figures. See also Félix, *Finances et politique au siècle des Lumières*; and Guéry, "Les finances de la monarchie française sous l'Ancien Régime."

43. The works of David D. Bien, Rafe Blaufarb, and Julia Osman focus on this subject during the period in question. See Bien, "Army in the French Enlightenment"; Bien et al., *Caste, Class, and Profession in Old Regime France*; Bien, "Military Education in 18th Century France"; Bien and Godneff, "Les offices, les corps et le crédit d'état"; Bien and Rovet, "La réaction aristocratique avant 1789"; Blaufarb, *French Army*; Blaufarb, "Noble Privilege and Absolutist State Building"; Osman, "Ancient Warriors on Modern Soil," 175–96; and Osman, "Patriotism as Power." See also Doyle, *Aristocracy and Its Enemies*.

44. Buffington, *Second Hundred Years War*. France's "natural frontiers" consisted of the Alps, the Pyrenees, and the Rhine. See Richelieu, *Political Testament*; and Thiers, *Histoire du Consulat et de l'Empire*. For a contemporary analysis of the relative strengths of the Austrian, Prussian, and French militaries, see "Mémoire abrégé sur l'armée de France," SHAT, 1 M 1791, 46.

45. See Middleton, "French Policy and Prussia after the Peace of Aix-la-Chappelle"; and H. Scott, *Birth of a Great Power System*.
46. Citino, *German Way of War*, 72–76; Kennett, *French Armies in the Seven Years War*, 15–16; Szabo, *Seven Years War in Europe*, 94–98.
47. Szabo, *Seven Years War in Europe*, 94–98. See also Citino, *German Way of War*, 76–82; Showalter, *Wars of Frederick the Great*, 186–92; and Waddington, *La guerre de sept ans*, 1:617–30.
48. Szabo, *Seven Years War in Europe*, 94–98. See also Citino, *German Way of War*, 76–82; Showalter, *Wars of Frederick the Great*, 186–92; and Waddington, *La guerre de sept ans*, 1:617–30.
49. Mackesy, *Coward of Minden*; Szabo, *Seven Years War in Europe*, 258–61; Waddington, *La guerre de sept ans*, 3:42–68.
50. Savory, *His Britannic Majesty's Army in Germany during the Seven Years War*, 309–28; Szabo, *Seven Years War in Europe*, 350–53; Waddington, *La guerre de sept ans*, 5:85–139.
51. Savory, *His Britannic Majesty's Army in Germany during the Seven Years War*, 309–28; Szabo, *Seven Years War in Europe*, 350–53; Waddington, *La guerre de sept ans*, 5:85–139.
52. See R. Palmer, "Frederick the Great, Guibert, Bülow."
53. Robert Citino notes, "The French army displayed huge weaknesses from the lowliest soldier to the highest commander; its officers were venal and corrupt, its rank and file half-hearted, its doctrine in a state of utter confusion." *German Way of War*, 81.

Chapter 2

1. Jaurgain, *Notice sur les familles Vallet et Villeneuve-Guibert*, 44. The conseillers du roi served as regional judicial officials, a role also partially filled by the gardes des sceaux. The latter officials also served as censors of written material. See Barbichc, *Les institutions de la monarchie française à l'époque moderne*.
2. Groffier, *Le stratège des lumières*, 23.
3. "Charles-Benoît Guibert," in *Biographie universelle*, 28:86. See also Jaurgain, *Notice sur les familles Vallet et Villeneuve-Guibert*, 45–46; Lauerma, *Guibert*, 12–15.
4. Browning, *War of the Austrian Succession*; "Charles-Benoît Guibert" 86; Jaurgain, *Notice sur les familles Vallet et Villeneuve-Guibert*, 45–46, 47; Lauerma, *Guibert*, 12–15. The daughters were Antoinette-Suzanne, future madame de Salès; Antoinette-Angélique, future comtesse de Pluvié; Antoinette-Christine; Françoise; and Hélène-Antoinette, future madame d'Azincourt.
5. Granier, "Où est né le Maréchal Guibert?"; Lauerma, *Guibert*, 12–15. Guibert included Apolline among those he gave to his daughter. He also published many of his works under the name François-Apolline; several editions still bear it. Granier rejects speculation that Guibert had a brother who died before maturity, thus accounting for the two names. He concludes that only Guibert knew the reason for the confusion.
6. Lauerma, *Guibert*, 14–15; Toulongeon, "Notice historique de Jacques-Antoine-Hippolyte Guibert," 1–4.

7. "Charles-Benoît Guibert," in *Biographie Universelle*, 18:86; Jaurgain, *Notice sur les familles Vallet et Villeneuve-Guibert*, 44–45; Lauerma, *Guibert*, 15–21.
8. "Charles-Benoît Guibert," in *Biographie universelle*, 18:86; Jaurgain, *Notice sur les familles Vallet et Villeneuve-Guibert*, 44–45, 47–48; Lauerma, *Guibert*, 16–17. See also "Mémoires détaillés de l'armée du roi de Prusse et sa tactique," "Notes et observations," "Mémoires sur des troupes prussiennes," and "Principes des prussiens sur différents objets militaires," SHAT, 1 M 1793, 13–16. These are all memoranda drafted by Guibert's father detailing the subject for the official record and for the education of his son.
9. "Jacques-Antoine-Hippolyte, comte de Guibert," in *Biographie universelle*, 18:86–87; Jaurgain, *Notice sur les familles Vallet et Villeneuve-Guibert*, 44–45. Guibert's friend François-Emmanuel Toulongeon makes this argument. See "Notice historique de Jacques-Antoine-Hippolyte Guibert," 1–4. See also Groffier, *Le stratège des lumières*, 23–24; and Lauerma, *Guibert*, 16.
10. Toulongeon, "Notice historique de Jacques-Antoine-Hippolyte Guibert," 4.
11. Lauerma, *Guibert*, 19–20; Citino, *German Way of War*, 81.
12. Friedrich Wilhelm von Seydlitz famously ignored orders at the Battle of Zorndorf on 25 August 1758. Frederick ordered the cavalry commander to attack a Russian position; Seydlitz demurred, explaining that the situation was not ripe for an attack. After receiving further orders to attack, Seydlitz replied, "Tell the king that after the battle my head is at his disposal, but in the meantime I hope he will permit me to exercise it in his service." Robert Citino sees this as an example of an autonomous and flexible operational way of war within the Prusso-German tradition. See *German Way of War*, 91–100.
13. Green, *Histoire du peuple anglais*, 2:333 (quote); Guibert, *Essai général de tactique*, 1:1–31.
14. Guibert, *Essai général de tactique*, 2:302.
15. Lucien Poirier in *Les voix de la stratégie* presents an intriguing counter to Toulongeon's point in arguing that bravery and brave acts were ubiquitous during the period, thus rendering them banal.
16. Groffier, *Le stratège des lumières*, 26–28; Lauerma, *Guibert*, 16–21; "Charles-Benoît, comte de Guibert," in *Biographie universelle*, 18:86; Jaurgain, *Notice sur les familles Vallet et Villeneuve-Guibert*, 44–45. The rank of maréchal de camp represented a junior general-officer's rank in the French system of the Old Regime. Subordinate to a lieutenant general on campaign, the maréchal de camp served a kind of protostaff position, particularly in drafting operational plans and arranging the army for battle.
17. See Charles-Benoît de Guibert, "Perpignan ce 1766," SHAT, 1 M 1794, 5; Lauerma, *Guibert*, 20–21.
18. Charles-Benoît de Guibert, "Perpignan ce 1766," SHAT, 1 M 1794, 5; Lauerma, *Guibert*, 20–21; Quimby, *Background of Napoleonic Warfare*, 175–84; Lauerma, *Guibert*, 20–21.

19. See Scott and Simms, *Cultures of Power in Europe*, especially Julian Swann, "'Silence, Respect, Obedience': Political Culture in Louis XV's France," 225–48; and Munro Price, "The Court Nobility and the Origins of the French Revolution," 269–88.
20. "Victor-François, duc de Broglie," in *Biographie universelle*, 5:594–96.
21. Colin, *L'infanterie au XVIIIe siècle*, 73–134; Quimby, *Background of Napoleonic Warfare*, 90–105. See also V. Broglie, *Campagnes*; and V. Broglie, *Correspondance inédite*.
22. Groffier, *Le stratège des lumières*, 28. On the influence of Broglie, see Guibert, *Voyages de Guibert*, 146–49.
23. Choiseul served as secretary of state for foreign affairs from 1758 to 1761 and again from 1766 to 1770, secretary of state for war from 1761 to 1770, and secretary of state for the marine from 1761 to 1770. See Choiseul, *Mémoires*. See also "Etienne-François de Choiseul," in *Biographie universelle*, 8:182–86.
24. "Charles-Benoît Guibert," in *Biographie universelle*, 86. "Mémoire sur la Nouvelle Consitution" (SHAT, 1791, 3) is likely written by the elder Guibert and contains much of the military theory and reform spirit that would underlie the Choiseul reforms.
25. Collins, *State in Early Modern France*, 176–256. For the continuing financial crisis, see ibid. For Choiseul's ministry, see Choiseul, *Mémoires*; and Latreille, *L'œuvre militaire de la révolution*, 1–25.
26. Colin, *L'infanterie au XVIIIe siècle*, 73–134; Quimby, *Background of Napoleonic Warfare*, 90–105. See also Choiseul, "Compte que j'ai rendu au roi de mon administration depuis 1757 jusqu'à 16 mars 1770," in *Mémoires*, 218.
27. Colin, *L'infanterie au XVIIIe siècle*, 73–134; Quimby, *Background of Napoleonic Warfare*, 90–105; Choiseul, "Compte que j'ai rendu au roi de mon administration depuis 1757 jusqu'à 16 mars 1770," in *Mémoires*, 218.
28. Colin, *L'infanterie au XVIIIe siècle*, 73–134; Quimby, *Background of Napoleonic Warfare*, 100–105.
29. Colin, *L'infanterie au XVIIIe siècle*, 73–134; Quimby, *Background of Napoleonic Warfare*, 100–105.
30. L. Puységur, "On croit devoir joindre à cet extrait des livres sur l'art militaire des Chinois, l'examen de la tactique d'un ouvrage nouveau, qui a pour titre: Essai général . . . ," in *Etat actuel de l'art et de la science militaire à la Chine*, 217–23. The author can find no evidence that Puységur produced the letters in question, and the issue of authorship of both the 1769 instructions and Guibert's later works did not recur until the twentieth century.
31. Colin, *L'infanterie au XVIIIe siècle*, 106–13. "N'a-t-il [Guibert père] pas collaboré à cette Instruction de 1769 pour les troupes légères, où figurent les colonnes serrées inventées par son fils, et qui portent son nom?" (Did he not collaborate on this Instruction of 1769 for light troops, displaying the closed columns invented by his son, and that bear his name?)

32. See Castries, *Madame du Barry*; Saint-Victor, *Madame du Barry*; and especially Mirabeau, *Mémoires du ministère du duc d'Aiguillon*.
33. See Goebel, *Struggle for the Falkland Islands*; Laver, *Falklands/Malvinas Case*, 19–50; and Rice, "British Foreign Policy and the Falkland Islands Crisis." Britain ceded its claims on the islands to the Spanish but retained its settlement, laying the foundation of the later and ongoing dispute with Argentina.
34. Latreille, *L'oeuvre militaire de la révolution*, 1–25; Wilkinson, *French Army before Napoleon*, 89.
35. "François-Jean, marquis de Chastellux," in *Biographie universelle*, 8:9–10. See also Chastellux, *De la félicité publique*; and Chastellux, *Voyages*.
36. Dumouriez, *Life*, 1:170–72.
37. Hall, *France and the Eighteenth-Century Corsican Question*.
38. Dumouriez, *Life*, 1:132–37; Dwyer, *Napoleon*, 19–21.
39. Dumouriez, *Life*, 1:132–37; Dwyer, *Napoleon*, 19–21; Peter Adam Thrasher, *Pasquale Paoli*, 129–32.
40. "Jacques-Antoine-Hippolyte, comte de Guibert," in *Biographie universelle*, 18:87; Groffier, *Le stratège des lumières*, 28–30; Lauerma, *Guibert*, 20–23; Toulongeon, "Notice historique de Jacques-Antoine-Hippolyte Guibert," 3–4; Dwyer, *Napoleon*, 18–25.
41. Dwyer, *Napoleon*, 18–25; Thrasher, *Pasquale Paoli*, 150–54.
42. Toulongeon, "Notice historique de Jacques-Antoine-Hippolyte Guibert," 4; Dumouriez, *Life*, 1:135–41.
43. Voltaire, *Précis du siècle de Louis XV* (1792), in Voltaire, *Œuvres complètes*, 1:485–503. See also Dwyer, *Napoleon*, 21; and Voltaire, *Œuvres complètes de Voltaire*, 46(14):425n1. Moland references a letter written by Guibert to Voltaire in August 1769, which was "pleine de détails très-piquants, sur Paoli et ses lieutenants, dont la férocité égale la lâcheté" (full of very piquant details on Paoli and his lieutenants, whose ferocity equal their cowardice).
44. The Corsican Legion, despite its name, was a regiment in function. See "Jacques-Antoine-Hippolyte, comte de Guibert," in *Biographie universelle*, 18:87; Groffier, *Le stratège des lumières*, 28–30; Lauerma, *Guibert*, 20–23; and Toulongeon, "Notice historique de Jacques-Antoine-Hippolyte Guibert," 3–4.
45. See Lauerma, *Guibert*, 22–23. Following the move to the Continent, the legion was transferred to various posts. In 1771 it was moved to Montauban, in 1772 to Strasbourg, and in 1775 to Livorno, where it was renamed the Legion de Dauphiné.
46. J. Puységur, *Art de la guerre par principes et par règles*; Folard, *Histoire de Polybe*; Folard, *Nouvelles découvertes sur la guerre*; Folard, *Traité de la colonne*.
47. Bois, "Notice sur Charles Graindorge d'Orgeville."
48. Mesnil-Durand, *Projet d'un ordre français en tactique*. For a contemporary analysis that reflects the pedantry and inefficiency of both Mesnil-Durand's system and l'ordre profond in general, see "Réflexions

critiques sur Folard addressées à un major d'infanterie" and "Observations sur le système de tactique de Monsieur de Mesnil-Durand," SHAT, 1 M 1791, 47, 49.
49. Colin, *L'infanterie au XVIIIe siècle*, 50–72; Quimby, *Background of Napoleonic Warfare*, 62–79.
50. "Pierre-Joseph Bourcet," in *Biographie universelle*, 5:353. Most prominently, Bourcet, *Mémoires historiques sur la guerre*; Bourcet, *Mémoires militaires sur les frontières de la France, du Piémont, et la Savoie*.
51. Bourcet, *Principes de la guerre de montagnes*. This work only achieved publication on the date listed, at the height of the polemical debate about military theory and thus the apex of public interest in the subject.
52. Ibid., particularly "Raisons du premier mouvement de l'armée d'offensive," 148–49.
53. Ibid., 148. The particular campaign described by Bourcet concerned the extreme southern portion of the Alpine border due north of the Mediterranean coast. The Col de Tende (Colle di Tenda in Italian) is a famous mountain pass, likely cut by the Romans, that provides the easiest passage from France into the Italian plains via the road from Cuneo to Breil-sur-Roya (modern D6204/E74) and was thus guarded by the "place," modern Fort Central, mentioned by Bourcet. The "Esture" is the Stura di Demonte, a river originating in the Alps approximately ten miles west of the Col de Tende and flowing east-northeast into the Tanaro, a tributary of the Po, to the east of Cherasco.
54. Bourcet's writings contain repeated calls for commanders to seize the offensive. See, for example, *Principes de la guerre des montagnes*, 18–19. Numerous works expound on his contributions to operational-level warfare. Particularly relevant is Telp, *Evolution of Operational Art*, esp. 5–34. See also Chandler, *Campaigns of Napoleon*, 133–204; Citino, *German Way of War*, 34–62; Martin van Creveld, "Napoleon and the Dawn of Operational Warfare," in Olsen and van Creveld, *Evolution of Operational Art*; and Dennis Showalter, "Prussian-German Operational Art, 1740–1943," in ibid. For an introduction to the subject, see Wasson, *Innovator or Imitator*.
55. "Jean-Baptiste Vaquette de Gribeauval," in *Biographie universelle*, 18:473–75; Lauerma, *L'artillerie de campagne française*; and McConachy, "Roots of Artillery Doctrine," 619–20.
56. "Jean-Baptiste Vaquette de Gribeauval," in *Biographie universelle*, 18:473–75; Lauerma, *L'artillerie de campagne française*; and McConachy, "Roots of Artillery Doctrine," 619–20. See also Rothenberg, *Art of Warfare in the Age of Napoleon*, 24–26.
57. "Jean-Baptiste Vaquette de Gribeauval," in *Biographie universelle*, 18:473–75; Lauerma, *L'artillerie de campagne française*; and McConachy, "Roots of Artillery Doctrine," 619–20. See also Rothenberg, *Art of Warfare in the Age of Napoleon*, 24–26.
58. Latreille, *L'œuvre militaire de la révolution*, 1–25; McConachy, "Roots of Artillery Doctrine," 619–20.

59. France's last true defeat prior to the eighteenth century was the Italian expeditions of Charles VIII and Louis XII beginning in 1494. Between 1520 and 1763, France was not decisively defeated in war. Even arguable defeats, most notably the Habsburg-Valois Wars of 1520–59, the Wars of Louis XIV from 1667 to 1713, and the Polish Succession produced benefits for France, including territorial gain and continued political hegemony in western Europe.
60. Collins, *State in Early Modern France*, 240–89.
61. Johann Ernst, baron von Pirch, "Mémoire raisonné sur les parties les plus essentielles de la tactique," SHAT, 1 M 1712.

Chapter 3

1. Groffier, *Le stratège des lumières*, 31–34; Lauerma, *Guibert*, 25–30.
2. Bourcet, *Mémoires historiques sur la guerre*; Bourcet, *Mémoires militaires sur les frontières de la France, du Piémont, et la Savoie*; Bourcet, *Principes de la guerre de montagnes*; Mesnil-Durand, *Projet d'un ordre français en tactique*.
3. Guibert, *Essai général de tactique*, 2:220. For an in-depth discussion of this point, see Roche, *France in the Enlightenment*, 11–108 (esp. 41–74). The Enlightenment's architects much concerned themselves with the issue of definition and ordering according to rational principles. The chief effort in this in France was the *Encyclopedia* of Jean le Rond d'Alembert and Denis Diderot, first published in 1751 and continuing until the 1770s, with still later editions. See *Encyclopédie ou dictionnaire raisonné des sciences, des arts, et des métiers*.
4. Guibert, *Essai général de tactique*, 1:v–lxxxvii.
5. Ibid., 1:v–xliii.
6. Ibid., 1:x–lxxviii. See also Lee, *Thirty Years War*; Parker, *Thirty Years War*; Roberts, *Gustavus Adolphus*; and Wedgwood, *Thirty Years War*.
7. Guibert, *Essai général de tactique*, 1:xxii–xxviii. On Colbert, see Ames, *Colbert, Mercantilism, and the French Quest for Asian Trade*; Cole, *Colbert and a Century of French Mercantilism*; Collins, *State in Early Modern France*; Inès Murat, *Colbert* (Paris: Fayard, 1980); and Sargent, *Economic Policy of Colbert*. For a penetrating analysis of the costs of Louis XIV's search for military hegemony, supported by Louvois, see Collins, *State in Early Modern France*. See also Corvisier, *Louvois*; Lynn, *Giant of the Grand Siècle*; and Lynn, *Wars of Louis XIV*.
8. Guibert, *Essai général de tactique*, 1:v–xii, xxvi–xxviii, xliv–l (esp.). For introductions to Enlightenment Classicism, see Cassirer, *Philosophy of the Enlightenment*; and Gay, *Enlightenment*. See also Rosenblum, *Transformations in Late Eighteenth Century Art*.
9. Guibert, *Essai général de tactique*, 1:xliv–l.
10. Vegetius, *Epitome of Military Science*; Vegetius, *Institutions militaires de Végèce*, ed. Claude-Guillaume-Bourdon de Sigrais (Paris: Prault, 1743).
11. Guibert, *Essai général de tactique*, 1:xii–xiv.
12. Ibid., 1:xiii.

13. This analysis has become the standard for Guibertian studies in English-language and most French sources, and this selection is often the only portion of the *Essai* directly quoted in secondary works, rendering it the most famous of Guibert's words to nonspecialists. See, to name but a few of the sources that carry this argument, Bertaud, *Army of the French Revolution;* Colin, *L'education militaire de Napoléon;* Gat, *History of Military;* Griffith, *Art of War in Revolutionary France;* Liddell-Hart, *Strategy;* Heuser, "Guibert: Prophet of Total War?"; Wilkinson, *French Army before Napoleon;* and especially Colin, *L'infanterie au XVIIIe siècle*. Colin famously refers to Guibert as the "prophet of the Revolution." See *L'education militaire de Napoléon,* 107. As an intriguing counterpoint to the above, R. R. Palmer argues that Guibert never "show[ed] much practical foresight, as distinguished from lucky predictions, or any sense that the ideas that he favored ... would become realities for the generation then alive." "Frederick the Great, Guibert, Bülow," 112.
14. Guibert, *Essai général de tactique,* 1:xii–xiv.
15. Ibid.
16. Ibid., 1:lxix–lxxviii.
17. Ibid., 1:xl.
18. See Guibert, *Eloge du maréchal de Catinat* and *The Patriot-Minister.* Both were written originally for essay competitions sponsored by the Académie française. In them Guibert lauds each minister's rationality, professionalism, virtue, and dedication to duty. See also Catinat, *Vie;* and Crouzet, *La sagesse et le malheur.*
19. Between 100 and the 20s B.C.E., various politicians successfully undermined the constitution of the Roman Republic until the seizure of imperial power by Gaius Octavius Julius Caesar between 30 and 20 B.C.E. See Scullard, *From the Gracchi to Nero.* Perhaps ironically, a militia resembling Guibert's appeared during the French Revolution in the National Guard. Gilbert du Motier, marquis de Lafayette, attempted a coup as its leader in 1791 before being exiled. See Doyle, *Oxford History of the French Revolution.*
20. Guibert, *Essai général de tactique,* 1:lxiv–lxviii.
21. Ibid., 1:xcvii–xcix, 3–24, 25. For present purposes, "speed" will be referred to interchangeably with the terms "mobility" and "maneuverability." "Mobility" refers to operational and strategic speed, "maneuverability" to tactical speed.
22. Guibert, *Essai général de tactique,* 1:35.
23. Ibid., 1:30, 33. See Colin, *L'infanterie au XVIIIe siècle,* 55–72.
24. Guibert, *Essai général de tactique,* 1:33–34.
25. Quimby, *Background of Napoleonic Warfare,* 117.
26. Guibert, *Essai général de tactique,* 1:29–37.
27. Ibid., 1:37–42.
28. Ibid., 1:42, 48–70.
29. Ibid., 1:90–94. Technically, "ployment" refers to maneuvers from march order to battle order and "deployment" the reverse, as the prefix

indicates. The former term has fallen from parlance, and the latter has come to encompass both meanings in nontechnical publications.
30. Guibert, *Essai général de tactique*, 1:94. *En bataille* is an elusive term that can be translated in multiple ways, chiefly as either "in battle order" or "in line." The former use is suggested by Guibert's context, particularly as the two would be virtually synonymous to a proponent of l'ordre mince. See Lynn, *Bayonets of the Republic*.
31. Guibert, *Essai général de tactique*, 1:94–165.
32. Ibid., 31, 131–60. See also Colin, *L'infanterie au XVIIIe siècle*, 113–34.
33. Guibert, *Essai général de tactique*, 1:110–68.
34. Ibid., 169–83.
35. Ibid., 199–214.
36. Ross, *From Flintlock to Rifle*, 27–28; Quimby, *Background of Napoleonic Warfare*, 133–39. Cavalry was generally employed against enemy cavalry or isolated enemy infantry. More rarely, it formed a mass of decision designed to break enemy lines; this was the most prominent use of cuirassiers. In almost every use the cavalry served as its own master rather than being incorporated with the two other arms at the operational or tactical levels.
37. Guibert, *Essai général de tactique*, 1:231–72 (esp. 231–32, 239–42).
38. Ibid., 1:253–72.
39. Duffy, *Military Experience in the Age of Reason*, 268–79; Guibert, *Essai général de tactique*, 1:215–31 (esp. 218–19). See also Rothenberg, *Military Border in Croatia*.
40. Guibert, *Essai général de tactique*, 1:70–90.
41. Much of volume two of the *Essai général de tactique* elaborates Guibert's doctrine in this regard.
42. Guibert, *Essai général de tactique*, 2:1–149 (quotes, 8, 24).
43. Ibid., 2:6–36.
44. Ibid., 2:8–38 (quote, 11).
45. Ibid., 2:12–24, 39–60. See Duffy, *Military Experience in the Age of Reason*, 151–88.
46. Bourcet, *Principes de la guerre de montagnes*; van Creveld, *Transformation of War*.
47. Robert Citino articulates this argument and the surrounding historiography. See *German Way of War*, 34–36.
48. Telp, *Evolution of Operational Art*, 26; R. Palmer, "Frederick the Great, Guibert, Bülow," 110.
49. Guibert, *Essai général de tactique*, 1:24–39, 90–94, 2:13.
50. See Telp, *Evolution of Operational Art*; and van Creveld, *Transformation of War*.
51. Guibert, *Essai général de tactique*, 1:39–44, 61–69.
52. Ibid., 2:50–60. While Guibert credits Frederick with the invention of this particular formation, much of it owed not to the Prussian but rather to Vegetius. His writings speak of an "oblique order" that bears a striking similarity to Guibert's. Given the ubiquity of Vegetius's work in contemporary military theory, this link is understandable. See Vegetius, *Epitome of Military Science*, 47–48, 83–106.

53. Guibert, *Essai général de tactique*, 2:45–60.
54. Ibid., 1:85, 2:45–60. Concerning the *Schwerpunkt*, see Frieser, *Blitzkrieg Legend*, 156–57. See also Clausewitz, *On War*, 566–76.
55. Guibert, *Essai général de tactique*, 2:199–214.
56. Ibid., 2:256–72.
57. Ibid., 2:88–115.
58. Ibid., 1:v–lxxix, 2:7 (quote).
59. Duffy, *Military Experience in the Age of Reason*, 268–79; Guibert, *Essai général de tactique*, 2:184. See also Guibert, "Extrait des mémoires du maréchal de Saxe," SHAT, 1792, 19.
60. Guibert, *Essai général de tactique*, 2:180–18.
61. Ibid., 2:180–218. See also Vauban, *New Method of Fortification*; Duffy, *Fire and Stone*; and Ostwald, *Vauban under Siege*.
62. Guibert, *Essai général de tactique*, 1:70–89. The philosophes strongly emphasized individualism in their writings. See Dumont, *Essai sur l'individualisme*, 92–102; Roche, *France in the Enlightenment*, 538–63; and Starobinski, *Invention of Liberty*, 131–38.
63. Guibert, *Essai général de tactique*, 1:70–89.
64. Montbarey, *Mémoires autographes*, 3:296; Guibert, *Essai général de tactique*, 1:21–71.
65. S. L. A. Marshall's *Men against Fire* provides the most significant historiographical study of individuals in combat. Marshall concludes that the vast majority of soldiers of any period did not observe fire discipline after battle began and rarely shot at the enemy, much less in a disciplined manner like a volley. While his conclusions apply best to a modern army, the psychological effects he notes have antecedents in Guibert's day, leading at least in part to his emphasis on individual fire.
66. Guibert, *Essai général de tactique*, 1:90. The *feu à volonté* was also referred to as the *billebaude*.
67. Ibid., 2:61–80 (quote, 70).
68. Ibid., 2:61–137.
69. Ibid., 1:v–lvxxix, 1–9, 2:2 (quote), 61–70, 113–36. David Bien discusses the role of génie and moyen in contemporary education in "Military Education in 18th Century France," 51–59.
70. Guibert, *Essai général de tactique*, 2:4, 139–61, 220.
71. See, for example, ibid., 2:109.
72. Ibid., 2:184.
73. Ibid., 1:xiii, xliv–lxxviii, 5–31, 254–306, 2:254–306.
74. Ibid., 1:xiii.
75. Clausewitz, *On War*, 78, 80, 87 (esp.): "War is merely the continuation of policy by other means."
76. See Groffier, *Le stratège des lumières*, 33–42; and Lauerma, *Guibert*, 25–63.
77. See Guibert to Lespinasse, 18 Oct. 1775, Lespinasse, *Love Letters*, 398–400.
78. Lauerma, *Guibert*, 63. The marquis de Chastellux noted: "[General William Heath] has read our best authors on tactics, and especially the

Tactics of Mr. Guibert, which he holds in particular estimation." *Travels in North America*, 48.
79. Frederick II, "Remarques sur l'ouvrage intitulé Essai général de tactique par le roi de Prusse," 4 Oct. 1772, SHAT, 1 M 1793, 20; Frederick to d'Alembert, n.d., printed in Shoberl, *Frederick the Great*, 2:142.
80. Frederick to Voltaire, 26 Nov. [1773], Voltaire, *Œuvres complètes*, 52:214-15.

Chapter 4

1. See S. Necker, *Mélanges extraits*, 2:207-18. Necker refers to "Guibert's wealthy parents." See also Collins, *State in Early Modern France*, 176-215; and Roche, *France in the Enlightenment*, 390-419.
2. The author can find no evidence of Charles-Benoît Guibert having been involved in the salons or in other social pursuits in any way.
3. Charles-François de Broglie, comte de Ruffec, brother of Marshal Victor-François, duc de Broglie, served as one of Louis XV's trusted advisors, including as head of the shadowy Secret du roi. See A. Broglie, *Le secret du roi*. See also "Charles-François, comte de Broglie," in *Biographie universelle*, 5:594-96; and "Victor-François, duc de Broglie," ibid., 596-97. As much of Charles-François de Broglie's actions remain veiled, given his position in the government, no evidence exists of a direct relationship between him and the Guiberts, but the family relationships would have brought them into the same political networks.
4. Dumouriez refers to himself and Guibert as "the two rats in the fable." See *Life*, 1:170-71. The reference is to "Le rat de ville et le rat des champs," a ubiquitous fable from renowned fabulist Jean de la Fontaine. See Fontaine, "Le rat de ville et le rat des champs," in *Fables*, 10-11.
5. Dumouriez, *Life*, 1:186-89; Groffier, *Le stratège des lumières*, 33-34; Gambier-Parry, *Madame Necker*, 110. From late 1770 to early 1771, Chancellor René Nicolas Charles Augustin de Maupeou forcibly suppressed the parlements of France. He forbade them to meet, which signaled a shift in the policy of Louis XV to more direct, and seemingly despotic, control of government. The parlements remained suppressed until the king's death in 1774, prompting calls for the Estates-General to mediate the power of the crown. See Flammermont, *Le chancelier Maupeou et les Parlements*; and Swann, *Politics and the Parlement of Paris*.
6. Staël-Holstein, "Eloge de M. de Guibert," in *Mémoires*, 339-61; Julie de Lespinasse to Marie-Jean-Antoine Nicolas de Caritat, marquis de Condorcet, 24 July [1772], Lespinasse, *Lettres inédites*, 81; Lespinasse to Condorcet, [July 1772], ibid., 85.
7. S. Necker, *Mélanges extraits*, 2:207-18.
8. Staël-Holstein, "Eloge de M. de Guibert," 355. See also Haussonville, *Le salon de madame Necker*, 2:174.
9. Staël-Holstein, "Eloge de M. de Guibert," 218; Grimm, *Historical and Literary Memoirs and Anecdotes*, 2:216-17. See also Goodman, *Republic of Letters*, 5-63.

10. Lespinasse to the comte de Crillon, 4 Jan. 1774, Lespinasse, *Lettres inédites*, 192; Guibert to Lespinasse, 18 Oct. 1775, Lespinasse, *Love Letters*, 398–400. "The comte de Guibert, a soldier full of military order, intelligence, and knowledge, thirsting after glory of every description, who had, whilst still young, arrived at superior rank by his activity, published an essay on tactics, which, from the great and new ideas it contained, acquired a rapid celebrity." L. Ségur, *Memoirs and Recollections*, 1:121.
11. See Goodman, *Republic of Letters*; and Roche, *France in the Enlightenment*.
12. Goodman, *Republic of Letters*, 53. See also Beasley, *Salons, History, and the Creation of Seventeenth-Century France*; Spencer, *French Women and the Age of Enlightenment*; Goncourt and Goncourt, *La femmme au dix-huitième siècle*; Lougee, "Le paradis des femmes"; Schiebinger, *The Mind Has No Sex?*; Steinbrügge, *The Moral Sex*; Wiesner, *Women and Gender in Early Modern Europe*.
13. Roche, *France in the Enlightenment*, 641–74. See also d'Alembert, *Œuvres*; Diderot, *Œuvres complètes*; Hume, *History of England*; Hume, *Treatise of Human Nature*; Montesquieu, *De l'ésprit des lois*; Montesquieu, *Lettres persanes*; Rousseau, *Les confessions*; Rousseau, *Du contrat social*; Rousseau, *Emile*; and Voltaire, *Œuvres complètes*. For excellent summaries of each author's work and philosophy, see Gay, *Age of Enlightenment*; Gay, *Enlightenment*; and especially Cassirer, *Philosophy of the Enlightenment*.
14. Goodman, *Republic of Letters*, 58, 74–83; Charles-Augustin Sainte-Beuve, introduction to Lespinasse, *Love Letters*, 32.
15. R. Palmer, "Frederick the Great, Guibert, Bülow," 106; Staël-Holstein, "Eloge de M. de Guibert," 340; Guibert, *Œuvres dramatiques*, 297–301. Georges-Louis Leclerc, comte de Buffon, was a philosophe who specialized in mathematics and the natural sciences and is regarded as the father of natural science. Antoine-Leonard Thomas worked primarily as a poet and sometime contributor to the *Encyclopedia*.
16. Lespinasse to Guibert, Nov. 1774, Lespinasse, *Love Letters*, 259. "Mme de M. . . ." refers to Jeanne Thiroux de Montsauge.
17. Condorcet referred to himself as Julie's "second secretary" after d'Alembert. Condorcet to Turgot, June 1771 (2), Condorcet, *Correspondance inédite*, 48–50. The *Encyclopedia* project was Diderot and d'Alembert's effort to define and order the natural world, including French society and the state. Hundreds of authors contributed, making it the largest and arguably most significant element of the Enlightenment project. See Darnton, *Business of the Enlightenment*; Morley, *Diderot and the Encyclopedists*; and Roche, *France in the Enlightenment*, 578–607. Turgot served as finance minister from 1774 to 1776, Necker from 1776 to 1781 and 1788 to 1789. Despite being ideological and political enemies, they traveled in the same social circles. See Collins, *State in Early Modern France*, 216–56; Groenewegen, *Economics of A. R. J. Turgot*; and J. Necker, *Sur l'administration de M. Necker*.

18. See Goodman, *Republic of Letters*, 53–58, 75.
19. D'Alembert to Frederick, 1 June 1772, d'Alembert, *Œuvres*, 5(1):323–24. The quote is an excerpt of a cover letter d'Alembert sent to Frederick, presumably with a copy of *Essai général de tactique*.
20. D'Alembert to Frederick, 17 May 1773, ibid., 338–40. The letter was later carried by Guibert and presented to Frederick upon the former's arrival at Potsdam.
21. D'Alembert to Frederick, 30 July 1772, ibid., 340–41. The letter is labeled 1772 but likely dates from 1773, given the reference to Guibert's and Frederick's meeting.
22. Turgot to Condorcet, 17 Dec. 1773, Condorcet, *Correspondance inédite*, 150–51.
23. Diderot, *Œuvres complètes*, 11:80. Naigeon, a failed painter and sculptor, joined the salon of Paul-Henri Thiry, baron d'Holbach, and became one of Diderot's closest collaborators on the *Encyclopedia*, including editing and contributing numerous articles and editing Diderot's work. His major philosophy centered on an attack on religion, calling for atheism and the destruction of the Christian church. See "Jacques-André Naigeon," in *Biographie universelle*, 30:540–44; and Kors, "Atheism of d'Holbach and Naigeon."
24. Julie de Lespinasse to Guibert, 20 Sept. 1774, Lespinasse, *Love Letters*, 180. She also mentioned, "M. d'Alembert and the comte de Crillon often speak to me of you."
25. Julie de Lespinasse to Guibert, 1 Aug 1773, ibid., 78; Groffier, *Le stratège des lumières*, 102.
26. *Revue des deux mondes*, 29:33–34; Lauerma, *Guibert*, 123. "Jeanne Bouret married Philibert Thiroux de Montsauge in 1758, who was named director and administrator of posts in 1778. The date of her birth and of her death are unknown. One only knows that she passed to England in the time of the Revolution." *Revue des deux mondes*, 29:832n1. Lauerma dates the affair from 1774, Groffier from 1771. The earlier date is much more likely as the affair seemed well established by the latter date. See Lespinasse to Guibert, Nov. 1774, Lespinasse, *Love Letters*, 259.
27. Lauerma, *Guibert*, 123. See also P. Ségur, *Julie de Lespinasse*, 199. As with much of Guibert's correspondence, these letters have been lost. Lespinasse's letters to Guibert chronicle this continuing association and possible affair. See, for example, Lespinasse to Guibert, 1 July 1773, in Lespinasse, *Love Letters*, 57–63. She asks: "But how comes it that that woman [Montsauge] does not love you to desperation? As you would like to be loved?"
28. Guibert, "Elegy of Eliza," in Lespinasse, *Love Letters*, 310; Louis-Henriette-Charlotte Philippine de Durfort, duchesse de Duras, to Rosalie de Constant, 15 Sept. 1809, in Duras, *La duchesse de Duras et Chateaubriand*, 64. Duras's portrayal of Guibert is not kind, assigning to him "a good villain's role."
29. Craveri, *Madame du Deffand and her World*; P. Ségur, *Julie de Lespinasse*, 16–127; Julie de Lespinasse to Guibert, 23 Sept. 1774, Lespinasse, *Love Letters*, 186–87.

30. P. Ségur, *Julie de Lespinasse*, 127–30.
31. Guibert, "Elegy of Eliza," 310, 317.
32. P. Ségur, *Julie de Lespinasse*, 154.
33. Ibid., 132–42.
34. Ibid., 72–77, 230–86. See also Courteault, *La mort du marquis de Mora à Bordeaux*.
35. Bardin, *Notice historique sur Guibert*, 13–14; Colin, *L'infanterie au XVIIIe siècle*, 118–19; Lauerma, *Guibert*, 71–72.
36. Guibert, *Journal d'un voyage en Allemagne*, 1:98–131.
37. Ibid., 1:132, 146.
38. Ibid., 1:160–70, 177. The phrase recurs frequently in his descriptions of Berlin.
39. The odd nickname purportedly resulted from a dispute with Frederick. As the two discussed the Battle of Pharsalus, Frederick misidentified a centurion in the battle, which Guichard corrected to Quintus Icilius. Frederick called Guichard this name in all future official documents. See Carlyle, *Friedrich the Second*, 113–14.
40. Guibert, *Journal d'un voyage en Allemagne*, 1:200–214, 217–20.
41. Ibid., 1:218–48. Henry was the thirteenth child of Fredrick William I and younger brother of Frederick II. He served alongside his brother in the War of Austrian Succession and Seven Years War. See Easum, *Prince Henry of Prussia*; and Szabo, *Seven Years War in Europe*.
42. Guibert, *Journal d'un voyage en Allemagne*, 1:249, 272–74, 1:284, 1:313–24.
43. See Grimsley, *Philosophy of Rousseau*; and Horowitz, *Rousseau, Nature, and History*.
44. Guibert, *Journal d'un voyage en Allemagne*, 2:1–114. See also Rothenberg, *Military Border in Croatia*.
45. See Guibert, *Essai général de tactique*, 2:70.
46. Guibert, *Journal d'un voyage en Allemagne*, 2:127, 156, 161. The king's opponent was probably Leopold Ludwig von Anhalt, a member of Frederick's staff, although Guibert is unclear on the point.
47. Guibert, *Journal d'un voyage en Allemagne*, 2:125–234.
48. Or what Clausewitz would refer to as "friction." See *On War*, 119–21.
49. Guibert, *Journal d'un voyage en Allemagne*, 2:202–203.
50. Ibid., 2:244–76.
51. Beginning in the 1740s, Louis XV contrived to place Louis-François de Bourbon, prince de Conti, on the throne of Poland. Dumouriez secretly gathered a military force to impose Conti's candidacy in 1773, which quickly became public, leading to the scandal. See A. Broglie, *Le secret du roi*. Favier traveled extensively in eastern Europe and wrote of his experiences, providing an invaluable source of information for the region. See Favier, *Doutes et questions sur le traité de Versailles*; and Favier, *Conjectures raisonnées sur la situation actuelle de la France*. See also "Jean-Louis Favier," in *Biographie universelle*, 13:445–47.
52. Groffier, *Le stratège des lumières*, 84–93. Charles-Francois, comte de Broglie, director of the Secret du roi, accompanied Guibert on at least part of the journey, according to Géorgel, *Mémoires*, 1:283.

53. Guibert, *Journal d'un voyage en Allemagne*, 1:276. Dumouriez believed Guibert to be a member of the Secret du roi, as he recorded in his memoirs. See *Life*, 1:335-36. Louis XV wrote several cryptic letters intimating Guibert's participation. See Louis XV to Charles-Francois, comte de Broglie, marquis de Ruffec, 21 Aug. 1773, Louis XV, *Correspondance secrète*, 361-62; and Louis XV to Dubois-Martin, 16 Oct. 1773, ibid., 368-69. See also A. Broglie, *Le secret du roi*, 430-33, 448, 472, 482.
54. Guibert, *Journal d'un voyage en Allemagne*, 2:263-64; Dumouriez, *Life*, 1:335-36; Groffier, *Le stratège des lumières*, 93-96. See also Géorgel, *Mémoires*, 1:283.
55. P. Ségur, *Julie de Lespinasse*, 321. The author can find no record of this quote in any published version of Lespinasse's letters; Ségur perhaps had access to unpublished material containing the line.
56. Lespinasse to Guibert, 22 Oct. 1774, Lespinasse, *Love Letters*, 235-38. Italics are Lespinasse's, indicating the importance of the opera box to their relationship and supporting Ségur's conjecture.
57. Lespinasse to Guibert, 30 May 1773, ibid., 42; Lespinasse to Guibert, dated "at every moment of my life," ibid., 101; Lespinasse to Guibert, [late spring] 1774, ibid., 116-17.
58. Lespinasse to Guibert, 13 Nov. 1774, ibid., 255; Lespinasse to Guibert, [late spring] 1774, ibid., 111.
59. Biographies of Lespinasse focus on this dissonance as a chief avenue of attack on Guibert, portraying him as a philandering figure who toyed with her feelings. Ségur's work contains much of this form of criticism. See also Janine Bouissounouse, *Julie de Lespinasse: Ses amitiés, sa passion* (Paris: Hachette, 1958); and Mitchiner, *Muse in Love*. The results of his theatrical interest are contained in Guibert, *Œuvres dramatiques*.
60. Lespinasse to Guibert, 4 July 1775, Lespinasse, *Love Letters*, 337; Lespinasse to Guibert, 22 Aug. 73, ibid., 89. Lespinasse was conscientious about burning Guibert's letters, which proved unfortunate for posterity as few of them remain. Guibert, despite constant assurances to the contrary, seems to have preserved the majority of Lespinasse's letters.
61. See d'Alembert, "To the Manes of Mlle. de Lespinasse," Lespinasse, *Love Letters*, 326-31.
62. Lespinasse to Guibert, 6 Oct. 1774, ibid., 207 (italics hers).
63. Lespinasse to Guibert, 6 July 1774, ibid., 120 (italics hers); Lespinasse to Guibert, 6 Sept. 1773, ibid., 90. The gap in Guibert's letters is substantial for the most intense periods of their relationship. It is possible that he communicated his feelings in a manner equal to Lespinasse's in the lost letters.
64. Guibert to Lespinasse, 9 Sept 1774, Lespinasse, *Love Letters*, 167-68. The earlier citation of Staël's letter noting his "wealthy parents" stands in direct contrast to Guibert's missive. Either she was not privy to the family finances, or they had greatly improved in the intervening decade. Alternatively, Guibert simply could have lied to Lespinasse in an attempt to quell her anger.
65. Guibert to Lespinasse, 22 Oct. 1774, ibid., 237. The events that kept Guibert from Paris included an illness that struck his mother and the

deployment of his regiment near Montauban, allowing him to remain on his family estate at Fonneuve. "Comte de Crillon" refers to François Félix Dorothée de Berton, duc des Balbes et de Crillon.
66. Alexandrine was born in 1758, presumably on the family estate. "Alexandrine-Louise Boutinon de Courcelles," in *Biographie universelle*, 18:90–91. The marriage allowed Guibert to enter the Berry nobility, as the estate there became his primary residence.
67. Lespinasse to Guibert, May 1775, Lespinasse, *Love Letters*, 315; Groffier, *Le stratège des lumières*, 103–27; Lauerma, *Guibert*, 127–29.
68. Lespinasse to Guibert, 1 July 1775, Lespinasse, *Love Letters*, 326–28.
69. Ibid.; Lespinasse to Guibert, 3 July 1775, ibid., 333–34.
70. See, for example, Lespinasse to Guibert, Aug. 1775, ibid., 358–61. Here Lespinasse records that she is "so used to suffering and to feeling only pain."
71. See Brégeon, *Le Connétable de Bourbon*.
72. Louise Honorine, duchesse de Choiseul, to Marie-Anne de Vichy-Chamrond, marquise du Deffand, 5 Sept. 1775, in Deffand, *Correspondance complète*, 3:194–95; Groffier, *Le stratège des lumières*, 137; Mettra, *Correspondance secrète, politique, et littéraire*, 17:75.
73. Bachaumont, *Mémoires secrets*, 8:160–61; Lauerma, *Guibert*, 107–12; Grimm et al., *Correspondance littéraire, philosophique, et critique*, 1:280 (June 1773).
74. Groffier, *Le stratège des lumières*, 137–40; Campan, *Mémoires sur la vie privée de Marie-Antoinette*, 1:150–51; Papillon de la Ferté, *L'administration des menus*, 385–86.
75. La Harpe, *Correspondance littéraire*, 1:144–45; Papillon de la Ferté, *L'administration des menus*, 390–91; Necker, *Mélanges extraits des manuscrits*, 2:271; Bachaumont, *Mémoires secrets*, 8:161–62, 279. See also la Harpe, *Œuvres*, 18:5–6, 199–202.
76. Voltaire to Deffand, 16 Nov. 1773, Deffand, *Correspondance complète*, 2:366; Voltaire to Charles-Augustin de Ferriol d'Argental, 15 Nov. [1773], Voltaire, *Œuvres complètes*, 13:224.
77. Voltaire to Comte de Schomberg, 3 Sept. [1775], Voltaire, *Œuvres complètes*, 13:305. He continues: "I found in this discourse a grand profundity of true, noble, fine, and sublime ideas; the morsels of eloquence quite moving, a courageous pride, and the enthusiasm of a man who secretly aspires to replace his hero. This feeling pierces every line."
78. G. Morris, *Diary and Letters*, 1:254.
79. D'Alembert to Frederick, 17 May 1773, d'Alembert, *Œuvres*, 5(1): 339; Voltaire to Frederick, 28 Oct. [1773], Voltaire, *Œuvres complètes de Voltaire*, 26:487–8.8.
80. Voltaire to Frederick, 28 Oct. [1773], Voltaire, *Œuvres complètes de Voltaire*, 26:487–88.

Chapter 5

1. Collins, *State in Early Modern France*, 79–124, 176–256 (esp.); Doyle, *Origins of the French Revolution*, 43–52.
2. Collins, *State in Early Modern France*, 176–215.

3. Ibid.; Doyle, *Jansenism*, 68–90; McManners, *Church and Society in Eighteenth-Century France*, 481–564; Rogister, *Louis XV and the Parlement of Paris*; Stone, *French Parlements and the Crisis of the Old Regime*; and Swann, *Politics and the Parlement of Paris*.
4. Désessarts et al., *Nouvelles ecclésiastiques*. See also Doyle, *Origins of the French Revolution*, 36–38, 57–91; Lefebvre, *Coming of the French Revolution*; and especially Echeverria, *Maupeou Revolution*.
5. Doyle, *Origins of the French Revolution*, 36–38, 57–91; Echeverria, *Maupeou Revolution*; Flammermont, *Le chancelier Maupeou et les Parlements*; Roche, *France in the Enlightenment*, 209–484 (esp. 390–419, 449–84).
6. Bien and Godneff, "Les offices, les corps et le crédit d'état"; Bien and Rovet, "La réaction aristocratique avant 1789"; Blaufarb, *French Army*; Blaufarb, "Noble Privilege and Absolutist State Building."
7. Bien and Godneff, "Les offices, les corps et le crédit d'état"; Bien and Rovet, "La réaction aristocratique avant 1789"; Blaufarb, *French Army*; Blaufarb, "Noble Privilege and Absolutist State Building."
8. Latreille, *L'œuvre militaire de la révolution*, 1–25.
9. Hardman, *Louis XVI*, 27–56; Semichon, *Les réformes sous Louis XVI*; Stone, *French Parlements and the Crisis of the Old Regime*, 252–70.
10. Groffier, *Le stratège des lumières*, 33–34; Lauerma, *Guibert*, 20–24, 86–88, 123; P. Ségur, *Julie de Lespinasse*; Guibert, *Essai général de tactique*, 1:v–lxxxiv. Charles Guibert apparently concerned himself with family finances during this period. "My father," Guibert recorded, "is worried and embarrassed by family affairs, and is still upset by them." The colonel also noted that he himself did not receive an expected pension, causing his sister to add her worries to their father's. See Guibert to Lespinasse, [Mar.–Apr.] 1776, Lespinasse, *Love Letters*, 507–508.
11. See, for example, Broglie to Montbarey, 20, 26 June 1778, SHAT, 1 M 1819, 60, 71. These detail Charles Guibert's expertise and indispensable organizational skill. See also Latreille, *L'œuvre militaire de la révolution*, 265–73; and Lauerma, *Guibert*, 20–21.
12. Latreille, *L'œuvre militaire de la révolution*, 26–66; Groffier, *Le stratège des lumières*, 149; Guibert to Lespinasse, 18 Oct. 1775, Lespinasse, *Love Letters*, 396–401. This letter details the excitement at the Fontainebleau court as the king debated who to appoint to the vacant leadership post of the Ministry of War and Guibert's thoughts on the issue.
13. Guibert to Lespinasse, 18 Oct. 1775, Lespinasse, *Love Letters*, 400. "Is it not clever of me," Guibert notes, "to have quarreled with him [Vaux]?" He gives no further indication of the reason for the falling out.
14. Ibid., 398–400.
15. Guibert, "Discours préliminaire," *Essai général de tactique*, 1:v–lxxxvi.
16. "Claude-Louis, comte de Saint-Germain," in *Biographie universelle*, 37:321–25; Saint-Germain, *Mémoires et commentaires*.
17. See Guibert to Lespinasse, 27 Oct. 1775, Lespinasse, *Love Letters*, 419–24.
18. Saint-Germain, *Mémoires et commentaires*, 31. See also Véri, *Journal*, 1:380; and Guibert to Lespinasse, 27 Oct. 1775, Lespinasse, *Love Letters*, 419–24.

19. Lauerma, *Guibert*, 88. See also Guibert to Lespinasse, 27 Oct. 1776, Lespinasse, *Love Letters*, 419–24. "I attached [to Saint-Germain] one of the memoranda I drew up for M. Turgot, the most important one." Ibid., 420. Turgot apparently served as both Guibert's patron and editor, likely adding his financial expertise to the colonel's proposed reforms. On Turgot see Bouton, *Flour War*; Groenewegen, *Eighteenth-Century Economics*; Thompson et al., *La guerre du blé au XVIIIe siècle*; and R. Palmer, "Turgot."
20. Latreille, *L'œuvre militaire de la révolution*, 72; Lauerma, *Guibert*, 88–90. For his explanation of the council and its functions, see Saint-Germain, *Mémoires et commentaires*, 25–65.
21. "Louis-François, baron Wimpffen-Bornebourg," in *Biographie universelle*, 44:668–69.
22. See Haechler, *L'encyclopédie de Diderot et de Jaucourt*; M. Morris, *Le Chevalier de Jaucourt*; Schwab, "Extent of the Chevalier de Jaucourt's Contribution"; and Wimpffen-Bournebourg, *Commentaires des mémoires de M. le comte de Saint-Germain*, 168–70. In the last Saint-Germain describes Jaucourt as "negligent."
23. Guibert, *Essai général de tactique*, 1:231–69; Lauerma, *L'artillerie de campagne française*; McConachy, "Roots of Artillery Doctrine," 619–20.
24. Saint-Germain, *Mémoires et commentaires*, 35–36.
25. Guibert to Lespinasse, 18 Oct. 1775, Lespinasse, *Love Letters*, 398–400; Guibert to Lespinasse, [Nov.] 1775, ibid., 444–45; Guibert to Lespinasse, [Nov.] 1775, ibid., 449–50.
26. For Guibert's analysis of the structural problems facing French society and the army, see "Observations relatives à la nouvelle constitution," "Vices de l'ancienne constitution et avantages de la nouvelle constitution," and "Project de travail relatif . . . ," SHAT, 1 M 1791, 13–15. Much of the thought reflects his writing in the "Discours préliminaire" of the *Essai*.
27. Guibert to Lespinasse, [Dec.] 1775, Lespinasse, *Love Letters*, 453; Lauerma, *Guibert*, 90. Even at this stage Guibert threatened to retire if "he [saw] that [Saint-Germain] lacked courage." The plan mentioned is probably "Observations relatives à la nouvelle constitution," SHAT, 1 M 1791, 15.
28. Bien, "Army in the French Enlightenment"; Blaufarb, *French Army*, 29–30; Blaufarb, "Noble Privilege and Absolutist State Building"; Osman, "Patriotism as Power."
29. Bien, "Army in the French Enlightenment"; Blaufarb, *French Army*, 29–30; Blaufarb, "Noble Privilege and Absolutist State Building"; Osman, "Patriotism as Power"; Latreille, *L'œuvre militaire de la révolution*, 76–80.
30. A relic of the period of pike and shot from the late sixteenth and early seventeenth centuries, the mousquetaires were one of the oldest units in the Maison militaire du roi. Grenadiers montés were elite infantry mounted for rapid movement, essentially dragoons. The chevaux légers were light-horse units capable of skirmishing. The gardes du corps and gendarmerie originated in the traditional role of elite soldiers, namely

to guard the person of the king. All served little practical use and had not been deployed in battle for decades.

31. Lauerma, *Guibert*, 90. See also *Commentaires des mémoires de M. le comte de Saint-Germain* (Paris, 1780), 73, 94–97. This work is generally attributed to Wimpffen, although a small chance exists that it could be the product of one of his many brothers also called "baron de Wimpffen".

32. Guibert to Lespinasse, [Feb. 1776], Lespinasse, *Love Letters*, 499–500; Groffier, *Le stratège des lumières*, 266–71; Lauerma, *Guibert*, 90–91; Bien, "Army in the French Enlightenment"; Bien, "Military Education in 18th Century France"; Blaufarb, *French Army*, 12–45. See also "Lettre de M . . . à Mme la comtesse de . . . ," SHAT, 1 M 1791, 18.

33. Guibert to Lespinasse, [Feb. 1776], Lespinasse, *Love Letters*, 499–500; Groffier, *Le stratège des lumières*, 266–71; Lauerma, *Guibert*, 90–91; Bien, "Army in the French Enlightenment"; Bien, "Military Education in 18th Century France"; Blaufarb, *French Army*, 12–45. See also "Lettre de M . . . à Mme la comtesse de . . . ," SHAT, 1 M 1791, 18; James Leith, *Facets of Education in the Eighteenth Century* (Oxford: Voltaire Foundation, 1977); Doyle, *Jansenism*, 68–78; and especially McManners, *Church and Society in Eighteenth-Century France*, 509–64.

34. See Bien, "Army in the French Enlightenment"; and Blaufarb, *French Army*, 12–29. Building on Bien's work, Blaufarb argues that the reformers were attempting to implement promotion by merit based on the Old Regime notion of military merit that passed from a worthy ancestor to his descendants. While Blaufarb does not couch his argument in the same language as Guibert, their arguments are essentially identical.

35. See Guibert, "Discours préliminaire," *Essai général de tactique*.

36. *Commentaires sur les mémoires de monsieur le comte de Saint-Germain*, 74; Guibert to Lespinasse, Dec. 1775, Feb. 1776, [Feb. 1776], [May 1776], Lespinasse, *Love Letters*, 461, 494–95, 499–500, 517–18; Latreille, *L'œuvre militaire de la révolution*, 87–93.

37. Mousnier, *Institutions of France under the Absolute Monarchy*. See also Blaufarb, *French Army*, 5–26; Corvisier, *Armies and Societies in Europe*; Dewald, *Aristocratic Experience*; Dewald, *French Nobility in the Eighteenth Century*.

38. Mousnier, *Institutions of France under the Absolute Monarchy*. See also Blaufarb, *French Army*, 5–26; Corvisier, *Armies and Societies in Europe*; Dewald, *Aristocratic Experience*; Dewald, *French Nobility in the Eighteenth Century*.

39. Bien, "Army in the French Enlightenment"; Bien, "Military Education in 18th Century France"; Latreille, *L'œuvre militaire de la révolution*, 1–25.

40. See *Commentaires sur les mémoires de monsieur le comte de Saint-Germain*, 73; Lauerma, *Guibert*, 90–97.

41. "Vices de l'ancienne constitution et avantages de la nouvelle," SHAT, 1 M 1790, 14. See also Bien, "Army in the French Enlightenment"; and Blaufarb, *French Army*, 12–45, 33–37 (esp.).

42. Latreille, *L'œuvre militaire de la révolution*, 98–102.
43. Ibid., 98–108; Blaufarb, *French Army*, 30–31.
44. Despite recognizing the need for these measures, Guibert expressed his personal distaste for them: "If I take the regiment I shall vegetate there for six months, and the inevitable expense will be an embarrassment to me; I shall have neither the type of occupation nor the activity which suit me." Guibert to Lespinasse, [Mar.] 1776, Lespinasse, *Love Letters*, 508.
45. Groffier, *Le stratège des lumières*, 179; Guibert to Lespinasse, [winter 1776], [Apr. 1776], Lespinasse, *Love Letters*, 507–10, 512–13.
46. Colin, *L'infanterie au XVIIIe siècle*, 135–84; Quimby, *Background of Napoleonic Warfare*, 205–209; Johann Ernst von Pirch, "Mémoire raisonné sur le parties les plus essentielles de la tactique," SHAT, 1 M 1712. Pirch's memoir was published later as *Instruction que le roi a fait expédier pour régler l'exercice de ses troupes d'infanterie* (1776). See also Colin, *L'infanterie au XVIIIe siècle*, 98–136.
47. Quimby, *Background of Napoleonic Warfare*, 205; Guibert to Lespinasse, [Mar. 1776], [winter 1776], [winter 1776, esp.], Lespinasse, *Love Letters*, 505, 507, 510–11; Lauerma, *Guibert*, 92–97.
48. Guibert, *Essai général de tactique*, 2:109, 184–90; Latreille, *L'œuvre militaire de la révolution*, 114–18. See also Duffy, *Military Experience in the Age of Reason*, 96–103.
49. Roche, *France in the Enlightenment*, 283–84; Van Kley, *Damiens Affair*; Foucault, *Discipline and Punish*, 3–72. On 5 January 1757 Damiens stabbed Louis XV with a small knife, drawing blood but not seriously wounding the king. Damiens was imprisoned and brutally executed in March. He was first tortured with burning pokers and hot sulfur, then quartered by tying each limb to a horse. The last proved ineffective, requiring the executioner to manually separate Damiens's limbs with an axe. Following the dismemberment, his torso was burnt at the stake. While this treatment was in keeping with traditional punishment for regicide, it proved horrific to many in the large crowd who witnessed it. Perhaps the most famous record of the event comes from Giacomo Girolamo Casanova, who recorded "the horrors [that] are an offense to our common humanity" in *Memoirs*, 5:32–34. See also Breton, *Pièces originales et procédures du procès fait à Robert-François Damiens*; Doyle, *Jansenism*, 65; and especially Van Kley, *Damiens Affair*.
50. Running the gauntlet was a procedure whereby an offending soldier was made to walk slowly between two lines of the other soldiers of his unit. They would beat him, often severely, as punishment for his offense. The goal of the punishment was to establish a corporate basis for discipline by involving the entire unit in both the crime and the punishment. Duffy, *Military Experience in the Age of Reason*, 96–103.
51. Guibert to Lespinasse, [Nov.] 1775, [Dec.] 1775, [Mar. 1776], Lespinasse, *Love Letters*, 449, 453, 505.
52. Guibert to Lespinasse, [Mar.] 1776, [Apr.] 1776 (esp.), ibid., 507, 510–11; Lespinasse to Guibert, 10 Nov. 1775, ibid., 441.

53. Groffier, *Le stratège des lumières*, 163–64; Toulongeon, "Notice historique de Jacques-Antoine-Hippolyte Guibert," 23–28. See also Cottret, *La révolution américaine*; Jourdan, *La révolution, une exception française?*; Merlant, *La France et la guerre de l'indépendance américaine*; and Sagnac, *La fin de l'ancien régime et la révolution américaine*. These works contain arguments for French support of the American Revolution, contending that it embodied the principles of the Enlightenment and also presented an opportunity for France to strike back at Britain for its defeat in 1763.
54. "Mémoire sur les affaires présentes," "Expédition d'Angleterre de 1779," and "Notes de Lecture du comte de Guibert," SHAT, 1 M 1792, 4, 11, 12; Groffier, *Le stratège des lumières*, 163–66.
55. Latreille, *L'œuvre militaire de la révolution*, 119–34.
56. Blaufarb, *French Army*, 33–35. Montbarey castigates Saint-Germain's "germanisme." See *Mémoires autographes*, 3:289. See also Girard, *Les cahiers*, 19–21; Saint-Germain, *Mémoires et commentaires*, 258–64; and L. Ségur, *Memoirs and Recollections*, 1:125–34.
57. See Doniol, *Histoire de la participation de la France à l'établissement des Etats-Unis d'Amérique*.
58. Several documents in SHAT, 1 M 1792, contain these memoranda. See especially "Mémoire sur les affaires présentes," "Expédition d'Angleterre de 1779," and "Notes de Lecture du comte de Guibert," ibid., 4, 11, 12. The first notes that "the revolution [in America] was inevitable because the two states were separated by an ocean of two-thousand leagues." Interestingly, "revolution" originally read "separation" before Guibert scratched it out and replaced it.
59. Groffier, *Le stratège des lumières*, 167.
60. "Solde et l'entretien des troupes," SHAT, 1 M 1791, 16; Guibert to Lespinasse, [winter 1776], Lespinasse, *Love Letters*, 508; Doniol, *Histoire de la participation de la France à l'établissement des Etats-Unis d'Amérique*, 2:652–52; Véri, *Journal*, 1:436–37; L. Ségur, *Memoirs and Recollections*, 1:128–29.
61. Saint-Germain, *Mémoires et commentaires*, 258–63. Ségur tempers his account by noting that "all such as admired the German discipline with as much enthusiasm as they had before displayed in favor of the English fashions, now contended that, with the strokes of the flat of a sabre, our army would shortly arrive at as high a pitch of perfection as that of the great Frederick; whilst their opponents considered it only as degrading humiliation, altogether incompatible with French honor. A third party expressed only surprise and doubt." See P. Ségur, *Memoirs and Recollections*, 1:123.
62. Lauerma, *Guibert*, 97–99.
63. Ibid. See also Saint-Germain, *Mémoires et commentaires*, 258–63; and P. Ségur, *Memoirs and Recollections*, 1:123–25.
64. See Latreille, *L'œuvre militaire de la révolution*, 115–31; Lespinasse to Condorcet, 9 Oct. 1775, Lespinasse, *Lettres inédites*, 178–79.

Chapter 6

1. She laments "the effects of constant opium" in Lespinasse to Guibert, 3 Oct. 1774, Lespinasse, *Love Letters*, 202.
2. P. Ségur, *Julie de Lespinasse*, 377–90 (quote, 384).
3. Guibert to Lespinasse, winter 1776, Lespinasse, *Love Letters*, 502.
4. Guibert to Lespinasse, May 1776, ibid., 518.
5. Lespinasse to Guibert, Saturday, Tuesday, May 1776, ibid., 519, 520. Count Villeneuve-Guibert notes that "this, in all probability, was the last letter Mlle. de Lespinasse wrote." See *Julie de Lespinasse*, 520n1.
6. P. Ségur, *Julie de Lespinasse*, 384–401; Guibert, "Elegy of Eliza," in Lespinasse, *Love Letters*, 310.
7. See d'Alembert, "Aux mânes de Mademoiselle de Lespinasse." This document is perhaps the most poignant of the entire affair, as it reveals d'Alembert's devastation, not only at Lespinasse's death but also his learning the truth of her affairs with Guibert and the marquis de Mora.
8. See Pellisson-Fontanier et al., *Histoire de l'Académie française*; and Roche, *France in the Enlightenment*, 102–108.
9. "Jean-François de la Harpe," in *Biographie universelle*, 22:541–49. See also Todd, *Voltaire's Disciple*. For the aforementioned plays, see volume 3 of Jean-François de la Harpe, *Œuvres choisies et posthumes*, 4 vols. (Paris: 1806).
10. "Jean-François de la Harpe," in *Biographie universelle*, 541–49; Todd, *Voltaire's Disciple*; Grimm et al., *Correspondance littéraire, philosophique, et critique*. The great literary critic Charles-Augustin Sainte-Beuve places la Harpe among the greatest teachers and critics of seventeenth-century French literature. See Sainte-Beuve, *Etude littéraire sur Chateaubriand*, 332–33.
11. Guibert, *Eloge de Maréchal de Catinat*; Guibert, *Eloge historique de Michel de l'Hôpital*; Abrantès, *Une soirée*, 63–65. Laure Martin de Permon was born in 1784 to a matrilineal line of the ancient Greek family, the Comnenes, and entered the volatile Parisian society of the Revolution as a young woman. She claims that Napoleon Bonaparte himself requested her hand in marriage in 1794; it was later given to Jean-Androche Junot, future general of the empire and duc d'Abrantès. After Napoleon's fall, she devoted her remaining decades to writing histories of the late Old Regime, of which she evinced a marked fascination. See ibid. and Abrantès, *Mémoires*.
12. Lespinasse to Condorcet, 28 Sept. [1775], Lespinasse, *Lettres inédites*, 175; Mettra, *Correspondance secrète, politique, et littéraire*, 5:401–402; Lauerma, *Guibert*, 116. See also Guibert, *Eloge historique de Michel de l'Hôpital*.
13. Colin, *L'infanterie au XVIIIe siècle: la tactique*, 225–40; Quimby, *Background of Napoleonic Warfare*, 199–209.
14. Guibert, *Essai général de tactique*, esp. 1:29–47, 90–93.
15. Mesnil-Durand, *Projet d'un ordre français en tactique*.
16. Mesnil-Durand, *Fragments de tactique*.
17. Ibid., 17–23, 45–48, 65–107. See also Quimby, *Background of Napoleonic Warfare*, 210–32.

18. Quimby, *Background of Napoleonic Warfare*, 17–187 (esp. 24–31, 65–107).
19. Mesnil-Durand, *Fragments de tactique*, 108–87.
20. Middlekauff, *Glorious Cause*, 153–332. See also Buffington, *Second Hundred Year War*; and Gipson, *British Empire before the American Revolution*.
21. See Bemis, *Diplomacy of the American Revolution*; Dull, *Diplomatic History of the American Revolution*; Gipson, *Triumphant Empire*; Gipson, *Coming of the Revolution*; and Stinchcombe, *American Revolution and the French Alliance*.
22. See Spurlin, *French Enlightenment in America*; May, *Enlightenment in America*; and Tocqueville, *Democracy in America*.
23. See "Mémoire sur les affaires présentes," "Expédition d'Angleterre de 1779," and "Notes de Lecture du comte de Guibert," SHAT, 1 M 1792, 4, 11, 12.
24. See D. Palmer, *George Washington's Military Genius*, 103–58.
25. Middlekauff, *Glorious Cause*, 363–433. On Saratoga, see Elting, *Battles of Saratoga*; and Mintz, *Generals of Saratoga*.
26. See Guibert, *Essai général de tactique*, 1:90–93, 2:130–229.
27. Montbarey, *Mémoires autographes*, 3:287; L. Ségur, *Memoirs and Recollections*, 1:127. See also Colin, *L'infanterie au XVIIIe siècle*, 213–18; and Latreille, *L'œuvre militaire de la révolution*, 135–53.
28. The official records of the Vaussieux camp are contained in SHAT, 1 M 1819. Of the approximately 250 documents in the carton, at least 150 are letters from Broglie to Montbarey discussing issues of supply, food, and finance. See especially "Correspondance entre Broglie et Montbarey, Mai–Juin 1778," ibid., 36–57. No official narrative of the camp exists, though Jean Colin provides an excellent narrative epitomized from extant sources. See *L'infanterie au XVIIIe siècle*, 213–45. Robert Quimby largely reproduces Colin's work in English. See *Background of Napoleonic Warfare*, 223–48. The last is the most recent and useful source for the exercises, particularly the tactical debate.
29. See "Correspondance entre Broglie et Montbarey, Mai–Juin 1778," SHAT, 1 M 1819, 36–57; and "Mémos et lettres," ibid., 59–80.
30. See, for example, letters from Broglie to Montbarey, May–Aug. 1778, ibid., 45–50, 63, 94–109 (esp.). These letters intermittently address an issue that much vexed the general in the summer concerning possible legal action against an officer named "La Rozière," probably Louis-François Carlet, marquis de la Rozière.
31. See Latreille, *L'œuvre militaire de la révolution*, 75–90.
32. Montbarey to Broglie, July–Aug. 1778, SHAT, 1 M 1819, 113. This contains an order whereby Montbarey grants Broglie the authority to decide the doctrinal issue as he sees fit. See also communications from Montbarey to Broglie, May–Aug. 1778, ibid., 77, 79, 97, 113–14, 125–26.
33. Quimby, *Background of Napoleonic Warfare*, 233–41. See also June–Aug. 1778, *Mercure de France* (Paris: Chez Panckoucke, 1778), 110–12, 349–50.

34. Broglie to Montbarey, 5 Sept. 1778, SHAT, 1 M 1819, 173; Moreau, *Mes souvenirs*, 1:314; Broglie to Montbarey, 7 Sept. 1778, SHAT, 1 M 1819, 178.
35. Broglie to Montbarey, 12 Sept. 1778, SHAT, 1 M 1819, 191; Wimpffen, "Lettre de Wimpffen," ibid., 20. See also Colin, *L'infanterie au XVIIIe siècle*, 213-45; and Quimby, *Background of Napoleonic Warfare*, 223-48.
36. Broglie to Montbarey, 12 Sept. 1778, SHAT, 1 M 1819, 191; Wimpffen, "Lettre de Wimpffen," ibid., 20. See also Colin, *L'infanterie au XVIIIe siècle*, 213-45; and Quimby, *Background of Napoleonic Warfare*, 223-48.
37. Broglie to Montbarey, 14 Sept. 1778, SHAT, 1 M 1819, 192; Rochambeau, *Mémoires*, 1:228-29; Wimpffen, "Lettre de Wimpffen," SHAT, 1 M 1819, 20.
38. Quimby, *Background of Napoleonic Warfare*, 236-37.
39. Ibid.; Wimpffen, "Lettre de Wimpffen," SHAT, 1 M 1819, 20.
40. Broglie to Montbarey, 18 Sept. 1778, SHAT, 1 M 1819, 209; Rochambeau, *Mémoires*, 1:230-31; Quimby, *Background of Napoleonic Warfare*, 238-41.
41. Broglie, "Ordre du 20 au 21 Septembre 1778," SHAT, 1 M 1819, 226. This and the following cited documents are the only complete and detailed accounts of the exercises in the official record.
42. Ibid., 9-20.
43. Broglie, "Ordre du 24 Septembre 1778," ibid., 231; Broglie to Montbarey, 25 Sept. 1778, ibid., 242; Broglie, "Manœuvres exécutées le 28 septembre 1778 au camp de Vaussieux," ibid., 255. As many of the exercises of the period were concerned with infantry tactics, combined-arms maneuvers rarely occurred. See SHAT, 1 M 1812, for records of other camps held during the period.
44. Montbarey to Broglie, 15, 17 Sept. 1778, ibid., 196, 203.
45. Bohan, *Examen critique du militaire français*, 1:9, 233-34, 297-98; Montbarey, *Mémoires autographes*, 3:287.
46. Broglie to Montbarey, 18, 25, 28 Sept. 1778, SHAT, 1 M 1819, 209, 242 (quote), 258; Rochambeau, *Mémoires*, 1:231.
47. Rochambeau, *Mémoires*, 1:231; Wimpffen, "Lettre de Wimpffen," SHAT, 1 M 1819, 20; Colin, *L'infanterie au XVIIIe siècle*, 243-44.
48. Colin, *L'infanterie au XVIIIe siècle*, 243-44; Quimby, *Background of Napoleonic Warfare*, 233-48.
49. See Bachaumont, *Mémoires secrets*, 14:131-32; and especially Moreau, *Mes souvenirs*, 1:314. Moreau opines that Guibert's advocacy led to Broglie's embarrassment at court, perhaps costing him a ministerial position.
50. See Ferling, *Almost a Miracle*, 477-539; and Lumpkin, *From Savannah to Yorktown*. Sartine remained in office until late 1780, whereupon Charles-Eugène-Gabriel de la Croix, marquis de Castries, took charge of the department, holding the post until after the end of the war. See "Charles-Eugène-Gabriel de la Croix, maréchal de Castries,"

in *Biographie universelle*, 7:190–91; and "Antoine-Raimond-Jean-Gualbert-Gabriel de Sartine," ibid., 38:36–38.
51. Groffier, *Le stratège des lumières*, 164–96.
52. Ibid. See also Broglie to Montbarey, 20, 26 June 1778, SHAT, 1 M 1819, 60, 71.
53. Guibert, *Défense du système de guerre moderne*.
54. Ibid., 1:2–3. In referring to himself as "not a maker of a system," Guibert did not demur from creating a doctrinal system. Rather, he meant that he was not building a polemical system in the vein of Pirch or Mesnil-Durand.
55. Ibid., 1:1–18.
56. Ibid., 1:23–24. The phrase "accidental formation" recurs numerous times in Guibert's analysis of l'ordre profond throughout the work.
57. Ibid., 1:19–75.
58. Ibid., 1:77–89, 1:90.
59. Ibid., 1:90–147, 1:152–61.
60. Ibid., 1:101–25 (quote, 121).
61. Ibid., 1:119–25, 170–212.
62. Ibid., 1:212–20.
63. Ibid., 1:218; Ayton et al., *Battle of Crécy*; Barker, *Agincourt*; Hewitt, *Black Prince's Expedition*. The best survey of the larger conflict remains Sumption, *Hundred Years War*.
64. Guibert, *Défense du système de guerre moderne*, 1:215–24.
65. See Colin, *L'infanterie au XVIIIe siècle*, 213–45; and especially Quimby, *Background of Napoleonic Warfare*, 249–68.
66. Guibert, *Défense du système de guerre moderne*, 2:1–36 (quote, 3), 59–70. See also Guibert, *Essai général de tactique*, vol. 2.
67. Guibert, *Défense du système de guerre moderne*, 2:37–46. On Turenne and his campaign, see Eckberg, *Failure of Louis XIV's Dutch War*; and Lynn, *Wars of Louis XIV*, 105–59.
68. Guibert, *Défense du système de guerre moderne*, 2:47–202. See also Bourcet, *Mémoires historiques sur la guerre*; Bourcet, *Mémoires militaires sur les frontières de la France, du Piémont, et la Savoie*.
69. Guibert, *Défense du système de guerre moderne*, 2:209–34, (quote, 212).
70. See Colin, *L'éducation militaire de Napoléon*, 1–108 (esp. 107); and Lauerma, *Guibert*, 155–67.
71. R. Palmer, "Frederick the Great, Guibert, Bülow," 112.
72. Guibert, *Essai général de tactique*, 1:xiv.
73. Lauerma, *Guibert*, 168–74.
74. Dumouriez, *Life*, 1:432. Dumouriez also argues that Guibert "procured himself many enemies in consequence of the regulations he drew up because he wished to change everything, and he prepared the way for the Revolution by disgusting the army." Ibid., 2:172.
75. Lauerma, *Guibert*, 97–102.

NOTES TO PAGES 140–45   235

Chapter 7

1. Guibert, *Voyages de Guibert*, 5.
2. See, for example, Voltaire to René-Nicolas-Charles Augustin de Maupeou, 14 Aug. 1774, Voltaire, *Œuvres complètes de Voltaire*, 17:57–59.
3. Darnton, *Literary Underground*, 15, 41–147. See also Mason, *Darnton Debate*.
4. Goodman, *Republic of Letters*, 131; J. Necker, *Treatise on the Administration of the Finances of France*. On Suzanne Necker's salon, see Bredin, *Une singulière famille*. On Jacques Necker's career, see Harris, *Necker*; and Harris, *Necker and the Revolution of 1789*.
5. J. Necker, *Compte rendu au roi*; See also Harris, *Necker*; Harris, *Necker and the Revolution of 1789*; and Swann and Félix, *Crisis of the Absolute Monarchy*.
6. J. Necker, *Compte rendu au roi*; See also Harris, *Necker*; Harris, *Necker and the Revolution of 1789*; and Swann and Félix, *Crisis of the Absolute Monarchy*.
7. Bredin, *Une singulière famille*; Goldsmith and Goodman, *Going Public*; Goodman, *Republic of Letters*, 53–54, 80–82, 100–107; Haussonville, *Le salon de Madame Necker*.
8. Groffier, *Le stratège des lumières*, 249–64, 277–92.
9. Suard, *Essais de mémoires*, 141; "Jean-Baptiste-Antoine Suard," in *Biographie universelle*, 40:373–77.
10. "Jean-Baptiste-Antoine Suard," in *Biographie universelle*, 40:373–77; Suard, *Correspondance inédite*; Suard, *Essais de mémoires*. See also Bertaut, *Egéries du XVIIIe siècle*.
11. Groffier, *Le stratège des lumières*, 297–301.
12. No author confirms an affair between Guibert and Montsauge at this time, but Groffier allows for such. See ibid.
13. "Alexandrine-Louise Boutinon de Courcelles, comtesse de Guibert," in *Biographie universelle*, 18:86–90; Jaurgain, *Notice sur les familles Vallet et Villeneuve-Guibert*, 51. Appolline married François-Réné Vallet, comte de Villeneuve, in 1795 and served as a *dame du palais* to Hortense, queen of Holland, during the Napoleonic period. Her husband became a prominent politican in the Second Empire and, more importantly for present purposes, inaugurated the Villeneuve family as custodians of Guibert's legacy. His descendants changed the family name to Villeneuve-Guibert and produced edited volumes of Guibert's work for generations.
14. Craveri, *Madame du Deffand and Her World*; Deffand to Voltaire, 3 Jan. 1774, Deffand, *Lettres*, 4:380–82.
15. Deffand, *Lettres*, 2:388n1.
16. Louis XVI to Marie-Antoinette, 26 Sept. 1781, in *Correspondance secrète inédite sur Louis XVI, Marie-Antoinette, la cour et la ville de 1777 à 1792*, 2 vols. (Paris: Plon, 1866), 1:435–36.
17. Niox, *Hôtel des Invalides*; Groffier, *Le stratège des lumières*, 265–73.
18. For example, see Guibert, *Voyages de Guibert*, 224.
19. Ibid., 37–54, 88 (quote), 161–219, 301–51. Several documents in the Guibert Papers also contain records of his voyages during the period,

chiefly 1783–84. See "Mémoire concernant un projet de réunion des canonniers Invalides avec les gardes côtes," "Observations pour mon [père]," "Mémoire sur les compagnies détachées d'Invalides et sur les soldats pensionnés de tout espace," "Mémoire sur les forts et chevaux du Royaume," and "Papier concernant les Invalides," SHAT, 1 M 1791, 23–29.
20. Guibert, *Voyages de Guibert*, 342. See also "Inspection des compagnies détachées des Invalides dans les provinces du Royaume," SHAT, 1 M 1791, 55.
21. Guibert, *Les Gracques*, in *Œuvres dramatiques*, 97–160. In 1775 Jacques Turgot eliminated the fixed price on grain in an effort to improve the kingdom's economy. Prices thus rose drastically, and riots broke out across northeastern France; they continued for several days until forcibly put down. This "flour war" demonstrated the danger of mob violence in relation to grain prices, which would prove a significant spark for the Revolution. See Doyle, *Oxford History of the French Revolution*, 21–22.
22. Grimm et al., *Correspondance littéraire, philosophique, et critique*, 12:420–21.
23. Guibert, *Anne de Boleyn*, in *Oeuvres dramatiques*, 161–242; Groffier, *Le stratège des lumières*, 145–47.
24. Jean-Paul Charnay, "Amour et inceste dans *Anne de Boleyn*—ou la catharsis de Guibert: fragments de la tragédie présentés par Jean-Paul Charnay," in *Guibert ou le soldat philosophe*, 41–62. See also P. Ségur, *Julie de Lespinasse*, 32–65.
25. La Harpe, *Œuvres*, 12:304.
26. Guibert, "Histoire de la constitution militaire de France depuis la fondation de la monarchie jusqu'à nos jours," SHAT, 1 M 1791, 20; Groffier, *Le stratège des lumières*, 252–58.
27. Guibert, "Histoire de la constitution militaire de France," 2.
28. Ibid., 12–13.
29. Necker, *Nouveaux mélanges extraits*, 1:273–75.
30. Abrantès, *Une soirée*, 63–65; Herold, *Mistress to an Age*, 89 (quote); Staël-Holstein, "Eloge de M. de Guibert," 348; Moreau, *Mes souvenirs*, 1:526. Germaine proved a leading figure in French society during the Napoleonic period. She also played a significant role in the cementing of Guibert's legacy. See Fairweather, *Madame de Staël*; and Herold, *Mistress to an Age*. On the possible romance, see especially Mrs. Phillips to Mrs. Arblay, 3 Apr. 1793, in Arblay, *Diary and Letters*, 5:188–89: "M. Guibert, an author and one who was, Madame de S[taël] told me, passionately in love with her before she married."
31. Quoted in Fairweather, *Madame de Staël*, 73.
32. See Groffier, *Le stratège des lumières*, 290. Groffier suggests that Guibert provided the chief inspiration for Staël's *Zulmé*.
33. Guibert and Ségur's son, Louis-Philippe, comte de Ségur, valued their relationship. "I was indebted, young as I was, for the friendship of [Jean la Rond] d'Alembert, of abbé [Guillaume-Thomas-François] Raynal,

[and] of the comte de Guibert." L. Ségur, *Memoirs and Recollections*, 1:55-56.
34. Latreille, *L'œuvre militaire de la révolution*, 171-236.
35. Bien, "Army in the French Enlightenment"; Bien et al., *Caste, Class, and Profession in Old Regime France*; Bien and Rovet, "La réaction aristocratique avant 1789"; Latreille, *L'œuvre militaire de la révolution*, 180-91.
36. Blaufarb, *French Army*, 33-36. See also *Commentaires des mémoires de M. le comte de Saint-Germain*, 152.
37. Bien and Rovet, "La réaction aristocratique avant 1789," 23-29; Blaufarb, *French Army*, 33-37. See also Johnson, *French Society and the Revolution*; and Smith, *French Nobility in the Eighteenth Century*.
38. See Soboul, *Sans-Culottes*.
39. Bien and Rovet, "La réaction aristocratique avant 1789"; Smith, *French Nobility in the Eighteenth Century*.
40. Bien, "Army in the French Enlightenment," 75-84.
41. See Bien and Godneff, "Les offices, les corps et le crédit d'état."
42. Ibid.; Latreille, *L'œuvre militaire de la révolution*, 76-80.
43. Bien and Rovet, "La réaction aristocratique avant 1789," 515-19.
44. Ibid.
45. Lauerma, *Guibert*, 90.
46. "Antoine-Léonard Thomas," in *Biographie universelle*, 41:401-406; Pellisson-Fontanier et al., *Histoire de l'Académie française*.
47. Groffier, *Le stratège des lumières*, 293-94.
48. Ibid., 288-90.
49. Grimm et al., *Correspondance littéraire, philosophique, et critique*, 13:34, 295. See also Pellisson-Fontanier et al., *Histoire de l'Académie française*, 239-51; Bachaumont, *Mémoires secrets*, 31:101-105; and la Harpe, *Correspondance littéraire*, 5:41-53.
50. Bachaumont, *Mémoires secrets*, 31:102-106; Grimm et al., *Correspondance littéraire, philosophique, et critique*, 13:33-45; la Harpe, *Correspondance littéraire*, 5:42-52; Pierre-Victor, baron Malouet, *Mémoires*, 2 vols. (Paris: Plon, 1874), 1:194.
51. Groffier, *Le stratège des lumières*, 296-97.
52. Ibid.
53. Ibid.; Abrantès, *Mémoires*, 2:320.
54. See, for example, Guibert, *Journal d'un voyage en Allemagne*, 2:276, which closes his 1773 voyage to Germany with a hymn to Nature.
55. "Charles-Benoît Guibert," *Biographie universelle*, 18:86; Guibert, *Eloge du roi de Prusse* (London: 1787).
56. Darnton, *Forbidden Bestsellers*; Darnton, *Literary Underground*. See also Mason, *Darnton Debate*.

Chapter 8

1. For a penetrating analysis of the monarchy's need for, and loss of, the monopoly on force during the early Revolution, see S. Scott, *Response of the Royal Army*.

2. Doyle, *Origins of the French Revolution*, 41–114 (esp. 43–56), 115–38; Lefebvre, *Coming of the French Revolution*, 7–40. Collins, *State in Early Modern France*, 53; Lefebvre, *French Revolution*, 1:19–53.
3. Flammermont, *Le chancelier Maupeou et les Parlements*; Lefebvre, *French Revolution*, 1:97–115.
4. Egret, *French Pre-Revolution*, 6–19; Hardman, *Overture to Revolution*; Lefebvre, *Coming of the French Revolution*, 21–40.
5. Egret, *French Pre-Revolution*, 12–19; Hardman, *Overture to Revolution*, 20–55.
6. Hardman, *Overture to Revolution*, 148–81.
7. Ibid., 29–40. See also Perrin, *Le cardinal de Loménie de Brienne*; and Schama, *Citizens*, 236–41.
8. Latreille, *L'œuvre militaire de la révolution*, 231–35; "Note pour monsieur le maréchal de Ségur," SHAT, 1 M 1790, 1.
9. See "Mémoire servant à la fois d'intruction et résumé au plan général de réforme du département de la guerre," "Plan général, Bureaux (Plan général)," and "Idées particulières," SHAT, 1 M 1790, 4, 5, 6, 10. Albert Latreille argues that Guibert authored all three and presented them to the king in Ségur's name. See *L'œuvre militaire de la révolution*, 231–35.
10. Doyle, *Origins of the French Revolution*, 96–114; Egret, *French Pre-Revolution*, 40–41; Witt, *Une invasion prussienne en Hollande en 1787*, 170–220.
11. Doyle, *Origins of the French Revolution*, 96–114; Egret, *French Pre-Revolution*, 40–41; Witt, *Une invasion prussienne en Hollande en 1787*, 170–220.
12. Doyle, *Origins of the French Revolution*, 96–114; Egret, *French Pre-Revolution*, 40–41; Witt, *Une invasion prussienne en Hollande en 1787*, 170–220.
13. S. Scott, *Response of the Royal Army*, 1–34. See also Murphy, *Diplomatic Retreat of France and Public Opinion on the Eve of the Revolution*, 80–96.
14. "Note particulière pour M. l'Archevêque de Toulouse," SHAT, 1 M 1790, 3; "Bureau du S. d'Aurange," ibid., 11.
15. "Instruction du roi pour le Conseil de la Guerre," n.d., ibid., 14, p. 10. This document illustrates Louis XVI's nature as a collaborator on reforms rather than a strong absolutist monarch driving or leading them.
16. Ibid.; Pierre Victor, baron de Besenval de Brünstatt, *Mémoires*, 4 vols. (Paris: Buisson, 1805), 3:294.
17. Besenval, *Mémoires*, 3:294; Esterhazy, *Mémoires*, 208.
18. See "Proposition au roi relative au Conseil de la Guerre and Résumé de la première division du travail du Conseil de la Guerre," n.d., SHAT, 1 M 1790, 16, p. 18.
19. "Résumé de la première division du travail du Conseil de la Guerre," ibid., 18, p. 5.
20. The supernumerary rank of colonel en second was ostensibly created decades earlier to provide an education for future colonels in the art and

science of commanding their own regiments. In practice it became a rank purchased simply for the prestige associated with the military and served no practical use in training the officer or commanding the army. The replacement of colonels en second with majors en second returned the supernumerary position to its origins as an educational position, requiring all officers to spend the five-year term apprenticed to a major to learn that officer's responsibilities.

21. Latreille, L'œuvre militaire de la révolution, 255–62, Lauerma, Guibert, 195–97. See "Première séance—rapport pour Octobre 1787," "Infanterie, Séance du 20 Novembre," and "Mémoire du Conseil de la Guerre à sa majesté sur les places des colonels-généraux et autres changes d'état-major," SHAT, 1 M 1790, 22, 23, 24.
22. See "Notes relatives aux officiers généraux employés dans les divisions, Maison du Roi," and "Mémoire concernant les gardes francisées," SHAT, 1 M 1790, 44–46. See also Latreille, L'œuvre militaire de la révolution, 239–42; and Lauerma, Guibert, 197–200.
23. Lauerma, Guibert, 200–201.
24. "Commandements dans les provinces," SHAT, 1 M 1790, 30. The zones were Flandres et Hainaut; Evêchés; Alsace; Lorraine; Franche-Comté; Dauphiné; Provence; Corsé; Languedoc; Roussillon; Guyenne; Poitou, Saintonge, et Aunis; Bretagne; Normandie; Picardie, Boulonnais, Calaisis, et Artois; Bourgogne; and the cours de la Loire et provinces de l'intérieur. Ibid., 4–5, 15. See also Latreille, L'œuvre militaire de la révolution, 262; and Miot de Melito, Mémoires, 1:2.
25. Latreille, L'œuvre militaire de la révolution, 262–66; "Rapport à faire au Conseil de la Guerre sur la formation de l'Armée," SHAT, 1 M 1790, 25; Lauerma, Guibert, 203–205. For details on the formation, deployment, and population of the divisions, see "Commandements dans les provinces," SHAT, 1 M 1790, 30.
26. "Commandements dans les provinces," 10–11, 12.
27. "Instruction du roi pour le Conseil de la Guerre," SHAT, 1 M 1790, 14.
28. Colin, L'infanterie au XVIIIe siècle, 311–30; Quimby, Background of Napoleonic Warfare, 301. See Saldern, Eléments de la tactique de l'infanterie.
29. Quimby, Background of Napoleonic Warfare, 302–303; Latreile, L'œuvre militaire de la révolution, 245–57; Saldern, Eléments de la tactique de l'infanterie, 5, 37, 253; Colin, L'infanterie au XVIIIe siècle, 257–59.
30. Quimby, Background of Napoleonic Warfare, 302–303; Latreile, L'œuvre militaire de la révolution, 245–57; Saldern, Eléments de la tactique de l'infanterie, 5, 37, 253; Colin, L'infanterie au XVIIIe siècle, 257–59.
31. Quimby, Background of Napoleonic Warfare, 302–303; Latreile, L'œuvre militaire de la révolution, 245–57; Saldern, Eléments de la tactique de l'infanterie, 5, 37, 253; Colin, L'infanterie au XVIIIe siècle, 257–59.
32. "Rapport à faire au conseil de la guerre sur la formation de l'Armée," "Armée—Infanterie," and "Commandements dans les provinces,"

SHAT, 1 M 1790, 25, 26, 30. See also Latreille, *L'oeuvre militaire de la révolution*, 269–84.
33. See Bouillé, *Souvenirs et fragments*, 1:83–88; and Miot de Melito, *Mémoires*, 1:2–4. Bouillé notes "un trait . . . insubordonné" (an insubordinate sense) at the camp, and Miot de Melito cleverly draws an allusion between the Swiss regiments and Prussian discipline, pronouncing the foreign units the best at the new system. This casts doubt on its "French" nature and thus its propriety.
34. "17 July 1788, Metz," SHAT, 1 M 1812, 2. This document, as the ones that follow, were drawn up in the summer of 1788 as guidelines for the camp.
35. Several loose documents in SHAT, 1 M 1812, detail these plans and maneuvers.
36. "Décision du roi relative au camp de Metz," ibid.
37. Ibid., 289–303. See also Esterhazy, *Mémoires*, 208; and Hardman, *Overture to Revolution*, 199–284.
38. Doyle, *Origins of the French Revolution*, 15–138; Hardman, *Overture to Revolution*, 257–84; Lefebvre, *French Revolution*, 1:102–15.
39. Doyle, *Origins of the French Revolution*, 15–138; Hardman, *Overture to Revolution*, 257–84; Lefebvre, *French Revolution*, 1:102–15. See also Doyle, *Oxford History of the French Revolution*, 86–111; and Garrett, *Estates-General of 1789*.
40. Guibert, *Projet de discours d'un citoyen, aux trois Ordres de l'assemblée de Berry*, 17–18.
41. Doyle, *Oxford History of the French Revolution*, 86–111; Doyle, *Origins of the French Revolution*, 128–38.
42. See Dawson, *Revolutionary Demands*.
43. Doyle, *Oxford History of the French Revolution*, 86–111; Doyle, *Origins of the French Revolution*, 128–38.
44. Allonville, *Mémoires secrets*, 1:135; Lauerma, *Guibert*, 217–19.
45. Allonville, *Mémoires secrets*, 1:135; Lauerma, *Guibert*, 217–19.
46. See Charles-Elie, marquis de Ferrières, to madame de Ferrières, 26 Apr. 1789, in Ferrières, *Correspondance inédite*, 29–30. Ferrières connects Guibert's fall to the dismissal of Necker from the Ministry of Finance, which would not occur until July 1789; indications before the May meeting of the Estates-General were that he would not long survive.
47. Jacques-Antoine-Hippolyte, comte de Guibert, *Précis de ce qui s'est passé à mon égard à l'Assemblée du Berry*; Lauerma, *Guibert*, 222–25; Guibert, *Projet de discours d'un citoyen aux trois Ordres de l'Assemblée de Berry*.
48. See SHAT, 1 M 1791, 31. This is a letter written, presumably to Guibert, in February 1789 and criticizing the Council of War for perpetuating "un régime vicieux dans tous les points et qu'il est impossible de défendre" (a vicious regime on all points and that is impossible to defend).
49. Groffier, *Le stratège des lumières*, 336; Lauerma, *Guibert*, 227.
50. Guibert, *Mémoire adressé au public et à l'armée*.
51. Guibert, *De la force publique*, 5–28.

52. Ibid., 30–45.
53. Ibid., 5–20, 30–45.
54. Ibid., 5–25.
55. Ibid., 9–10.
56. Doyle, *Oxford History of the French Revolution*, 118–39; Lefebvre, *French Revolution*, 1:129–52.
57. Guibert, *De la force publique*, 30–41.
58. Ibid., 40–50.
59. Ibid., 51–62.
60. Ibid., 53–61.
61. Ibid., 62.
62. Lauerma, *Guibert*, 247; Toulongeon, "Notice historique de Jacques-Antoine-Hippolyte Guibert," 70–85.

Chapter 9

1. See, for example, Carnot, *Mémoires*; Robespierre, *Speeches*; and Saint-Cyr, *Mémoires*.
2. See, for example, Bertaud, *Army of the French Revolution*; Jaurès, *Histoire socialiste de la révolution française*; Michelet, *Histoire de la révolution française*; Mathiez, *La victoire en l'an II*; Soboul, *Les soldats de l'an II*; Sorel, *L'Europe et la révolution française*; and *Napoleon and the French Revolution*. Bonaparte lamented that "the works of Folard, . . . Guibert, . . . and several other authors are only incomplete compilations and too voluminous to be read with any profit. . . . We have not yet a single work which can with justice be called the *Art of War*. We possess a masterpiece entitled *Le Réglement sur les manœuvres de l'infanterie du 1er Août, 1791*. Any officer who would employ himself in forming a companion to this work, by collecting in a similar manner an account of whatever related to the plans and operations of an army in campaign, would be incontestably entitled to the gratitude of every military man." Quoted in Sarrazin, *Confession of General Buonaparté*, 142. See also Marmont, *Spirit of Military Institutions*, 179; and Napoleon, *Memoirs of the History of France during the Reign of Napoleon*, 3:327–28.
3. Brown, *War, Revolution, and the Bureaucratic State*, 19–23; Colin, *L'infanterie au XVIIIe siècle*, 260–78; Ross, *From Flintlock to Rifle*, 51–56.
4. Lacroix, *Rules and Regulations*, 169–290.
5. Ibid.
6. Quimby, *Background of Napoleonic Warfare*, 300–307.
7. Saint-Cyr, *Mémoires*, 1:xliii–xlv; Dumas, *Précis des événements militaires ou essais historiques sur les campagnes de 1799 à 1814*, 12:30–32; Morand, *De l'armée selon la Charte et d'après l'expérience des dernières guerres*, 142–47; Pelet, "Essai sur les manœuvres d'un corps d'armée d'infanterie." See also Quimby, *Background of Napoleonic Warfare*, 320–27.
8. François Roguet, "Etude sur l'ordre perpendiculaire," 528.
9. See Colin, *L'infanterie au XVIIIe siècle*, 200–201; Quimby, *Background of Napoleonic Warfare*, 145–231; and SHAT, 1 M 1812 and 1819. Too

much is made of the participation of some elite units in the early riots of the Revolution, particularly elements of the Maison militaire du roi in the attack on the Bastille. Despite the threats of caesarism and a few famous examples of disciplinary lapses like the murder of Gen. Théobald Dillon after a minor defeat in 1792, the bulk of the army retained its professional core and never truly lost its discipline. For in-depth discussions of the problems of discipline early in the Revolution, see Lynn, *Bayonets of the Republic*; and S. Scott, *Response of the Royal Army*. John Money records the dubious discipline and morale of the French armies in 1792, noting that they required a lively fire and defensive entrenchments to prevent breaking. *History of the Campaign of 1792*, 78–86.

10. See, for example, Bricard, *Journal*, 35–36, 71; Dupuis, *La campagne de 1793*, 2:30; Fricasse, *Journal de marche*, 68; Lombard, *Un volontaire de 1792*, 153; Thiébault, *Mémoires*, 5:454–55; and especially Lynn, *Bayonets of the Republic*, 287–300 (table).

11. Marbot, *Memoirs*, 1:131. See also Berthier to Davout, 5 Sept. 1803, Davout, *Correspondance*, 1:6–8; Davout to Napoleon, 8 Oct. 1803, ibid., 24–26; Davout to Napoleon, 12 Mar. 1804, ibid., 66–70; Davout to Napoleon, 24 May 1804, ibid., 82–84; and Davout to Napoleon, 23 Mar. 1805, ibid., 105–109. Marshal Ney describes how his "men were becoming daily more skillful in their evolutions." See Ney, *Memoirs*, 186–231. Scott Bowden provides a well-researched description of the quotidian business at Boulogne. See *Napoleon and Austerlitz*, 11–94.

12. Blanning, *French Revolutionary Wars*; Griffith, *Art of War of Revolutionary France*, 221–22. For the possible origin of Griffith's argument, see "Marshal Ney's Military Studies," in Ney, *Memoirs*, 2:291–384.

13. Blanning, *French Revolutionary Wars*. Forty-nine major battles occurred in Europe from 1703 to 1762, covering the major conflicts of the eighteenth century. Spectacular defeats by armies with massive numerical superiority, like the French at Villafranca or Rossbach, illustrate the folly of using a single deterministic factor as the basis for a historiographical argument. Although Blanning's argument carries some weight during the Revolutionary period, particularly as the French were better able to absorb defeats than their various opponents, the nature of combat throughout the eighteenth century reduced numerical superiority to a minor advantage decisive only if both armies and commanders were of equal ability and quality. See Corvisier, *Dictionary of Military History*; Lynn, *Wars of Louis XIV*; Sutton, *King's Honor and the King's Cardinal*; and Szabo, *Seven Years War in Europe*.

14. Dupuis, *Les opérations militaires sur la Sambre*, 289–92; SHAT, B1, 34. These numbers also appear in Hayworth, "Evolution or Revolution on the Battlefield?," 5, 14.

15. Boycott-Brown, *Road to Rivoli*, 194–96; Chandler, *Campaigns of Napoleon*, 193–99. Despite suffering serious defeats, particularly after 1794, Austria and the other allies matched French manpower in quantity, if perhaps not in quality. For an excellent analysis of the Austrian army

during the period, see Rothenberg, *Napoleon's Greatest Adversaries.* Despite this work, the subject of Allied manpower, both its quantity and its quality, remains largely unexplored in English-language historiography and remains in need of intensive research.

16. Griffith, *Art of War of Revolutionary France,* 221–22; Muir, *Tactics and the Experience of Battle,* 72–74; Rothenberg, *Art of Warfare in the Age of Napoleon,* 117. Open-order shock assaults were used exclusively against fortified positions, usually cities. Soldiers fixed bayonets and deployed in open order, fighting in small teams or as individuals to clear the enemy position. See, for example, Ney, *Memoirs,* 2:282. For a recent example of this ongoing historiographical debate, see Arnold, "Reappraisal of Column versus Line in the Peninsular War."

17. Fricasse, *Journal de marche,* 39. See also Bricard, *Journal,* 146–47, 220–21, 225–30; Colbert, *Le général Auguste Colbert,* 2:15–18, 21, 335–37; Fricasse, *Journal de marche,* 21–22, 32, 90, 114; Leclaire, *Mémoires et correspondance,* 43–44; Lejeune, *Memoirs,* 21; and Ney, *Memoirs,* 1:59–60, 2:364.

18. Ney, *Memoirs,* 1:110–12; On the alleged lack of tactics, see Coignet, *Narrative,* 131–34; Money, *Campaign of 1792,* 210. For the latter argument, see Chandler, *Campaigns of Napoleon,* 479–502; Marshall-Cornwall, *Napoleon as Military Commander,* 146–66; and Yorck, *Napoleon as a General,* 1:267–302.

19. Davout, *Opérations du 3e Corps 1806–1807,* 30–48; Ney, *Memoirs,* 1:186. See also Chandler, *Campaigns of Napoleon,* 479–502; Gallaher, *Iron Marshal,* 116–50; Marshall-Cornwall, *Napoleon as Military Commander,* 146–66; Petre, *Napoleon's Campaign in Prussia,* 149–64; Ross, *From Flintlock to Rifle,* 99–104; and Yorck, *Napoleon as a General,* 1:296–300. Yorck notes that the French troops "calmly delivered fire."

20. Louis-Paul Baille, "Rapport du colonel Baille, commandant le 51e d'infanterie de ligne, à M. le général Morand, commandant la 1re Division du 3e Corps," 8 Feb. 1807, in Davout, *Operations du 3e Corps,* 282–84; Davout to Berthier, 6 Feb. 1807, Davout, *Correspondance,* 410–11; Davout to Napoleon, 26 Dec. 1805, ibid., 202–206; Fricasse, *Journal de marche,* 33–38; Money, *Campaign of 1792,* 78–86; Ney, *Memoirs,* 1:174–79; Rovigo, *Memoirs,* 1:178. See also Goetz, *1805, Austerlitz,* 255–70; Chandler, *Campaigns of Napoleon,* 286–97; Marshall-Cornwall, *Napoleon as Military Commander,* 108–14; Muir, *Tactics and the Experience of Battle,* 51–67; Nosworthy, *With Musket, Cannon, and Sword,* 245–62; and Yorck, *Napoleon as a General,* 164–97.

21. See Phipps, *Armies of the First French Republic,* 2:184–87. See also Hayworth, "Evolution or Revolution on the Battlefield?"

22. Nosworthy, *With Musket, Cannon, and Sword,* 82–97.

23. See Colin, *L'éducation militaire de Napoleon,* 47–64; R. Palmer, "Frederick the Great, Guibert, Bülow"; and Telp, *Evolution of Operational Art,* 35–58.

24. Colin, *L'éducation militaire de Napoleon,* 353–82; Rothenberg, *Art of Warfare in the Age of Napoleon,* 95–164; Telp, *Evolution of Operational*

Art, 35–144. See also Boycott-Brown, *Road to Rivoli*; and Ferrero, *Gamble*. Bonaparte used the emerging operational art most notably in the Lake Garda campaigns from August 1796 to January 1797. On three occasions the Austrian army marched south along the major roads. Bonaparte screened each route with a division and placed his headquarters in the center. When the direction of the main enemy effort became apparent, he gathered his divisions to meet it. This occurred in August 1796 at Castiglione, in November at Arcola, and in January 1797 at Rivoli. See Boycott-Brown, *Road to Rivoli*, 360–405.

25. Chandler, *Campaigns of Napoleon*, 133–204; Elting, *Swords around a Throne*, 55–66; Rothenberg, *Art of Warfare in the Age of Napoleon*.
26. Chandler, *Campaigns of Napoleon*, 133–204; Elting, *Swords around a Throne*, 55–66; Rothenberg, *Art of Warfare in the Age of Napoleon*; Telp, *Evolution of Operational Art*, 35–38.
27. Chandler, *Campaigns of Napoleon*, 443–508; Davout, *Operations du 3e Corps*, 30–48; Yorck, *Napoleon as a General*, 1:267–302.
28. Bertaud, *Army of the French Revolution*, 231–65; Brown, *War, Revolution, and the Bureaucratic State*; Carnot, *Mémoires*, 126–29; Griffith, *Art of War of Revolutionary France*, 207–25.
29. Guibert, *Essai général de tactique*, 2:180–218. He appropriates the quote that "war should nourish war" from Cato, who made the remark during the Punic Wars, referring to Carthage.
30. Despite melodramatic letters from soldiers and pronouncements from Bonaparte, the Army of Italy retained adequate supply and wanted only for organization and regularization of its logistical systems, to which Louis-Alexandre Berthier quickly attended. See Boycott-Brown, *Road to Rivoli*, 123–61.
31. Louis-Joseph Bricard notes several instances of public capital punishment for relatively minor crimes related to pillage and predation on the native populations of the various countries in which he campaigned. On 27 Fructidor an 2 (13 September 1794) he records, "[we] shot on the line a corporal of the fifth battalion of light infantry, convicted of pillage." The following 4 complémentaire (20 September): "[We] shot a volunteer. . . . [T]his execution was cruel to watch: he began to shout and made an escape; they were obliged to kill him as fleeing game." Such executions continued throughout his service and seemed to reduce pillage. He notes few instances of disciplinary breakdown, even in the harsh Egyptian environment. *Journal*, 132, 231–32.
32. See Guibert, *Essai général de tactique*, 2:105–14. Guibert laments the "horreurs de la campagne" (109).
33. Ibid., 2:61–70; Guibert, *Journal d'un voyage en Allemagne*, 2:110–234.
34. For example, Adam-Philippe, comte de Custine, in 1793 led the Armée du Nord in a series of training exercises with large units, as Guibert had instructed, to train them in the tactical and operational art of large-unit warfare. See Lynn, *Bayonets of the Republic*, 216–40.
35. Bertaud, *Army of the French Revolution*, 80–97, 143–52, 171–90 (esp.).
36. He elaborates: "Soldiers have a thirst for war and citizens a love for

peace. Equality and liberty [*l'égalité et la liberté*] are the rights of the citizen. Subordination and passive obedience are the duties of soldiers. Soldiers cannot have the same courts, nor the same penalties, nor the same objects of emulation as citizens. Soldiers must have a sense of esprit-de-corps and professionalism. Citizens must have a public and national spirit. It is perhaps a little less impossible to make citizen-soldiers, that is to say to impart momentarily to citizens the functions of soldiers." Guibert, *De la force publique*, 9–10.
37. See Bien and Godneff, "Les offices, les corps et le crédit d'état"; Bien and Rovet, "La réaction aristocratique avant 1789"; Blaufarb, "Noble Privilege and Absolutist State Building"; and Blaufarb, *French Army*.
38. See Bertaud, *Army of the French Revolution*, 171–90.
39. Guibert, *Essai général de tactique*, 2:2–8, 219–27.
40. See Lynn, *Bayonets of the Republic*, 21–40, 97–118; and Bertaud, *Army of the French Revolution*, 39–43, 127–32.
41. Guibert, *Essai général de tactique*, 1:xii–xiv.
42. Heuser, "Guibert: Prophet of Total War?," 58.
43. Elting, *Swords around a Throne*, 5–67; Rothenberg, *Art of Warfare in the Age of Napoleon*, 124–47; Telp, *Evolution of Operational Art*, 35–56.
44. Elting, *Swords around a Throne*, 555–63.
45. Ibid., 554–71.
46. Bowden, *Napoleon and Austerlitz*, 11–142; Ross, *From Flintlock to Rifle*, 88–125; Colin, *L'éducation militaire de Napoléon*, 107.

Chapter 10

1. Broglie to Montbarey, 20, 26 June 1778, SHAT, 1 M 1819, 60, 71; Dumouriez, *Life*, 1:170–78; Toulongeon, "Notice historique de Jacques-Antoine-Hippolyte Guibert," 7–11.
2. Lespinasse to Guibert, 23 Oct. 74, Lespinasse, *Love Letters*, 240.
3. See Chambray, *Mélanges*, in *Œuvres*, 5:213–14, 434. Georges, marquis de Chambray, argues that the Guibert column formed the basis for French tactics and that the *Essai général de tactique* was one of the two most important works of the Old Regime, the other being Maurice de Saxe's *Mes rêveries*.
4. See Quimby, *Background of Napoleonic Warfare*, 57–205; and Guibert, *Essai général de tactique*, 1:v–lxxxvi.
5. Latreille, *L'œuvre militaire de la révolution*.
6. Most popular works skip from Frederick II to the Revolution or Napoleon, entirely ignoring the Old Regime. Scholarly works tend to devote small portions of their analysis to this period. For example, Basil Liddell-Hart and David Chandler both note Guibert's importance in developing the French system, but of over 1,500 pages in their two most famous works, fewer than ten address the Old Regime after the Seven Years War. See Chandler, *Campaigns of Napoleon*; and Liddell-Hart, *Strategy*.
7. Guibert, *Essai général de tactique*.

8. Latreille, *L'oeuvre militaire de la révolution*, 30–54, 172–289; Lauerma, *Guibert*, 86–106, 175–228; Lacroix, *Rules and Regulations*.
9. Citino, *German Way of War*, 34–103; Szabo, *Seven Years War in Europe*, 94–98. See also Duffy, *Military Life of Frederick the Great*; Schieder, *Frederick the Great*, 218–32; and Showalter, *Wars of Frederick the Great*. Guibert details a hypothetical failed advance in column that closely resembles the French formation at Rossbach. See *Essai général de tactique*, 1:117–18.
10. See Saxe, *Mes rêveries*. Robert Quimby's *The Background of Napoleonic Warfare* provides an excellent summary and discussion of the various works between 1720 and 1789.
11. See Guibert, *Essai général de tactique*, 1:2–4.
12. See Folard, *Nouvelles découvertes sur la guerre*, 4–6, 13–24; Folard, *Traité de la colonne*; and Saxe, *Mes rêveries*, 1:29–43, 73–119.
13. See G. Morris, *Diary and Letters*, 1:363, 410, 420–24, 444, 464. Morris recorded several dinners at Alexandrine Guibert's house in the mode of a salon; she must have maintained a small quasisalon during the Revolution that carried "the esprit Jacobin."
14. Groffier, *Le stratège des lumières*, 292, 363–64. See Marmontel, *Œuvres complètes*, 1:478; and Morellet, *Mémoires inédits*, 2:341–42.
15. Lauerma, *Guibert*, 249; Lespinasse, *Love Letters*.
16. Quimby, *Background of Napoleonic Warfare*, 306; Lacroix, *Rules and Regulations*.
17. See Lauerma, *Guibert*, 90–92.
18. See Guibert, *Essai général de tactique*, 1:v–xcix; Guibert, *Défense du système de guerre moderne*; and Guibert, *De la force publique*.
19. See Groffier, *Le stratège des lumières*, 345–67.
20. See Bouissounouse, *Julie*; Mitchiner, *Muse in Love*; and especially P. Ségur, *Julie de Lepinasse*.
21. See Groffier, *Le stratège des lumières*, 113.

Bibliography

Manuscript Sources
Service Historique—Armée de Terre (SHAT). Vincennes, France.

Guibert's Writings
Guibert, Jacques-Antoine-Hippolyte, comte de. *Considérations militaires et patriotiques.* Avignon, n.d.
———. *Défense du système de guerre moderne, ou réfutation complète du système de M[esnil] D[urand].* Vols. 3–4 of *Œuvres Militaires de Guibert.* Paris: Chez Magimel, 1803.
———. *De la force publique, considérée dans tous ses rapports.* Paris, 1790.
———. *Eloge de Maréchal de Catinat.* Edimbourg, 1775.
———. *Eloge du roi de Prusse.* London, 1787.
———. *Eloge historique de Michel de l'Hôpital, Chancelier de France.* 1777.
———. *Essai général de tactique.* 2 vols. Liege: C. Plomteaux, 1773.
———. *Journal d'un voyage en Allemagne.* 2 vols. Paris: Chez Treuttel et Würtz, 1803.
———. *Lettre à M. le comte de Guibert sur les précis de ce qui est arrivé à son égard à l'assemblée du Berry.* 1789.
———. *Mémoire adressé au public et à l'armée sur les opérations du Conseil de la Guerre.* 1789.
———. *Œuvres dramatiques.* Paris: Persan, 1822.
———. *The Patriot Minister: An Historical Panegyric on M. de l'Hopital, Chancellor of France.* London, 1778.
———. *Précis de ce qui s'est passé à mon égard à l'Assemblée du Berry.* 1789.
———. *Projet de discours d'un citoyen, aux trois Ordres de l'assemblée de Berry.* N.p., 1789.
———. *Voyages de Guibert, dans diverses parties de la France et en Suisse faits en 1775, 1778, 1784, et 1785.* Paris: D'Hautel, 1806.

Published Primary Sources
Allonville, Armand-François, comte d'. *Mémoires secrets de 1770 à 1830.* 6 vols. Paris: Werdet, 1838–45.
Arblay, Frances d'. *Diary and Letters.* 6 vols. London: Macmillan, 1905.
Bachaumont, Louis Petit de. *Mémoires secrets pour servir à l'histoire de la République des Lettres en France.* 36 vols. London: John Adamson, 1788.

Barère, Bertrand. *Mémoirs*. Paris: Nichols, 1896.
Bohan, François-Philippe-Loubat, baron de. *Examen critique du militaire français*. 3 vols. Geneva, 1781.
Bouillé, Louis-Joseph Amour, marquis de. *Souvenirs et fragments pour servir aux mémoires de ma vie et de mon temps*. 3 vols. Paris: A. Picard, 1906–11.
Bourcet, Pierre-Joseph. *Mémoires historiques sur la guerre que les français ont soutenue en Allemagne depuis 1757 jusqu'en 1762*. Paris: Maradan, 1792.
———. *Mémoires militaires sur les frontières de la France, du Piémont, et la Savoie, depuis l'embouchure du Var jusqu'au Lac de Genève*. Paris: Chez Levrault, 1802.
———. *Principes de la guerre de montagne*. Paris: Imprimerie Nationale, 1888.
Bricard, Louis-Joseph. *Journal du canonnier Bricard: 1792–1802*. Paris: Hachette, 1894.
Broglie, Victor-François, duc de. *Campagnes du maréchal duc de Broglie en Allemagne 1759–1761*. Frankfurt et Leipzig, 1761.
———. *Correspondance inédite*. Paris: A Michel, 1903.
Campan, Jeanne-Louise-Henriette Genet. *Mémoires sur la vie privée de Marie-Antoinette*. 3 vols. Paris: Baudouin frères, 1822.
Carnot, Lazare. *Mémoires historiques et militaires sur Carnot*. Paris: Baudouin frères, 1824.
Casanova, Giacomo Girolamo. *Memoirs*. 1844.
Catinat, Nicolas. *Vie*. Paris, 1770.
Chambray, Georges, marquis de. *Œuvres*. 5 vols. Paris: Pillet ainé, 1840.
Chastellux, François-Jean de Beauvoir, marquis de. *De la félicité publique, ou considérations sur le sort des hommes, dans les différentes époques de l'histoire*. 1772.
———. *Travels in North America*. New York: White, Gallaher, and White, 1827.
———. *Voyages de M. le Marquis de Chastellux dans l'Amérique septentrionale, dans les années 1780, 1781, et 1782*. 2 vols. Paris: Chez Prault, 1788.
Choiseul, Etienne-François, duc de. *Mémoires*. Paris: Mercure de France, 1982.
Coignet, Jean-Roch. *The Narrative of Captain Coignet*. Edited by Lorédan Larchey, translated by M. Carey. Thomas Y. Crowell, 1890.
Colbert, Auguste. *Le général Auguste Colbert (1793–1809): traditions, souvenirs, et documents touchant sa vie et son temps*. Edited by Marquis de Colbert-Chabanais. Paris, 1888.
Condorcet, Marie-Jean-Antoine Nicolas Caritat, marquis de. *Correspondance inédite de Condorcet et Turgot, 1770–1779*. Paris: Charavay frères, 1883.
D'Alembert, Jean le Rond. "Aux mânes de Mademoiselle de Lespinasse." In *Le tombeau de Mlle. de Lespinasse*, 77–90. Paris: Librairie des bibliophiles, 1879.
———. *Œuvres de d'Alembert*. Paris: Belin, 1822.

Davout, Louis-Nicolas, duc d'Auerstädt, prince d'Eckmuhl. *Correspondance de maréchal Davout*. Paris: E. Plon, 1885.
———. *Opérations du 3e Corps, 1806–1807: rapport du Maréchal Davout, duc d'Auerstädt*. Paris: Calmann Lévy, 1896.
Deffand, Marie-Anne de Vichy-Chamrond, marquise de. *Correspondance complète de mme du Deffand avec la duchesse de Choiseul, l'abbé Barthélemy, et M. Craufurt*. 3 vols. Paris: Michel Lévy frères, 1877.
———. *Lettres de la marquise du Deffand à Horace Walpole, depuis comte d'Orford, écrites dans les années 1776 à 1780, auxquelles sont jointes des lettres de Madame du Deffand à Voltaire, écrites dans les années 1759 à 1775*. 4 Vols. Paris: Chez Ponthieu, 1824.
Désessarts, Alexis, et al., eds. *Nouvelles ecclésiastiques; ou mémoires pour servir à l'histoire de la constitution Unigenitus*. Louvain, 1728–1803.
Diderot, Denis. *Œuvres complètes*. 20 vols. Paris: Garnier frères, 1876.
Dumas, Mathieu. *Précis des événements militaires ou essais historiques sur les campagnes de 1799 à 1814*. 19 Vols. Paris: Treuttel et Würtz, 1817.
Dumouriez, Charles-François. *The Life of General Dumouriez*. 3 vols. London: J. Johnson, 1796.
Duras, Louis-Henriette-Charlotte Philippine de Durfort, duchesse de. *La duchesse de Duras et Chateaubriand: d'après des documents inédits*. Edited by Gabriel Pailhès. Paris: Perrin, 1910.
Encyclopédie ou dictionnaire raisonné des sciences, des arts, et des métiers. Paris, 1751–72.
Esterhazy, Valentin Ladislas, comte d'. *Mémoires*. Paris: Plon, 1905.
Favier, Jean-Louis. *Conjectures raisonnées sur la situation actuelle de la France dans le système politique de l'Europe*. Paris, 1793.
———. *Doutes et questions sur le traité de Versailles entre le roi de France et la reine de Hongrie*. 1778.
Ferrières, Charles-Elie, marquis de. *Correspondance inédite*. Paris: A. Colin, 1932.
Folard, Jean Charles, chevalier. *Histoire de Polybe*. 6 vols. Amsterdam, 1774.
———. *Nouvelles découvertes sur la guerre, dans une dissertation sur Polybe, où l'on donne une idée plus étendue du commentaire entrepris sur cet auteur, et deux dissertations importantes détaches du corps de l'ouvrage*. Paris: Jean-François Josse and Claude Labottiere, 1726.
———. *Traité de la colonne, la manière de la former et de combattre dans cet ordre*. Amsterdam, 1774.
Fontaine, Jean de la. *Fables*. Boston: Jâques Munroe, 1841.
Fricasse, Jacques. *Journal de marche du sergent Fricasse de la 127e demi-brigade, 1792–1802*. Paris, 1882.
Géorgel, Louis-François. *Mémoires pour servir à l'histoire des événements de la fin du dix-huitième siècle depuis 1760 jusqu'en 1806–1810*. 6 vols. Paris: Alexis Eymery, 1817.

Girard, Etienne-François. *Les cahiers du Colonel Girard, 1766–1846.* Paris: Plon, 1951.
Graham, John Murray. *Memoir of Lord Lynedoch, G.C.B.* London: William Blackwood and Sons, 1877.
Graham, Thomas. *The Despatches of Colonel Thomas Graham on the Italian Campaign of 1796–1797.* Edited by J. Holland Rose. English Historical Review 16. New York: Longmans, Green, 1899.
Grimm, Friedrich Melchior, baron von, et al., eds. *Historical and Literary Memoirs and Anecdotes.* 2 vols. London: Henry Colburn, 1814.
Grimm, Friedrich Melchior, baron von, et al., eds. *Correspondance littéraire, philosophique, et critique.* 1747–93.
Hume, David. *The History of England: From the Invasion of Julius Caesar to the Revolution in 1688.* Indianapolis: Liberty Classics, 1983–85.
———. *A Treatise of Human Nature.* New York: Oxford University Press, 1978.
Lacroix, Irenée Amelot de. *Rules and Regulations for the Field Exercise and Maneuvers of the French Infantry Issued August 1, 1791; and the Maneuvers Added which Have Been since Adopted by the Emperor Napoleon; also, the Maneuvers of the Field Artillery with the Infantry.* Boston: T. B. Wait, 1810.
La Harpe, Jean-François de. *Correspondance littéraire adressée à son altesse impériale Monseigneur le Grand Duc, aujourd'hui Empereur de Russie et à M. le comte André Showalow, Chambellan de l'Impératrice Catherine II, depuis 1774 jusqu'à 1789.* 6 vols. Paris: Migneret, 1801–1807.
———. *Œuvres.* 16 vols. Paris: Verdière, 1820.
Leclaire, Théodore. *Mémoires et correspondance du général Leclaire, 1793.* London: Librairie militaire R. Chapelot, 1904.
Lejeune, Louis-Francois, baron. *Memoirs of Baron Lejeune.* Translated by Arthur Bell. New York: Longmans, Green, 1897.
Lespinasse, Julie de. *Letters of Mlle. Julie de Lespinasse.* New York: Versailles Historical Society, 1899.
———. *Lettres de Mademoiselle de Lespinasse écrites depuis de l'année 1773, jusqu'à l'année 1776.* Edited by Bertrand Barère. Paris: Leopold Collin, 1809.
———. *Lettres inédites de Mlle. de Lespinasse à Condorcet.* Paris, 1887.
———. *The Love Letters of Mlle. de Lespinasse to and from the Comte de Guibert.* Edited by Armand Villeneuve-Guibert, translated by E. H. F. Mills. London: Routledge and Sons, 1929.
Lombard, Jean. *Un volontaire de 1792: psychologie révolutionnaire et militaire.* Paris: A. Savine, 1892.
Louis XV. *Correspondance secrète du comte de Broglie avec Louis XV, 1756–1774.* Paris: Klincksieck, 1956.
Marbot, Jean-Baptiste-Antoine Marcellin, baron de. *Memoirs of Baron Marbot.* 2 vols. Translated by Arthur John Butler. London: Longmans, Green, 1892.
Marie-Antoinette. *Correspondance secrète entre Marie Thérèse et Marie Antoinette.* Paris, 1874.

Marmont, Auguste-Frédéric-Louis Viesse de, duc de Raguse. *The Spirit of Military Institutions*. Translated by Frank Schaller. Columbia, S.C.: Evans and Cogswell, 1864.
Marmontel, Jean-François. *Œuvres complètes*. 19 vols. Paris: Verdière, 1818–20.
Mercure de France. Paris: Chez Panckoucke, 1786.
Mesnil-Durand, François Jean de Graindorge d'Orgeville, baron de. *Projet d'un ordre français en tactique, ou la phalange coupée et doublée soutenue par le mélange des armes*. Paris: Antoine Boudet, 1755.
———. *Fragments de tactique: ou six mémoires*. Paris, 1774.
Mettra, Louis-François. *Correspondance secrète, politique, et littéraire*. 3 vols. London: John Adamson, 1787.
Miot de Melito, André-François, comte. *Mémoires*. 3 vols. Paris: Michel Lévy frères, 1858.
Mirabeau, Honoré-Gabriel de Riquetti, comte de. *Mémoires du ministère du duc d'Aiguillon*. Paris, 1792.
Money, J[ohn]. *The History of the Campaign of 1792, between the Armies of France under Generals Dumouriez, Valence, Etc. and the Allies under the Duke of Brunswick*. London, 1794.
Montbarey, Alexandre-Marie-Eléonor de Saint-Mauris, prince de. *Mémoires autographes*. 3 vols. Paris: Alexis Eymery, 1827.
Montesquieu, Charles-Louis Secondat, baron de la Brède et de. *De l'esprit des lois*. Paris: Gallimard, 1995.
———. *Lettres persanes*. Paris: Garnier, 1960.
Morand, Charles-Antoine-Louis Alexis. *De l'armé selon Chartre et d'après l'expérience des dernières guerres*. Paris: Anselin, 1929.
Moreau, Jacob-Nicolas. *Mes souvenirs*. 2 vols. Paris: Plon, 1901.
Morellet, André. *Mémoires inédites de l'abbé Morellet suivis de sa correspondance avec M. le comte de R-, ministre des finances à Naples*. 2 vols. Paris: Baudoin frères, 1823.
Morris, Gouverneur. *Diary and Letters*. 2 vols. New York: C. Scribner's Sons, 1888.
Napoleon. *Memoirs of the History of France during the Reign of Napoleon*. Vol. 3. London: H. Colburn, 1823.
Necker, Jacques. *Compte rendu au roi*. Paris, 1781.
———. *Sur l'administration de M. Necker*. Paris, 1791.
———. *A Treatise on the Administration of the Finances of France*. 3 vols. London, 1787.
Necker, Suzanne. *Mélanges extraits des manuscrits de Mme. Necker*. 2 vols. Paris: Genets, 1801.
Ney, Michel, duc d'Elchingen, prince de la Moskova. *Memoirs of Marshal Ney*. 2 vols. London: Bull and Churton, 1833.
Observations on the Military Establishment and Discipline of his Majesty the King of Prussia. London: Fielding and Walker, 1780.
Papillon de la Ferté, Denis-Pierre-Jean. *L'administration des menus: journal de Papillon de la Ferté, 1756–1780*. Paris, 1887.
Puységur, Jacques-François de Chastenet, marquis de. *Art de la guerre par principes et par règles*. 2 vols. Paris, 1749.

Puységur, Louis-Pierre de Chastenet, comte de. *Etat actuel de l'art et de la science militaire à la Chine*. Paris: Didot, 1773.
Richelieu, Armand Cardinal Jean du Plessis, duc de Fronsac et de. *The Political Testament of Cardinal Richelieu*. Translated by Henry Bertram Hill. Madison: University of Wisconsin Press, 1961.
Robespierre, Maximilien. *Speeches of Maximilien Robespierre*. New York: International, 1927.
Rochambeau, Jean-Baptiste-Donatien de Vimeur, comte de. *Mémoires militaires, historiques, et politiques*. 2 vols. Paris: Fain, 1809.
Roguet, François. "Etude sur l'ordre perpendiculaire." *Spectateur militaire* 18 (1834): 528.
———. *Mémoirs militaires du lieutenant-général comte Roguet, Colonel en second des Grenadiers à pied de la vieille garde, Pair de France*. 2 vols. Paris: Librairie militaire, 1862.
Rousseau, Jean-Jacques. *Du contrat social*. Paris: Garnier-Flammarion, 1966.
———. *Emile: ou de l'éducation*. Paris: Garnier-Flammarion, 1966.
———. *Les confessions*. Paris: Editions Garnier frères, 1964.
Rovigo, Anne-Jean-Marie René Savary, duc de. *Memoirs of the Duke of Rovigo*. 2 vols. London: Henry Colburn, 1828.
Saint-Cyr, Laurent Gouvion, marquis de. *Mémoires pour servir à l'histoire sous le directoire, le consulat, et l'empire*. Paris: Anselin, 1831.
Saint-Germain, Claude Louis, comte de. *Mémoires et commentaires*. London, 1781.
Saldern, Friedrich-Christof von. *Eléments de la tactique de l'infanterie, ou instructions d'un lieutenant-général prussien pour les troupes de son inspection*. 1783.
Sarrazin, Jean, ed. *Confession of General Buonaparte to the abbé Maury*. London, 1811.
Saxe, Maurice de. *Mes rêveries*. Paris: Librairie Militaire, 1895.
Ségur, Louis-Philippe, comte de. *Memoirs and Recollections of the Count Ségur*. 3 vols. London: Henry Colburn, 1825.
Staël-Holstein, Anne-Louise-Germaine de. *Mémoires of Madame de Staël*. Paris: Charpentier, 1843.
———. *Zulma*. London, 1813.
Suard, Amélie. *Correspondance inédite de Condorcet et Mme. Suard (1771–1791)*. Edited by Elisabeth Badinter. Paris: Fayard, 1988.
———. *Essais de mémoires de M. Suard*. Paris: Didot, 1820.
Thiebault, Paul-François. *Mémoires*. 5 vols. Paris: Plon, 1893.
Toulongeon, François-Emmanuel. "Notice historique de Jacques-Antoine-Hippolyte Guibert, écrit en 1790." In Guibert, *Journal d'un voyage en Allemagne*, 1–85. Paris: Chez Treuttel et Würtz, 1803.
Vauban, Sébastien le Prestre, seigneur de. *The New Method of Fortification*. Translated by Abel Swall. London, 1691.
Vegetius, Flavius Renatus. *Epitome of Military Science*. Translated by N. P. Milner. Liverpool: Liverpool University Press, 2001.
Véri, Joseph Alphonse de. *Journal de l'abbé de Véri*. 2 vols. Paris: Jules Tallandier, 1928–30.

Voltaire. *Henriade*. Geneva: Institut et Musée Voltaire, 1965.
———. *Œuvres complètes*. 60 vols. Edited by Louis Moland. Paris: Carez, 1820.
———. *Œuvres complètes de Voltaire*. 52 vols. Edited by Louis Moland. Paris: Garnier frères, 1877–85.
———. *Le siècle de Louis XIV*. Paris: Garnier Flammarion, 1966.
———. *Sequel to the Age of Louis XIV, to Which Is Added, a Summary of the Age of Louis XV*. Translated by R. Griffith. London: Fielding and Walker, 1781.
Wimpffen-Bournebourg, Louis-François, baron de. *Commentaires des mémoires de M. le comte de Saint-Germain*. London, 1780.

Secondary Sources

Abel, Jonathan. "Jacques Antoine Hippolyte, comte de Guibert." Last modified 28 Apr. 2014. *Oxford Bibliographies Online*. http://www.oxfordbibliographies.com/view/document/obo-9780199791279/obo-9780199791279-0037.xml?rskey=TqyudG&result=1&q=Jacques+Antoine+Hippolyte%2C+comte+de+Guibert#firstMatch.
———. "Jacques-Antoine-Hippolyte, comte de Guibert's Military Reforms: Enlightened Evolution or Revolutionary Change?" *Napoleonic Scholarship* (2010): 26–38.
Abrantès, Laure Junot, duchesse d'. *Mémoirs*. 2 vols. London: Napoleon Society, 1895.
———. *Une soirée chez Mme. Geoffrin*. Paris: Gallimard, 2000.
Adlow, Elijah. *Napoleon in Italy, 1796–1797*. Boston: William J. Rochefort, 1948.
Allmand, Christopher. *The De re militari of Vegetius: The Reception, Transmission, and Legacy of a Roman Text in the Middle Ages*. Cambridge, U.K.: Cambridge University Press, 2011.
Ames, Glenn Joseph. *Colbert, Mercantilism, and the French Quest for Asian Trade*. DeKalb: Northern Illinois University Press, 1996.
Anderson, Fred. *A People's Army: Massachusetts Soldiers and Society in the Seven Years War*. Chapel Hill: University of North Carolina Press, 1984.
Anderson, M. S. *War and Society in Europe of the Old Regime, 1617–1789*. New York: St. Martin's, 1988.
Antoine, Michel. *Louis XV*. Paris: Fayard, 1989.
Arnold, James R. *Marengo and Hohenlinden: Napoleon's Rise to Power*. Lexington, Va.: J. R. Arnold, 1999.
———. "A Reappraisal of Column versus Line in the Peninsular War." *Journal of Military History* 68 (2004): 535–52.
Asprey, Robert. *Frederick the Great: The Magnificent Enigma*. New York: Ticknor & Fields, 1986.
Ayton, Andrew, et al. *The Battle of Crécy, 1346*. Woodbridge, U.K.: Boydell, 2005.
Barbiche, Bernard. *Les institutions de la monarchie française à l'époque moderne*. Paris: PUF, 1999.

Bardin, Etienne-Alexandre. *Notice historique sur Guibert*. Paris: Corréard jeune, 1836.
Barker, Juliet. *Agincourt: Henry V and the Battle That Made England*. New York: Little, Brown, 2006.
Beasley, Faith. *Salons, History, and the Creation of Seventeenth-Century France: Mastering Memory*. Burlington, Vt.: Ashgate, 2006.
Bemis, Samuel. *The Diplomacy of the American Revolution*. Bloomington: Indiana University Press, 1957.
Bertaud, Jean-Paul. *The Army of the French Revolution: From Citizen-Soldiers to Instrument of Power*. Translated by R. R. Palmer. Princeton, N.J.: Princeton University Press, 1988.
Bertaut, Jules. *Egéries du XVIIIe siècle: madame Suard, madame Delille, madame Helvétius, madame Diderot, mademoiselle Quinault*. Paris: Plon, 1928.
Best, Geoffrey. *War and Society in Revolutionary Europe, 1770–1870*. New York: St. Martin's, 1982.
Bien, David D. "The Army in the French Enlightenment: Reform, Reaction, and Revolution." *Past & Present* 85 (1979): 68–98.
———. "Military Education in 18th Century France: Technical and Non-Technical Determinants." In *Science, Technology, and Warfare: Proceedings of the Third Military History Symposium, U.S. Air Force Academy, 8–9 May 1969*. Edited by Monte D. Wright and Lawrence J. Paszek, 51–59. [Washington, D.C.]: Office of Air Force History, Headquarters, USAF, 1971.
Bien, David D., and Nina Godneff. "Les offices, les corps et le crédit d'état: l'utilisation des privilèges sous l'Ancien Régime." *Annales. Histoire, Sciences Sociales* 43 (1988): 397–404.
Bien, David D., and J. Rovet. "La réaction aristocratique avant 1789: l'exemple de l'armée." *Annales Histoire, Sciences Sociales* 29, no. 2 (1974): 23–48; no. 3 (1974): 505–34.
Bien, David D., et al. *Caste, Class, and Profession in Old Regime France: The French Army and the Ségur Reform of 1781*. St. Andrews: Centre for French History and Culture, 2010.
Biographie universelle ancienne et moderne. Edited by Louis Gabriel Michaud. 45 vols. Paris: C. Desplaces, 1842–65.
Black, Jeremy. *European Warfare, 1660–1815*. New Haven, Conn.: Yale University Press, 1994.
———. *Warfare in the Eighteenth Century*. London: Cassell, 1999.
Blanning, T. C. W. *The French Revolutionary Wars, 1787–1802*. New York: Arnold, 1996.
Blaufarb, Rafe. *The French Army, 1750–1820: Careers, Talent, Merit*. New York: Manchester University Press, 2002.
———. "Noble Privilege and Absolutist State Building: French Military Administration after the Seven Years War." *French Historical Studies* 24 (2001): 223–46.
Bois, Louis du. "Notice sur Charles Graindorge d'Orgeville, baron de Ménil-Durand." In *Almanach de la ville et de l'arrondissement de Lisieux pour 1839*, 75–80. Lisieux: Veuve Tissot, 1839.

Bouissounouse, Janine. *Julie: The Life of Mademoiselle de Lespinasse: Her Salon, Her Friends, Her Loves.* Translated by Pierre de Fontnouvelle. New York: Appleton-Century-Crofts, 1962.

Bouton, Cynthia. *The Flour War: Gender, Class, and Community in Late Ancien Régime French Society.* State College: Pennsylvania State University Press, 1993.

Bowden, Scott. *Napoleon and Austerlitz.* Chicago: Emperor's, 1997.

Boycott-Brown, Martin. *The Road to Rivoli: Napoleon's First Campaign.* London: Cassel, 2001.

Bredin, Jean-Denis. *Une singulière famille: Jacques Necker, Suzanne Necker, et Germaine de Staël.* Paris: Fayard, 1999.

Brégeon, Joël. *Le Connêtable de Bourbon: le destin tragique du dernier des grands féodaux.* Paris: Perrin, 2000.

Breton, Alexandre-André le. *Pièces originales et procédures du procès fait à Robert-François Damiens.* Paris: Pierre-Guillaume Simon, 1757.

Broglie, Albert. *Le secret du roi.* New York: Cassel, 1879.

Brougham, Henry. *Lives of the Philosophers of the Time of George III.* Edinburg: Adam and Charles Black, 1872.

Brown, Howard. *War, Revolution, and the Bureaucratic State: Politics and Army Administration in France, 1791–1799.* New York: Oxford University Press, 1995.

Browning, Reed. *The War of the Austrian Succession.* New York: St. Martin's, 1993.

Buffington, Arthur H. *The Second Hundred Years War, 1689–1815.* New York: Holt, 1929.

Caillois, Roger. *Bellone ou la pente de la guerre.* Fata Morgana, 1994.

Camon, Hubert. *Napoleon's System of War.* Translated by George Nafziger. West Chester, Ohio: Nafziger Collection, 2001.

———. *Quand et comment Napoléon a conçu son système de bataille.* Paris, 1935.

———. *Quand et comment Napoléon a conçu son système de manœuvre.* Paris, 1931.

Carlyle, Thomas. *History of Friedrich the Second, Called Frederick the Great.* 8 vols. New York: John B. Alden, 1885.

Cassirer, Ernst. *The Philosophy of the Enlightenment.* Boston: Beacon, 1955.

Castries, René de la Croix, duc de. *Madame du Barry.* Paris: Hachette, 1967.

Chandler, David. *The Campaigns of Napoleon.* New York: Macmillan, 1966.

———, ed. *Napoleon's Marshals.* New York: Macmillan, 1987.

Charnay, Jean-Paul, ed. *Guibert ou le soldat philosophe.* Paris: Chateau de Vincennes, 1981.

Chartier, Roger. *The Cultural Origins of the French Revolution.* Durham, N.C.: Duke University Press, 1991.

Childs, John. *Armies and Warfare in Europe, 1648–1789.* New York: Holmes and Meier, 1982.

———. *Warfare in the Seventeenth Century*. Washington, D.C.: Smithsonian Books, 2006.
Citino, Robert. *The German Way of War: From the Thirty Years War to the Third Reich*. Lawrence: University Press of Kansas, 2005.
Clausewitz, Carl von. *La campagne de 1796 en Italie*. Translated by Jean Colin. Paris: Librairie militaire de L. Baudoin, 1899.
———. *On War*. Edited by Michael Howard and Peter Paret. Princeton, N.J.: Princeton University Press, 1984.
Cole, Charles Woolsey. *Colbert and a Century of French Mercantilism*. Hamden, Conn.: Archon Books, 1964.
Colin, Jean. *L'éducation militaire de Napoléon*. Paris: R. Chapelot, 1901.
———. *L'infanterie au XVIIIe siècle. La tactique*. Paris: Berger-Levrault, 1907.
Collins, James. *The State in Early Modern France*. New York: Cambridge University Press, 1995.
Condon, Patricia, Marjorie B. Cohn, and Agnes Mongan. *In Pursuit of Perfection: The Art of J.-A.-D. Ingres*. Louisville, Ky.: J. B. Speed Art Museum, 1983.
Connelly, Owen. *Blundering to Glory: Napoleon's Military Campaigns*. Wilmington, Del.: Scholarly Resources, 1987.
Corvisier, André. *Armies and Societies in Europe, 1494–1789*. Translated by Abigail T. Siddall. Bloomington: Indiana University Press, 1979.
———. *A Dictionary of Military History and the Art of War*. Revised by John Childs. Translated by Christ Turner. Cambridge, Mass.: Blackwell, 1994.
———. *Louvois*. Paris: Fayard, 1983.
Cottret, Bernard. *La révolution américaine: la quête du bonheur 1763–1787*. Paris: Perrin, 2003.
Courteault, Paul. *La mort du marquis de Mora à Bordeaux*. Bordeaux: Féret, 1927.
Craveri, Benedetta. *Madame du Deffand and Her World*. Translated by Teresa Waugh. Boston: David R. Godine, 1994.
Crouzet, Denis. *La sagesse et le malheur: Michel de l'Hospital, Chancelier de France*. Seyssel: Champ Vallon, 1998.
Darnton, Robert. *The Business of the Enlightenment: A Publishing History of the "Encyclopédie."* Cambridge, Mass.: Harvard University Press, 1979.
———. *The Corpus of Clandestine Literature in France, 1769–1789*. New York: W. W. Norton, 1995.
———. *The Forbidden Bestsellers of Pre-Revolutionary France*. New York: W. W. Norton, 1995.
———. *The Literary Underground of the Old Regime*. Cambridge, Mass.: Harvard University Press, 1982.
Dawson, Philip, et al., eds. *Revolutionary Demands: A Content Analysis of the Cahiers de doléances of 1789*. Stanford, Calif.: Stanford University Press, 1998.
Delbrück, Hans. *History of the Art of War*. Lincoln: University of Nebraska Press, 1990.

———. *Medieval Warfare*. Lincoln: University of Nebraska Press, 1982.
De Vries, Kelly. *Guns and Men in Medieval Europe, 1200–1500: Studies in Military History and Technology*. Burlington, Vt.: Ashgate, 2002.
———. *Infantry Warfare in the Early Fourteenth Century: Discipline, Tactics, and Technology*. Woodbridge, U.K.: Boydell, 1996.
Dewald, Jonathan. *Aristocratic Experience and the Origins of Modern Culture: France, 1570–1715*. Berkeley: University of California Press, 1993.
———. *The French Nobility in the Eighteenth Century: Reassessments and New Approaches*. University Park: Pennsylvania State University Press, 2006.
Doniol, Henri. *Histoire de la participation de la France à l'établissement des Etats-Unis d'Amérique*. 6 vols. Paris: Imprimerie nationale, 1886–92.
Doyle, William. *Aristocracy and Its Enemies in the Age of Revolution*. New York: Oxford University Press, 2009.
———. *Jansenism: Catholic Resistance to Authority from the Reformation to the French Revolution*. New York: St. Martin's, 2000.
———. *The Origins of the French Revolution*. New York: Oxford University Press, 1980.
———. *The Oxford History of the French Revolution*. New York: Oxford University Press, 1989.
Duffy, Christopher. *Fire and Stone: The Science of Fortress Warfare, 1660–1860*. Edison, N.J.: Castle Books, 2006.
———. *The Military Experience in the Age of Reason*. New York: Atheneum, 1988.
———. *The Military Life of Frederick the Great*. New York: Atheneum, 1986.
Dull, Jonathan. *A Diplomatic History of the American Revolution*. New Haven, Conn.: Yale University Press, 1985.
Dumont, Louis. *Essai sur l'individualisme: une perspective anthropologique sur l'idéologie moderne*. Paris: du Seuil, 1983.
Dupuis, Victor. *La campagne de 1793: à l'armée du Nord et des Ardennes*. Paris: R. Chapelot, 1906–1909.
———. *Les opérations militaires sur la Sambre en 1794, bataille de Fleurus*. Paris: R. Chapelot, 1907.
Durand, Georges. *Etats et institutions, XVIe–XVIIIe siècles*. Paris: Colin, 1969.
Duval, César. "Le 2e bataillon du Mont-Blanc, la 19e demi-brigade de bataille, et la 69e de ligne a l'armée d'Italie." *Mémoires et Documents* 36 (1897): 510–54.
Dwyer, Philip. *Napoleon: The Path to Power*. New Haven, Conn.: Yale University Press, 2008.
Easum, Chester Verne. *Prince Henry of Prussia, Brother of Frederick the Great*. Madison: University of Wisconsin Press, 1942.
Echeverria, Durand. *The Maupeou Revolution: A Study in the History of Libertarianism, France, 1770–1774*. Baton Rouge: Louisiana State University Press, 1985.

Eckberg, Carl J. *The Failure of Louis XIV's Dutch War.* Chapel Hill: University of North Carolina Press, 1979.
Egret, Jean. *The French Pre-Revolution, 1787–1789.* Translated by Wesley Camp. Chicago: University of Chicago Press, 1994.
——. *Louis XV et l'opposition parlementaire, 1715–1774.* Paris: A. Colin, 1970.
Elting, John. *The Battles of Saratoga.* Monmouth Beach, N.J.: Philip Freneau, 1977.
——. *Swords around a Throne: Napoleon's Grande Armée.* New York: Free Press, 1988.
Epstein, Robert M. *Napoleon's Last Victory and the Emergence of Modern War.* Lawrence: University Press of Kansas, 1994.
Ergang, Robert. *The Potsdam Führer, Frederick William I, Father of Prussian Militarism.* New York: Columbia University Press, 1941.
Esdaile, Charles J. *Napoleon's Wars: An International History, 1803–1815.* New York: Viking, 2008.
Eysturlid, Lee W. *The Formative Influences, Theories, and Campaigns of the Archduke Carl of Austria.* Westport, Conn.: Greenwood, 2000.
Fairweather, Maria. *Madame de Staël.* New York: Time-Life Books, 1981.
Félix, Joël. *Finances et politique au siècle des Lumières: le ministère L'Averdy, 1763–1768.* Paris: Comité pour l'histoire économique et financière de la France, 1999.
Ferling, John. *Almost a Miracle: The American Victory in the War of Independence.* New York: Oxford University Press, 2007.
Ferrero, Guglielmo. *The Gamble: Bonaparte in Italy, 1796–1797.* Translated by Bertha Pritchard and Lily C. Freeman. London: G. Bell and Sons, 1961.
Fitzsimmons, Michael P. *The Night the Old Regime Ended: August 4, 1789, and the French Revolution.* University Park: Pennsylvania State University Press, 2003.
Flammermont, Jules Gustave. *Le chancelier Maupeou et les Parlements.* Paris: A. Picard, 1883.
Forestié, Emerand. *Biographie du Cte. de Guibert.* Montauban, 1855.
Forrest, Alan. *Conscripts and Deserters: The Army and French Society during the Revolution and Empire.* New York: Oxford University Press, 1989.
——. *Napoleon's Men: The Soldiers of the Revolution and Empire.* New York: Hambledon and London, 2002.
——. *The Soldiers of the French Revolution.* Durham, N.C.: Duke University Press, 1990.
Foucault, Michel. *Discipline and Punish: The Birth of the Prison.* Translated by Alan Sheridan. New York: Vintage Books, 1995.
Frieser, Karl-Heinz. *The Blitzkrieg Legend: The 1940 Campaign in the West.* Translated by John T. Greenwood. Annapolis, Md.: Naval Institute Press, 2005.
Gallaher, John G. *The Iron Marshal: A Biography of Louis N. Davout.* Mechanicsburg, Penn.: Greenhill Books, 2000.

Gamberini, Andrea. *The Italian Renaissance State*. Translated by Isabella Lazzarini. Cambridge, U.K.: Cambridge University Press, 2012.
Gambier-Parry, Mark. *Madame Necker: Her Family and her Friends*. London: W. Blackwood and Sons, 1913.
Garrett, Mitchell. *The Estates-General of 1789: The Problems of Composition and Organization*. New York: D. Appleton-Century, 1935.
Gat, Azar. *A History of Military Thought: From the Enlightenment to the Cold War*. New York: Oxford University Press, 2001.
Gates, David. *The Napoleonic Wars, 1803–1815*. New York: Arnold, 1997.
Gay, Peter. *The Age of Enlightenment*. New York: Time, 1996.
———. *The Enlightenment: A Comprehensive Anthology*. New York: Simon and Schuster, 1973.
———. *The Enlightenment: An Interpretation*. Vol. 1, *The Rise of Modern Paganism*. New York: Knopf, 1966.
Gipson, Lawrence Henry. *The British Empire before the American Revolution*. 15 vols. New York: Knopf, 1936–70.
———. *The Coming of the Revolution, 1763–1775*. New York: Harper and Row, 1965.
———. *The Triumphant Empire: The Rumbling of the Coming Storm, 1766–1770*. New York: Knopf, 1965.
Goebel, Julius. *The Struggle for the Falkland Islands: A Study in Legal and Diplomatic History*. New York: Oxford University Press, 1927.
Goetz, Robert. *1805, Austerlitz: Napoleon and the Destruction of the Third Coalition*. Mechanicsburg, Penn.: Stackpole Books, 2005.
Goldsmith, Elizabeth, and Dena Goodman, eds. *Going Public: Women and Publishing in Early Modern France*. Ithaca, N.Y.: Cornell University Press, 1995.
Goncourt, Edmond, and Jules de Goncourt. *La femme au dix-huitième siècle*. Paris: Flammarion, 1982.
Gooch, G. P. *Louis XV: The Monarchy in Decline*. New York: Longmans, 1956.
Goodman, Dena. *The Republic of Letters: A Cultural History of the French Enlightenment*. Ithaca, N.Y.: Cornell University Press, 1994.
Granier, Raymond. "Ou est né le Maréchal Guibert?" *Actes du congrès des sociétés savantes. Section d'histoire moderne et contemporaine* 77 (1952): 29–33.
Green, John Richard. *Histoire du peuple anglais*. 2 vols. Paris: Plon, 1888.
Griffith, Paddy. *The Art of War of Revolutionary France, 1789–1802*. Mechanicsburg, Penn.: Stackpole Books, 1998.
Grimsley, Ronald. *The Philosophy of Rousseau*. New York: Oxford University Press, 1973.
Groenewegen, Peter D. *The Economics of A. R. J. Turgot*. The Hague: Martinus Nijhoff, 1977.
———. *Eighteenth-Century Economics: Turgot, Beccaria, and Smith and their Contemporaries*. London: Routledge, 2002.
Groffier, Ethel. *Le stratège des lumières: le comte de Guibert (1743–1790)*. Paris: Editions Champion, 2005.

Gruder, Vivian. *The Royal Provincial Intendants: A Governing Elite in Eighteenth-Century France*. Ithaca, N.Y.: Cornell University Press, 1968.

Guéry, Alain. "Les finances de la monarchie française sous l'Ancien Régime." *Annales Histoire, Sciences Sociales* 33 (1978): 216–39.

Habermas, Jürgen. *The Structural Transformation of the Public Sphere: An Inquiry into a Category of Bourgeois Society*. Cambridge, Mass.: MIT Press, 1989.

Haechler, Jean. *L'encyclopédie de Diderot et de Jaucourt: Essai biographique sur le chevalier Louis de Jaucourt*. Paris: Champion, 1995.

Hall, Thadd E. *France and the Eighteenth-Century Corsican Question*. New York: New York University Press, 1971.

Hardman, John. *Louis XVI*. New York: Cambridge University Press, 1993.

———. *Overture to Revolution: The 1787 Assembly of Notables and the Crisis of France's Old Regime*. New York: Oxford University Press, 2010.

Harris, Robert. *Necker: Reform Statesman of the Ancien Régime*. Berkeley: University of California Press, 1979.

———. *Necker and the Revolution of 1789*. Lanham, Md.: University Press of America, 1986.

Hassall, Arthur. *Louis XIV and the Zenith of the French Monarchy*. New York: G. P. Putnam's Sons, 1895.

Haussonville, Paul-Gabriel d'. *Le salon de Madame Necker*. 2 vols. Paris: Calmann-Lévy, 1882.

Hayworth, Jordan. "Evolution or Revolution on the Battlefield? The Army of the Sambre and Meuse in 1794." Unpublished paper, 2011.

Herold, J. Christopher. *Bonaparte in Egypt*. New York: Harper and Row, 1962.

———. *Mistress to an Age: A Life of Madame de Staël*. New York: Time-Life Books, 1958.

Heuser, Beatrice. *The Evolution of Strategy: Thinking War from Antiquity to the Present*. New York: Cambridge University Press, 2010.

———. "Guibert: Prophet of Total War?" In *War in an Age of Revolution, 1775–1815*. Edited by Roger Chickering and Stig Forster, 49–68. New York: Cambridge University Press, 2010.

Hewitt, H. J. *The Black Prince's Expedition of 1355–1357*. Barnsley, U.K.: Pen and Sword Military, 2004.

Higonnet, Patrice Louis-René. "The Origins of the Seven Years War." *Journal of Modern History* 40, no. 1 (1968): 57–90.

Hoefer, Ferdinand. *Nouvelle biographie générale*. Paris: Firmin-Didot, 1866.

Hooper-Hamersley, Rosamond. *The Hunt after Jeanne-Antoinette de Pompadour: Patronage, Politics, Art, and the French Enlightenment*. Lanham, Md.: Lexington Books, 2001.

Horowitz, Asher. *Rousseau, Nature, and History*. Buffalo, N.Y.: University of Toronto Press, 1987.

Houssaye, Arsène. *Est-il bon? Est-il méchant?* Paris, 1884.

Humbert, Jean-Marcel. *The Hôtel des Invalides*. Paris: Editions de la tourelle, 1978.
Huntington, Samuel P. *The Soldier and the State: The Theory of Politics and Civil-Military Relations*. Cambridge, Mass.: Harvard University Press, 1957.
Jaurès, Jean. *Histoire socialiste de la révolution française*. Paris: Editions sociales, 1968–73.
Jaurgain, Jean de. *Notice sur les familles Vallet et Villeneuve-Guibert*. Paris: Imprimerie de la Cour d'Appel, 1893.
Jebb, Camilla. *The Star of the Salons: Julie de Lespinasse*. New York: G. P. Putnam's Sons, 1908.
Johnson, Douglas. *French Society and the Revolution*. New York: Cambridge University Press, 1976.
Jomini, Antoine Henri, baron de. *Précis sur l'art de guerre*. Paris, 1836.
Jourdan, Annie. *La révolution, une exception française?* Paris: Flammarion, 2004.
Kagan, Frederick W. *The End of the Old Order: Napoleon and Europe, 1801–1805*. Cambridge, Mass.: Da Capo, 2006.
Kale, Steven. *French Salons: High Society and Political Sociability from the Old Regime to the Revolution of 1848*. Baltimore: Johns Hopkins University Press, 2004.
Kennett, Lee. *The French Armies in the Seven Years War: A Study in Military Organization and Administration*. Durham, N.C.: Duke University Press, 1967.
———. *The French Forces in America, 1780–1783*. Westport, Conn.: Greenwood, 1977.
Kettering, Sharon. *French Society, 1589–1715*. Harlow, U.K.: Pearson Education, 2001.
Knox, MacGregor, and Williamson Murray. *The Dynamics of Military Revolution, 1300–2050*. New York: Cambridge University Press, 2001.
Kopperman, Paul E. *Braddock at the Monongahela*. Pittsburgh: University of Pittsburgh Press, 1977.
Kors, Alan Charles. "The Atheism of d'Holbach and Naigeon." In *Atheism from the Reformation to the Enlightenment*. Edited by Michael Hunter and David Wootton, 273–300. New York: Oxford University Press, 1992.
Lachouque, Henry. *Napoleon's Battles: A History of His Campaigns*. Translated by Roy Monkcom. London: George Allen and Unwin, 1964.
Lacourtre, Jean, and Marie-Christine d'Aragon. *Julie de Lespinasse*. Paris: Ramsay, 1980.
Latreille, Albert. *L'oeuvre militaire de la révolution: l'armée et la nation à la fin de l'ancien régime; les derniers ministres de la guerre de la monarchie*. Paris: Librairie Chapelot, 1914.
Lauerma, Matti. *L'artillerie de campagne française pendant les guerres de la révolution*. Helsinki: Suomalainen Tiedeakatemia, 1956.
———. *Jacques-Antoine-Hippolyte de Guibert (1743–1790)*. Helsinki: Suomalainen Tiedeakatemia, 1989.

Laver, Roberto C. *The Falklands/Malvinas Case: Breaking the Deadlock in the Anglo-Argentine Sovereignty Dispute.* The Hague: Martinus Nijhoff, 2001.
Lee, Stephen J. *The Thirty Years War.* New York: Routledge, 1991.
Lefebvre, Georges. *The Coming of the French Revolution, 1789.* Translated by R. R. Palmer. New York: Princeton University Press, 1949.
———. *The French Revolution.* Translated by Elizabeth Moss Evanson. 2 vols. New York: Columbia University Press, 1962–64.
Le Roy Ladurie, Emmanuel. *The Ancien Régime: A History of France, 1610–1774.* Cambridge, Mass.: Blackwell, 1996.
Liddel-Hart, Basil. *Strategy.* New York: Praeger, 1967.
Ligou, Daniel. *Jeanbon Saint-André, membre du Grand Comité de Salut Public, 1749–1813.* Paris: Messidor/Editions sociales, 1989.
Lougee, Carolyn C. *"Le paradis des femmes": Women, Salons, and Social Stratification in Seventeenth-Century France.* Princeton, N.J.: Princeton University Press, 1976.
Lumpkin, Henry. *From Savannah to Yorktown: The American Revolution in the South.* Columbia: University of South Carolina Press, 1981.
Luvaas, Jay. *Napoleon on the Art of War.* New York: Simon and Schuster, 1999.
Lynn, John. *The Bayonets of the Republic: Motivation and Tactics in the Army of Revolutionary France, 1791–94.* Urbana: University of Illinois Press, 1984.
———. "The Evolution of Army Style in the Modern West, 800–2000." *International History Review* 18 (1996): 505–45.
———. *Giant of the Grand Siècle: The French Army, 1610–1715.* New York: Cambridge University Press, 1997.
———. "Recalculating French Army Growth during the Grand Siècle, 1610–1715." *French Historical Studies* 18 (1994): 881–906.
———. "Toward an Army of Honor: The Moral Evolution of the French Army, 1789–1815." *French Historical Studies* 16 (1989): 152–73.
———. *The Wars of Louis XIV, 1667–1714.* New York: Longman, 1999.
Mackesy, Piers. *The Coward of Minden: The Affair of Lord George Sackville.* London, 1979.
Mallet, Michael, and Christine Shaw. *The Italian Wars: 1494–1559.* Harlow, U.K.: Pearson Education, 2012.
Marshall, S. L. A. *Men against Fire: The Problem of Battle Command in Future War.* Norman: University of Oklahoma Press, 2000.
Marshall-Cornwall, James. *Napoleon as Military Commander.* London: Batsford, 1967.
Mas, Raymond. "L'éssai général de tactique (1770) de Guibert ou le rationalism des Lumières face à la guerre." In *La Bataille, l'armée, la gloire, 1745–1871: actes du colloque international de Clermont-Ferrand.* Edited by Paul Viallaneix and Jean Ehrard, 1:119–34. Clermont-Ferrand, Fr.: Association de publications de la Faculté des lettres et sciences humaines, 1985.
Mason, Haydn, ed. *The Darnton Debate: Books and Revolution in the Eighteenth Century.* Oxford: Voltaire Foundation, 1998.

Mathiez, Albert. *La victoire en l'an II*. Paris: Alcan, 1916.
May, Henry. *The Enlightenment in America*. New York: Oxford University Press, 1976.
McConachy, Bruce. "The Roots of Artillery Doctrine: Napoleonic Artillery Doctrine Reconsidered." *Journal of Military History* 65 (2001): 617–40.
McLaren, Moray. *Corsican Boswell: Paoli, Johnson, and Freedom*. London: Secker and Warburg, 1966.
McManners, John. *Church and Society in Eighteenth-Century France*. New York: Oxford University Press, 1998.
Menard, Colonel. "De la force publique ou le testament militaire du comte de Guibert." *Revue de défense nationale* (1969).
Merlant, Joachim. *La France et la guerre de l'indépendance américaine (1776–1783)*. Paris: F. Alcan, 1918.
Michelet, Jules. *Histoire de la révolution française*. Paris: Gallimard, 1952.
Middlekauff, Robert. *The Glorious Cause: The America Revolution*. New York: Oxford University Press, 1982.
Middleton, Robert Nelson. "French Policy and Prussia after the Peace of Aix-la-Chappelle, 1749–1753." Ph.D. diss., Columbia University, 1968.
Mintz, Max. *The Generals of Saratoga: John Burgoyne and Horatio Gates*. New Haven, Conn.: Yale University Press, 1990.
Mitchiner, Margaret. *A Muse in Love: Julie de Lespinasse*. London: Bodley Head, 1962.
Morley, John Viscount. *Diderot and the Encyclopedists*. 2 vols. Ann Arbor: University of Michigan Press, 1923.
Morris, Madeline. *Le chevalier de Jaucourt: un ami de la terre (1704–1780)*. Geneva: Droz, 1979.
Mousnier, Roland. *The Institutions of France under the Absolute Monarchy, 1598–1789*. 2 vols. Chicago: University of Chicago Press, 1979–84.
Mousset, Sophie. *Women's Rights and the French Revolution: A Biography of Olympe de Gouges*. New Brunswick, N.J.: Transaction, 2007.
Muir, Rory. *Tactics and the Experience of Battle in the Age of Napoleon*. New Haven, Conn.: Yale University Press, 1978.
Muller, Cathy, and José-Louis Bocquet. *Olympe de Gouges*. Paris: Casterman, 2012.
Niox, G. *The Hôtel des Invalides*. Paris: Delagrave, 1924.
Nosworthy, Brent. *The Anatomy of Victory: Battle Tactics, 1689–1763*. New York: Hippocrene Books, 1990.
———. *With Musket, Cannon, and Sword*. New York: Sarpedon, 1996.
Olsen, John Andreas, and Martin van Creveld, eds. *The Evolution of Operational Art: From Napoleon to the Present*. New York: Oxford University Press, 2011.
Osman, Julia. "Ancient Warriors on Modern Soil: French Military Reform and American Military Images in 18th Century France." *French History* 22 (2008): 175–96.

———. "Patriotism as Power: The Old Regime Foundation for Napoleon's Army." *International Congress of Military History Conference Proceedings 2009* (2010).
Ostwald, Jamel. *Vauban under Siege: Engineering Efficiency and Martial Vigor in the War of Spanish Succession*. Boston: Brill, 2007.
Outram, Dorinda. *The Enlightenment*. New York: Cambridge University Press, 1995.
Palmer, Dave. *George Washington's Military Genius*. New York: Regnery History, 2012.
Palmer, R. R. "Frederick the Great, Guibert, Bülow." In *Makers of Modern Strategy: From Machiavelli to the Nuclear Age*. Edited by Peter Paret, 91–122. Princeton, N.J.: Princeton University Press, 1986.
———. "Turgot, Paragon of the Continental Enlightenment." *Journal of Law and Economics* 19 (1976): 607–19.
Paret, Peter. *Clausewitz and the State*. New York: Oxford University Press, 1976.
Paret, Peter, ed. *Makers of Modern Strategy: Military Thought from Machiavelli to Hitler*. Princeton, N.J.: Princeton University Press, 1952.
———. *Makers of Modern Strategy: Military Thought from Machiavelli to the Nuclear Age*. Princeton, N.J.: Princeton University Press, 1986.
Parker, Geoffrey. *The Military Revolution: Military Innovation and the Rise of the West, 1500–1800*. New York: Cambridge University Press, 1988.
Parker, Geoffrey, ed. *The Thirty Years War*. Boston: Routledge, 1984.
Pelet-Clozeau, Jean-Jacques-Germain. "Essai sur les manœuvres d'un corps d'armée d'infanterie." *Spectateur militaire* 4 (1828-29).
Pellison-Fontanier, Paul, et al. *Histoire de l'Académie française*. Paris: Didier, 1858.
Perrin, Joseph. *Le cardinal de Loménie de Brienne, archevêque de Sens*. Sens: P. Duchemin, 1896.
Petre, F. Loraine. *Napoleon's Campaign in Poland, 1806–7: A Military History of Napoleon's First War with Russia*. London: J. Lane, 1907.
Phipps, Ramsay. *The Armies of the First French Republic and the Rise of the Marshals of Napoleon I*. 5 vols. London: Oxford University Press, 1926–39.
Poirier, Lucien. *Les voix de la stratégie*. Paris: Fayard, 1985.
Quimby, Robert. *The Background of Napoleonic Warfare: The Theory of Military Tactics in Eighteenth-Century France*. New York: Columbia University Press, 1957.
Revue des deux mondes. Paris: Bureau de la revue des deux mondes, 1905.
Rice, G. W. "British Foreign Policy and the Falklands Islands Crisis of 1770–71." *International History Review* 32 (2010): 273–305.
Riley, James. *The Seven Years War and the Old Regime in France: The Economic and Financial Toll*. Princeton, N.J.: Princeton University Press, 1986.
Roberts, Michael. *Gustavus Adolphus*. New York: Longman, 1992.

Roche, Daniel. *France in the Enlightenment.* Translated by Arthur Goldhammer. Cambridge, Mass.: Harvard University Press, 1998.
———. *Le siècle des lumières en province: académies et académiciens provinciaux, 1680–1789.* Paris: Mouton, 1978.
Rogers, Clifford J., ed. *The Military Revolution Debate: Readings on the Military Transformation of Early Modern Europe.* Boulder, Colo.: Westview, 1995.
Rogister, John. *Louis XV and the Parlement of Paris, 1737–1755.* New York: Cambridge University Press, 1995.
Rosenblum, Robert. *Transformations in Late Eighteenth Century Art.* Princeton, N.J.: Princeton University Press, 1967.
Ross, Steven T. *From Flintlock to Rifle: Infantry Tactics, 1740–1866.* London: Frank Cass, 1979.
Rothenberg, Gunther. *The Art of Warfare in the Age of Napoleon.* Bloomington: Indiana University Press, 1978.
———. *The Military Border in Croatia, 1740–1881: A Study of an Imperial Institution.* Chicago: University of Chicago Press, 1966.
———. *Napoleon's Greatest Adversaries: The Archduke Charles and the Austrian Army, 1792–1814.* Bloomington: Indiana University Press, 1982.
Rowlands, Guy. *The Financial Decline of a Great Power: War, Influence, and Money in Louis XIV's France.* New York: Oxford University Press, 2012.
Royde-Smith, Naomi Gwladys. *The Double Heart: A Study of Julie de Lespinasse.* New York: Harper, 1831.
Sagnac, Philippe. *La fin de l'ancien régime et la révolution américaine (1763–1789).* Paris: Presses universitaires de France, 1941.
Sainte-Beuve, Charles-Augustin. *Etude littéraire sur Chateaubriand.* Vol. 1 of *Œuvres complètes de Chateaubriand.* Paris: Garnier frères, 1859.
Saint-Victor, Jacques de. *Madame du Barry, un nom de scandale.* Paris: Perrin, 2002.
Sargent, A. J. *The Economic Policy of Colbert.* New York: B. Franklin, 1968.
Savkin, Vasilii Efimovich. *The Basic Principles of Operational Art and Tactics: A Soviet View.* Washington, D.C.: Government Printing Office, 1974.
Savory, Reginald Arthur. *His Britannic Majesty's Army in Germany during the Seven Years War.* Oxford: Clarendon, 1966.
Schama, Simon. *Citizens: A Chronicle of the French Revolution.* New York: Knopf, 1989.
Schiebinger, Londa. *The Mind Has No Sex? Women in the Origins of Modern Science.* Cambridge, Mass.: Harvard University Press, 1995.
Schieder, Theodor. *Frederick the Great.* Translated by Sabina Berkeley and H. M. Scott. New York: Longman, 2000.
Schneid, Frederick C. *Napoleon's Conquest of Europe: The War of the Third Coalition.* Westport, Conn.: Praeger, 2005.
Schur, Nathan. *Napoleon in the Holy Land.* Mechanicsburg, Penn.: Stackpole Books, 1999.

Schwab, Richard N. "The Extent of the Chevalier de Jaucourt's Contribution to Diderot's *Encyclopédie*." *Modern Language Notes* 22 (1957): 507–508.
Scott, H. M. *The Birth of a Great Power System, 1740–1815*. Harlow, U.K.: Pearson Longman, 2005.
Scott, Hamish, and Brendan Simms, eds. *Cultures of Power in Europe during the Long Eighteenth Century*. New York: Cambridge University Press, 2007.
Scott, Samuel. *From Yorktown to Valmy: The Transformation of the French Army in the Age of Revolution*. Niwot: University Press of Colorado, 1998.
———. *The Response of the Royal Army to the French Revolution: The Role and Development of the Line Army, 1787–93*. Oxford: Clarendon, 1978.
Scullard, H. H. *From the Gracchi to Nero: A History of Rome from 133 B.C. to A.D. 68*. London: Methuen, 1970.
Ségur, Philippe-Marie-Maurice Henri, marquis de. *Julie de Lespinasse*. New York: E. P. Dutton, 1927.
Semichon, Ernest. *Les réformes sous Louis XIV: Assemblées provinciales et parlements*. Paris: Didier, 1876.
Shoberl, Frederic. *Frederick the Great: His Court and Times*. 2 vols. London: Henry Colburn, 1844.
Showalter, Dennis. *The Wars of Frederick the Great*. New York: Longman, 1996.
Shy, John. *A People Numerous and Armed: Reflections on the Military Struggle for American Independence*. New York: Oxford University Press, 1976.
Smith, Jay. *The French Nobility in the Eighteenth Century: Reassessments and New Approaches*. University Park: Pennsylvania State University Press, 2006.
Soboul, Albert. *The Sans-Culottes*. New York: Doubleday, 1972.
———. *Les soldats de l'an II*. Paris: Club français du livre, 1959.
Sorel, Albert. *L'Europe et la révolution française*. Paris: Editions sociales, 1968–73.
———. *Napoleon and the French Revolution*. Edited by H. L. Hutton. New York: Nelson, 1928.
Spencer, Samia I., ed. *French Women and the Age of Enlightenment*. Bloomington: Indiana University Press, 1984.
Spurlin, Paul, ed. *The French Enlightenment in America: Essays on the Time of the Founding Fathers*. Athens: University of Georgia Press, 1984.
Starkey, Armstrong. *War in the Age of Enlightenment, 1700–1789*. Westport, Conn.: Praeger, 2003.
Starobinski, Jean. *The Invention of Liberty, 1700–1789*. New York: Rizzoli, 1987.
Steinbrügge, Liselotte. *The Moral Sex: Woman's Nature in the French Enlightenment*. New York: Oxford University Press, 1995.

Stinchcombe, William C. *The American Revolution and the French Alliance*. Syracuse, N.Y.: Syracuse University Press, 1969.
Stone, Bailey. *The French Parlements and the Crisis of the Old Regime*. Chapel Hill: University of North Carolina Press, 1986.
Sumption, Jonathan. *The Hundred Years War*. 3 vols. Philadelphia: University of Pennsylvania Press, 1999.
Sutton, John L. *The King's Honor and the King's Cardinal: The War of the Polish Succession*. Lexington: University Press of Kentucky, 1980.
Swann, Julian. *Politics and the Parlement of Paris under Louis XV, 1755–1774*. New York: Cambridge University Press, 1995.
Swann, Julian, and Joël Félix, eds. *The Crisis of the Absolute Monarchy: France from the Old Regime to Revolution*. New York: Oxford University Press, 2013.
Szabo, Franz. *The Seven Years War in Europe, 1756–1763*. New York: Pearson/Longman, 2008.
Telp, Claus. *The Evolution of Operational Art, 1740–1813: From Frederick the Great to Napoleon*. New York: Frank Cass, 2005.
Thiers, Adolphe. *Histoire du Consulat et de l'Empire*. Paris: R. Laffont, 1972.
Thompson, E. P., et al., eds. *La guerre du blé au XVIIIe siècle: la critique populaire contre le libéralisme économique au XVIIIe siècle*. Monteuil: Editions de la Passion, 1988.
Thrasher, Peter Adam. *Pasquale Paoli, an Enlightened Hero, 1725–1807*. Hamden, Conn.: Archon, 1970.
Tocqueville, Alexis de. *L'ancien régime et la Révolution*. Paris: Flammarion, 1988.
———. *Democracy in America*. Translated by J. P. Mayer. New York: Perennial Classics, 2000.
Todd, Christopher. *Voltaire's Disciple: Jean-François de la Harpe*. London: Modern Humanities Research Association, 1972.
Van Creveld, Martin. *Supplying War: Logistics from Wallenstein to Patton*. New York: Cambridge University Press, 1984.
———. *The Transformation of War*. New York: Free Press, 1991.
Van Kley, Dale. *The Damiens Affair and the Unravelling of the Ancien Régime, 1750–1770*. Princeton, N.J.: Princeton University Press, 1984.
———. *The Jansenists and the Expulsion of the Jesuits from France*. New Haven, Conn.: Yale University Press, 1975.
Vivent, Jacques. "Un précurseur de la tactique moderne: le comte de Guibert." In *Revue historique de l'armée; revue trimestrielle de l'état-major de l'armée, service historique*. N.d.
Waddington, Richard. *La guerre de sept ans: histoire diplomatique et militaire*. 5 vols. Paris: Firmin Didot, 1899–1914.
Wasson, James N. *Innovator or Imitator: Napoleon's Operational Concepts and the Legacies of Bourcet and Guibert*. Fort Leavenworth, Kans.: U.S. Army Command and General Staff College, 1998.
Wedgwood, C. V. *The Thirty Years War*. New York: Doubleday, 1961.
Weigley, Russell. *The Age of Battles: The Quest for Decisive Warfare from Breitenfeld to Waterloo*. Bloomington: Indiana University Press, 1991.

Wiesner, Merry E. *Women and Gender in Early Modern Europe.* New York: Cambridge University Press, 2008.
Wilkinson, Spenser. *The Defense of Piedmont, 1742–1748: A Prelude to the Study of Napoleon.* Oxford: Clarendon, 1927.
———. *The French Army before Napoleon: Lectures Delivered before the University of Oxford in Michaelmas Term, 1914.* Oxford: Clarendon, 1915.
———. *The Rise of General Bonaparte.* Oxford: Clarendon, 1930.
Witt, Pierre de. *Une invasion prussienne en Hollande en 1787.* Paris: Plon, 1886.
Wolf, John B. *Louis XIV.* New York: Norton, 1968.
Yorck, Maximilian, von Wartenburg. *Napoleon as a General.* 2 vols. London: K. Paul, Trench, Trübner, 1902.
Zinsser, Judith P. *Emilie du Châtelet: Daring Genius of the Enlightenment.* New York: Penguin Books, 2007.

Index

Abrantès, Laure Junot, duchesse d', 121, 231n11
Académie française, 46, 85, 118, 120, 140; Guibert's nomination, 142–43, 152–55, 202–203
Aiguillon, Emmanuel-Armand du Plessis de Richelieu, duc d', 45
American Revolution. *See* War of American Independence
"Anhalt," 89, 223n46
Anne de Boleyn, 145–46
anoblis, 26, 108–10, 149–52, 162
Archives de la Guerre, 8, 12, 200
Argenson, Marc-Pierre de Voyer de Paulmy, comte d', 21
"Aristocratic Reaction," 9, 149–51
Armée de Sambre et Meuse, 179
Army of Italy, 186, 244n30
Army of the Lower Rhine, 37
Army of the North, 178, 180, 244n34
Art of War by Principles and Rules, 21
artillery, 26, 125, 130, 176; in the *Défense du système de guerre moderne*, 134; developments in, 13, 15; in the *Essai général de tactique*, 64–66, 69; in Gribeauval's reforms, 49, 51–52, 55, 104, 117; in the reforms of Ségur/Brienne, 161, 163; in the Regulations of 1776, 111; in the Revolutionary and Napoleonic wars, 183, 186; in the Seven Years War, 28–32, 40; in the works of Folard, 19
Assembly of Notables, 156, 158–60, 166
Augereau, Pierre, 184

Bardin, Etienne-Alexandre, 7
Barère, Bertrand, 7, 200
Barry, Jeanne Bécu, comtesse du, 45

bataillon carré, 183–84, *185*
Battle of Auerstadt, 181, 184–85, 192–93
Battle of Dettingen, 35
Battle of Jena, 184–85, 192–93
Battle of Minden, 3, 28–31, 30, 32, 37–38, 135
Battle of Neerwinden, 180
Battle of Ponte Nuovo, 4, 48, 205n6
Battle of the Roer, 182
Battle of Rossbach, 3, 29, 34, 98, 198; description of, 27–28; as driver of reform, 36–38, 53, 108, 111, 195–96; effects on participants, 40, 103; fallout from, 31–33
Battle of San Pietro, 35
Battle of Vellinghausen, 3, 30–33, 32, 37–39
Berlin, 86–87
Bernadotte, Jean-Baptiste, 184
Bertaud, Jean-Paul, 12
Bien, David D., 9
Blanning, T. C. W., 11
Blaufarb, Rafe, 11
Bonaparte, Napoleon. *See* Napoleon (emperor of France)
Bordeaux, 85
Bourbon, Charles III, duc de, 94
Bourbon Restoration, 7
Bourcet, Pierre-Joseph, 39–40, 55, 74; influence on operational warfare, 49–51, 67, 136, 182
Breslau, 88–89
Brienne, Etienne-Charles de Loménie de, Cardinal, 108, 158–60, 166
Brienne, Louis-Marie-Athanase de Loménie, comte de, 156, 160–61, 166, 197, 201
Brissot, Jacques-Pierre, 141, 155
Broglie, Charles-François, comte de, 90, 138–39, 220n3

269

270   INDEX

Broglie, Victor-François, duc de, 46, 49, 55, 74, 165–66; developing the division system, 40–41, 66; family connections, 78, 138–39, 140; in the Ministry of War, 102, 121–22; in the Seven Years War, 28–31; at Vaussieux, 125–34, 232n28
Buonaparte, Carlo, 47

cadenced step: absence of, 17, 19, 21; development of, 22, 24, 53–65, 175, 195
cadet-gentilhomme, 110
Caesarism, 60, 172, 241n9
cahiers des doléances, 167–68
Calonne, Charles-Alexandre, vicomte de, 157–59
Camp of Vaussieux, 9, 118, 140, 143, 146, 154, 166; description of, 125–39, *127, 129, 121*, 232n28
Carlyle, Thomas, 24
Carnot, Lazare, 184–88, 199, 201
Castries, Charles Eugène Gabriel, marquis de, 102, 153, 160, 233n50
Catinat, Nicolas, 59, 121
cavalry, 116, 125, 218n36; in the *Défense du sytème de guerre moderne*, 134–35; development of, 13–16, 18; in the *Essai général de tactique*, 62–66, 68–69; in Guibert's later writings, 172; in the Prussian system, 88–89; in the reforms of Ségur/Brienne, 162–64; in the Revolutionary and Napoleonic wars, 176, 181, 183, 186; in the Seven Years War, 28–32, 39, 40; at Vaussieux, 130; in the works of Folard, 19
Chabot, Louis-François-Jean, 128
Chamrond, 84, 146
Charles Emmanuel IV (prince of Piedmont), 95
Charles XII (king of Sweden), 86

Charnay, Jean-Paul, 10
Charôst, Armand-Joseph, duc de, 168
Chartier, Roger, 10
Chastelleux, François-Jean, marquis de, 46, 219n78
Chenonceaux, 200
Choiseul, Etienne-François, duc de, 8, 12, 55, 86, 213n23; and the Gribeauval System, 51–52, 104; legacy of, 109, 158, 192, 195; ministry of, 4, 39, 62, 75; reforms of, 11, 41–42, 45–47, 100–102
Clausewitz, Carl von, 7–8
Clement VII (pope), 94
Colbert, Jean-Baptiste, 56–57
Colin, Jean, 8–9, 45, 132, 165
Collé, Charles, 78
Collins, James, 157, 205n9, 210n41
Comédie française, 95, 105, 202
Compte rendu au roi, 141–42
Condé, Louis de Bourbon, prince de, 15
Condorcet, Nicolas, marquis de, 81–82, 96, 121, 221n17
Connêtable de Bourbon, 79, 94–97, 105, 144–46, 153–54
Conseil de la Guerre, 4, 12, 192, 197; effects on Guibert, 173–74; later evolution, 175–76, 184, 189; under Saint-Germain, 98–99, 103–119, 123, 139; under Ségur, 148, 152–54, 156, 159, 160–66, 168–69
Conseiller du Roi, 34–35, 211n1
Contades, Louis Georges Erasme, marquis de, 28–30, 37
corporal punishment, 111–12, 116, 165
corps d'armée, 178, 183–84
Correspondance littéraire, philosophique, et critique, 79, 95, 121, 145, 152–53
Corsica: Guibert's deployment on, 4, 34, 55, 77, 94, 96, 132, 194; pacification of, 46–49, 96, 194
coup d'oeil, 73, 189

Courcelles, 93, 139, 143, 168
Crébillon, Claude Prosper Jolyot de, 78
Crillon, François-Félix-Dorothée, comte de, 81, 93, 153, 224–25n65
Cross of Saint-Louis, 104

D'Alembert, Jean la Rond, 80–82, 84, 121, 142, 221n17, 222n24, 236n33; correspondence with Frederick II, 75, 96; relationship with Julie de Lespinase, 85, 91, 119–20, 206n19, 231n7
Damiens affair, 112, 229n49
Davout, Louis-Nicolas, 181, 184
Declaration of the Rights of Man and the Citizen, 171
Défense du système de guerre moderne, 118, 133–39
Deffand, Marie Anne, marquise du, 81, 84, 95, 121, 142, 143–44
De la force publique, 156–57, 170–73
Delbrück, Hans, 8, 206n20
Department of the Marine, 26, 56–57, 132
De re militaris, 57
Diderot, Denis, 80–81, 96, 142, 152, 194–95; as defender of Guibert, 82–83, 121; as *Encyclopedist*, 85, 221n17
"Diplomatic Revolution," 27
division system, 25, 166; development by Bourcet, 41, 50–51; in the *Défense du système de guerre moderne*, 134, 136; in the *Essai général de tactique*, 66–68, 70–72; under Napoleon, 183–84, 186; during the Revolution, 182–83, 186; during the Ségur-Brienne ministry, 159, 163–64, 174
doctrine, 6, 10–12, 55, 153; in the *Defense du système de guerre moderne*, 133–38; development of, 13–14; in the *Essai général de tactique*, 55–76; Guibert's legacy in, 175–93, 194–201; later developments in Guibert's writings, 169–74; personal, 17–20, 31–33, 37–38, 40–41; reforms of under Saint-Germain, 109–16; reforms of, under Ségur, 161–66; systemic, 21–24; at Vaussieux, 126–32
Dresden, 75, 86, 88
Dumas, Mathieu, 169, 177
Dumouriez, Charles-François, 12, 96, 139, 201, 234n74; friendship with Guibert, 4, 46, 78; in the Secret du roi, 89–90, 223n51, 224n53
Duras, Emmanuel-Félicité, duc de, 78
Duras, Louis-Henriette-Charlotte Philippine, duchesse de, 84
Dutch Crisis of 1787, 156, 160, 165–66

École militaire, 35, 108–109, 163, 201
Elegy of Catinat, 96, 121
Elegy of Eliza, 120
Elegy of Frederick, 154
Elegy of l'Hôpital, 121
Elting, John, 12
English Channel, 125, 178
Enlightenment, the, 3–5, 26, 120; and America, 114, 124; Classicism in, 60, 145; and the Damiens affair, 112; and the French Revolution, 167; Guibert's influence on, 7, 202–203; historiography of, 9–11; influence on Guibert, 55–57, 75, 187, 194, 196; and the *parlements*, 98–99, 107–109; sociability in, 80–81; waning of, 141–43, 152–55
Essai general de tactique, 12, 45, 146; analysis of, 55–76; effects of, 78, 86–87, 116, 155, 175, 197, 201; influence on Guibert's later writings, 133, 135–38, 165, 190–92; as

Essai general de tactique (*continued*)
inspiration for reforms, 99–105, 112, 121–22; publication of, 4; writing of, 95–97
Estates-General, 78, 156–58, 166–69, 174, 201

Favier, Jean-Louis, 78, 89–90, 223n51
Ferdinand (prince of Brunswick), 28–32
fermiers-généraux, 99–100
Ferney, 89, 121
feu à volonté/billebaude, 71–72, 219n66
First Battle of Fleurus, 179
First Italian Campaign, 182–83, 186, 193, 199, 244n30
First (Napoleonic) Empire, 7, 176, 180
First World War, 8
Folard, Jean-Charles, Chevalier: Guibert's criticism of, 133–34; influence on military theory, 24–25, 28, 42, 49, 53–54, 121–22, 198–99; writings, 18–21
Fonneuve, 35–36, 39, 224n65
Fontainebleau, 102–103, 226n12
Forestié, Emerand, 7
Francis I (king of France), 53
Frederick I (king of Prussia), 20
Frederick II (king of Prussia), 40, 207n41, 223n39, 223n41; and operational warfare, 68, 218n52; and the Prussian army, 11, 13, 20, 31, 53, 67, 194, 198–99, 212n12, 230n61, 245n6; relationship with Guibert, 75, 7, 82, 87, 96, 154; at Rossbach, 27–28, 116; in training camps, 72, 88–89
Frederick William (crown prince of Prussia), 87
Frederick William I (king of Prussia), 20, 223n41
Frederick William II (king of Prussia), 159

French Revolution, 6–8, 11, 46, 104, 141, 155, 200; army of, 11, 58–59, 117, 175–76, 178–79, 181–93, 197, 199, 201, 203; Guibert and, 137–38, 156–74; philosophy of, 48, 149, 151–52
Friant, Louis, 181
Fronsac, Louis-Antoine-Sophie de Richelieu, duc de, 78

Gay, Peter, 10
garde des sceaux, 34–36
general staff, 103, 148, 164, 184–86
Geneva, 75, 141
génie (engineers), 26, 160–61
génie (innate skill), 72–73, 107–109, 199, 219n69
Geoffrin, Marie Thérèse Rodet, 80–81, 84, 142–43
Goodman, Dena, 10, 80–81
Graffigny, François de, 203
Grande Armée, 6–7, 11; development of, 174, 175–76, 178–79, 182–86, 191–93, 199
Great Britain/England, 3, 26, 48, 145–46; in the War of American Independence, 113–15, 123–25
Grenadiers of Languedoc, 47
Grenzer, 65
Gribeauval, Jean-Baptiste Vaquette de, 55; in the Choiseul ministry, 49, 51–52; in Guibert's writing, 64–65, 88; in the Ministry of War, 104–105, 111–12, 116–17, 161
Griffith, Paddy, 11–12
Grimm, Friedrich Melchoir, baron von, 152
Groffier, Ethel, 10–11, 90, 201
Gudin, Charles-Etienne, 181
Guerre des farines, 145, 236n21
Guibert, Alexandrine, 7, 73, 143, 199–200, 225n66, 246n13
Guibert, Appolline, 143, 200, 235n13
Guibert, Charles-Benoit, 3, 45, 77, 138, 153, 194–95, 220n2; career, 35–37, 39–41, 101–102, 144

Guibert, Jean, 34–36
"Guibert columns," 53–54, 111, 175; development of, 42–45, 195; in Guibert's writings, 62, 66–68, 135; in the Regulations, 165, 177, 180–82
Guichard, Karl Gottlieb, 87, 223n39
Gustavus Adolphus (king of Sweden), 56, 86

Habsburg dynasty, 65, 87–88
Hamm, 30–31
Hanover, 27–28
Hénault, Charles-Jean-François, Président, 84
Henry (prince of Prussia), 87
Heuser, Beatrice, 11, 190
Hildburghausen, Joseph Maria Frederick Wilhelm, 27–28, 37
Hoche, Lazare, 189
Hohenzollern dynasty, 19–20
Holy Roman Empire, 27–28, 94
homme de genie: in Guibert's writing, 72–73, 136; in practice, 189, 191, 193, 197, 199
Hume, David, 80
Hundred Years War, 14

Industrial Revolution, 52
infantry (light), 244n31; in the *Essai général de tactique*, 65–66, 68–69; in the Revolutionary and Napoleonic wars, 176, 183. *See also* Grenzer
infantry (line), 125, 175, 218n36, 227–28n30, 233n43; in the *Défense du système de guerre moderne*, 134–35; development of, 13–18; in the *Essai général de tactique*, 60–66, 68–69; in the Prussian practice, 88–89; in the reforms of Saint-Germain, 109; in the reforms of Ségur/Brienne, 163–64; in the Revolutionary and Napoleonic wars, 176, 181, 185–86; in the Seven Years War, 28–33, 38, 40; at Vaussieux, 128–30; in the works of Folard, 18–19; in the works of Mesnil-Durand, 49
Intendance, 191–92
Invalides, Les, 101, 106–107, 112, 144–45, 160–61

Jansenism, 99, 205n5
Jaucourt, Louis de, Chevalier, 104–105, 161
Joly de Fleury, Jean-François, 108
Jomini, Antoine-Henri, baron, 7–8, 10
Jourdan, Jean-Baptiste, 182, 189

La Châtre, Claude-Louis, comte de, 168
Lafayette, Gilbert, marquis de, 133, 217n19
La Harpe, Jean-François de, 202, 231n10; as Guibert's nemesis, 95, 120–21, 139, 146, 152
Lannes, Jean, 184
la patrie, 48, 171
Latreille, Albert, 8–9, 104
Lauerma, Matti, 9, 11, 138
La Vallière, Louis-César, duc de, 52
League of Augsburg, 3
Les Gracques, 145, 153, 202
Lespinasse, Julie de, 11–12, 77, 173, 206n19, 224n59, 224n60, 224n64, 231n7; correspondence with Guibert, 101, 102, 113, 200; death, 139–43; description of Guibert, 78–79, 194–95; posthumous influence of, 146–48; relationship with Guibert, 7–8, 83–85, 90–94, 96–97, 105, 119–20, 202–203; as salonnière, 10, 80–82, 121, 160
L'Hôpital, Guillaume de, 59, 121
Liège, 75
logistics, 101; government reforms of, 111–13, 159; in Guibert's writings, 70, 74–75; Revolutionary and Napoleonic reforms of, 185–88, 191–92. *See also* Intendance
Louis III (king of France), 153

Louis XIV (king of France), 1, 25, 35; age of, 20, 99–101; 106, 144, 150; wars of, 17, 41, 56–57, 179
Louis XV (king of France), 3, 39, 41, 142; age of, 57, 99–101; and the Damiens affair, 112, 229n49; 220n5, 223n51, 224n53; and the Malvinas crisis, 45; and the Secret du roi, 89–91; wars of, 25
Louis XVI (king of France), 95, 101–102, 144, 238n15; and the Council of War, 103, 117, 160–61; in the French Revolution, 156–58, 166–68, 169, 176; in the War of American Independence, 124–25
Louis XVIII (king of France), 200
"Louis XXIX" (fictional king of France), 147
Louvois, François-Michel, marquis de, 56–57
Lynn, John, 12, 14, 18, 178

Madrid, 85
Maison militaire du roi, 26, 106–107, 117, 151, 160–63, 227n30
maîtresse-en-titre, 45
Malvinas Crisis, 45–46, 214n33
Marbot, Jean-Baptiste-Antoine, baron de, 178–79
maréchaussée, 160–61, 170–72
Maria-Theresa (archduchess of Austria), 88
Marie Antoinette (queen of France), 95
Masséna, André, 189, 199
Maupeou, René Nicolas Charles Augustin de, 100–101, 114, 141, 157, 220n5
"Mémoire adressé au public et à l'armée sur les operations du Conseil de la Guerre," 169–70
Mes rêveries, 24
Mesnil-Durand, François-Jean, baron de, 74; as Guibert's rival, 122–23, 132–35, 139; military theories, 49–50, 55, 198–99; at Vaussieux, 118, 126–32
Military Committee, 176
Military Revolution, 14–16
militia, 189–90, 217n19; in Guibert's writing, 58–59, 137, 162, 170–72
Montauban, 3, 34–36, 194, 224–26n65
Montbarey, Andre-Marie-Eléanor, prince de, 25, 114–15, 125–26, 130–32, 148, 196, 232n28
Montecuccoli, Raimondo, graf, 136
Montesquieu, Charles-Louis, baron de, 4–5, 80, 124, 170, 196
Monteynard, Louis François, marquis de, 101, 196
Montsauge, Jeanne Thiroux de, 81, 83, 91–93, 143
Montsauge, Philibert Thiroux de, 83
Mora, marquis de, 85
Morand, Charles-Antoine-Louis Alexis, 177, 181, 189
Morris, Gouverneur, 96, 246n13
Moulin-Joly, 83, 85
moyen, 72–73, 107–109
Muir, Rory, 11
Muy, comte de, 102

Naigeon, Jacques-André, 82–83, 222n23
Napoleon (emperor of France), 10–11, 125, 200, 231n11; age of, 175–76, 245n6; creation of the Grande Armée, 178–79; development of operational warfare, 182–87; logistical reforms, 191–92; Napoleonic warfare, 6–8, 67–68, 173, 189, 193, 199, 201–203
"national character," 16–17; as criticism of Guibert, 115–17; French, 20–21, 24, 38, 71, 123, 135–36, 196
National/Constituent Assembly, 169–70, 176, 200–201

Necker, Germaine. *See* Staël-Holstein, Germaine de
Necker, Jacques, 82, 97, 141–42, 155, 166, 221n17, 240n46
Necker, Suzanne, 78, 80–81, 121, 141–43, 147, 152
Neustria Regiment, 110, 163
Ney, Michel, 181, 184, 242n11
Nosworthy, Brent, 182
Nouvelle ecclésiastiques, 99

oblique order, 68, 89, 218n52. *See also* operations/operational warfare
Officiers employés à la reconnaissance du pays, 39–40
open order (en tirailleur), 65–66, 180–81, 243n16
operations/operational warfare, 72–72, 156; development under Broglie, 40; in the *Defense du système de guerre moderne*, 133–39; in the *Essai général de tactique*, 66–70; Guibert's legacy in, 175, 181–82, 198–99; Prussian innovations in, 88–89; reforms of under Saint-Germain, 109–13; reforms of under Ségur, 159, 161–66; in the writings of Bourcet, 50–51; at Vaussieux, 126–32
ordre mince, 9, 19, 154, 206n24; development of, 20–21; in Guibert's writing, 60–61, 63, 68, 133–36, 139; in mid-century debates, 49–50; in the Ségur-Brienne ministry, 164; in the 1776 Regulations, 111–13; in the 1791 Regulations, 176–82; at Vaussieux, 121–26, 128
ordre mixte, 139, 154, 197, 200; development of, 63–64; in the 1791 Regulations, 176–82; at Vaussieux, 121–26
ordre profond, 9, 206n24; in the Choiseul ministry, 41–42; development of, 19, 20–22; in Guibert's writing, 60–61, 63–64, 75, 133–36, 139; in mid-century debates, 49–50, 198; in the Ségur-Brienne ministry, 164; in the 1776 Regulations, 111–13; in the 1791 Regulations, 176–82; at Vaussieux, 118, 121–26, 128
Osman, Julia, 11
Ottoman Empire, 65, 88, 144

Palais-Bourbon, 95
Palais-Royal, 95
Palmer, R. R., 8–9, 11, 67, 81, 138
Paoli, Pasquale, 47–48
Paradis de Moncrif, François-Augustin de, 78
parlements, 210n38; in the French Revolution, 157–59, 166–67, 169; in the Maupeou crisis, 78, 99–101, 141, 220n5
paulette, 26. *See also* venality
Pelet-Clozeau, Jean-Jacques-Germain, 177
Perpignan, 39, 107
Pirch, Johann Ernst, baron von, 53, 111, 113, 122, 126, 132, 164
plésion, 21, 49
Poirier, Lucien, 9–10
Pompadour, marquise de, 45
Potsdam, 87
"Précis de ce qui s'est passé à mon égard à l'Assemblée du Berry," 169
Principes de la guerre de montagne, 50
"Projet de discours d'un citoyen aux trois Ordres de l'Assemblée de Berry," 169
Prussia, 3–4, 77, 82, 96, 103, 126, 133, 140, 154, 187; in accusations levied against Guibert, 168–69; army of, 13–14, 19–24, 41–43; in the French Wars, 181, 184, 192–93; in Guibert's writings, 60, 67–68, 71–72, 86–89, 135; influence on French reforms, 108–18, 122–24,

Prussia (continued)
164–66, 194–201; influence on French theorists, 49–50, 53, 99; invasion of the Dutch Republic, 156, 159–60; in the Seven Years War, 27–33, 34, 36–40.
Puységur, Jacques-François de Chastenet, marquis de, 21, 25, 42, 49, 121
Puységur, Louis-Pierre de Chastenet, comte de, 44–45, 161, 164, 166, 197, 213n30

Quimby, Robert, 9, 11, 19, 64, 111, 165
Quintus Icilius. *See* Guichard, Karl Gottleib

Regiment d'Auvergne (Auvergne Regiment), 35–36, 39, 46, 138
Regiment of Navarre, 49
Regulations (Réglements): of 1753–1755, 21–22, 61; of 1764 and 1766, 41–42, 164; of 1774–1775, 111, 122, 126, 164; of 1776, 111–12, 122–23, 126–28, 132–33, 164; of 1787 and 1788, 9, 156, 164–66, 175, 177, 192; of 1791, 4–6, 9, 12, 175–78, 181, 183, 197, 199–200
Republic of Genoa, 46–47
Republic of Letters, 4–7; Guibert's entry into, 77–78, 82–83, 94–97; Guibert's participation in, 118–19, 120–24, 137, 151–54
Rhine River, 14, 27, 30, 36–37, 40, 86, 193, 199
Richelieu, Armand, duc de, 27
Rivail, François de, 35
Rivail, Suzanne, 45
Rochambeau, comte de, 128–33
Roche, Daniel, 10
Roguet, François, 177
Rome: city of, 94, 145; Republic and Empire, 14, 19, 50, 57, 60, 72, 157

Ross, Steven T., 11–12
Rothenberg, Gunther, 11
Rousseau, Jean-Jacques, 5, 124; death of, 141, 152, 155; influence on Corsica, 47; in the Republic of Letters, 80–82; as Romantic, 88, 203
Royal Legion, 47

Saale River, 27
Saint-Germain, comte de, 98–99, 118, 197, 200; nomination as Minister of War, 103–106, 227n27; reforms of, 109, 111–17, 230n56; legacy of, 125–26, 144, 148, 161
Saint-Lambert, marquis de, 153, 161
Saldern, Friedrich Christof von, 164–65
salons, 4–5, 196; Guibert's participation in, 77–89, 95–97, 101, 118–19, 120–21, 138, 140–45, 147, 152–54, 160; historiography of, 10–12. *See also* Republic of Letters
Sartine, comte d'Alby, 113–14, 132, 233n50
Saxe, Maurice de, 49, 50, 103; influence on theory, 53, 55, 66, 122, 198–99; *Mes rêveries*, 24–25
Saxony, 27, 86–88
schwerpunkt, 69
Second Battle of Fleurus, 179
Second Hundred Years War, 27, 123
Secret du roi, 89–90
Ségur, Louis-Philippe, comte de, 115, 236n33
Ségur, Philippe Henri, marquis de, 140, 153, 196, 201; as Minister of War, 148–49, 156, 159–60, 162, 174
Ségur, Philippe-Marie-Maurice Henri, marquis de, 7–8, 89, 90, 119
Ségur Decree, 9, 140, 149–51, 162, 168, 206n27

1769 Instructions for Light Troops (L'instruction de 1769 pour les troupes légères), 34, 42–45, 112–13
Seven Years War, 3–4, 103–104; battles of, 27–33, 34; Guibert's role in, 36–42, 46–47, 132–33, 194; in Guibert's writing, 56, 66, 72, 138, 164; legacy of, 49–52, 100, 106, 113, 115, 117, 128, 151, 160, 192
Seydlitz, Friedrich Wilhelm von, 28–31, 212n12
Soubise, Charles, prince de, 27–31, 36–37, 86, 198
Soult, Nicolas, 184
Spain, 3, 15, 45, 123
Staël-Holstein, Erik, 148
Staël-Holstein, Germaine, 12, 78–79, 81, 153, 224n64; relationship with Guibert, 147–48, 200, 236n30, 236n32
Strasbourg, 35, 86
stratégique, 136
strategy, 70, 74, 136–38
Suard, Amélie, 142–43, 152, 200
Suard, Jean-Baptiste-Antoine, 85, 141, 142–43

tactics, 36, 71–72, 88–89, 118, 154, 156; debates on in the mid-1770s, 120–23; in the *Défense du système de guerre moderne*, 133–35, 139; early modern developments, 14–19; in the *Essai général de tactique*, 60–66; Guibert's legacy in, 175–82, 184, 159–201; reforms of under Saint-Germain, 109–13; reforms of under Ségur, 161–66; in the Regulations of the 1750s, 22–24; in the Regulations of the 1760s, 41–42; in the 1769 Instructions for Light Troops, 42–44; in the work of Mesnil-Durand, 49–50; at Vaussieux, 126–32
Tarascon, 48
Telp, Claus, 11, 67

tercio, 15, 19
Thomas, Antoine-Leonard, 81, 124, 152–53
Toulongeon, François-Emmanuel, 7, 48, 200, 212n15
Traité de Polybe, 18
Treaty of Paris 1763. *See* Seven Years War
Trésoriers généraux de l'extraordinaire des guerres, 26
Turenne, vicomte de, 17, 136
Turgot, Jacques, 82, 84, 97, 113–14, 141, 158, 221n17, 236n21; relationship with Guibert, 103–104, 155, 227n19

University of Clermont-Ferrand, 10

Vauban, siegneur de, 18
Vaux, comte de, 4, 47–48, 102, 228n13
Vegetius, 57–58
venality: of offices, 26, 34–36; within the military, 16, 100–101, 106–109, 114, 140, 149–51, 238–39n20
Versailles, 79, 81, 89, 92, 115, 158
Vichy, Gaspard de, 146
Vienna, 87–88, 89–90
Villeneuve, Vallet de, 200, 235n13
Voltaire, 80, 82, 121, 124, 144, 207n41; commentary on Corsica, 48; death of, 141, 152, 155; relationship with Guibert, 76, 77, 81, 89, 95–96, 225n77

Walpole, Horace, 144
War of American Independence, 160; debates about, 113–15, 121, 123–25, 132–33, 142; French officers in, 46, 117, 118, 139
War of Austrian Succession, 39–40, 50; Charles Guibert in, 35–37; legacy of, 24–25, 52, 106; Prussia and, 13, 20–21, 194
War of the First Coalition, 181, 183, 189

War of Polish Succession, 25, 35, 50, 210n40
War of the Spanish Succession, 3, 18
Watelet, Claude Henri, 83–84
Weser River, 28
Wilkinson, Spenser, 8–9
William V, prince of Orange-Nassau (stadtholder of the United Provinces), 159–60
Wimpffen, baron de, 104–105, 116–17, 128, 132, 137, 184